J. Fletch Woodward

Uncle Sam's Bible

Part First

J. Fletch Woodward

Uncle Sam's Bible
Part First

ISBN/EAN: 9783743419438

Manufactured in Europe, USA, Canada, Australia, Japa

Cover: Foto ©Lupo / pixelio.de

Manufactured and distributed by brebook publishing software (www.brebook.com)

J. Fletch Woodward

Uncle Sam's Bible

AMERICAN SCRIPTURES.

VOLUME THE FIRST.

120 Y.A.I.

UNCLE SAM'S BIBLE.
PART FIRST.

Containing the Declaration of Independence, the Constitution of Uncle Sam, Washington's Farewell Address, an Analysis, or an Essay on man, with an Introductory history of Bibles and Religions, with the Yankeeite Creed; or, Standard of Justice!

,NOTE! I believe I have chosen, and compiled more great truthes, in this book, than has been done in any Bible. That I was shaped, and influenced to do so by God, as much so, as any. That the works chosen, are as much Inspired as any of the books chosen for other Bibles; and that I am as much Inspired, and I have as good a right to choose these books and compile them into a Bible for the American Freeman, as had that Jew, or that Roman, or that Englishman, or that Mohammedan, or that Mormon; or, that host of others. That was the way they got their Bibles, and that is all there is in it.

COMPILED BY
J. FLETCH WOODWARD, M.D.
McMINNVILLE, TENN.
Advertiser Print —1890.— and Sterotype.

ENTERED according to act of Congress, in the year 1893, by J. Fletch. Woodward, M. D., in the office of the Librarian of Congress, at Washington, D. C. All rights reserved.

PREFACE.

I DID NOT write this book. It is the writings, and beliefs of many, many great, wise, and good men and w︎︎︎ from all parts of the world. It is a doki... of Liberal, Free or Individual government ; that is for giving man a chance to read, study, investigate, and to enjoy the different ideas and opinions of their fellow men or their own. If it is wrong, then freedom is wrong, and I have a grate deal of good company.

How does the lives and characters of Paine, Jefferson, Franklin, Washington, Lincoln, Sherman, Grant, and a host of our Infidel Fathers compare to those of Abraham, Lot, Isaac, Jacob, Moses, Solomon, and that set of enslaving, murdering, lieing, thieving, whoreing, devastateing, set of god-sent Jews and Christians?

I am not alone in this wide, wide world, and my bible is just and rational! Not so with the Jew Christian, King Jim's bible! It runs counter to the nature, of man and things; it is wretchedly self-contradictory, both in history, facts, and circumstantial evidence!

What I have said about religionists and their bibles is nothing compared to what they first said about my liberty and infidelity! They that live in glass houses ought not to throw rocks! Or he that is without sin let him throw the first rock! It is a mighty ill wind that blows no one any good! I believe, however, that this Jew-Christian-King-Jim-bible is that kind of an ill wind! It has always injured its friends worse than its foes! I believe it is too foul, vicious, obscene, and dangerous for man to generaly keep for our youth to read!

And, if you will investigate this subject as it is presented to you from page 108 to 122, of book Our Beginningless, you will find that this is enough references for you!

Religion is an awful mental disease! And its mortality has been greater than all other diseases put together! And this is why I have dwelt so much on this subject.

This book is entended as a private medical and legal guide. It contains many choice subjects that can be read on all readable occasions; as at births, weddings, funerals, or at the sick bed.

We hold that religion is an acquired disease, a craziness! I have endeavored to prove it from their own fruits! For by their crab-apple fruits we know them! And I have endeavored to point out a remedy; not only for it, but, for our ever ill.

It is entended as a chart and prescription, and it should be kept as private property—private and secure, under lock and key! The destroying hand of religionists will ever be after it and you!

I object to the old Jew bible, because it was only a garbled extract from the old snake, fish, ghost, and legendary fables of the ancients. I reject the Christian‚s bible, because it rests on the same old mythical foundation. They reject all of the old except its foundation; therefore, this gives me the right to reject it and their ghostly foundation! And to declare in favor of Hylotheism, or that there is no god except universal matter! And that he is universal goodness and intelligence!

Each plant is an individual, filled with deity! They are male and female, they love and hate, suffer and enjoy, they display an intelligence, they work and they rest, they live and they die. Plants and trees are but stationary animals, for in the great chain of life it is impossible to tell where the plant life ends and the animal life begins!

So, from plant life we come, and back to it our body does go, while our intelligence back to deity doth flow!

 MAN IS ONLY A DETACHED PLANT!

PREFATORY REMARKS.

Religion is a sign of weakness, caused from the predominance of our infernal infirmaties. It being an unbalanced or diseased condition it is not reliable nor trustworthy, and leads to craziness. We should never cry, grieve, fret, nor unnecessarily complain. This, too, is an expression of our unbalanced, or weakened condition. Religion has never improved, nor elevated man. We only have to refer you to the road traveled by it from the first religious altar—Cain's and Able's, on down to the Sabatarian and Prohibitionists of today.

Religionists descend the scale. They never climb. They descend from a lord of all they survey, to a church-ridden subject, and from a subject to a priest-ridden slave, and from a slave to a beast of burden. From an Eden to a hell. It is a fact, although the Adamites claim to be God-first and God-chosen, and God-perfect, yet they have but little in prose, song, law or gospel but what they gleaned from others. And being last, from the hind tit, they are runts, and imbibe our vices more than our virtues. They claim to be God-perfect, and cannot discover, or learn any more.

According to their own history, after God had made everything, then he made male and female man, in his own image and placed them in the world, (not a garden nor an Eden), but the world, and commanded them to be fruitful and multiply, and replenish and subdue the earth. And that it was good. Now, this was on Saturday, or the 6th day. Of course, God is a white man, and that was when the white man was made. Now, the next chapter tells us that the Lord God, not God, early Sunday, made this colored man, Adam, from the dust, rubbish, and nubbin end of creation, and put him in a garden, to keep it. In proof of the above assertion that Adam was made from the dust, dirt, and colored rubbish, left from a hard week's work, there was nothing to make Eve, so he had to take a piece of Adam. And then he was so tired he had to rest! Leaving them half made, naked, ignorant, and at the mercy of an awful Devil! And this awful curse remains on all Adamites, or Christians to this day.

Can you not see, they are different men, made by a lot of different gods, out of different material, at different times, and put in quite a different place, and given very, very different commands?

The Adamites cannot prove their origin, when nor where they got their laws, songs or gospel. They were so obscene and wretched that they were afraid to sign their names to them, or give dates; but like a thief claim to have found them. (See 22c., 2 kings.) And it was a bitter pill to the king, 11v. Who knows or can prove this is the law given to Moses?

These Adamites were mere infants to the nations that existed prior to them. Their bible is a mere almanac compared to the bible of mother India. It is so extensive that a man cannot read it in a lifetime. Yet, this world was full when these lieing, thieveing, murdering, piratical, presumptuous Adamite bigots started out. This world was full when that murder Cain started out, and found a wife. It was full when old drunken Noah had the deliriumtremens, and imagined that awful flood. It was full when that old lying, obscene, vagrant Abraham tramped about. It was full when that idiotic Jacob worked fourteen years for two treacherous wives. It was full when that murdering, bastard Moses claimed two mams and nary dad. And, although he wandered 40 years, he could not find a vacant or unclaimed spot! The world was full when their descendants, in 1492, landed on our beautiful American shores. Although we have given them religious, political and civil freedom and protected them with equal and exact justice—nowhere else, or never before enjoyed, yet, they seem to retain that same old hydro-phobia religious virus that confuses, maddens, and destroys both great and small now, as much so as in the days of Sodom and Gomorrha.

Even John the babsouser, Jesus the man God, and Paul the law giver, struggled to reform the errors of Moses, David and Soloman. Paul summed the Law and Gospel up in these few words: 'Thou shalt not committ adultry, kill, steal, bear false witness, nor covit. And if there be any other commandments it is, to love thy neighbor as thyself. Rom. 13. Let no man judge you in meat, drink, holy days, the new moon, or the Sabbath days. Col. 2. That one man esteemeth one day above another, and that another man esteemeth every day alike. Let every man be fully pursuaded in his own mind Rom. 14. That Christ abolished the Commandments, Laws, and Ordinances. And that we are now delivered from the law. Lu. 16, 16. Eph. 2, 15. Rom. 7, 6.' Isaiah said such laws was an iniquity; so said our revolutionary fathers. And they gave us their Declaration of freedom. Our Constitution forbids all religious laws and ordinances.

Our Stars and Stripes, thank God, wave above the image, the eagle, the cressant and the cross! The Declaration of Independance rules above all bibles, words of God and religion—and it claims to be from a just God; declaring equal and exact justice to all man-kind. A privilege never before granted.

These Adamites have a lot of religious songs, their God songs, from Moses, David and Soloman, yet they won't sing them, and the most unscrupulous Christian seems to be ashamed of them.

All these things being declared by Jason in five, books, we abridge in one, says 2nd., Mccabees. It is said, so and so, in the books of the wars of the lord, and in the books of Arnon, says the 21st.,chapter of Numbers. So, it has always been. The first man wrote his books. And so has all men and tribes. They wrote them on stone, bark, leaves, on whatever come handy; on the ground, and on their own living skin. A tattoo is a character that signifies something, as much so as our Phenician characters, a, b, c, or our Arabic characters, 1, 2, 3. Derber of ancient Phenicia was called the book city, To them we owe the present alphabet, and to the Arabs we owe our present arithmetical figures. So the Christians, did not know much about geology, astronomy, geography, physiology, nor the simplist lnws of nature. And, worst of all, it turns out that all that their god told them turns out false.

So, it does not tell well for Mr. Jew, and Mr. Christian, who claim to be the origin of every thing and every body.

The great trouble is, man has a disposition to lie, cheat, and to defraud, to claim his is superior, or the best. This desire led to the claim of a help from God, or a super-human power. This caused the killing of Able, This caused the downfall and the destruction of every country ruled by religion. It caused the dark ages. It will take the bright light of American freedom many, many years to re-discover, and to replace what religion has destroyed.

I have seen three versions of this Jew-Christian King's bible. They contradicted each other, and themselves. Yet, we are told they are very perfect, and come from a perfect god. So, it is with Christians, they claim to have been made perfect, and the serpent played the devil with them. Yet, their bible at the 3rd., chapter, 22ond.,verse of Genesis tells us that the serpent learned them good from evil. And their god punished them, and their posterity awfuly for learning. Then Luke tells us at

16th., c. 8th., v., that the children of this world are wiser than the children of light, or the Adamites. Then, from personal and historical acquaintance with Christians I fail to see that they are as good, nor, that their muchness, is any more reliable than other people.

It cannot be disputed but what every word that was in their first bible, that they claimed Moses got from his god, was a thousand years older than he or his people And was common property, of the snake, fish, and ghost stories, of the five cent type.

It is an old saying, "as long aa the moral law". It applied to the sacred laws of mother India, of which there is 12 thousand volums, and no mans life is long enoughf to read them! The Pagans abridged them into one sentence—" Do to others as you would they should do unto you". Moses abridged them into 10 commandments. Paul abridged them into 5 commandments. And Uncle Sam abridged it all down into one glorious word— " freedom".

And yet, it is stranger than fiction to say it—yet, it is too true—this declaration of freedom, although established over 100 years—yet, it is flatly denied, by every government, and contradicted, and cunningly thwarted, and withheld by every party, clique, church, and order under the sun. And there can scarcely be found —a free man— or one that even believes in a free people. In other governments you only have to support one party. In this they willingly, without need, in rags, and poverty feed, clothe, and strut, as idle, ignorent, gods, many many, parties, cliques, churches, nnd orders!

The theology of mother India, is not only the old est, but the best yet offered. It is Pantheistic, that is, whatever is, is a part of God; and if natural, or well balanced, it is right. That we have the godhead of the Creator, a Preserver, and a Changer.

This last, gives us the transmigration, that is, the matured, or perfected man or woman, will be absorbed to rest in God, while the immatured, or imperfect man, woman, or child will be given another chance. This is the most rational and scientific, and then it is just. While a Jew savior, and an everlasting Christian hell, of fire, is simply the output of mans becrazed infernal infirmities.

What the Greeks, and Romans, found in mother India, is just what meets the eye of the traveler today. A teeming population, gentle and peacable, fabulous riches; the arts and the industries passing from generation to generation unchainged. The same is so of the oldest city—Damascus, the capitol of ancient Syra. She has never been changed, nor destroyed! The same was found in this country, in 1492. It was a perfect garden, inhabited by a sinless race of people, that were as numerous as the ants upon the ant hills. But now how is it? View the contrast, wherever the cross has been raised!

Loss, theft, murder, robbery, forgery, rape, suicide, mob law, gag law, force law, prohibition law, sunday law, moral law, civil law, common law, out law, money law, always at law, inforcing unconstitutional, and uncalled for laws; along with the sudden and premature deaths, premeditated and death by poison, a drunken death, death by law, a spirtual death, and an eternal death—is the hue and cry from one end of this continent to the other.

And religious, political misrule, with their thousand and one secret oath bound orders, that has usurped our civil rule, and trampled down our constitutions, has caused it.

The papers cannot record the awful tragidies as, fast, and as truthfully, as they rapidly occur. The death roll for this presidetial campaign, and on up to now, never was equaled on earth! Yes, only think, that a great, and respectable part of our good peaceable, law-abiding citizens, yes, citizens of these great and mighty FREE states, secretly rallied and arrayed by secret oath-bound, oath-breaking, religious, political, paternal CLANS — declaring destruction to our fixed, free institutions; the God given rights of other citizens—for the avowed and determined purpose of RULING and controlling of them without their consent, representation, or knowledge! Forcing us to sanction, give, and support a subsidiary robbery, or be boycotted, or, castrated, that is, made in-to a cut fice-dog, at best, if you please!

And this is one of the reasons why we have such a howl, such a bowyow, just now. For all that the largest majority can now do, is stint, starve, suffer; stand-a fair off, and view those oath-bound, secret touchmenot, privileged fields of sweet Eden, over and over, jump around, whine, play dog—and die like a dog; and this is life among the Christians in a land long a go declared FREE!

To prove that I am not exaggerating Pres. Clveland on the 30th., of June, 1893, called the congress of the United States together for the purpose of relieving the people from their great distress, and to prevent further loss, by repealing the unwise laws, as he termed them.

This government, under Gen. Grant, being induced by the Christians, some 20 years ago, to contribute money, and government help, to convert the world; and especially the south, the Negro, and the Indian. An Inquisitorial Christian crusade was generaly inaugerated, whenever, and wherever it was possible. A kind of a religious, paternal government has been forced upon us for 20 years; with an army of hidden accusers, that force us into the courts; all of which is unconstitutional. Myself being dragged before the federal court, the attorney-general with hidden accusers, acted the double and rediculous farce of prosecutor and defender. I making a witness of him and won the case, as is recorded in my book Brutality and Humanity.

The most outrageous taxes have been collected, and the vilest laws enforced. No representation, and little protection.

They destroyed the peoples greenback money. It had saved the country against a great rebellion. It had inspired new hope, and started it again in prosperity and peace. They estabelished a system of speculating banking —give them capital; and exempted them from taxes; and levied an outrageous privilege tax on all the trades, arts, and industries. They increased their army of government officers, and employes. They increased their salaries. They turned all offices, both national, state, county, and corporations, into a speculative business, and soon amassed fabulous fortunes.

This soon begun the shutting down the wheels of honest industry, and started a million army of begging. thieving, robbing, ravishing, and murdering tramps. In less than a year, the thousand and one, sectarin churches, built themselys mighty cathedrells and palacious parsonages. And all of this fabulous wealth has been given to then, and is alowed to shine, and strut free of taxation. While the poor labor pays outrageous rents, taxes, and lives in a hovel, a disgrace to these lords stables! And when a storm comes they are blown away.

Just one church, Trinity, in New York, owns a league of land, right in the heart of the city, free from taxes. Wall street with its tuns of gold, the millionaires homes, the great shows, theaters, and all free from taxes!

No wonder the Itallians, Chineses, Indians, Negroes, and subjugated southerners, have grown clanish and uncertain. Mob law had to be resorted too by the Chineses and Indians, to get rid of these unbearable Christian missionaries. Mob law had to be resorted too by the south to get rid of the impudent and lawless Negroes, Itallians, and Simite Christians! And although the government was so foolish as to dabble, and invest in religious matters, she was also, so unjust as to select just one sect, the Quakers, to make "honest Injin." And yet, after gobbling up a few millions, in less than no time they run the poor Indians crazy, made them idle, had them looking for a saviour. And as he was to be an Indian conquor, and not a subjugated Jew, they begun the bloody war dance, for the destruction of every body but "good Injin. Finally the government sent an army out there and slew them; not sparing the women nor children ;nad the rivers run red with their blood! And religion done it!

These are only a few facts among the many where this religious, paternal class, with their unconstitutional class laws, has proven disasterously. Right now while I am penning this page, the decision of our highest court is that the worlds fair can keep open on Sunday! This outrageous attempt of the Sundyites to inforce their filthey crazey religion, caused a loss of thouands of dollars, ruined the fair, disgraced the nation, add made a braying jack ass of themselves.

It would take 25 hundred teams each carrying a tun of money, to pay for one years expenses that these "unwise laws," has taxed the people with— that's squandered in uncalled for religious lawsuits! It would take the same to haul a years interest for these banking bond lords!! It will take tuns of money to pay these democrat and republican gods, their outrageous sallcries, while they were placing these "unwise laws" upon us, and whose interest it is to keep such upon us!!! Now,' Grover, where are you going to get this noney ? Remember the money-changers, your saviour fussed with, and you will see you are confronting exactly the same Jew money-changers, and the same state of affairs. If you give these speculative money-changers a new lease, and get the money; then you re-place the nation in a worse slavery than the old Negro slavery, and you know it, and you know that the people know it. And the sequel will be told of us as it was told of Rome, Persia, Babylon, Egypt, and others.

☞ When Rome went down these same religious money-changers, that run Christ crazy, owned all the then known world! When Persia went down one per cent. of the population owned the money, and all the land! When Babylon went down two per cent. of the people owned all of the wealth. When Egypt went down three per cent. of her population owned ninty-seven per cent. of the wealth! In every instance the common people were church ridden slaves, and starved to death!

For the last twenty years the United States has rapidly followed in the steps of these old preast-ridden religious nations! And religion caused it! And yet, our constitution positively forbids religous legislation. Every honest citizen forbids it. And our experience forbids it.

This is a big countrey. The 827,844 square miles of the original 13 states, would have long a go been exhausted had it not been for the fresh additions.

Jefferson bought Louisiana of Napoleon, and added more than a million square miles of western territory to the union. Monroe purehased Florida of Spain, and brought 59,268 additional square miles under the stars and stripes. The annexation of Texas increased our territory by 376,921 square miles. The annexation of the provinces of northen Mexico increast it by 535,783 square miles. The Gadsden purchas in the southern part of Arizona gave us 45,535 square miles more. Sewards purchased Alaska, from the Czar of Russia, added 577,930 square miles of territory, and brought the area of this free and independent union up to its present extensive possessions, of 3,603,884 square miles. More than three-fourths of which has been added by annexation during the present century.

The fourth of July, 1893, marks the 117th birth. day of the first, and only free nation, under the sun a mighty nation. Every sound, every sight, should remind us of that fourth of July, 1776, when that band of heroic men, rebelled against the tyranny of the English church, and subscibed their names to a declaration of the ETERNAL right to independence and self-government! A privilege that all nations had denied man, from the fact, that they were under church rule, and not self-rule!

Yet, their preast-ridden subjects, aided us in gaining our freedom, and served in our ranks in defending it! And our pension money goes out freely to every country under the sun!

State after state has been added, until the thirtey are now forty-odd. ☞ Let no one forget the length of time, and the cost at which freedom and liberty were secured!

Reader, it is awful to teach, that all that our revalutionary fathers done, and all that our country has done, is hellish! Yet, this is exactly, what all churches teach!

Remember, this is a civil government. It is not a religious, nor a political one. It was intended to be run by the civil magistrates; under the peoples written constitution. They should be elected by the people, and not by, nor in the interest of any party, clique, church, or order.

☞ The church is our most dangerous enemy, from the fact, that they deny the supremacy of our magistrates, and teach that the pope, the bishop, the preast, the preacher, and the king, are divine, and recieve a commission from God to rule man. We deny a divine class to rule. Yet, they claim that they must spit, and dabble in every thing before it can be legally eat, drank, or used. That you are not living a legal life, unless they have circumcised you into the old original Jew meat, blood and money route to heaven. Or, the sweet Jesesites water route of bapsousing, wine bibing, and money begging, to heaven. That you are not legally begot, nor legally born, unless they tied the gordian knot, and got big pay for it.

To illustrate: When I was 21 years old, my father a methodist preacher, come to me and asked me if I wanted to be baptised. I asked, why do yo ask me that? He replied, answer me, and then I will explain. I replied, no, nor circumcised. He then said, your mother would not alow you baptised, and made me promise her, on her death bed, not to alow it, and to ask you this question, when you were of age!

So, to this day, I thank my God that I never have BELONGED to any THING and can truthfully say, I am an American. Of course, for fifteen long years, I was begged, and solicited, by others, but, not by my father, to become a Christian. But, from my firs recollections, I abhorred such an idea.

Yet, I so respected my father, that I never made known my convictions until after his death. His old bible, manuscripts, prayers, and sermonds, fell into my hands, and informed me that he too, was an Infidel! That the Methodist Conference, had discharged him, because he would not quit singing those old songs, praying those old prayers, and preaching those old sermonds! So, he died an Infidel, and was not buried with his wife and children but, buried by the Masons, in a Presbyterian graveyard, near the grave of one of the wickedest men I eve knew. I have heard his curse-oathes a mile!

When my mother, a sister, and a brother died; and as I had not been bapsoused, as one of the lords kids, I was not considered worth, nor worthey, of a doctors bill. Thus, I not only, escaped initiation to Christian slavery, but, medical murder! After seeing that I would not die, my father gave me to a sister of charity, and her Christian charity, was as true as the needle to the pole, for she gave me to an old town sow, the old sow carried me to her nest of pigs! But, like poor old Daniel, I was so infernaly hellish that the hogs would not eat me!

My grandfather, an old Irish Infidel, found me in the hogs bed, and carried me in his arms, eight miles to his country home, and gave me a black mamma. She was an Infidel, from the fact that her only child had been torn from her bosom, and carried south by these southern Methodist Christians, who claimed a Negro had no soul, to save!

Religionists, and especially, Christians respect not the feelings, nor the concience of others, but are eternally yelping about theirs. I dont believe it is possible to hold a court, without having some old long faced, hypocritical complaining Christian before it.

Their savior says at Luke 14c. 26v, that you, to become a Christian, must HATE your father, mother, wife, children, brethern, sisters, and your own life! This is actually the first symptom of craziness! If you are truly a Christian you are certainly crazey! The mind hast to be wrought up to that pitch of excitement that partly, or wholy unbalances it. This is, what they call, "gitin ligin". It is having the organic quality of your brain chainged from a healthey to an unhealthey condition. From rest, to unrest! and you are ever afterwards restless, and miserable.

The faith, hope, and charity of our government is more just, stable, and trustworthy, and this makes us better than Christianity. We bestow full faith, hope, and charity to all mankind, to every thing! All other religions, bestow only to their sect, and only to paying members at that; giving discouragement to others throughout life, and dooming you to an eternal hell throughout eternity!

☞ As soon as a member, or, slave, to any party, clique, church, or order fail to pay their dues, then charity stops! And the poor suffering becrazed creatures that has served them all their life has to die in an old Infidel poor-house! We do not condem a man for what his ancestors done. Christianity does. " Visiting the iniquity of the fathers upon the children. Ex. 20c. Gen. 3c, 17. 9c, 25. Lev. 25c, 45, 46. Jo. 3c, 8. Lu. 21c, 17. 2 Tim. 3c, 12. Heb. 12c, 68. Rom. 5c,12." Many more could be given.

These are wretched facts, before every bodies eyes, and yet, they will give, give to the church all their life, and at last, be deserted, and have to die in our old Infidel asylum; in full view of those magnificent churches, and those palacious parsonages, Only think, how many, many towns and counties, there are in this union; and every one has its asylum. Did you ever see a church that had an asylum ? Yet, they are all the time begging for the poor heathen; and sit and whistle jigs, and see their members carried to our asylums every day.

Our civil magistrates meet every month, to hear your complaints, and to provide for your wants. Does your pretending great friends, the church, ever do so? Even Trinity Church, of New York, with millions of exempt property, has no asylum! but many, many a saloon, and gambling hell!

Websters dictionary tells us that the heathens had their asylums for the vilest criminals. The Jews had their cities of refuge." But, you Christians are a lot of wealthey lying beggars! Feasting on falce pretenses, and exacting submission by threatening every body with an eternal hell, but they would use force to-day, brute force, were they in power. The 109 psalm is a fair sample of a Christians prayers. And think of it being ordered, and inspired by God. I composed, and prayed a similar one when a child. I here give you both.

"Let the extortioner catch all that he hath—and let the stranger spoil all his labor. Let there be none to extend mercy unto him—let his posterity be cut off. But, O, God, deliver thou me!"

I chimed in : " O, God, I would there were a Christian hell; and that I was a favord fiend, to feed' and feast, upon their immortal gizzards. O, how I would chunk 'em."

It now seems to me that I am in a Christian hell and O, dont I chunk 'em?

The seduction of young girls, and mens wives, in the church, by preachers, are far more often than by saloonists, or gamblers. Take your history of your fathers; Abraham, Isaac, Jacob, David, Solomon; and on down to Wesley, Beacher, and others. Then just call to mind, any church in your time, and answer this question.

And where do you go to get a redress of your injuries? To the church? No, never; but to our old Infidel, Court House. The only place you can get a notice, and a protection. And you know it. Did your bible, or any religious government, ever respect, or protect your life, liberty, happiness, and virtue? Never, never, no never? The Catholics settle a case of rape for 2 or 3 dollars.

Solomon in all his glory, would not respect, nor protect, your childhood, innocence, nor virtue. He, himself, would violate any female child, he choose, and even imprison them, as long as he wished! He would send out his soldiers and take of your fair daughters, just who, and as many as he pleased, and do with them just when, where, and as he pleased! Just read his history, and then get some old drunk fool to sing his songs, and hug you at the same time; and see if you would not like to be one of his 7 hundred strange wives, or one of his 3 hundred young concubines! Read the 1st. verse of the 11th. chapter of 1st. Kings, and it tells you that he loved many strange women, together [in a whore house] with the daughters of Pharaoh, women of the Moabites, Ammonites, Edomites, Zidonions, and Hittites. Contrary to his gods orders. And he loved other gods; also, contrary to orders.

Then you Christians of to-day, add to this infamy a glaring lie, on his songs, and on your maker, by adding to them, and make them say it is the churches love for Christ. When he, nor none of his people had yet thought of a religion that included a Christ.

Just such whoreing religion was going on in the south, and was forced on the Negro. The same in Utah. And, would be forced on us to-day if it were not for our Infidel government. And they have the bible for it. The 6th. chapter of Genesis tells us the sons of God took them wives of the daughters of men as they choose.

Solomon, according to the laws of nature, could not have used that number of women in a life time, at broken doses, much less, all at one dose. The facts are, he was the keeper of a mammoth whore house! He was a great big, black, hoo-doo, Jew Negro. He practiced spells, and charmes. And, in the short space of a 40 years life exhausted the fabulous wealth, the plunder from nation, after nation; that their god had murdered, in cold blood, and give to him, through Moses, Aaron, and Joshua. And, although his god had destroyed all his former creation, and created Jeruselam specially for him, and had promised to dwell there, perpetually, for ever. Yet, this wine, woman, and song, crossmark, hoo-doo religion downed them all. Millions of her men, women, and children wer slaughterd within her walls, and the rest sold into slavery!

And, religion in your wiseest man caused it. O! my, what a mashing lover, for the church, was Solomon. He loved love. His love was free-love; and thrown away on those undeserving. Christs was love exacted through a threat, a reward, or a price; bought love; slave love! Both were the extremes of craziness. While our love is a universal love, a rational, reasoning love, founded on what is due you; or justice to all mankind.

Yes, we say, as does Pope, at page 36 : "Take Nature's path, and mad opinion's leave; All states can reach it, and all heads can concieve; Obvious her goods, in no extreme they dwell; There needs but thinking right, and meaning well; And mourn our various portions as we please, Equal is common sense, and common ease.

Remember, man, "the Universal Cause Acts not by partial, but by general laws;" And makes what happiness we justly call Subsist not in the good of one, but all."

But, this proposed Christian savior, or, man-god, taught, as did his fathers, a special election only for the Jews, and a special damnation for every body else! Matt. the 15c., 24 tells us that Christ was only sent to the lost sheep of the house of Israel. And at the 26 verse he calls others DOGS! The 1 c., 11 of John tells us that his own recieved him not.

Yes, your bible teaches, and so does tradition, that the house of Israel rejected him, and claimed that he was a bastard, a fraud; and the moneychangers said he was a regular he billey goat, and butted over their tables; and the old women declared he was a mad dog, and slaped them about.

So, his craziness had become dangerous. He had not only thretened his people, and their temple with destruction, and preached sedition, but, he had laid on violent hands! He had committed the sin, and the crime, that caused the officers of their god to hunt him up. They found him hiding out, trying to elude an arest, as you are told by Luke, at 14 c., 46, 48, Now, if they were not the officers of God, then your bible is a lie, and if they are officers of God, then your man-god is crazy, mistaken, or an imposter. At any rate, he was offering both an earthley, and a heavenly Jeruselam, on a credit, and at short promissory payments at that. He could get only ignorent men for his apostles. And they were all the time asking about an earthley instead of a heavenly kingdom.

He even said publically, that: "There was some standing there that would not tast death until they sean him coming in his kingdom," Matt., 16c.,28. Mar., 9c., 1. Lu., 9c., 27. And, although, they wated, hoped, and looked, yet he never came. And from that day to this, fools only expect him. And although they claim the earth, and the temple was rent, and the heavens darkened, the dead walked around; is not supported by the records; and is an unreasonable lie. As to his resurection, the apostles did not look for that, nor did they believe it. Lu.16c 13, 14. But they knew they had betrayed him, deserted him; and seen him die like a dog on the cross of infamy. They had seen him drink gall and vinegar. They had seen him slaped, kicked, stabed, and spit upon. And after they had allowed all this, and as they had all deserted him, they heard him desparingly cry out. as he was dying—in a loud voice:—"My god! my god! why hast thou forsaken me?

His own recieved him not, but, according to God's Holy Law, John the bapsouser, had done it ALL! According to this self-same law, they murdered him! And according to his own law they made wine out of his blood, happy bread of his body, and they eat, and drink, him to this day!

Only think! forsaken by his people, by his apostles, and by his god! What an awful lif and death was his, and all of his followers, even to this day!

☞ O! my, what mistakes for gods to make! John was to be his forerunner, to prepare the way, so Christ could set up his kingdom. And although he had couverted, and bapsoused, in the little river Jorden, in one summer, ALL Judea, ALL Jeruselam, and every body round a bout there—which was millions, and millions, of all races of people. Matt. 3c., 5. Mar. 1c., 5. Lu. 3c., 1 to 21. John did no miracles, John 10c., 41. Then, who told this lie?

When Jesus arived he found John in prison, and could not have been bapsoused by him, Matt. 11c. 2, 3. And the way not prepared, so he undertook to prepare it. Poor fellow; Peter cursed him, and disowned him! Judas sold him! And the medical students dissected him! The peddlers baught his old clothes! Yet, in the face of all this we are told he rose from the dead; that he upbraded them for their unbelief; then he gave them a greater command.

By this time he was awful charitable, for Lu. the 16th. c. and 14 15 verses, tell us that he appeard to the dirty 11 ; this even included old 'cussing,' 'denying,' 'crying,' Peter, " And he said unto them, Go ye into ALL the world, and preach the gospel to every ☞ CREATURE. ☜

Creature included the Musketo, the Flea, Chinch, the Louse, the Devil, and your deadliest enemies! It includes the Hog, the Dog, and the Jackass, our best friends!

These are the signs of this new, Catholic, or, believe or bedamed religion. " In his name they were to cast out devils, speak new tongues, [to acommodate every CREATURE,] handle serpents, drink poisons, and heal the sick." But lo, and behold, these like all signs failed, and they all soon met awful deaths!

Hundreds of years after a simelar Catholic religion was restarted, by Constantine, emperor of the Romam Empire. And yet no bible! Christ had not only failed to make them understand; but, he himself could not read, nor write, and left not the scratch of a pen!

Reader, remember this is proof gleaned from themselves, and not from others. And remember, also, that the bible is only a lot of novels, a fabrication, got up by a Roman King, from old traditionary fish, and snake stories, of the five cent type. It is an outrage to contribute it to the Devil, muchless our Maker. From its original self, you could not distinguish it from the scratches of an old hen. It is only fragments, or broken doses, of those old traditionary fables, and stories of the ancients. Nothing is original, nor is any subject faithfully given, nor is it complete. This is why you cannot make any thing out of it but a jumbled up mass of Self-Contradictions!

THIS CUT represents the religionists of this King's Bible smashing out a poor mans brains, just for picking up a few sticks on Sunday. See Numbers, Chapter xv. Verse 32 to 37.

They done so till stoped by the Romans. So did the Roman Christians till destroyed by the Arabs. The English and the American Christians done so till stoped by the United States. So, Mr. Christians what power to protect, or to inforce your

Gods, God-Kings, Lords, Lord-Gods, Christs, Christ-Jesus', or Saviors laws when you, yourselvs do not keep, nor even respect them?

You have always, in every country under the Sun, changed your gods laws just to suit man and the Devil. Noah, Abraham, Moses, Joshua, and others were Lords and Saviors. Jesus tried to be a Lord and a Savior, but failed— his own people disowned, and killed him by beating his brains out for violating their Sunday and other laws, just as this picture represents. He was not crucified!

This 4th Commandment has two objects. Hard labor, and pretended rest. And, this is precisly, the way it has been inforced, whenever, and wherever religionists had the power. "Six days SHALT thou labor." it demands! One is as much enjoined as the other.

The first object is to force you to labor every day or pay a fine. And to give a part of that days wages to the church, or pay a fine. The next is, to force you to observe their Sabbath, and many other church days, as they say, or pay a fine. And to force you to their church, and your children to the Lord's school, as they say, or pay a fine.

How presumptuous, how hypocritical, how absurd, and self-contradictory in religionists to claim that they obey the 4th, or any of the commandments! Or, that a God with a spark of sense, would give us a commandment that conflicts with the unchangable laws of nature. God has given us HALF of TIME for REST! He even marked it with a dull, heavy, somber hue; or, darkness, called night, and you with a tired, yawning, stretching, relaxed, stupid condition— a desire to rest, slumber, snooze, or sleep. None, no, not one can dispute nor mistake this time, nor its necesity. Then, why will you be a fool? and a beast of burden? for a lot of knaves, and evil designing rascals?

You never hear these blasted, blating, braying,

Jackass, once a week, Sunday clean up, go to meeting, whitewashed, Christian, hypocritical knaves, and fools, say one word about the desecration of man's God given, one half of time, for rest. No, you never heard such a thing! And yet, without it every bit of it—man becomes an unhealthey, unbalanced, or crazy being! And this condition has to be reached; and established, before any man will profess Christianity!

Most of our diseases, and troubles, arise from this disregard of man's God given, one half of time for rest. And this everlasting meddling, wanting to change our wives and children into Christians. Wanting to attend to God's business, wanting to change the noblest work of God, or Nature; as if they were beholding to man. This meddling with peoples private affairs. This meddling with young married people. This meddling with old people, after they are in their dotage. This meddling with sick people. This meddling with people after they are dead. Yes, this smelling around generally; this eavesdsopping, this intimidating, and meddlesom practice of Christians, as in the days of Rome, have not only become an unbearable nuisance, but a curse! And we have reached a point where forbarence has ceased to be a virtne; and retaliation has to be resorted to in self defence.

This so-called, mis-called, man styled Lord's day for rest, is a lie; and the people know it. It is a day for preacher feasting, money begging, winebibing, bibblebabling, backbiting, proselyting, and meddling with people generaly!

It actually debilitates, deranges, and injures man and beast; and they feel less like work the next day than any day in the whole week; and are more or less sick, or addled from the loss of sleep, intemperance, glutony, or over exertions, and excesses, and the awful jealousy that is pecular to this courting day, and time for dress display. It is a grand day for saloons and doctors!

Only review the humiliating situation that rallied to be the God-sent Agent to open, and controle the World's Fair. Only think! hundreds of different religions, or God sent Agents, with their Standard of Justice, or rules of faith, were there!

☞ And every one dimetrically opposed to the other, to God and Nature, to our Declaration of Independence, to our Constitution, and to our individual conscience, and chances, as free independent Sovereigns.

Yes, they were ALL there demanding that they, and they alone, were the genuine elect, or God's chozen Agent, and the only one that God would alow to open, and controle the Great World's Fair! and thus, the whole World be made to bow obedience to their peculiar little, nearsighted, sectarian songs, prayers, and sermons! or genuine rout to Heaven!

What a crazy, humiliating condition was this. The President of the United States had to interfear and open, and control the Fair himself! Then O! my, what a howl! what a bowyow! of shame, and slander, and insolence went up, throughout this crazy! crazy! religious world: saying that the great World's Fair was so big that it aimed to get along without the help of God. This was a dastardly, and a cowardly insult, to our Free American God, and to every free American citizen.

☞ Then cam the hiena howl, we will boycot you, that is, we will premeditatingly, in secret, murder yur Fair! We will close you on Sunday! Then the query came, whose Sunday? For lo, and behold, there were more different Sundays offerd than there are days in a week! Then pray tell us whose Sunday can we keep? Mine, mine, yelled a legion of crazey cranks, from every quarter under the Sun.

And to their viciousness, shame, and disgrace, and our stupidity, they did illegally, and contrary to all law, God's or man's, they forced a partial close, two or three times; knowing that it could not be observed; and thank God it was not. But, around their own churches, and homes, indignantly, and defiantly, caroused the maddened rabble. It almost rivaled the storming of the Bastile, in Paris, in 1789. And they demanded that it be no more closed on any Man's, Lord's, nor God's days.

Reader, all this proves beyond a doubt that God is not like a man; neither does he lie, repent, and change. Neither was man made in the image and likeness of God Man is only an atom of God. God neither hears nor answers prayers. This was not only tested, and thoroughly proven, to its fullest extent, by the united prayers of all the religions throughout the whole world, to close the gates of World's Fair on Sunday, or the Christian's Jew-Lord's day. Yes, history is full, and running over, with just such tests. Take the fall of Jeruselam, and religion in that day. Take the fall of Rome, and religion in that day. Take the fall of the Crusades, that ☞ MURDERED ☜ millions of their own Christian children, by endeavoring to regain Jeruselam. Take the fall of England when praying and fighting, for OUR INFIDEL FATHERS destruction; and from that day to this, praying, and working for the destruction of the only free government under the sun.

☞ This praying to an imaginary god has been going on for ages, and not one instance is on record where their prayeas were answered—or that God has made himself known to man.

Prayer, faith, and works were all thoroughly tested at the Great World's Fair. They not only spent week after week, praying and working, but they spent millions of dollars! Yet their god, like their Jesus' god, anwered not his nor their prayers. He shirked, and prayed for the cup of death to be withheld, and when he felt the cold, relentlus hand of death was upon him, he askingly cried in a loud voice; " My God! my God! why hast thou forsaken me?" Reader, God knows no religion, no bible, nor Sunday. Uncle Sam knows no religion, no bible, nor Sunday; nor no sane man does. Why should God make a day for rest and worship, and not mark it, so that all Nations, and Tribes of man could not mistake his time and wish? Nature nor no other animal, but this crazy animal man knows any such a day. Ample proof was furnished of religion being a daingerous crazy curse, during the World's Fair. ☞ It opened with rapine and murder! It lived beset with rapine and murder! It closed with rapine and murder! And religion caused it!

The Sun of the Preacher of Congress, while at the Fair, cuts his throat, and catches his blood in a bowl, and dies like a dog! The Mayor of the city of Chicago, as the Great World's Fair was being shroud d, was shot down dead, like a brute. And my dear reader, this is only an item of what taken place in tihs Priestridden City, where every officer is a Catholic! And why? or what is the cause of all this chaos? Because Christians, and especially the Catholics, deny our form of government, and hate our freedom! When our Revalutionary Fathers, whiped the Christian, King George, and freed us from their crazy, hellish rule; the religonists, one, and all, from that day to this, has saught to confuse, and to destroy our freedom: our personal, inalienable sovereignty.

The American Sentinel, of New York, in its ishue of March 1, 1894, on page 66 says: " This Inquisitor-General Parkhurst has scattered through this city 1, 137 spies—one in each election district—who spend their time KNOT simpley in discovering crimes which have been alrerdy committed, but in inducing people to commit crimes, and even in COMMITTING crime themselves, in company of others, or on the premises of others, in order to entrap, to prosecute, and to imprison those others. And the worst feature about it is that THE COURTS give it the support and sanction of law."

This is practically running and controlling us by religion, and its main object is to make money by the Sale of Indulgence, and Black-mail, as of old.

It is the same old crazy religion, that claim sin or, murder may be committed if good is entended.

Now, although this is very common, and has become the predominating religious theory, yet, it is very, very unnatural, miserable, inhuman; and is the common aggravating, well known cause of all our misfortunes, and destructions. They claim to be God perfect, and cannot be altered, changed, improved; nor learned any thing; no, they claim to know all about God, and must know all about your private business; they even sware that God has made them our guardian. They preach to us the 48th verse of the 5th chapter of Mathew, that says: "Be ye as perfect, as your Father in heaven." And when we preach to them the 19th verse of the 7th chapter of Hebrews, that says: "That the law made nothing perfect." And the 20eth verse of the 7th chapter of Ecclesiastes, that says: "There is not a just man upon the earth, that doeth good." And the 10th verse of the 3rd chapter of Romans, that says: "There is none righteous, no, not one."

They chime in, O! it dont mean that; it is not a contradiction; dont you believn in a god?

Yes, Christianity teaches that every body but the members of their sect are TOTALY depraved; that is, you are as mean as hell, and sure to go to hell if you dont 'git' their peculiar religion, and it must be got in their peculiar way. No matter how good, pure, and virtuous you may be, your goodness, and honesty is worth nothing, and will not save you. This sends every church to hell but ONE.

☞ Then they all unite in one inglorious curse and send every body to hell that does not profess religion. Thus it was that the churches, one and all, preached our revolutionary fathers to hell. And the rebel church preached our emancipating defenders of this Union to hell. And if Christianity, and its Jew-Kings, Slavery Bible is true they are in hell. But, thank God, dear reader, you know that they all cannot be true; then, is it not possible, when we see, and know so many great and popular churches, or roads to heaven, are wrong, then, is it not possible that they are ALL mistaken?

If there is a personal god, and if he choose such a plan of salvation, then why is it that man grows, matures, dies, and passes away without ever thinking about it; and laws have to force us to even respect it? If it was not for the preachers there would be no religion. Mankind, even where rased by religious parents, the largest majority of them would die without a preacher, a prayer, or any uproar, if allowed to do so. But, they seek us, dog us through life, and will not allow us to even have a peaceful death bed. You dont have to tell man he is hungry. No, whatever God, or Nature, wanted you to do you do it, and it takes no preacher to show you.

Only think, nation after nation, has past away, not knowing the now proposed only road to heaven. And but few, now in existence, will ever be informed. Sam Jones said there are 6 hundred millions of people on this earth who never heard the name of God.

Jesus said unto his deciples, follow me and I will make you fishers of men! But it seemed that he, and them, were a mear lot of Sardiens, themselves, and was immediatly caught! and killed; notwithstanding a promis of security from all manner of harm. See Mark xvi, 17, 18.

Tteir first fishing was at night, secretly, in Jeruselam; where Jesus, Judas, Paul, and the two James' wer caught, and killed! The rest of them fled to foreign countreys, but caught and killed!

Yet, in the face of all this, they tell us that we have to get our religion, or our passport, for heaven from this boasting, bastard, Jew fisherman. And he wont let you have it unless you approach him in a dog shivering, humileating way; in old sackcloth, filth, and ashes; saluting him as king; bowed down wailing, mourning, begging; and worst of all, acknowledging, to the whole world, that you are as mean as hell! Great God, reader, can you accept this? And when you have got it, you must yell like a demon; 'jine de church,' 'pay de preacher', 'de missionary,' and the lieing Sunday school teacher! Or, they give you another chance; you may rob, rape, murder, and steal, all your life, and when you get so old and worthless that the devil wont have you, then like a young Jay Bird, you can throw open wide your hellish mouth, and for the first time, and the only time, and the last time, on earth, gasp out: O! LORD'A! And the angels of this Jew Lord will come and get you, and carry you right slap dab to Heaven.

Or, when you are caught, and to be hung, all you have to do is to ' git, or re-git dis ligion, jine, or re-jine de church,' and go to bemeaning, and villifying, every body and every thing; die like a fool, and go to eternity in an uproar! Or, they give us another chance: pay them, and they will even pray us out of hell! This is why so much is given and willed to the churches!

Great God, this is an insult to my free sovereign identity, and to the dignity of every free American citizen. ☞ Tell me that I was born totally blind, and totally depraved, and as mean as hell, and must go to hell, for an old fabulous accurst Jew's sins; or, for something that I had nothing to do with! But, these Christian devils, that are blasting our homes and our lives; enslaving us; raping, and murdering our mothers, sisters, wives, and daughters: as history amply records. And yet these murdering devils are sure for heaven, so the preachers say. For all they have to do is to send for ' de parson,' look to that Jew Lord, be bapsoussed, bid defiance to your victims, and swing from the gallows, right slap dab into heaven!

☞ And I an innosent, sinless, little bastard, or raped, and murdered being, have to burn in an endles, and eternal hell! And as I am kicked, and slaped from flame to flame, I can look up to heaven and see that great big, burley Christian demon, that made me a bastard, that raped and murdered me! a bright shining angel in heaven. So say all Christendom!

THIS is Christian morality and justice! Great God let us sweep such religion from the face of this beautiful earth.

Christians only pretend to a religion! and a day for rest! Yes, pretend! They do not rest themselves, nor, do they allow any body, or any thing to rest. Rest, quiet, perchance slumber, or sleep? Ah! my God, where is any of this when a lot of chicken eating, Sunday feasting, wine bibing, bibblebabling, proselyting, Christians are about?

They are all the time, wolf like, sculking around pretending to be a lamb, and God's lamb at that, but, the facts are, they are gaining privileges, power, and wealth, under false pretenses. They, nor none of their children have got any confidence in one another, and go abroad to marry and to do business, as did Moses, Isaac, Jacob, and others. They will marry the Devil, or any of his children; a saloonist, a gambler, a bigamist, a harlot, or any thing, or any body lord, just to get away from a Christian home!

Only think, hundreds of different religions surround us, all declaring each other false, and every body but themselves on the road to hell! And especially our United State's Standard of Justice, or RELIGION, is wrong: when it is the ONLY Standard of Justice, or Religion, ever known to man, where all are alike protected in their religious freedom! Think of that you ungrateful, proselyting hypocrits!

How did God rest! Was he deafening you with the thunder of great belles? Was he pounding an old clapboard pulpit, screaming like a Panther; telling the rich man that it is easier for a Camel to go through the eye of a cambric needle than for a rich man to go to heaven? Or, that God blest, and saved only the liberal giver? And thus extort from weak minded people, old women, children, widows and orphans, blood money?

THIS so-called Lord's Day could not be made practical, beneficial, nor general, that is, universal, from the fact that time is not the same all over the world at the same time, and at all places. This fact was not known to the getters up of bibles!!!! This fact, got them, and their god in to a scrape of presumptuous ignorance. Even that winding up book of horror of horrors, murder of murders, in that awful revealed prophecy, of this Christian god, to his only son, and from him to his brother John of what would shortly come to pass, has not come to pass. See Revelation·

They taught that the earth was held up by its four corners. They did not know it was round, and when day here it was night there. So, a general day of rest would stop not only communication, but commerce, travel and trade. It would do it between the states— for they are free and independent souvereigns on all such questions, and could not, or would not agree, on the same Lord, nor the same Lord's day. Tellegrams, nor letters could not be exchanged. This craziness was carried so far by the Jews that they would not fight on Sunday, so the enemy slaughtered them. They swallowed their money, and their enemy riped them open and got it; destroyed their house of god, that was to stand forever. And to-day the Infidel holds all of it, all that God once alowed the Jewe and Christians to bost of, as a God given home.

Being driven from their so-claimed god-given homes, long before 1492, they fled, not knowing where they were going, and landed on our beautiful Yankee Continent: that we called Americus-Vespucius, or the twin brothers, or the Amerikas · We recieved them, with all human charity, and now just view their fruits, and hear their hellish boasting, and threats; that this countrey is theirs, and that they are going to controle it: when the facts are, they are crazey, and cannot controle themselves.

Fifteen years ago I said that if this state of affairs continued that soon nobody but the lawyer and the bond holder would controle this countrey, right or no right. And it is so! I now say that if this state of affairs continue; that is, alowing religion to have any control of us whatever, that destruction will soon follow ! !!! ! !

If this state of affairs continue every Magistrate will have his Preacher, to pray before he begins a trial. Every old Granny will have a Chaplain to pray before a cild can be legally born.

There is now more singing, praying, and preaching done in our Tax-tackey-schools, than in our churches· Every school is run for the special interest of the church. And they are teaching our children lies and they know it! The facts are all public matters are run in the special, individual interest of some special indiviuals, as some party, clique church, or a secret oath bound order. And at awful salαr es. And things are run illegally, and unjust; and they know it! This is worse than slavery, or a king; for you have hundreds of kings and bond-lords to support; with a rapid increasing army of beggers and paupers.!

They, your masters, do not want a fair and a honest government! You don't want it! And this is why we do not have it! The simplest individual if he will but stop and think, for himself, just one moment, will see that it is the peoples addled, becrazed, and enslaved, preacher-ridden condition that feds, struts, and clothes with unlimited power the Polititions, the Lawyers, the Doctors, the Popes, the Priests, the Preachers, the Gamblers ; and a thousand and one, of their parties, cliques, churches, and their secret oath bound orders ! ! ! !

☞ Good laws do not feed polititions! Peace does not feed lawyers! Health does not feed doctors! A clear concience does not feed the pope, the priest, the deacon, the chaplain, the preacher, the missionary, and the lieing Sundy school teacher! A good government would not feed a thousand and one of these presumpteous, parasitical, piratical, so-called, self-styled, God sent guardians !

They are the law brakers, and the accusers of the

loyal, and the innocent! They murdered Morgan, in New York; Lincoln, and Garfield, in Washington; Cronin, and Harrison, in Chicago, and Hennesy, in New Orleans!

Religion is only an emotional insanity, a weakness that leads to craziness. History, both sacred and secular, tells us that religion never improves, nor elevates man, as is claimed! It makes man descend the scale; from a God-given, free moral agent or an independent sovereign, of all they survey, down from a lord to a church-ridden subject, and from a subject to a priestridden slave, and from a slave to a beast of burden. They are the destroyer of the good, the true, and the beautiful!

This is the historical descent, or downfall, of every nation, that has ever existed! and religion caused it! ☞ Deny it and you make your bible a lie ; admit it and you at once prove it a dangerous curse!

I do not know whether man ascended from a Porwigle; or descended from a god; but one thing I do know, and that is, religionists descend from free men to slaves ! ! ! !

The doctrin of Franklin, Paine, Jefferson, and our Revolutionary Fathers, that all men was created free and equal, was blasphemous to religionists, and their King George's Bible·

☞ Tom Paine-ism, or Infidelity, or Independence, found this Yankee Nation's neck under the despotic, religious heal of King George; and his bond-lords! It found the people then, as we find them now—howling from oppression— praying for the privilege of being his slave—not a free man !

Freedom had never entered their empty pates. They were not trying to be free men— no, they were only trying to soften the gall-gizzard of their masters. Ifidelity found them plowing with a stick, and reaping with their fingers—just as they were doing in the days of their Moss Jesus; and it was an awful sin to say he had not learned us all ! ☞ With sticks and stones, Infidelity made the first attact on King George's soldiers ! And after seven long years of awful suffering, death, starvation, and bloodshed, they give to the whole world the first privilege to be, or not to be a freeman! Yet, to-day, in the broad, bright light of the one hundredth year of the Independence of the United States, there can scarcely be found a free man! Never was there such a scramble for office as now. To be the hired purgered slave of some clique, party, church, or secret oath-bound order!

As far back as time can date all nations got their ideas from Egypt, and not from God. And Egypt got her's from Mother India; who got her's from the devil! So our evidenc has reached us through the third witness, and not God. And the worst of all: not one principle taught by this wandering Jew-god, of the Christians, was original; no, but it was the common ideas of those old countries. So now where, O, where is your thief of a god?

This temporal ruling of man by an earthly god, that religionists, and especially, the Catholics, aim to so amend our Constitution as to so rule us, was in the form of a god-head in Egypt. It was a trinity, composed of the Father, the Mother, and the first born Son. This is royal and not free religion. Here is where this royal idea of the first born son was of God: that is, begot by God: and an heir to his earthly throne: that is, he is born a god and you a beast of burden!

Tis was Jesus' claim; and he actualy insulted a poor penitent woman and called her a dog: See the 21st to 27th verses of the 15th chapter of Matt. That the rest of the children were nothing, not reliable, for they were only the children of men, or the bastard children of the gods. This made Isaac the only begotten son of Abraham. At least, that is the principle, that all governments prior to our's was founded. We see this principle aimed at when Cain slew Abel; he being the first born son, was declared got from God, but they dont tell us where they got Abel. Cain could not stand to hear Abel claim to be god-favored, or respected, as Abel claimed: O, no, this was blasphemy, so he slew Abel.

We see it in old Juda, who made Onan, his second son marry his first son Er's widow, that an heir may be born to Er. Er was killed by the Lord, and when Onan failed to give the Lord a royal heir the Lord slew him. Just read the 19th, and the 38th chapters of Genesis; and see the kind of morrality, it teaches our sons 'and daughters. ☞ Onan-isim, royal-isim, obscenity, and murder! is the composition of Christianity and its Lords Gods, and followers! ☞ My God! reader, just read the 19th and the 38th chapters of Genesis. ☞ Only think, of an all-wise God, having any thing to do with such abominations. ☞

Er and Onan, killed by this Christian Lord, or God, because they would not be a party with him in sin, shame and crime! Sodom and Gomorrah was burned alive! innocent mothers, and infants that had never thought of crime, much less committed it was burned alive, by this Christian god because they would not ☞ take and use old Lots girls. They, after being driven from Sodium, in the plains of Gomorrah, take refuge in the mountains, and play the devil with their old daddy!

Look at the Stone-forts, in South, in Central and North America, and they tell of the struggles of Virtue against this abominable Christian god!!

There is not one foot of ground, as far as I can see but what has drank the life blood of some Slave to this Christian God! I was begat, borned, and rased within their domain; and know of what I say.

And history tells us that precisley so is recorded of all the now known world!

Egyptian history, tells us of a god-head, of three. And here it was that the Jews and the Christians got their ideas; and not from God: and then they changed the old god-head into a father, son, and a holy ghost. Mixing a haunt, a ghost, or an embodied spiret with the physical, and the mental. And from Egypt Jesus got his idea of a Christ: for they have a fable of a god, Osiris, that went about the world doing good.

Even after King George was whiped, and his church driven from our land; the aristocracy of tne slave owning South, under the influence of Hamelton, and the preachers, and especially the Puritans, with their awful blue religious laws, united as Federalists, and come very near overthrowing our Infidel form of government.

Since the Amerikas, or Twin Brothers, have been known to Europe, Asia, Africa, and the Islands, sixteen wars have raged in what are now the United States. The Dutch war of 1655, King Philip's war of 1675, King William's war of 1689, Queen Anne's war of 1713, French and Indian war of 17 57, the Revolution of 1775, the Indian war of 17 90, tha Barbary war of 1803, the Tecumseh war of 1811, the war of 1812, the first Seminole war 1817, the second Seminole war in 1832, the Black Hawk war of 1835, the Mexican war of 1846, and the Rebelion in 1861.

The duration and cost of the four great wars were : Revolution, seven years, and cost over one hundred million dollars ; 1812, two and a half years and cost over one hundred million dollars; Mexican, two years, and cost $66 millions; the Rebelion, four years, and cost over 3 billions.

In the revolution were over 2 hundred thousand Yankee, or American troups ; while in the Rebelion there was over 2 billions of troops, from all parts of the world, fought for this Union ; and to-day, 33 years after, our pension money still goes out freely to them— to many a foreigner, away in a distant land ! ! !

There have been a perpetual desire to overthrow this government; and many attempts have been made. The first was in 1782, when some officers of the federal army tried to consolidate the thirteen states into one and confer supreme power on Washington ; in 1787, Shay's Insurection ; in 1794, Whiskey Insurection; in 1814, the Federalists again ; in 1820, Missouri Teritory ; in 1820, Georgia and the Creek Indians ; in 1820, Georgia and the Cherokees ; in 1832, South Carolina; in 1842, Rhode Islaud; in 1856, the Mormons; in 1859 John Brown; in 1861, the Southern Rebelion; in 1890, the Sinites, in Ala., and the Indians out west ; while the Briceville Insurection in Tenn. in 1891 and 2 was only a repetition of similar Insurections throughout the whole Union; and this everlasting, crazy, meddlesom practice of pie hunters; or fishers of men, seek to cause it !

Every four years, these fishers of men, struggle for the largest pie—the Presidential Pie—that is worth five hundred thousand dollars ! Then, every two years, the various states, are run wild by these pie hunting, fishers of men !

So, it is a fact, that as fast as the old fools die out the young fools grow up! Yes, we will have plenty of fools with us always; school or no school; and you yourself being the fool ! It is easy to fool all the people, but impossible to keep them from finding it out: and woe! to the smart Alecks when caught! Yes, while these large fish are gobbling up the smaller fish, the smaller ones are grabbing mouthful after mouthful from the larger ones, until like a snow pile their muchness melts away, and they, and it, return to the devil who gave it; religion, or no religion.

So, after all, whatever is, is right, and aim at— change your partners—and balanc all : you too, can do well if you will but attend to your own home, the dearest, and the most sacred place on earth.

So, when cast upon the great sea of life, we find it a sea of strife, and just like some little boat, some are cast upon the rocks and never get to float. And, yet, you can if you will make it Home, sweet home : for at best, all men have to study, fret, and work, early and late, and when they get one of those palaces it is mearly to die in; and be left for these pie hunting fishers of men. But few by their own honest labor can even make a comfortable home. He has no time to loose; to give away; nor to work for some body else. ☞ Then where did these palaces, temples, churches, mansions, and great buildings come from ? In answer, I say, that millions of poor human beings have been robbed of their time, labor, and life to build them. Then as they come by plunder, history and experience, tell us that they too, will go to ruin and destruction. This is no superhuman prophecy, but it is a moral fact; and the moral is this— the man who builds honestly himself an humble home, buildes the noblest temple to his country and to his God! It is home, sweet home, the noblest, the dearest, and the most sacred spot in existence; yes—

"Those who will may wed the lands,
 And the princely dower;
Bind themselves a lifetime too
 Some brick and mortar tower.
Yet, the bitter tear will start,
 And the soul will rue,
Better fair than riches all,
 Is the honest heart that is true.

Freedom, health, or tranquility is the wish of all sane people. The good, the bad, the great, the small, one and all, long and sigh for peaceful tranquility. It is this heaven of rest that all hope to attain, both in this life and the life hoped for.

"Some calm sequestered spot,
The world forgetting, by the world forgot."

☞ This was the happy condition of all tribes of man when first discovered by these Jew-Jesusite, missionary malcontents. This happy condition was this blissful Eden of peacefulness; when discovered by the Christians. Now, just view the fruits of Christian avarice on one side and Infidel charity on the other. After Christianity had killed out the whole then known world, and caused the dark, dismal, ignorant age— then it was that Infidelity in the deserts of Arabia; and the wildes of the Amerikas gave us Liberty!

I seen the very identical results reached in my father's family. My father, a preacher, married an Infidel's daughter· It so happened that the parson was to stay at home for a season, and accordingly give us Christian rule— that ended in ruin! As I was coming home, late one evening, I saw the parson chop off a cat's head. What on earth, father can be the matter? I asked. She was trying to kill the martins, he exclaimed. Time went on, and one long summer's afternoon I constantly heard the firing of his shot gun; and all hands wondered if the parson had turned sportsman. And on arriving at the house we found the parson had been killing martins. What is the trouble, father, I asked? The martins are eating up the bees, he replied· Time roled on, and soon cider-making came on. Work over we went to making cider. Here come the bees. They sucked the old sowered pomace, got drunk, made no honey, and starved, and froze to death. My dear black mamma's only child was torn from her bosom, by the parson, and sold to the South; and soon she with a broken heart died. Scrofula, like a hyena, seased me; and when a long dark, cold and dismal winter had past, the parson had completely exhausted our summer's harvest, by giving feasts, and charity to the beggars· And when the bright and joyous spring--time was come to make glad and happy, our home, sweet home, but, ah! alas, there was not one ray, nor sound of gladness there!

The last prayer I heard the parson pray was: "Servants, obey your masters, for such is the commands and the will of high heaven, etc." And although I was rotting with scrofula, and could not wear my shirt, I fled to New York, where I for the first time seen Tom Paine's followers marching in a large procession, under the Stares and Stripes, pealing forth exciting strains of martial music; celbrating the memory of that great and good patriot, Thomas Paine; I had so often heard slandered ·

Here it was that I wandered from temple to temple; from church to church; from palace to palace; from den to den; from school to school; asking what is truth. I seen, tasted, felt, smelt, and heared for myself the beliefs, ways and ideas of this world. Early Sunday morning I heard the clink-ety-clink, simelar to the ironed hoofs of horses on the pavement. It was the catholics going to mass. I fell in and went too. An intimacy formed between the priest and myself, and I actually know of ship loads of property that he gathered from his dupes. The Spirtualists told me that they would paint my mothers picture; but could not tell me if she was white or black. The Miller ites were predicting the world to end then; just as the first fools done thousands of years ago. The Mormons on one end of this dilemma declaring religion was increase and multiply; while the Shakers occupied the opposit, declaring it was not to increase and multiply. Hundreds of contradicting religions and beliefs were there, all contending to be our masters, and like king-gods rule us. They all but the Paine or Yankeeites; hate our free, or Infidel form of rule. They deny to the people, equal and exact justice, in labor, wages, ability, and privilages.

Although our Revolutionary fathers proclaimed this; lived, suffered and died, struggling to inforce it. Yet, King Dollar's republican castration form of rule never alowed it. By it the people, like dogs, are kept castrated; that is, some clique must vote you for president, and he your servant, appoints or, sells to the highest bidder all the rest or our offices. This is catholicism, the opposit to freedom!

A dollar is just so much no matter who has it. A measured days work is just so much no matter who dose it. It may be a president, it may be a peasant; yet, they are both hirelings, and should recieve the same for a days work. They dont! This rascality is the cause of bonds and taxes. They are for no other purpose than to sumptuously support the rascal. King Dollar knew he could not bribe, nor fool a nation, but, get them to agree to a mediator, a go between, that is, to be ruled and fooled by a representative, then he had them at the will of his money, his majority rule, his veto and pardening powers.

Our only safty is in equal and exact justice in labor, wages and privilages. And allow no law nor officer of the law, only by a direct vote of the people: and a large two-third majority rule at that.

Yes, this is what ails us—the people by law furnish their officers not only what they need, but, what they want! Then their officers, by law, will not allow the people what they need, much less that which they want! This is a Christian bell-weather disease. Follow me and I will make you fishers of men! sayeth their man-god! Yes, the Christian mans actions prove they hath no pre-eminance above a beast !

The religious man, like sheep, go in flocks, and like them have their bell-weather leaders. Reader, who is your bell-weather? Who have you sworn to follow; and by so doing forfited your freedom and manhood ? It is quite natural and right that children and idiots should have bosses and leaders. It was so arranged by our Revolutionary Fathers, and expected that when a man was grown he would think for himself, throw off slavish restraints, and in the light of his own conscience, keep himself and his country forever thereafter free.

☞ But, ah, alas, who can say I am an American?

Truly, this is an age of great progress, an age of change, where the survival of the fitest seems to be struggling for a higher life. At any rate, no time, according to history, and circumstantial evidence, was the world so free from superstition as now, and from the glaring absurdities which have for all ages degradingly enslaved it. The free man is a thinking man that is not satisfied with a sounding brass, nor a tingling symbol, or a dead letter in a sealed book, as is the Christian's Jew bible.

Yes, what matter is it if such teachings and customs were believed and practiced by our fathers for ages? That does not go to prove them true, or make them right for us. Do we not see that we are rational, reasoning, accountable, immortal beings of progress, of development, destined never to stand still ? Do we not now see that which was necessary and sufficient to satisfy the demands of ages past and gone, is wholy alarming and injurious to the present? Do we not plainly see that we can now do with our works of art, in a few days, for a few dollars, what it took our fathers months, at an outlay of vast labor and mony to do? Then where is there any saftey, or any good practical common sense to stick to those old routine, sham-conventional and delegatory powers, and such like paternal rule, that is not only a monopoly in the hand of some persecuting, treacherous party, clique, order, or church, whoes rule is hellish, that debars not only the onward progress of freedom and reform, but it crushes out every spark of freedom, invention, or improvement, of whatever growth or kind! Yes, even in the broad bright light of American experienc, we see people stinting, starving, or half clothing their children and at the same time wasting their money, food and time on barbacues, church festivals, and the missionary hoax!

I am opposed to all this, for a famine always follows a feast. I am opposed to all, to everything whose tendency is to mislead, fetter, or in the least rob, or enslave the mind, the body or the conscientious aspirations of man! I am opposed to all, to everything that cannot come out honest and square into the broad open light of day, and stand equally the scrutinizing tests of their fellow man.

PAINE AND INGERSOLL.

CUT 1 Represents Ingersoll, and CUT 2 Represents Paine.

CUT 1. | CUT 2.

THE Free Thinkers of New York and Brooklyn on Decoration Day, 118, unveiled a monument to Thomas Paine, near New Rochelle, New York. Col. Ingersoll was the orator of the occasion. And said: " More than 118 years ago Thomas Paine came to our shores. He was an Englishman, and while I remember the history of that people, and their savage brutality; while I remember their crowned idiots and robed hypocrits; while I remember all that is bad and all that is great and glorious, I say here to-day that no better blood than the English blood never coursed in human veins. [Yet the English people grew out of a notorious band of thieving, piratical murders! just as the Jews did! Ed]

"The first article Paine wrote was on and against Negro slavery. He wrote against dueling. He wrote in favor of the wrights of woman, to marriage and to divorce. He wrote on international arbitration, and the treatment of prisoners while in prison. He wrote on human reason, called the—

Age of Reason. He wrote the Declaration of Independence. He was the first to write the words "United States of America." He was first to suggest a government of the people, by the people, and for the people instead of one by the gods, and for the gods! He was the first to suggest a constitution of the people, in place of the one by the aristocratic god-favored few He did more to establish this republic than any other man."

"He was a greater thinker and a greater power than all the pulpits and rostrums combined. And why? because he was just. In France, when the question of the execution of King Louis came up he said; "Kill the monarch, but not the man Louis;" and for this he was imprisoned.

There is not a doctor of divinity, (and it is not wonderful that such a divinity needs doctors,) for there never has been one great enough, ingenious enough, educated enough, to answer the argument of Thomas Paine, as found in his book, The Age of Reason. The priests began to attact him and they are at it now. Every pulpit has been a mint where slander and lies have been coined against the greatest of American patriots! Will it never cease? Sometimes I think truth is the scarcest thing in the world. Sometimes I think that a lie is the healthiest thing that is ever told to this world. No matter how old or absurd it is, it appears without a wrinkle, with ears undulled, and with eyes undimed, fresh as dew in the heart of a rose.

The ministers have lied about Paine's last sickness until they got blue in the face. They say he died regretting that he wrote against God and the Bible. He never did any such a thing. And if he had that would not have made the bible right, religion sane, nor a personal man-god certain. He never wrote against God, but he said he believed in one God and no more, and he had a hope for a blissful life after death. He died calmly, regretting nothing of that kind. While his faculties remained he was true to the teachings that inspired him in the days of his pride and power. But the clergy are given so much to misrepresentation that they cannot discern the difference between the truth and falshood. Sometimes I get a little sorry for the preachers. I have lived to see the brand of inferiority put on every orthodox brain. I have lived to see the time when the real thinkers, the philosophers, the men of thought, are on the other side. So I tell you to-day that in the great battle between reason and superstition we have passed midnight. In the great battle between government by the people and government by God through kings we have past midnight. The tendency of the world to-day is towards representative govenment. It is towards absolute intellectual liberty, towards intellectual hospitality, towards allowing every human being to make the best guess he can on a subject he knows notning about. In the great battle between living for this worldand soem other we have passed midnight, and we are living for this world. We want homes, sweet homes, good food and good clothes, we want friends, we want books, we want pictures, we want music, with its thrilling voice We want everything there is of joy, and gladness beneath the sky, and when we come to another world, if we ever do, we will have plenty of time to attend to that. We are believers in the home here, in the family here; and we think more of our families than all the so-called spirtual rulers you can cram into infinite space; and the man who did as much as any other to help on the human race, along this great highway of intellectual and physical progress is the man we honor to-day.

He was one of our greatest soldiers in the grand old army of human progress, and his reputation is increasing every day; and in a few more years as the American people meet on the fourth of July to pay honors to the memory of the great; and when they speak of Washington, Jefferson, Franklin, they will also speak of Thomas Paine."

WASHINGTON AND LINCOLN.

The Liberators of Man.

CUT 1 Represents Lincoln, and CUT 2 Represents Washington.

CUT 1. | CUT 2.

It is an old saying that Washington was the first in war, the first in peace, and the first in the hearts of his countrymen, but second in the hearts of his countrywomen, for after having his first love refused he led his countrymen victorious through a long bloody war, and then married a widow, and then served them many years in helping to organise the first free government ever known.

Yet, he nor his countrymen had not advanced far enough in humanity to advocate, or to grant a universal freedom. And it was even eighty odd years after a perpetual struggle over the question of universl human freedom before the opportunity of the single stroke of Lincoln's pen gave us univeral freedom! So Lincoln, the old Infidel, (who the rebel preachers say their god killed in a theater, because he repealed their god's laws and set the soulless, beast of a nigger free!) was actually the first successful saviour of man. He gave to man the first privilege of a universal religion or no religion; and a universal bible or no bible! Yet, but few can to-day say I am a free man; for we have not yet fought for a universal suffrage! We have no voice in fixing values, rents, wages, and privilegs; and by these agencies mankind is yet enslaved!!! Enslaved privileges and enslaved money make an enslaved people!!

It is to Jefferon and Franklin that we owe very, much. They stood firm for equal and exact justice in suffrage and privileges, while Washington lent a great deal to the god-favord few. Yet he was a deist, therefore, not a believer in religion, but his military bump made him as vain as a peacock, and he courted the smiles of the hypocrits, and was for great pomp and formality.

Jefferson was the first President inaugerated at Washington, and he was a materialist, or a hylotheist. Franklin was a deist and robed the Christian's gods of their thunder amd lightning, and to-day we are using it as fuel, for light, for heat, and for engine power. So, our Ben. not only denied and rebeled against the earthly rule of the gods, but robbed them of their artillery!

And if we only had a free' money, a money that could not be bought and sold, or hoarded up in the banks, to speculate upon our miseries and misfortunes; if we had uniform wages, and privileges as advocated by Jefferson, the father of democracy, or home rule, we would be prosperous freemen in deed and truth.

A dollar is just so much no matter who has it, nor what it is made out of. A days work is just so much done, no matter who done it, or how long it took them to do it. It may be a President it may be a Peasent involved, yet, both are hirelings and should recieve the same amount of the same kind of money for tnat days work. They do not, and this rascality is the cause of bonds, taxes and poverty! bond and tax slavery!!!!

THE DEEDS.

FIRST, A DEED for a town lot, on the south side of the public square, Mc. Minnville, Tenn. Fronting 23 feet and 5 inches—thence south 40 feet—thence west 23 feet 5 inches—thence to the beginning.

Recorded in Mc. Minnville, Tenn., 1st., day of July, 1867.

SECOND, a deed from the corporation of Mc. Minnville, for a cemetery lot, No. 153, as shown on plot, and as now used by said Woodward, this the 20th., day of August, 1880.

MY WILL and WISH is that these two pieces of mother earth, and their fixtures, be protected by the LIBERALS throughout the world. That is, that they be held and used by them for their special benefit. That my wife Emma, and our four sons Isaac, Fletch, Frank, Tom, and my son Lavater, or those of them that are Liberals, and survive me, they are the first Trustees to watch after, and to see to the renting of said town property, paying of taxes, repairing and improving of the same, and receiving a reasonable pay as they may agree on.

All disputes must be settled, all truetees elected by a majority vote of the trustees.

The place should be known as— Woodard's Liberal School and Asylum. And its Library of Liberal books, manuscripts, papers, pictures, patents copyrights and fixtures should be constantly used for this purpose by some one or more teachers as the trustees may see fit to lease out or support.

As the object is the maintenance of our Liberal form of Government, therefore, all Liberty Loving people everywhere should struggle for its growth by donating property and money to it, and by establishing of other schools, libraries and asylums.

It does not matter what others may think, say, do or threaten, the thing is, for us to do and to keep doing. If you have but one Liberal book, but one glorious truth, then use them. Teach them by the wayside, or as you work your way along, even by the flickering light of a camp fire. This is your privilege and no blating, bulldozing, crazy Christian has any right to attempt to make you ashamed or afraid. The thing is, say your say! do your do! it matters not what others believed or knew!

☞ It wont be long until the name of Christian, like that of their hateful dady the self-accursed Jews will be but a hiss and a curse!

☞ O! my, what a great help would an acre of ground with a spring of good water be to your Libbarty and to the educating of your children, and what a small amount to you that has thousands of just such places unoccupied. Give us such as that for a Library and for burrial purposes and we will furnish a house and books—books of all kinds.

☞ When my earthly life is ended, then burry me on this lot 153. A neat, straight or parallel coffiin with four hand holds so four friends can carry me to the grave. Burry me on my left side facing the magnet, or north-east. Play or sing some good lively air as Yankee doodle, Star-Spangled Banner and all go home rejoiceing.

This the 4th., day of the 7th., month and the 120 th., year of our American Independence.

   J. Fletch. Woodward, M, D,
Mc. Minnville, Tennessee. 7, 4, 120.

The Sweet By-and-by.

Ther's a land that is fairer than day,
And by faith we can see it afair,
For the Father waits over the way,
  To prepare us a dwelling-place there.

CHORUS.

In the sweet by-and-by,
We shall meet on that beautiful shore;
In the sweet by-and-by,
We shall meet on that beautiful shore.

We shall sing on that beautiful shore.
  The melodious songs of the blest.
And our spirits shall sorrow no more:
  Not a sigh but pure blessings of rest.
    In the sweet by-and-by, etc.

To our bountiful Father above
  We will offer the tribute of praise
For the glorious gift of his love,
And the blessings that hallow our
  days. In the sweet by-and-by, etc.

We shal rest on that beautiful shore:
  In the joyes of the saved we shall share;
All our pilgrimage-toil will be o'er,
  And the conqueror's crown we shall wear. In the sweet etc.

We shall meet, we shall sing, we shall reign,
  In the land where the saved nver die;
We shall rest free from sorrow and pain,
  Safe at home, in the sweet by-and-by. In the sweet by-and-by, etc.

Home, Sweet Home.

'Mid pleasures and palaces
　Though we may roam,
Be it ever so humble,
　There's no place like home;

A charm from the skies
　Seems to HALLOW us there,
Which, seek through the world,
　Is ne'er met with elsewhere.

CHORUS.

Home, home, sweet, sweet home,
Be thou ever so humble,
There's no place like home.

I gaze on the moon,
　As I chace the dear wild,
And feel that my parent
　Now thinks of her child;

She looks on that moon
　From our own cotage door,
Through woodbines whose
　　fragrance
Shall cheer me no more.--Chorus.

An exile from home,
　Splender dazzles in vain,
Oh, give me my holy,
　Thatched cottage again;

The birds singing gayly,
　That come at my call,
Give me then, with sweet peace,
　Mine dearer than all.—Chorus.

OUR BEGINNINGLESS.

HISTORY, legendary traditions, ancient ruins, and written records, or direct and circumstantial evidence of the origin, nature, and destiny of mind, matter, mankind, and all other things.

In the beginningless of time, we have no chaos, no confusion, but one grand, vast, knowing, all-wise, creative, or invisible God--space! This was, has been, and is yet, the only form, shape, and nature of God! As is shown in cut 1.

CUT 1. | CUT 2.

And in the beginning we have but nebula, or a visible light; as shown in cut 2. Ttis God-illuminated nebulous matter begun to revolve on its own center or its equador, from west to east; and by the efforts of equa the matter composing the nebula gradually become condensed towards the center; the exterior portions thus had the velocity of their revolutions increased, until by the centrifugal force they wer seperated from the main mass, and left behind in the form of a ring; thus it was, that the materials of each of the planets was seperated from the main mass; while the remainder of the main mass was condensed towards the center, forming the sun; the famous and fabulous fountain of all life, or the source of all planets and life, as it relates to our solar system. And finally each of the planetary rings, by a similar process, was condensed into planets, depositing in the mean time rings out of which its secondaries, the moon or, its moons, etc., are formed.

And in process of time this earth may become an uninhabited, fixed, firy sun. Inhabited only by the firy, sinful souls of those people who once inhabited it in its present fast changing condition. And around which will revolve the moon—it having changed to an inhabitable earth—for the good, the true, and the beautiful.

Yes, it is highly probable that this earth is fast changing to a firy sun, and the moon to an inhabitable earth. But it is not reasonable to suppose that either it nor man will be blotted out, but only purifyed and changed. Theology and religion take the advantage of knowledge and science as much so as they do of innocence and ignorance, and presuppose frequently too much—for the progress of knowledge, science, discovery, and history has certainly knocked prop after prop from under them as fast as they presupposed them; leaving the first religion of our first fathers, the worshiping of the Creater through the sun, near the truth; and their legendary traditions more reliable.

Only think, thousands of such solar systems as ours have been discovered, all whirling through this vast, vast immensity of infinite God-space; in many things or ways fair grater and grander than that of ours. Sirius imparts many times more light than our sun; in Vega we have a heavenly body many, many times larger than our sun. Yes, yes, there are other suns in this ☞ knowing infinite God-creative space, that are infinitly larger than the one that which gives us light, heat, and life.

This all goes to sustain the legendary traditions, historys, records, and the stupendous remains of a mighty race of people that inhabited the Amerikas, or twin brothers, thousands of years before the sun appeared in the heavens. We yet have the most stupendeous remains of cities, walls, towers, temples, and grand paved thoroughfares, in these Amerikas that out date any thing on this earth, dating back before the sun appeared in the heavens!

The light from other heavenly bodies give them a

perpetual, grand, subdued, mild, equally balanced light for thousands of years before our present firy sun appeared in the heavens and set up a perpetual strife, both in man, animals, and all nature.

At that time the earth had another continent called the Atlantika. It was situated between Afrika and South Amerika, it almost connected them. It was sunk by an earthquake, and when it went down a flood of water dashed over a portion of Afrika to Asia, and in receding it caused the great desert. This was where Moses got Noah's flood.

There was no earthquakes, no great storms, no great cyclones, no great volcanic eruptions until the firy sun appeared in the heavens and set on fire the combustable gasses and substances of those lofty unprotected mountains. Then it was when the Atlantick Continent, with its mighty nations went down beneath the old oceans wave, to rise no more. Then it was that the great cities of Central South Amerika and Afrika was shaken down; and although their mighty inhabitants was giants, yet, those who survived this awful blinding, deafening becrazeing shock, fled to the shady dark woods and caverns of the mountains to protect themselves from the suns awful firy face! which was awful in a torrid zone! Then it was that they, the survivers begun to petition the Great Heavenly Father, through his mighty sun! A planet sun and not a man-sun as the Christians will hava it.

Yes, yes, there are other suns in space that are infinitly larger than the one wich gives us our heat, light, and life. Yet, the Jews and Christians claimed their bible deniend all this, and they even declared the moon was an independent light, immovably fixed, or hung up in the heavens, made just to rule the night; and the sun, just to rule the day; and it rose and set, and the earth was flat, and the bigest thing in existence, made especialy for the Jews. Then the Christians declared the same for themselves. They murdered in cold-blood the inhabitants of Mexico, Central, and South

Amerika, to rob them of their fabulous wealth, and their beautiful homes, and their accumulations of ages in knowledge."

The star Arcturas, was known to them, the anecient Aztec nations of the Amerikas. They knew it to be a mighty sun of a far, far a way solar system of planets; and that it was millions of miles further from us than is our sun; and thousands of miles larger than the sun that now, for the present time, gives us our light, heat, life, strife or changes.

Ah, yes, strife, for a repose, a paradise of idle ignorance is not the aim nor intention of the Creator; but education, which is a noble unrest, an ever renewed awakening from the dead, a ceasless questioning of the past for the proper interpretation of the future, and the urging on of the motions of life, which had better be accelerated into an Infidel fever than alowed to retrograde into a Christian stupidity. This is when, how, and where their Adam fell.

They did not worship them, these suns, no, but the Great Heavenly Father through these suns, as does their lineal descendants, the Arabians, Chinese, Japanese, Moors, and the Albino tribts. And why? because they believed them pure, therafore, they aimed at approaching the Great Heavenly Father through the purest and nearest medium. They held that the Christian's man-god was too impure, and unreliable for a savior. And here is where the Christians got their idea of a savior.

As early as tradition and history goes we find that the eastern world had been trading and mixing with the Amerikas, or twin brothers; and that their discovery by a Columbus, in 1492, is simply a Catholic Lie. There was no such a man as Columbus. But, when by intrigue, murder, and treason the Christians controled the Roman Empire, then it was that Ferdinand, the Catholic, inaugerated that awful thieving, robbing, death dealing Crusade. He sent over an overwhelmning army concealed them, and after having arrainged for a friendly commercial conference with the ruler. the various American governments, and whi. they were in friendly sea... n his army massacred them—fired on them from ambush! not sparing women and children. Having massacred most of their great men at one blow, these Christian devils then for years ravaged the Amerikas from center to circumference, never respecting nor sparing the women and children! Yes, yes, they these Christian devils claimed it their divine duty to thus rob, and murder mankind, and never ended their relentless blood curdleing crusades until the North Amerikan Revolution, in 1776, when all mankind was declared brothers, created free and equal; Adam or no Adam ... that no special slavery curses, marked by caste or color had been fixed upon some mankind as Christians and their bibles taught, and had enforced, whenever, wherever they could; till this earth was filled with ruins and the winds with the moning, wailing, howling, piteous voices of innocent, murdered victims!

Such had been the awful fate of the world until checked by our Amerikan Infidel Fathers in 1776, after three hundred years of perpetual war, the Condor, the Eagle, and the Cactus, bears aloft in high Heaven the Stars and Stripes, far, far above all religions of all bibles of the Lion and the Unicorn, the Crescent and the Cross—declaring from our exalted Equador, equal and exact justice—and at liberty to hold to a god, or no god, and no bloody, murdering, Christian hell hound had any rights to molest us, nor make us afraid!

And here we are, a mixed, Yankee, or Arab type of people, not as white as oua Albino Aztic fathers, nor as black as our Ethiopian mothers—but of a whitish color, and a more rational, sane, well balanced free man than a pure unmixed caste.

Note what history says of our fathers. Barnes in his general history of 1883, in his introduction to modern peoples at page 427, says: "Its laws were written in hieroglyphics; its judges were cho-

... for life; its army was fur... ...ed with music hospitals, and surg...ons; its cala.....r was more accurate than the Spanish; its people were skilled in agriculture and the arts, and its capital, Mexiko, was supplied with aqueducts, and adorned with palaces and temples. Peru was perhaps richer and more powerful than Mexiko. Two great military roads extended the entire length of the empire, and along them the public couriers carried the news 200 miles per day. A vast system of water-works, ... more extensive than that of Egypt, irrigated the rainless region, and agriculture had gained a high degree of perfection."

Volume after volume of good proof can be produced to show our priority and equality to any race, of man, and that Ecuador was the mother of all mankind. Yes, Ecuador situated at the head waters of the largest, most extensive, grandest and most powerful river on earth, the river Amazon, in South America, has the lake Titicaca, whoes island tradition says is the birth-place of man. And all nature being so equaly blended, and balanced, and the most favorably adapted and situated, far above the stormy clouds, the lightnings fearful flash, the thunders deafning roar, summers heat, winters ice, cold, frost and rain. Yes, literaly speaking it is in heaven, having vast grand old cities in the skies; and here is where the Christians songs come from.

Yes, yes, it is here we are told by traditions, and legends old and strange, that long, long before the sun ever shone, that six kinds of man was born or brought into existence here. ☞ And nowhere on earth is there a more favorable place for the originating, rearing, educating and starting out of man; nor has there ever been a more reasonable legendary tradition put forth.

Christians reject our legendary traditions, facts, history, and accept those of mythical Greece, Rome and the Britons; accepting their King James Jew and Roman bible, that is only a mear garbled fragmentary collection of obscene fish, snake, fox, blood

THE PACIFIC OCEAN.

PACIFIC, or peaceful, is the legendary name of the ocean situated between the Amerikas and Asia. It was so called on account of its exemption from violent storms.   CUT 1.

We here reproduce two maps of 1846 and quotations from a very old geography, to prove that the Amerikas or twin brothers was first, and from them we owe our very existence as illustrated on page 39. Cut 1 is the Pacific Ocean. It covers more than one third of the earths surface, making it the largest body of water on the globe.

It has a general current, near the equator, sweeping by the Sandwich Islands, that has the healthiest and the most delightful climate on the globe. This current is setting from the east to the west, that is, it flows from Amerika straight across to Asia. A canoe will waft from Amerika to Asia! And as far as tradition goes the Pacific Ocean was navigated from Amerika to Asia by canoes that plied from island to island, and expeditions coasted along the shore!

THE ATLANTIC OCEAN.

CUT 2 is the Atlantic Ocean, or that part of the ocean between Afrika and Europe on the east, and Amerika on the west.   CUT 2.

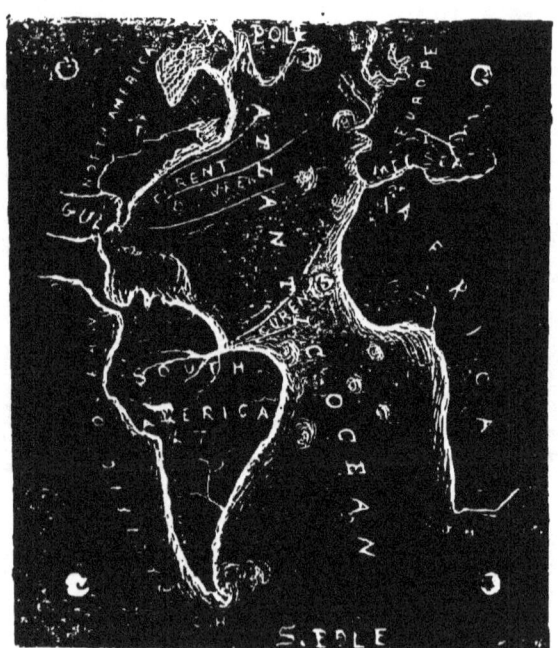

It occupies only about one tenth part of the surface of the globe. It has two remarkable currents flowing to Europe and Afrika from the Amerikas. The Gulf stream, of wind and water, that warm nourish, and sustain all Europe; and the Amazonian current that flows straight across to Afrika; and it is but a short distance, and easily followed even by a canoe. Then blow, spout, splutter, and talk about the discovery of the Amerikas! A greater lie never was palmed off on man than this Christopher Columbus Catholic lie! Its another Santa Claus lie!
☞ The facts are, only a shorter and a more practical route to the Amerikas was the only discovery!
☞ And that was sought by all parts of the world!

and thunder, or unnatural, and unreasonable ghost stories; collected up and compiled into a bible since the destruction of Jeruselam and Constantinople.

All of which is entirley immoral, vicious, destructive and entirly foreign to our free country, to our enlightened, minds; while this which is herein offered is in accordance to first class, sound, hard sense, backed by justice, freedon, rational reason, and the interest of all, both great and small, and is supported by better legendary traditions, by better history, and then by better living facts, as well as by ancient ruins, monuments, and picture-graphic records now in existence; notwithstanding the Christians pretended flood that destroyed theirs, even edstroyed the earth, and then their jealous wars, have for all time tried to destroy ours. See our illustrations.

Moroko in Afrika was peopled from South Amerika thousands of years before the present atmosphere cleared up enough for the sun to shine, or the stars to be seen. The Moors, knew and traded with their Aztec South Amerikan fathers. The Aztecs wer the lineal descendants of the original Albino or very white rase of people, that inhabited the mountainous country of South Amerika long before the sun, moon, or stars shone to guide wondering man elsewhere. They kept fires perpetually burning from all elevated mounds, hills, and mountains, to guide them in their travels and pursuits of life—hence, we call them mound builders, and fire worshipers.

Fire was firt discovered early by our first fathere while using reeds and stalks of corn; they found by vigerously rubbing them together they caught ou fire. And what a grand discovery, a friend of vast importance, well worthy admiration, love and worship.

So, you can see how easy it was for our first parents to travel, even before the sun, moon and stars to guied them. So, of our first sailors, they taken the advantage of currents, winds, and tides, and it was not as dificult to travel by water as by land. Then, look on the maps of the world, compare the facilities, resources, advantages and adaptability of South Amerika; see from her exalted altitude and Eden-like climate how favorable the place to people the entire world, both by land and by water. But, I will not be as low-flung, nor as low-bred as has been all Abraham ites and Jesus ites, and claim all, the whole earth, hell and heaven, to 'me self' alone. If you will look on the map of Afrika, right on the same tropical circle, as in South Amerika, you will find at the head waters of the river Nile a like adaptability to generate man.

But, nowhere on earth has there went forth as much proof, as has went forth to the world, in favor of any beginning place for man, as has, in all ages past, and as is yet being developed in favor of Mexiko, Central and South Amerika. It has always been a densely populated Eden, of inteligent, satisfied, stay at home, and attend to their own business kind of people. But, their priority, superiority, civilization and humanity, their fabulous mines of gold, silver, pearls, diamonds and precious things of this earth, so enraged the jealous and avaricious, and hellish hearts of the Christians that they with the mighty Roman Empire to back them saught their anihilation!

And yet, it is an Eden, and a heaven, to this evil hour! where people dwell in immense cities far above the clouds, in the bright clear skyes, where it is perpetual summer, and sunshine all day long, the year in the year out, and at night the sunlight from millions of other distant suns making it nearly as bright as day! Where storms, winds, rains, thunder and lightning is not known. Where it is one perpetual spring-time, of beautiful flowers, sweet bowers, of delicious fruits, georgeus butterflies, angelic birds, and every thing to make glad and satfied the heart of a noble man.

Yes, yes, nowhere else on this earth can another more favorable Eden or eartly Paradise be found.

— 9. —

And all nature not only surpasses all other places in magnitude and grandure, but being so equally balanced and blended as to prove its priority as a fit borning, rearing and starting out place of all mankind. All races, and colors seem to spontaneously spring up from here in the beginning, and to gradually branch out to people the globe.

Is it not easy to see where the nations of this earth got their traditions, songs and teachings? Those that committed sin and crime were banished from the [presencs of the father], from those earthly cities, far above the clouds, in the skyes, in the ever, or immediate presences of our heavenly father; and never to return in that life! So thousands, and thousands were driven out to people the world; or if they prefered to stay they wer sacrificed; or if they ever returned, they were sacrificed, and so they sacrificed all prisoners of war.

So every fable, custom, lie, wrong, or song can be traced back to this beginning; even hell oiriginated in those awful volcanic earthquakes, and those awful firy eruptions.

These refugees, criminals, and dare devil adventures, eventually found out the whole creation; and that it was only one grand merry-go-round at best. So, they soon found out each others hidden booger, and went for his pocket-book, hell, or no hell; until raid after raid, crusade after crusade, conquest after conquest, has so rapidly ravaged, pillaged and plundered the Amerikas until all learning, and all wealth has been traced back to our shores. Yes, we have been the golden Eldorado for the world, and they have given us their deadly Upas in return.

The gold and ornaments for Solomons Temple was shiped from here; the glory of India, Babylon, Greece and Rome was made and shiped from here! Take from the great Cathedral of Rome what the Spaniards stole and robed from Amerika, and it would sink into insignificance! Take from that great Trinity Church in New York what it has, by law, robed the people of, in no tix on a league of land and it would vanish! Only think it is the largest church, and the tallest steeple, in this country and yet, its an ant-hill when compared to the mammoth pile of stolen property— the Cathedral or St. Peter's of Rome. Harper's Monthly, July, 1872 says : " We pace the church, and find its length that of three ordinary city blocks! The front of the basilica is as broad as five of the largest American churches, and about as high as three such churches piled one above the other. The roof of the nave is as high as the top of one of the tallest of our city steeples. Above this mammoth pile towers the dome to such a hight that the steeple of Trinity Church, of New York, might be placed on the floor beneath it, and would only reach to the base of the walls of the dome; and another steeple, if placed upon the top of Trinity, would only pierce the dome and lantern, and just overtop the great gilded cross."

☞ Such could not be said until the builders of this mass of iniquity had plundered, robed, and destroyed our Temples in Amarika! ☞ And as this church came by iniquity and plunder, so, also, she will depart as iniquity and plunder; and her infamous people, like their infernal fathers, the self-accursed Jews, will pay the penalty, by being a hiss and an accursed word throughout all time!

These Christians were not hunting a new world, no, but a shorter route to the old world, so as to be able to ship more direct. This Columbus discovery business is a Catholic lie.

To prove what I here say see Barnes General History, on Phenicia. The Phenicians and Moors were Albino colonies from the Amerikas; and had carried with them the art of all arts, the art of picture-graphic and typographic printing. We were at that time the masters of the commerce of the world, and the Phenicians and Moors our common carriers. And when they fell into the hands of the Romon Christians, then it was, and this is how it was that they discovered Amerika, and then was it to their great discomforture that they found all of our Capitals situated on the most elevated Pacific shores; forceing them to traverse our Continent, or round our extream southern extremity— Cape Horn. He tells us on page 74 that: "They concealed the source of their supplies so carfully that once a Phenicirn captain, outward bound, finding himself followed by a Roman ship sent to discover his destined port, ran his own vessel on the rocks to lead his enemy to destruction, and prevent revealing the secret!"

All around this famous and fabulous fountain of perpetual youth, light, and life, are the grand and beautiful lakes of life, the lakes Lauricocha, Reyes, Titicaca, and their isles. The purest and most elevated water, vegetables, fruits, and flowers in the world, adorn, beautify, and make perpetnal spring time in and around their shores. Yes, on the high mountainous ranges, vallies and coves, of the Andes of Ecuador and Peru, are yet to be seen the ancient ruins of the first cities in the world, and the first temples ever dedicated to our heavenly Father, or the Creator, or the Beginningless of all.

The ruins of those mighty cities of the skies, and the temples of the sun, moon, stars and fire are still there, to bear ont the legendary traditions, and circumstantial proof of a mighty race of highly civilized, and enlightened, humane people, that has no doubt been murdered. Gone, thousands of years before the Peruvians come and went in a like manner from those delightful earthly mansions in the skies.

Millions of years have past and gone, yet, the ruins, the vallies, the ravines, the lakes, the islands, the everlasting mountains, the Eden climate, the land of perpetual light, all, all go to support these very reasonable legendary traditions of our dead fathers.

Here it was that the first Eggs of man was develcped and hatched. Nature having been supplied with a sufficient amount of Human Germs, or Eggs for the Borning of every Species of mankind, as the white, black, red, yellow and blue. And from these five primary or elementary colors have all now existing families, tribes, and nations have so sprung. So, also, was it so arranged for everything that hath vegetal life. A sufficient amount of original species was spontaneously brought forth, through the earth, wherever it was favorable. And here it was the most favorable spot on earth, for the generating, borning and rearing of man, and all vegetal life.

And then, from thence on, generation has been by sexual organs of generation, implanted in every thing having vegetal life, and controled by the natural laws of love affinity of the sexes. And from that day to this spontaneous generation, or divine begetting has not been possible; that is living matter cannot originate from non-living; that is, — when the earth tore loose from the sun it brought forth with it a certain limited amount, and kind of seed or egg germs for every living being, that hath come into existence, after its kind, as soon as suitable or favorable opportunities offerd.

Thus ended spontaneous geneartion, or a special creation; and now it is only transmitted generation. Hence, the theory of transmutabillity, and a special creation, or a special providence, outside of, or contrary to the laws of Nature, by a special man-god, yes, a special providence is wholy wrong.

Early in the history of man we find him capable of making perfect imitations of eggs and cells, that neither microscopic examination nor chemical analysis could detect the difference. Yet, they would not grow. Precisely so with transmutation, or the changing of one thing, or person into quite another thing, or person, having quite different natures. For a long time, the transmutation of base metals into gold was thought possible; and the changing of imperfect man into a perfect angel, but nature has proved pre-eminent, and man had to acknowledge a supreme unchangable fixed law, that he then could not reach. And although millions of years have given him time, yet, he cannot reach it, but, he can only approach it through the medium of some higher law ; and this is what give rise to this personal idol, god or savior; and being made over. Pretending to take the mediatorial place due all nature.

Now, you see the difference, all religions before the Ackteekites and Yankeeites acknowledged a very fickle, unreliable, ever changing personal man god; operated through a changable idol, myth-god, or a man mediator, or savior; while we acknowlledge an unchangable, allwise Creator-God, that borns, guides and controles only through the unerring and unchangeable, and immutable laws of nature; hence ALL Nature is our mediator or Savior.

Therefore, our religion is sumed up in the iv. epistle of Pope's Essay on Man, that says : "Take Nature's path and mad opinions leave, etc."

Yes, here it was, and here it yet is, in our earthly home, the tropics, that December is as pleasant as April or May, as the Christians sing, and sigh for in their anticipated heaven. Ah, yes, here their immaculate Mol would not have to hunt a stable in December, no, but, out on the green pastures all night long with the shepards lay ! And here it is where you get your Christmas, May-pole, and All-fools-day— a nine months gestation adzactly; making their immaculate conception day in April or May ! Fie, fie, fie, I do say !

See our cut of our Earthly Paradise, or our Land of Perpetual Light; see the Lake, the Isle, and the Celestrial Human Egg-plants; and the Trees of Life, or the waving, flapping, milkey Corn; and the great variety of milk, bread, meat, fruit and vegetable plants and trees, that not only grew there then, but, they yet grow in great variety, to nourish and to sustain man. Note the great varieties of bread and fruit Palms, and the clothing, utensils, tents, boats, houses, etc., that they furnish man there to this very, very remote day.

Hence, not only does living man prove that our

first fathers were not only white, black, red, yellow and blue, but natural sense teaches it, even our first food, the milky, green corn, was, and is yet, are of all these colors. And now all of these extremes have united, mixed and blended in every conceivable way, place and condition, making one grand equanimous, or equador, or a well proportioned, blended and balanced humane human being, known as the Yankee.

And as their government pushes onward and upward to the original starting point, Eucador, we see them assuming a well proportioned man of a flesh and blood color, far in advance in physical and mental excelence to their primitive fathers of many colors. This was proven by the voyages, expeditions, and crusades into the western world, or the Amerikas, and the isles of the seas. In every instance both black, white, red, yellow, anb blue, have given way to the Equadors, Arabs or Yankees. The traditions of our firit fathers, from Equador, or Eden, in South Amerika, prove that our first fathers were of the three elementary colors, as the red, yellow, blue, and the white and black blenders; and vegetated from the Celestrial Eggplant, the original undergrowth amid the trees of life, or the milky, sweet corn, and the bread and meat palms, that grew to such gigantic proportions, and in many varieties; on and around this island Titiaca.

We see the ugly wiggletail changed to the ungodly musketo. We se that horrid caterpillar also changed into a beautiful, angelic butterfly. Then, is it any more unreasonable that these same Laws of Nature should Vegetate man from the vegetable kingdom? or change him from a mammoth porwigle?

Are not these traditions far more reasonable than those that tell us that we were only half made? Made from the dust, rubbish and nubend of a hard weeks work? Just enough dust left to 'sorter' make Adam; and not a particle left to make Eve;

— 15. —

and by a lord-man-god, that got so tired that he had to rest. Which is the most reasonable tradition reader? No, from indestructible mind and matter thou wast made, and back to them thou wilt surely return.

The facts before us, and the existing ruins prove it, to say nothing of legends, traditions, and histories circumstantial proof. Circumstantial proof tell us that the first permanent buildings were of rock. Why? Simply because great rocks, medium rocks, small rocks were more plentiful, and more practical. Soft rocks that was easy carved and hardened when left to the sun and time. Chunks and wedges, strips and sheets of rocks, and hardened lava, in all shape and form, as sharp as a knife and as hard as steel was plentiful. They only had to choose their tools. Iron, Gold, copper, silver, and the mettles were plentiful, already melted and seperated from their oars, and fused along the volcanic crevices, right before their wondering eyes. The earth was teeming with all manner of food and drink; furnished in every conceiveable vessel; and all our primitive fathers had to do was to use these hard flints, lava, etc., for tools to work the rocks, mettles, clay, wood and things into what they fancied. So, soon all nature served them, enriched, adorned and butified them. Step by step they seen nature develop every thing before them, and all they had to do was, as is now, useing them and profiting by the unerring lessons of Mother Nature and suffering and loosing, in every instance, by the irring lessons of rulers, masters, man-made-gods; that run counter to the laws of our life.

Yes, their Paul says: "The Natural Man receiveth not the things of the spirit of god—" When the facts are, they know not God! muchless his spirit; for if they did they could not run contrary to the laws that made and sustain them. They do, see 1. Cor. ii. 14. Yes, their bastard of a man-god said: " Follow me, and I will make you fishers of men. Mat. iv. 19." Yes, this infamous Christian bastard of a man-god said to do this, to follow him, you must hate everybody, everything, and your own life. Lu. xiv. 26. And this is the first, and the main symptom of craziness. And their fruits from Cain and Abel on down prove it!

At the first age of the earth, and especially at the equator, every animal, insect, and thing, was so well provided for that they had no occasion to molest each other; and ages of peace and plenty come and went before strife, contention, fights and war set in. And this was caused by the sudden apperance of the firy sun in the heavens, that forced them to ventuereing necessarily and unnecessarily too far— out from under the presence of equa, or the land of perpetual light, out into the world of darkness, sickness, changableness, or where everything was in a less balanced condition.

This give rise to the story of the fall and curse of man and nature. Nearly every story of the sacred writings, of the east, is founded on facts that yet exist in the Amerikas.

The first men born from the Celestriael Eggplant, [cut 3,] were two white twin brothers. And they watched with breathless silence the borning of the next egg nearest to them, and when born, lo and behold they were two twin sisters. Or, men with a womb, hence, called the womb-man, from which was eventually dubbed the name woman·

Being near the waters of the lake they washed themselves, swam, splashed and spluttered about in the water with great joy. Seeing the difference in each other, and that this difference attracted the close attention of one to the other, so they made for themselves shibboleth belts and necklaces, from the corn shucks.

The shucks in the necklaces hanging down so as to cover the breasts; and the shucks in the belts covered their bellies, hips, buts, and privates. The men being more hairy they did not use necklaces. From the corn shucks they made themselves beautiful moccasins, mantles, mats, ornaments, bedding

PARADISE,

OR THE ORIGINAL HOME OF MANKIND.

➤PHOTO CUT THREE·⬅

PARADISE, OR THE LAND OF perpetual light. The cradle, and the original home of man. It is situated in Ecuador, South America, at the head-waters of the river Amazon, in and around the vale and lake Tiliacac.

It is the most delightful and the most elevated home ever occupied by man anywhere on the globe. It is perpetual spring, no chilling winter, no burning summer, no rain nor storm clouds. The leaf, the flower, and the fruit are perpetual; far up above the storm cloud in the heavens!!!

and covers. And from the corn and cain stalks they made themselves tents, wigwams, and inclosenres.

The milky corn, milky cocoa, and cow-trees, yielded them milk, the palm trees gave them cocanut and banana meat, and the plantain, corn, wheat and rice, furnished them mush and bread; figs, berries, mellon, fruits, delicious vegetables, nuts and seeds gave them an abundance of good food.

And, although, this was an eden of bliss, that gave man all that his animal and mental natures could possibly enjoy, yet, that continued change that ended in death, naturally rased the question does this end all ? No, ah, no, it makes him believe in, and long for another, and a still higher state of existence. And, he is undoubtedly, destined to another, and a higher state of existence.

We find as the body, and as the brain is developed the mind manifests its self. ☞ The minds, per-se, that is, in and of its self does not change, grow, increase, nor diminish; or die. Mind is immortal! Matter is mortal! and allways sick and dying; and although when young we cannot, and when old we cannot manifest the minds, as when in mature manhood, yet, the fault is in the body.

Yes, it is not lost, it is only pent up and cannot manifest its self, from the feeble, diseased or abnormal condition of the body. Yet, mind is mind, and I am certain that it is mind that manifests every function of matter throughout the entire universe.

Yes, knowing, rational, reasoning, never growing, never changing, never dying mind. Build the animal organs, or house, for the kind of, and quantity of mind you want and it will be occupied by that class of mind only.

The insect sees man crush it beneath his feet; it sees and knows this; but, does it know that man is inteligence? Man sees the elements crush him beneath their mighty force, but, does man know, and acknowledge, the elements, or their force is intelligence? If they were in the shape, and the body of a man then he would say yes, the elements have intelligence, and they do me an injustice! Then is it necessary that intelligence should be confined only to the shape of a man? Certainly not. There was necessarily bearriers, boundarys and limits put to all things. And I am convinced that mind in the form of nebulous matter exists within us, and can float away into the infinite immensity of God-space, from whence it originally came.

The first man called himself Ab, and the first woman Abba. The next called himself Baal, and the second woman called herself Baala. As they then had so mysteriously met, they naturally admired each other, and as they mutually aided each other, they soon loved and adored each other, and soon agreed to always respect, love and to live one for the other, and as one.

In course of time they met up with other men and women living near to them, and they could but relate to each other about the same borning, and happy existence. And as their numbers and skill increased soon it was ma-ma and pa-pa; and a vigorous child was born for each breast; and in a bout eight years that child, also, became a parent.

In due time their thatched cottages give way to massive cities of rock, the ruins to this day can be seen near the north eastern edge of Lake Titicaca, where arts, sciences and industries was cultivated and sent out throughout the world. How easy for the minds of the first men from their exalted and elevated homes, on the mountains of Ecuador, elevating them five miles, or more, above every thing and the sea. How easy for them to form an idea of the world beyond; even before the sun appeared in the heavens·

Ab's and Abba's generations followed the mountains and the Pacific coast, and eventually reached Afrika, where they met with Baal's and Baala's generations, who had followed the Amazon in their boats, and across to the Atlantica, where they soon reached Afrika. This is the Azteec and Phenecian traditions; and facts to this day, are in their favor.

— 19. —

The Encyclopedia Britanica acknowledges the priority of the Aztec existance, and sun worship, by saying: "The most holy and perfect rite in the Elusinian Mysteries was to show an ear of corn mowed down in silence, and this was a symbol of the incarnation of the sun, by the sun worshipers. It was the deification of, and the worship of the reproductive organs." Yes, the first men having been begot of God, through the Sun and Nature, and born from the Celestrial Egg-plant; and their first food being the milky corn, roasting--ears, Indian corn, or Zea Maize of the Aztecs.

This was the first and the most mysterious right and festival of the Aztecs sun and fire worship. It was a lesson entended to forever remember the actual origin of the first men through the Celestrial Egg-plant, and first nourished by the milky roasting ears ; and that the next men were from man's own reproductive organs.

Zea Celestrial, or the Celestrial Egg-plant, like Zea Maize, and Zea Caragua are mammoths of the graass family; and like the mammoths of the animal kingdom, the Behemoth, the Mastodon, and the Celestrial Egg-plant, have fulfilled their entended mission, and are now only fossail remains— a thing of tradition and history.

☞ And as the grass family first clothed and fed the earth, so the grass family first fed and clothed man. ☞ And as the grass family had attained to such a great age, and to such a mammoth size, being the most extensive and useful, having matured to a mammoth in extent, statue, variety and usefulness, in the Amerikás, is our knock-down proof, in our favor, for the borning and beginning place of vegetable, animal and human existence.

☞ My great grandfathea told me that when he was a child he stood on the Andes, and viewed the vally of the Amazon, and it was a vast pampas of mammoth shrubs and grasses. And when he landed in Tennessee, it was mostly a vast canebrake, dotted here and there, with mammoth grass and shrubs. Now it is covered with mammoth oaks, furnishing the eastern, or younger parts of the world with lumber, just as we furnished Solomon. Count the yearly strata of these oaks and they will tell you that my old grandfather was right.

We have always found the white, black, yellow, red, blue, and brown man, and their various mixtures, in the Amerikas.

 The Albino Irishman is the pure white man.
 The Negro African is the pure black man.
 The Florid Scotchman is the pure red man.
 The Nankeen Chineman is the pure yellow man.
 The Ethiopian African is the pure blue man.
 The American Indian is the pure brown man.

The Festival of Ceres, the goddess of corn, has been celebrated by all these tribes of man, whenever, or, wherever found. The Lord's supper is only this. So, which is first? Now, would I not rather represent my thankfullness to our Heavenly Father, for this first, and these continued blessings of this grass family, through this Goddess, Cerese, than through an imposture of a man.

To say that all these unfading, unchanging colors and types of man sprung from a Jew Adam is selfish and unreasonable, unjust, contrary to nature and without a shadow of evidence, and not one ray of proof. And worse still, is it to say that all the animal kingdom sprung from a water polyog, and all these families of man and animals, are circumstances of the gradual development of time, up from a polyp; or, what can be more shameful, cowardly, and humiliating, than to say they are curses put upon man, as the mark put on Cain, or the curse put on Ham; or an avaricious, greedy, thieving trick of Jacob made ring, streeked, striped and spotted cattle. Wonder who spotted the Leopard, and gave the georgeous colors to the birds and butterflies?

Reader, is it not more reasonable to take unering and unchanging natures path, and say, that as we can see that the vegetable kingdom connects with, and grows out of the mineral or earth, air, and water kingdoms, and as they, the vegetable world depends upon these for life and existence; so of man, animals and all warm blooded creatures— they depend upon the vegetable world for their origin and support.

Then is it not more in line to say they all originally sprung from these many, many Vegetable Egg-plants, that was of the first growths to clothe and cover the earth? the family of grasses, than to accept such a humiliated man-god creation, as is given in these King's Bibles?

The Christians tell us that their bible rests on the Jew's bible; and as I have shown that it rests on nothing, and tells us not of the Amerikas, the Atlanticas, nor their wonderful people, nor of the five or six kind of man that was at the beginning.

I will now speak of theirs, as it is of a later date. Now, their father, and his son, and a ghost, tell us through their infalible witness, the only remains of an executed malefactor, that could neither read nor write, a Mr. Mathew, a Roman, their first witness, they make him say that Jesus was the son of David and Abraham. He tell us, man by man, the generations up to Joseph, his law-evading, and law-breaking step-dad; saying that there were twenty-eight generations; see 1, 1 to 18.

Then this same father, and his son, and a ghost, tell us through another infalible witness, the very uncertain remains of an other executed malefactor that could neither read nor write, a Mr. Luke, a Roman, their third witness, they make him say at iii, 23, that Jesus was only ☞ supposed to be the sun of Joseph! ☞ So, it is only a supposition as to whoes bastard he was! or, whether he ever was!

He, too, gives their names, man to a man, from Joseph, his supposce dad, up to David, one of his many declared dads, making it out forty-three generations! ☞ A difference of fifteen generations! ☞ And agreeing in none but David's generation!

And Mr. Luke counts four Josephs, and Mr. Matthews but one! Two Mattathias and Mr. Matthew none! Two Matthats and Mr. Matthew none! making a complete momix! Proving that they are a set of presumptuous ignorameses, that know nothing of their own origin, much less the origin of the five or six races of man!

Now, my dear reader, how is all this for high? for infalible witnesses? or, to rest your souls salvation on? Mr. Matthew says positively that he was the son of two men, 1, 1; then, as positively, tell us that he is the son of a ghost, 1, 18. Then, Mr. Luke does not tell us whose son he is, but, says "As was supposed the son of Joseph."

Again, Mr. Matthew tells us at 1, 16, that Jacob begat Joseph; then Mr. Luke chimes in and tell us at iii, 23, Joseph is the son of Heli! So, you see.

A GOD-HEAD.

none of them knew their old dad, much less his; and, the father, the son, and that holy ghost, has played the devil in trying to tell us. And man has always played the devil when he has any thing to do with them.

John, at xiv, 28, tells us that the father was grater than the son; then at x, 30 he tells us that they are one. Then Mr. Mark, their second witness, at vi, 5, says he could do no mighty work, save heal a few sick folks.

Now, if man needs a savior it is more than Nature, or Nature's God knows; for all Nature is our saviour. And if you will stick to Nature's Path, and Mad Opinions leave, you will have no use for a blating missionary, nor a tax gathering preacher.

The above cut represents the Christians godhead it was in lieu of the ancient Aztecs, that was the Father, the Mother and the Child; and represents the perpetuation of man; and this is his Salvation.

TWO AWFUL SELF—CONTRADICTIONS——— We are told that Moses wrote the five first books of this King Jim's bible. These books say— " And the Lord spake unto Moses. These be the words which Moses spake. etc."

We find recorded at the xxxiv chapter, 5 and 6 verses of Deuteronomy, one of the books that they say Moses wrote, we find an account of the death and buriel of Moses! Then how could he have wrote about his own death and buriel? This fact and the finding of a book of laws as is recorded at xxii chapter, 8 verse of ii Kings, settles the hash as to the authenticity of the old Jew scriptures.

Then we are given as witnesses, a lot of books, to prove that there was a bastard son of a ghost and a lot of men, Jesue by name, said to be the only son of God, and that he was sent to save his people— the Jews, that had always claimed to be God's only people! Therefore, not lost! and did not need him— they kicked, and recieved him not, no, but they killed him for his impudence, as they had done many! many others!

☞ This was a trick of stratagy by the Romans to convert the Jews! Yes, they first said to their missionaries that they sent to the Jews— "Go not to the Gentiles, and into the cities of the Samaritans, enter not! But go to the lost sheep of Israel." And when they killed this imposter Jesus and his missionaries then it was that Rome sent out a very liberal claim of— "Go ye into all the world and pro claim the gospel to every creature! ".

We are given Matthew, Mark and Luke, Jesus' cousins, and his bastard brother John, the bapsouser, that was illegally begat and born about the same time as was Jesus, and by the same rake of a god! See Luke, i, 35, 36, 41. This makes them bastard brothers! i, 19, 36. And these fellows writing about their own infamous begeting and borning is as absurd as Moses writing about his own death and burial.

They marveled among themselves and contradicted each other as to who he was. They ask "Whoes son is he?" "By what authority does he violate the laws and threaten our destruction?" And well they may after reading how many dads he had and the kind of dads he had.

Now Matthew tell us in his second chapter that it was wise men from the east that called to see the babe; that they found him in a house and they give him gifts of gold, etc., from their treasures. And they picture it as a mansion; see cuts on the next page.

Then Luke their third witness tell us in his second chapter that it was shepherds that called to see the condemed basterd, and they found him in a manger with the cattle!

They picture the shepherds as out in the green pasture, in May, with their sheep, and they picture them at the open manger or feeding trough, in an open lot by the wayside and not in a house as Matthew says! And this in a cold December night, adorned with frost, snow and ice!

CUT 1, In the House. | CUT 2, In the Manger.

Then Matthew tells us at the 14 verse of his ii chapter that Joseph fled that night with the babe into Egypt!

Then Luke chimes in and contradicts Matthew by telling us at the 22 verse of his ii chapter that they carried the babe to Jeruselam!

Now, the question is, why should this god-favored woman be humiliated to a vagabond tramp and just at this very, very criticle stage of divine pregnancy?

Another awful self-contradiction is in Matthew saying Jesus rode an ass and her colt into Jeruselam. He said ye shall find an ass tied and her colt with her, bring them, xxi, 2. Now, Mark, Luke and John contradict this! Mark says a colt tied, xi, 5. Luke says a colt tied, xix, 30. And they both say bring him, not her or them as Matthew says. Now, his brother John that was beheaded long before this occurance is made to say— " As it is written, he, Jesus found a young ass and sat thereon, and he did ride into Jeruselam with a great crowd of wild, frantic ragamuffins yelling, hail! hail! thy King cometh, sitting on an ass's colt, xii, 14.

☞ Thus it was he committed the overt act of treason that cost him his dear life; and caused him to cry— " My god! my god! why hast thou forsaken me?" Then, and thus it was that he disturbrd the peace and defied the authorities of and the laws of both God, Rome and Judea, and by over throwing the tables of the money changers, and the seats of them that sold doves, at the temple, Matt. xxi, 12 !!

The Romen laws that ruled the Jews and the then whole known world, would not alow religious trmaps, public parading, public preaching, and excitement! This is the law then and there in force.——

"Whoever introduces new religions, the character and tendencies of which are unknown, whereby the minds of men may be disturbed, shall, if belonging to the higher rank, be banished, and if to the lower rank, they shall be put to death."

So the Jews and the Christians brought on their own destruction by meddling with other peoples business, and by defying the powers that be!

Reader, only think, yes, think! the Adamites, Abrahamites, Israelites, Jew-Jesusites, are one and the same, and claim to be the beginning! When authentic history, from old reliable governments, tell us that they, the filthey! obscene, vicious Jews were hatched from the mud of the river Nile, in Egypt thousand of years after the Amerikas, Indis, Egypt and other countries were in existence, with teeming millions of inteligent, civilized human beings!

Their own history tells you this from Genesis to Revelations, from Alpha to Omega, or, from A, to Izard! And then they were orriginally a kinkey-headed black, red lipped Negro, and of a very low down organization. They did not have as much sense as our Andes Shepherd Dogs!

Then Geology, botany and all branches of natural history tell us the same facts! ☞ Take their own testamony, it alone makes their own history! And why? Simpley because they were so infernaly infamous that no other nation on God's earth would degrade themselves by even mentioning of them! And God was so just that he made them record their own infamy in a book called the book of God!

And the first we hear of them is that after God had made Man! and evey thing [Gen. 1. 26.], then it was that the Lord-god, not God, made this Jew-Adam, from the dust or nubends of creation, [Gen. ii, 7.], which was the drying up of the mud of the river Nile! They were originally a mud Negro! The men God made had some sense and they were turned loose, a free, independent sovereign, into the world. See Gen. I. 28. Not so with the Jew-Adamites that the Lord-god, not God, and some body made early Sunday, from the nubends of creation! They were ignorent and put off in a garden in Eden, and not out in the world as man was; See. Gen. ii, 7, 8, 15   iii, 1 to 24; until driven out a cursed race; to which I do not belong; I am an Amerikan.

The tramping of Adam or Abraham into Egypt, the selling of Joseph into Egypt. The bondage of the whole race of Jews in Egypt volentarily! The longing for their flesh-pots. The being of slaves for the Medes and the Persians. The being led away slaves to Babylon. The being led a way captive slaves to Rome, to Turkey, to Russia, to Arabia, to Africa, to the Amerikas, all go to prove that they were, and still are a crazy, superstitious set of bastard mongrels, that know nothing only as they guess at it. They have been slaves for every known race of man; and therefore a vile mixture of them all; just as their bible says, see page, 163.

THE AMERICAN SLAVE!

THE SLAVE BLOCK!
Reader we refer you to page 87, 100, 123-9, 136-7-9 141-2, 156, 161-2-3; and to slavery in our index. And especially to page 123.

Reader, only think, over half of the world is at this moment growning under Christian slavery! Authorised from a book called the book of God!

They are of all races, casts, conditions, and color They are striped and sold to the highest bidder as is here pictured. They are sold publicly as is our cattle and horses. The mouth is opened, the teeth examined, they are striped and all parts examined.

This I have seen enacted in Mc Minnville, and Sparta, Tenn. Thus it was enforced from Main to Mexico! Now you can see it from Mexico to Australia! wherever Christianity is enforced! And if this Jew-Christian bible is the book of God as is claimed, then this stealing, kidnapping, buying and selling of human beings, to be used as beasts of burden is right! for it certanly does permit it and command it! And religion caused it! And is sustaining and defendihg it wherever Christianity rules!

WHAT IS GOD?

Moses' god was a jealous demon! A personal man-god; with all the animal passions, and infernal infirmities of man, hell, and the devil. A god of hate, revenge, cruelty, and desolation. That destroyed nation after nation, and then turned on his own people, and after destroying the most of them, giving their homes to their enemies, and their women as slaves, and the remnant he scattered as vagabonds throughout the earth.

There were all manner of gods long before his. There were gods for everything. The god of heaven, the sun, moon and stars. The god of earth, the winds, seasons, snows and storms. The god of love and marriage. Abraham carried his gods with him as he tramped and somebody stole them. Babylon's great god was Bel and the Dragon, that Daniel said was dead. His god was a live one that would not let the lions eat him. Jesus claimed the same god and when he seen he was not going to save him as he had Daniel, he in great agonies of despair askingly cried aloud: "My god, my god, why hast thou forsaken me?"

Aaron's god was a gold calf. His was worth something, and would command respect in any land. The Christians' god was a Jew, a born criminal, a bastard, a mongrel, a half breed; an ill-bred man-god, and was executed.

Then in a general use a god is what a man styles a King, the ruler, or the biggest thing in his perceptions. And his perceptions might not be any greater than a child, who believes its mother is the greatest god of all. Whatever controlling influence rules man, that is his god. Man's god has always been his rulling passion. Whatever he calls his god, may be to others a mere nothing. The gods of the Ancients have all lived their time, and are now dead. The Christians of to-day, their god was executed for treason, blasphemy, and high crime, before he was grown.

The philosophers, the scientist, and all well balanced, and informed men, in all ages, and in all races, had a GOD of PRINCIPAL. Their idea of a God was a Scientific Phenomena. That is, God fills the universe. Force is the measure and ultimate of matter—the measure and the ultimate of all existence. GOD fills the whole universe. There can be no point in space, in an element, or in an atom of matter, that is not filled with God. If GOD is not every where, then you have something greater than GOD—a space greater than GOD. Then to acknowledge any thing greater than GOD is to acknowledge there is no GOD.

☞ We can only approximatingly comprehend GOD. Through natural law. We cannot know, or see GOD as we se our selves, and one another. He has no parts. He is infinite. Not to be infinite would be not to be God; and to be infinite is to be mearly abstraction. So we cannot comprehend God as a whole, we can only comprehend him by piecemeals. We cannot comprehend beyond our sense, which only come to us through five different avenues; as 1 st., feeling, 2 nd., tasting, 3 rd., smelling, 4 th,, seeing, and 5 th., hearing.

And, although, these five avenues use the same nerves. and brain, yet you cannot see through any but the eye; neither can you smell through any but the nose. And whatever we can conprehend, we certainlcy have a right to analyze. But, to attribute an effect to a cause he cannot prove is foolishness. Yet, this is the religionists lamentable fix.

Their idea of a god, and a heaven, is of the very lowest down passions. Something that the lowest down rascal on earth craves, as gold, silver, meat, bread, drink, puppy love and idleness. It is a god of passion, and a heaven of idleness. They have neither principle, nor rational, human reason. They are a thousand years behind the dignity of an enlightened and free people, like the majority of the American people are. They are only to be made known to be hated, and banished forever. And as our Declaration of Independence sounded the last death knell to all religions, and their gods. They are now only fossil remains, and classed with the dead gods of the past.

The GOD of the present, and the future, is a GOD of dignity, of rational reason. A GOD of honor, of light, knowledge, love, justice, truth, and of universal freedom. Then, watch—see—our enemies as they watch and struggle, night and day, to place their little dead, defunct, bastard, criminal, Jew god—sweet Jesus they call him—see how they try to place themselves, and that hateful emblem of sin shame, and slavery—the cross—above our Stairs and Stripes, our emblem of freedom, and a just heaven. GOD is invisable, undividable, and unchangable. He is one and the same always. He does not exist as father, a son, and a ghost. But he exists in us as a father, a mother, and a child. So venerate, and worship your father, your mother, yourself and home, for by so doing you pay due homage to the great giver of all.

GOOD FATHER,
HEAVENLY FATHER, or the
GREAT INTELLIGENCE— GOD.

O THOU eternal One, whose presence bright
All space doth occupy, all motion guide,
Unchanged through Time's all-devastating flight,
Thou only God! there is no God besides!
Being above all beings! only One!
Whom none can comprehend and none explore,
Who fills space-existence with self alone,
Embracing all, supporting, watching o'er—
A Something we call God, and know no more.

In its sublime research, Philosophy
May measure out the ocean deep, may count
The sands or the sun's rays, but, God! for thee
There is no weight nor measure; none can mount
Up to thy mysteries; Reason's brightest spark,
Though kindled by thy light, in vain would try
To trace thy counsels, infinite and dark;
And thought is lost ere thought can soar so high,
Even pass like moments in eternity.

Thou from primeval godliness didst call
First nature, then existence; God, on thee
Eternity had its foundation; all
Spring forth from thee— of light, joy, harmony,
Sole origin; all life, all beauty, thine;
Thou didst create all, and yet create;
Thy splendor fills all space with rays divine;
Thou wast, thou art, and shalt be, glorious, great,
Life-giving, life-sustaining, or create!

Thy chains the unmeasured universe surround,
Upheld by thee, by thee inspired with breath;
Thou the beginning with the end hast bound,
And beautifully mingled life and death!
As sparks mount upward from the firy blaze,
So suns are born, so worlds spring forth from thee,
And as the spangles in the sunny rays
Shine round the crystal snow, the pageantry
Of heaven's bright children glitters in thy praise'

Trillions of torches, lit by thy command,
    Journey unwearied through the blue abyss;
They own thy power, accomplish thy command,
    All gay with life, all eloquent with bliss;
What shall we call them? Piles of crystal light?
    A glorious company of golden streams?
Lamps of celestial ether, burning bright?
    Suns lighting systems with their joyous beams?
But thou to these art as the noon to night.

Yes! as a drop of water in the sea,
    All this magnificence in thee is lost,
What are the trillion worlds compared to thee?
And what am I, then? Heaven's unnumbered host,
Though multiplied by myriads, and arrayed
    In all the glory of sublimest thought,
Is but an atom in the balance, weighed
    Against thy greatness— is a cipher brought
Against infinity! Oh, what am I, then? Naught.

Naught! But the effluence of thy light divine,
    Pervading worlds, hath reached my bosom too!
Yes! in my mental doth thy knowledge shine,
    As shines the sunbeam in a drop of dew;
Naught! but I live, and on hope's pinions fly
    Eager towards thy presence, for in thee
I live, and breathe, and dwell, aspiring high,
    Even to the throne of thy divinity;
I am, O God, and surely thou must be!

Thou art! directing, guiding all. Thou art!
    Direct my understanding, then, to thee;
Control my desires, guide my wandering heart;
    Though but an atom 'mid immensity,
Still I am something fashioned by thy plan!
    I hold a middle rank 'twixt heaven and earth,
On the last verge of mortal being stand,
    Close to Eden where beings had their birth,
Just on the boundary of the perfect-land!

The chain of being is complete in me;
    In me is MATTER'S last gradation lost;
And the next step is Spirit—Deity!

I can command the lightning; is this dust?
A monarch and a slave? a worm? a god?
Why came I here, and how? why so marvelously
Constructed and conceived? Unknown? This god
Lives surely through some higher energy!
For from itself alone it could not be!

Creator, changer, preserver,— my God,
You created me! Source of life and good!
My mind connects in links to thine O, God!
Thy light, thy love, in their bright plentitude,
Filled me with an immortal mind, to spring
O'er the abyss of death, and bade it wear
The garments of eternal day, and wing
Its heavenly flight beyond this little sphere,
Even to its Source— to thee— its Author, thee.

O thoughts ineffable! O vissions blest!
Though partial are our conceptions of thee,
Yet, may thy shadowed image fill my breast,
And waft homage to thy Divinity;
God! thus alone my lonly thoughts can soar;
Thus seek thy presence, Being wise and good!
Midst thy vast works admire, obey, adore!
And when this tongue is eloquent no more,
My mind will thank in strains of gratitude.

DERZHAVIN.

GOD, therefore, is not in any sense a substance; nor a person, neither is he an effect; but, he is the remote cause of force, pervading and underlying all the ceaseless changes of everything that hath either form, substance, or life. He is celestrial mental intelligence, full, complete, and without passions, or form; a circle complete, without beginning or end.

THE BAD MAN,
BAD SPIRIT, or the
EVIL ONE—the DEVIL.

:SE are a few modest names usually used
epresent that which is bad, or opposite to
d or God. They, like the names, for
l are many; and it proves them to be the
vth of mans literature. It proves that
ie creator of these many gods and devils,
re had been first, a god and a devel do-
id of them, then they would have been
all man by one name, one history, as is
Washington. As it is, their names, like-
ctions, and history are legion and myth-
ring that they never did exist, in human
zar and Washington; and that they are
)n of mans infernal infermities.
account we have of the evil one, in our
mythology, is in the war in the heavens
:he evil one and his army were cast out,
y winged their way to this earth the sun
em, coming nearer the earth than it ev-
e, making its light and heat so intense
)n fire the gasses in our most elevated,
₃l mountains, causing the most terific fi-
ering volcanoes, and destructive earth-
[t not only set on fire the thatched cotta-
shook down the massive cities, blinded,
nd caused great terror, suffering, and de-
) all Eden, the land of perpetual light,
id to all South Central, North Amerika,
les of the seas, but the whole earth was
from its center to its circumference.
the Atlantic Continent, where the most
of this evil one landed, causing a great
ter to sweep over Afrika, even into Asia
parts of the earth, which on receding it
₃rts, swamps, and prairies, leaving not
₃arths centers broken and changed, but,
in many places was imbeded with foss-

ils and remains from other distant parts of the world, making it very foreign to it.

Causing a more distinct night and day, summer and winter, winds and currents, causing the breathing, or flow and ebb of the sea, that twice a day meets and disputes with the mighty current of the fearful giant Amazon; at its mouth, causing the most terrific dashing volumn of water known on this earth. A volum of water fifty miles wide, and hundreds of feet deep, forcing its way for thousands of miles, across the South Amerikan Continent, from the very top of the Andes, from the actual Elen, where its headwaters are above the clouds, four or five miles higher than the sea, and being forced down such a grade, forces its fresh water current hundreds of miles out into the briny sea.

Twice a day, it and the ocean's flow disputes for masterdom, and in meeting, these enormous masses of water, a mountain of water, surf, and foam is dashed upward, and then held in all its terific fury hundreds of feet in the air!

Such was not known to the Antesollucents, or to those people who existed on earth before the sun made its appearence inthe heavens; setting all nature to a greater struggle, and to a more forcible axistence— not for each others destruction, no, but for the supremacy of those most fit. All this was a mear change of growth of nature, and no gods, devils, good nor evil ones had any thing to do with it. Yet, the massive ruins of cities and temples, that was ornamented with huge statues, and huge statue-shaped rocks, throughout the Amerikas, are pointed out to us to this day as petrified statues of these Antesollucent gods, and devils.

Yes, we are told that the sun turued the devil, and all of his host of officer-gods and goddess' as Jupiter, Vulcan, Pluto, Juno, Mars, Mercury, Neptune, Saturne, Minerva, Sirene, Triton, Urania, Venus, etc., into big stone statues, and that their wicked soules are left to swoop down upon us, and to howl across our continents, in tornadoes, herricans, cyclones, and the howling, shrieking, moaning, trembeling, freezing, death dealing wintery blasts— for such strife was not known to the Antesollucents.

The oldest book the Christians have, in their bible, is the old Arab Job, and it is only a garbled extract. It represents the devil as a fit associate with their god and his sons, see Job i. 6, 7; a kind of a detective, that went about killing and torment ing gods own folks. Then this evil one is not only the prince of the demons, but also, the prince of this world, see John xii. 31; xiv. 30; xvi, 11; and even the god of this world, see 2 Cor. iv. 4. Eph. vi. 12. And Rev. xii. 9, tell us that the Dragon, Serpent, Devil and Satin, is one, the four gods of this mighty godhead— the gods of this world, that was cast out of heaven, and [made] an unmerciful abuser and murder of its peaceful inhabitents!

Yes, this god of the Christians, and his sons, are very, yes, awful friendly with this devil after such a terrific row and war! I guess those tother sons, that Job mentions must have died for Jesus is said to be his only son, and he and this devil of a god was on awful friendly terms, for he layed out, without food, forty days, way out in a wilderness, with this devil; Jezy even let Nick tote him up to heaven, to the holy city, and stick him on the pinnacle of the steeple; Nick then flew with him, up into an exceeding high mountain, and showed Jezy what a whopping big world he was god over; saying now Jezy if you will just tumble down and worship me I will give you my gal Sal and all of this big world see Matt. iv.

Then Jezy told Nick if he would follow him he would make him a fisher of men, Matt. iv, 19, and to do this he must hate every thing, and every body, and even himself, and love nothing but sweet Jezy, Lu. xiv. 26. For, says he, Nick I am some devil meself: Think not I am come to send peace on earth, no, I came not to send peace! but a sword! Matt. x. 34. I am come to send fire on this earth;

Lu. xii, 49; so, you just git, or I will mall the stuf-. fing out of you; Matt. iv, 10. And he got, and this was more than he, Nick, the acknowledged king of this world, and a contending king for heaven could stand, so he declared war against sweet Jezy and as his father had given him all power of earth and heaven, giving all things into his hand, Mat. xxviii, 18. Jo. iii. 35; he was simply a sardine for Nick.

For we are told at iv. 26, of the Acts, that the Kings of this earth stood up, and the Rulers were gathered together against the Lord, and against his Christ. So the powers that was did not receive Jezy nor acknowledge him; his own received him not, and the powers that be killed him! And, although he called loud and lustily, for his god to save him yet, he died a malefactor to the higher powers; and Paul his apostle, their last witness, after seeing Jezy and Jony go up, he then declared he was a Roman, and said: "Let every soul be subject to the higher powers. For their is no power but of God: the powers that be are ordained of God, Rom. xiii."

So, take it up one side, and down the other, and for the life of me, I never was able to see any difference betwen the Christian's gods and devils. I am just as fraid of one as the other— and more afraid of them, for they are all a lot of crazy devils! for by their fruit we know them!

☞ Now, the Christian's bible have these devils here on earth at the beginning, monkeying with their idiotic mother, Gen. iii, 1,22. Then, they have the sons of their god taking the daughters of men for wives, Gn. vi,2. Then, to cap the climax, they have their gods and their devils fighting over a woman, in heaven, and the devil and his army of gods women and devils were cast out of heaven on earth to mix and to momix up man, Rev. xii ,6, 9. Then we see these gods of this earth so jealous of those tother gods that they killed poor Onan, because he would not beget them a royal son, as did Joseph! Gen. xxxviii, 8 to 1f. Then, we see their main god coming to earth and seducing Joseph's wife, and getting her a bastard, contrary to all justice, decency, and laws, of either God's, Man's or Nature's, see Matt. i, 18.

Reader, it looks to me like all these preachers, gods and devils are after is women—and this is their theory of our present races of man—a lot of bastards from these gods and devils! Then they tell us no bastard can go to their heaven, they even exclude all to the tenth generation! see Deut. xxiii, 2.

So under such falce theology and absurd religions is it any wonder our children are rased up fit subjects for slaves, scared to death, believing in all manner of spirits, haunts, ghosts, witches, and hobgoblins? Is it any wonder that such statuary as a God's Slave, that says: You shal be bought, sold or treated as Slaves, so see Deut. xxviii, 68. Joel iii, 8. Or, a King's concucbine Slave, see 1.Kings ,xi, 1, 3? Or, a Turkish, Greekess, Christian Slave; or a Mormon wives Slave; a Negro Slave, is now contrasted with the inspiring Amazonian Female warrior; or the New York, New Jersey, Virginir, North Carolina, Arkansas and the California Female Coats of Arms; or the United States Goddess of Liberty, and Justice!

View them, contrast them, and it is alone in the Land of Liberty that our mothers are duly worshiped and respected.

Then, is it any wonder Thomas Paine should declare himself free? and give us his 'Age of Reason? and a Declaration of Independence? And declare he believed in the Freedom of Woman and in One God and no more; and hoped for happiness beyond this life. Or, that our Revolutionary Fathers rebelled against this King's bible's assumed divine rights of Kings Gods and Devils?

THE MIGHTY RIVER AMAZON.

THIS giant among the rivers of the earth takes its rise among the glaciers of the Andes. The first hostile Europeans on its waters was confronted by a nation of people who had female warriors, hence the fables of the Amazons.

THE AMAZONIAN BILLOW!

After emerging from the Andes, swelled by tributary streams, this noble river winds through the vast savannahs of South America till it has run a course of nearly four thousand miles. Before reaching the Atlantic the vast flood of water is fifty odd miles wide, and in mid-channel the opposite costs are not visible. It seems more like a fresh-water sea than a river.

At its mouth a vehement struggle takes place between the river flowing down and the tide running up, as is represented in the above cut. Twice a day they dispute the pre-eminence, and in the meeting of the enormous mass of water a ridge of surf and foam is raised to a height of one hundred and eighty feet, as shown in the above cut.

At a distance of five hundred miles out at sea the waters of the Amazon are still perceptible. For the last four hundred and fifty miles of its course it is never less than four miles wide, while the depth is so great that large vessels may go up the channel for two thousand miles and still be in forty fathoms of water.

The researches of travlers have shown that the vegetable and animal productions of the basin of the Amazon outnumber in species and variety nearly all the products of the same kingdoms in Europe and North America taken together; and yet many tributaries of this mighty stream, flowing from the vast unknown interior to the north and south, have been only partially explored. What a noble field for enterprise, when even the fibers and nuts of a few species of palm afford valuable objects of trade! American Reader.

THE SEA AND ITS USES.

IT is a common thing in speaking of the sea to call it "a waste of waters." But this is a mistake. Instead of being a waste and a desert, it keeps the earth itself from becoming a waste and a desert. It is the worlds fountain of life, health, and beauty and if it were taken away, the grass would perish from the mountains, the forests would crumble on the hills. Water is as indispensable to all life, vegetable or animal, as the air itself. This element of water is supplied entirely by the sea. The sea is the great inexhaustible fountain which is continually pouring up into the sky precisely as many streams, and as large, as all the rivers of the world that are pouring into the sea.

The sea is the real birth-place of the clouds, the crystals, the icebergs, the glaciers, the snow-caped mountains, the springs, rills and rivers; yea, out of it comes all the frosts and dews of heaven. Instead of being a waste and an incumbrance, therefore, it is a vast fountain of fruitfulness, and the nurse and mother of all the living. Out of its mighty bosom come the resources that feed and support the population of the world. We are surrounded by the presence and bounty of the sea. It looks out upon us from every flower in our garden-bed; from every sprig of grass that drops upon our passing feet the morning's dew; from the bending grain that fills the arm of the reaper; from bursting presses, and from barns filled with plenty; from the broad forehead of our cattle, and the rosy faces of our beautiful children.

It is the sea that feeds us; it is the sea that clothes us. It cools us with the summer cloud, and warms us with the blazing fires of winter. We make immense wealth for ourselves and our children out of its rolling waters, though we may live a thousand leagues away from its shores, and never have looked on its crested beauty or listened to its eternal anthem. Thus the sea, though it bears no perceptable harvest upon its bosom, yet, sustains all the harvests of the world. If, like a desert itself, it makes all the other wildernesses of the earth to bud and to blossom as the rose. Though, its own waters are salt and wormwood, yet, it makes the clouds of heaven to drop with sweetness; it opens the springs of valleys and forces the rivers among the hills.

The sea is a perpetual source of health and life to the world. Without it there could be no drainage for the lands. It is the scavenger of the world. The sea is also set to keep pure the atmosphere. The winds, whose wings are heavy and whose breath is sick with the malaria of the lands over which they have blown, are sent out to range over these mighty pastures of the deep, to plunge and to play with its rolling billows, and to dip their pinions over and over in its healing waters. There they rest when they are weary; there they rouse themselves when they are refreshed. Thus their entire substance is drenched, bathed, and washed and winnowed, and sifted through and through by this glorious baptism. Thus they fill their mighty lungs once more with the sweet breath of ocean, and, striking their wings for the shore, they go breathing health and vigor.

The ocean is not the idle creature that it seems, with its vast and lazy length stretched between the continents, with its huge bulk sleeping along the shore or tumbeling in bowuless fury from pole to pole. It is a mighty giant, who, leaves his oozy bed comes out upon the land to spend his strength in the service of man. Thus the sea keeps all our factories and mills in motion. Thus the sea spins our thread and weaves our cloth.

It is the sea that cuts our iron bars like wax, and rools them into proper thinness or pile them up in the solid shaft strong enough to be the pivot of a revolving planet. It is the sea that tunnels mountains, and bores the mines, and lifts the precious ore and coal from their sunless depths. It is the sea that lays the iron track, that builds the iron horse, that fills his nostrils with firy breath and sends his tireless hoofs thundering across the continent. It is the power of the sea that is doing for man all those mightiest works that would otherwise be impossible.— Swain.

THE INFLUENCE OF THE SUN.

AS surely as the force which moves a clock's hands is derived from the arm which winds up the clock, so surely is all terrestrial power drawn from the sun. Leaving out of account the eruptions of volcanoes and the ebb and flow of the tides, every mechanical action on the earth's surface; every manifestation of power, organic and inorganic, vital and physical, is produced by the sun.

His warmth keeps the sea liquid and the atmosphere a gas; and all the storms which agitate both are blown by the mechanical force of the sun. He

He lifts the rivers and the glaciers up to the mountains, thus the cataract and the avalanche shoot with an energy derived immediatly from the sun. Thunder and lightning are also the transmitted strength of the sun. Every fire that burns, and every flame that glows, dispenses light and heat which originaliy come from the sun.

In these days, unhappily, the news of battle is familiar to us, but every shock and every change is an application or a misapplication of the mechanical force of the sun. He blows the trumpet, he urges the projectile, he bursts the bomb. And remember, this is not poetry, nor fiction, but rigid mechanical truth. He rears, as I have said, the whole vegetable world, and through it the animal; the lilies of the field are his workmanship, the verdure of the meadows and the cattle upon a thousand hills are his creation.

He forms the muscles, he urges the blood, and he builds the brain. His fleetness is in the lions foot; he springs in the panther, he soars in the eagle, and he slides in the snake. He grows the forest and he hews it down; the power which raised the tree and which wields the axe being one and the same. The clover sprouts and blossoms, and the scythe of the mower swings, by the suns force.

The sun digs the oar from our mines, he rolls the iron, he rivets the plates, he boils the water, and he draws the train. He not only grows the cotton, but he spins the thread and weaves the web. There is not a hammer raised, a wheel turned or a shuttle thrown, but what is raised, turned and thrown by the sun. His energy is poured freely into space, but our world is a halting-place where this energy is conditioned.

Here the Proteus works his spells; the self-same essence takes a million shapes and hues, and finaly disolves into its primitive and almost exhaustless forms. The sun comes to us as heat, he quits us as heat, and between his entrance and departure the multiform powers of our globe appear. They are all special forms of solar power—the moulds into which his strength is temporally pour'd in passing from its source through infinitude.— Tyndall.

RATE OF THE EARTHS MOTION.

AS the earth is nearly twenty-five thousand miles round at the equator, and as it takes twenty-four hours to turn from west to east on its axis, it is easy to see that every point of the equator is careering eastward at the rate of more than a thousand miles an haor. To understand this fully, fix your thoughts on a city such as Quinto, built on a high ridge midway between the Poles. Men, houses, spires, trees, and every thing are whirling round with such swiftness that they sweep over sixteen miles in a minute. While it whirls us onward at the incredible speed of a thousand miles a minute in its anual trip around the sun.

The fastest railway train, from which we start back in alarm as it thunders past creeps along, compared with this speed. Every thing on the great thick girdle of the earth is whirled round equally quick. Ships at sea, the angry tossing waves, the birds of the air, the clouds and vapors are hurried onward tward the east with the same amazing speed. The ocean currents being thus formed, creating a movement contrary to that of the earth,— that is, while the earth is moving from west to east it causes a current of the ocean to move from east to west.

There is no dainger of any of them being whisked off, as water is whisked off a mop when swiftly turned round. They are, as it were, firmley tied on to the earth by an unseen, unfelt chain which we call the force of gravity. Pulling all things toward the earth's center, it allows nothing to fall or to fly off. So long as the day remains of twenty-four hours in length, there is no cause for fear. If, hawever, the day were shortened to a seventeenth part of its present length, then this unseen chain, this force, called gravity, could no longer tie things to the earth. Men, animals, and all things, would soon loose their hold. We might be whisked into space, like water from a mop, or might fall off and be left behind, as the earth hurries forward on its incredible journey round the sun.

Although every thing at the equator is whirled around at the rate of more than a thousand miles an hour, in its daily revolution on its axes, to the sun, the rate is not the same in other parts of the earth. Midway between the equator and either Pole it is only seven hundred and forty miles an hour, or about twelve miles a minute. At the nearest point to the North Pole which man has yet reached, hills, icebergs, plains and seas are all traveling eastward only about as fast as an express railway train. A vast difference to the speed at the equator."

The period of twilight shortens towards the equator and lengthens toward the poles; while day and night lengthens towards the poles and shortens at the equator. The nights being from four to six months long near the poles, and only twelve hours long at the equator! What a difference! And only think, our World, Bible and Sunday makers did not know this! What an awful hell-of-a-day Sunday would be at the poles!

" We now come to the most wonderful part of the geography of Europe. If you should sail across the Atlantic, directly west from the German Empire, England, Scotland, Ireland, or North part of France, you would go from great and prosperous nations to a cold, desolate region called Labrador, where the inhabitants are snow-bound nearly all the year. These people of Labrador are no further from the hot zone than those of the countries just mentioned. Why, then this difference? It is simply because a great stream of warm water flows continually across the Atlantic towards those prosperous countries, and because warm winds blow over them. This warm current of water is called the Gulf Stream. Reverse this. If this warm, ocean current, the Gulf Stream, and the warm winds should be directed towards Labrador, instead of towards Europe, then the former would become productive, green and prosperous, while the latter would become snow-bound and desolate."

N. B. All this goes to prove that the altitude of the American Continent is so much greater than the European, and that its vast rivers, rushing its waters across to the Eastern Continent, proves beyond a doubt that the beginning was in the Americas, from whence all that is, has been supplied.

Shame! shame! on any man, or on any set of men, or a vast continent that would teach otherwise—right in the very face of an always, ever existing unimpeachable witnesses from all Nature. They not only owe us for their origin, but, they owe their very existence to us!

AMERICA, DEAR NATIVE LAND.

America, dear native land,
Of golden zone and silver strand;
Whoes mountains pierce unto the sun,
Whoes endless rivers seaward run;
How thrills my soul to hear thy name,
To sound thy kindeling deeds of fame;
Dear land of all our best desires,
Where freedom keeps her altar flars.

America, whose humblest sons
Are born as earths divinest ones,
With faces set unto the hights
Where honor crowns her faithful knights;
Whoes daughters wear the royal grace,
That clothe the queen of regal race,
Where hand in hand they hold unfurled
The Magna Charter of the world.

— 41 —

America, on many a plain,
The flower of thy youth lies slain,
But from the soil by valor fed,
The ripest grain is harvested.
☞——Our Father's God, we cry to thee,
O keep thy people pure and free,
And let the fires of freedom run,
To all the lands beneath the sun.

Written for the Acme Haversack, by Kate Brownlee Sherwood.

SWEET LAND OF LIBERTY.

Tune, America.

My countrey! 'tis of thee,
Sweet land of liberty,
  Of thee I sing;
Land where my fathers died,
Land of the Pilgrims' pride,
From every mountain side
  Let freedom ring.

My native country! thee,
Land of the noble free,
  Thy name I love;
I love thy rocks and rills,
Thy woods and templed hills;
My heart with rapture thrills,
  Like that above.

Let music swell the breeze,
And ring from all the trees,

Sweet freedom's song;
Let mortal tongues awake;
Let all that breathe partake;
Let rocks their silence break,
　The sound prolong.

My fathers' God! to thee,
Author of Liberty!
To thee we sing;
Long may our land be bright
With freedom's holy light:
Protect us in our right,
　Great God we sing!

Written by Samuel Francis Smith, of Boston, in 1832, to be sung at Fourth of July celebrations.

AMERICA IN THE FRONT RANK OF NATIONS.
BY DANIEL WEBSTER.

THIS lovely land, this glorious liberty, these benign institutions, the dear purchase of our fathers, are ours; ours to enjoy, ours to preserve, ours to transmit. Generations past, and generations to come, hold us responsible for this sacred trust. Our fathers, from behind, admonish us, with their anxious paternal voices. Posterity calls out to us from the bosom of the future; the world turns hither its solicitous eyes,— all, all conjure us to act wisely and faithfully, in the relations which we sustain.

We can never, indeed, pay the debt which is upon us; but by virtue, by morality, by religion, by the cultivation of every good principle and every good habit, we may hope to enjoy these blessings through our day, and to leave it unimpared to our children. Let us feel deeply how much, of what we are and what we possess, we owe to this liberty and to these liberal institutions of government.

It cannot be denied, but by those who would dispute against the sun, that with America, and in America, a new era commences in human affairs.

This era is distinguished by free representative governments, by entire religious liberty, by improved systems of national intercourse, by a new awakened and an unconquerable spirit of free inquiry, and by a diffusion of knowledge throughout the community, such as has been before altogether unknown and unheard of.

America, America, our country, our own dear and native land, is inseparably connected, fast, fast bound up, in fortune and by fate, with these great interests. If they fall, we fall with them; if they stand, it will be because we have upheld them.

Let us contemplate, then, the connection which binds the prosperity of others to our own ; and let us manfully discharge all our duties which it imposes. If we cherish the virtues and principles of our fathers, all Nature will assist us to carry on the work of Human Liberty and Human Happiness.

Auspicious omens cheer us. Great examples are before us. Our own firmament now shines brightly upon our path. Washington and our Revolutionary Fathers, as stars, are indelibly, and forever fixed in the clear upper sky. Many, many other bright and noble stars have now joined the American constellation ; they circle round their center, and the heavens beam with new light. Beneath this illumination let us walk the course of life, and at its close devoutly commend our beloved country the common parent of us all, to Divine Goodness.

HONESTY THE BEST POLICY.

Washington after Serving, [not ruling] his countrey for forty-five years, gives this as his farewell warning : " I hold the maxim no less applicable to public than to private affairs, that honesty is always the best policy. Can it be that Providence has not connected the permanent felicity of a nation with its virtue? Let it be asked where is the security for property, where is the security for reputation, where is the security for life, if a truthful and righteous obligation does not animate the oathes, which are the instruments of investigation in our courts of justice?" Again he asks: " Who that is a sincere friend to it, can look with indifference upon attempts to shake the very foundation of the whole fabric?"

HAIL REPUBLIC!

"Hail! thou Republic of Washington, Hail!
Never one star of thy Union shall pale,
Thou hope of the world! Every omen of ill
Must fade in the light of thy destiny still;
And Time brings but honor with increase to thee,
Thou land of the beautiful, home of the free."

THIS is a likeness of Washington, who with our Revolutionary Fathers, faught for years against the religious tyrants, of this Old Jew King's Bible, and its awful vicious, enslaving, crazy, and self-contradictory teachings! The churches, one and all, and all religionists, called them Traitors, Heratics, and Infidel Rebls! And they are in hell to-day if this awful King's Bible is true! But thank God, dear reader, it is not true. It is only a collection of sixty odd blood and thunder fish, snake, and ghost stories, from the Low-down, vicious, obscene, vulgar, Five Cent Novels of that day!

"Success, right or wrong, wins our sympathies. And this is why Washington, the Father of our Countrey's name is written with fame. Had he made a failure, who would have remembered him with honor and pride? Echo answers who? and any owl, or fool can say who."

PATRIOTISM THE SUBLIMEST OF ALL PUBLIC VIRTUES.

That patriotism which, catching its inspiration from on high and leaving an immeasurable distance below all lesser, groveling, personal interests and feelings, animates and prompts to deeds of self sacrifice, of valor, of devotion, and of death itself: that is public virtue; that is, it is the noblest, and the sublimest of all public virtues.— Henry Clay.

I BELONG TO THEM!

READER, the above cut represents what actually happened to one of our Govenors. In his canvass for election he actually boasted of the Secret Oath-bound Orders that he belonged too. Saying: I belong 1st. to the Church; 2nd. to the Masons; 3rd. to the Oddfellows; 4th. to the Democrats; 5th. to the Alliance; and of course, the church made him admit that he originally belonged to the 6th. fellow, Mr. Devil!

And it so happened that the Devil had the largest chain on him, and the flogging that old Job got was nothing to what this poor old Slave got from all of his masters!. Next accompanying cut represents an Indignation Meeting at Elm-street Curch, South Nashville, Tenn., where this "I belong to them" govenor Buchanan was sevearly denounced, and threatened with mob violence! They declared he had brought Shame and Disgrace on the whole State!

They declared that he spent his time at Sunday whiskey hells, and was frequently too drunk to attend to business, and yet, a deacon in the church!

The papers terribly denounced him as a trickster,

THE MEETING AT ELM-STREET CHURCH!

because he had not pleased any of his masters.

They say, that he, by the trickery of these oath-bound, secret-orders, got to be Govenor! That he now sets back in his office, and has his Officials out secretly working to maintain him, by fraud and unfair means! That he releases too many notorious convicts! That he let a notorious forger, Davis, that had forged himself in the Penitentiary, forge himself out! And worst of all the Banner says: "All this expense would have been avoided if the Legislature had done its duty and the Govenor had not Signed inportant Laws without reading them."

Only think, it would take a book as large as the largest to record the rascality, errors, and blunders of this oath-bound, secret-order, govenor, and his hayseed, foxtail, sagegrass, legislature! They have gutted the Treasury, and give the gripes to all of our pocket books.

And yet, after all this outrageous blundering, dissatisfaction, mob law, and confusion, he and his oath-bound, secret-order ringsters, has the impudence of the very Devil, and added insult to injury by asking the people to still trust him.

Great god, only think—the money that he and his religions, political, paternal, oath-bound, secret order, hayseed, foxtail, sagegrass, legislature has lost, and squandered, if made into silver barbed wire it would fence in the whole state. He gave two thousand dollars to a lawyer to do a little business that the banks offerd to do for nothing.

So the Democrats Stomped the Stuffing out of 'im; the Church gritted thir teeth, shook their fists, and made awful mouths at 'im, and forgot to pray for 'im; so, the Devil and the Tricksters went right and left for 'im; the Miners at Briceville, aided and backed by the whole county of Anderson, they after petitioning, and remonstrating to this Govenor to no relief, reached that point where forbarence ceased to be a virtue, and they rose up as a solid mob, turned out, drove away the Convicts and blowed up the prison, and burnt up the stockades, as our above picture represents. He and his religious ringsters draged me before the United States Court for Caricaturing of him and the situation in the state. Uncle Sam however, looked down on the wretched momixed up affairs of the State, and smilingly consoled himself by releasing me and saying: " Well it's an old saying, there is fools in all families; and there is Buck, just look at 'im, he is the biggest fool 'ive got.

And the very night after I was released, an awful mob, of thousands of infuriated citizens of Davidson County, attacted the Jail, tore down the gates, doors, shot the guards, and mobed a lot of prisoners, and the Govenor was there! and was heard to say, boys, boys, listen to me! But, no one would listen to him.

This is the Circular that waked them up, and caused my arrest and trial; and they entended to imprison and ruin me!

TO the Senate and the House of Representatives, and to the Attorney General, and Govenor of Tennessee.

For years your predecessors have disregarded our Constitution in toto! And you have done the same so far! Col. Savage forewarned you Smart Elecks of this wretched state of affairs. Declaring that the Legislature had no right to hire out the convicts or to make a law to extend beyond two years. It is this disregard for our laws by you that is fast demoralizing our people; and forbearance has ceased to be a virtue, and mob violence has to be resorted too in self defence; and you bet, God is always to be found with David! So you need nolonger console your galling gizzards with the delusive dogma " That the greatest good to the greatest number is right.". Every human being has his Constitutional Rights, and none of your ordinances is Law if it Conflicts with the Constitution!

Nor will God protect you in the enforcing of it, but he will turn you over to David Damnation just as certain as this state of affairs continue? How much Dynamite do you suppose there is now in the State of Tennessee?

GENTLEMEN are you aware that only ONE man could step down to any of our drug stores, and purchase just THREE ingredien's that OLD WOMEN use for dyeing, and in one hours time, have enough Dynamite made to blow your little Militta to eternity? Dont you remember the rumored earthquakes and volcanic eruptions in our mountains? Only think! this —Our Bob— ever since his term was up, has been shrieking around the State with an old fiddle trying to again rase a wind, and as he could not, he anounced to lecture on fools! But, ah, alas, presumpteous Bob! you are only a political mummy! And your royal successor Buck, after the stuffing was stomped out of him then the Alliance picked up what was left of him and run him for the second term, and thank God! he never carried a single county!

Had I not been one of the number of free men that you smart Elecks have Outlawed I would be mum. But, for you, when threatened, and forewarned, to thus knowingly make a more infernal set of royal class laws than your bruder Bob did is damnable! This picture represents his would like to be Cock of the walk—a trio of royal, religious, medical quacks, of his own creation! A headless, senseless, quack of a goose. The people he says have not got sense enough to choose their physician. He places us in the hands, and at the mercy of a set of fool quacks! He and they show their infamy by wanting a law to force people to employ them, and them only.

So it is quack! religion! medicine and politics!

YES, quack! quack! quack! goes Gov. Taylor's 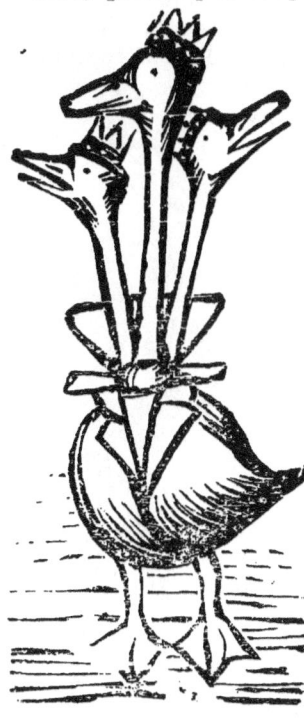 royal, medical, goose of a would like to be King. A divine favored triune dictator, or a three headed goose!

This goose is only one of the many, many unconstitutional laws Gov. Taylor, Buchanan, and Turney have signed!

They Know Our Constitutions positively forbids Religious, Medical, or, any Class laws!

They know that Our Constitution says: "Full faith and credit shall be given in each state to the public records of every other state.

That citizens in each state shall be entitled to all the privileges of citizens in the states. That perpetuities and monopolies shall not be allowed. That you are not to be made to observe any Religious ordinance, or rule."

Yes, they know that any body has got as good a right to practice their politics, religion, medicine, and to choose their day for rest, as they have to do any thing.

Yes, each of these good, religious Govenors have been remonstrated with, shown the unjust, unfair, unprecedented, and unconstitutionality of these laws. And they and the legislature have been petitioned to repeal all such laws; but, enstead of doing so they enact more! So, what hope is there for us when those empewered with the making, and executing of our laws are our greatest blunders hypocrits, and our vilest law breakers?

History and experience, tell us that nearly all improvements, discoveries have been given to us by some common Arab, Negro, Indian, or Individual. Opposed and persecuted by this self-same goose headen religious set, that is all the time quacking around our Courts, Congress, and Legislatures as this cut represents.

If they were only allowed to use just what they, what their goose headed set have gotten up they would be a thousand years behind! and have nothing better to offer man than the white Elephant, a sacred Bull, a pack Camel, a climbing Lama, African Slavery, an involuntary Bond or Tax Slave, horse shoe, cross mark, hoodo, I heare so, politics, religion, and medicine.

It was they that betrayed your sacred weaknesses, and infirmities, that by law you are forced to confess, and to uncover to the whole world. It was they that made that unconstitutional law forcing you to employ them in every case of measels, or pay a fine and be imprisoned! It was they that forced an illegal and unconstitutional clause in our Census Law that forced everybody to uncover and expose their sacrid rights and secrets to the public, to be published to the world— thus placing you in the power of, and at the mercies of any devil that might choose to devour you!

Some Govenors have been man enough not to sign such laws, and some have been repealed, while our higher courts are all the time busy repealing them!

April, 1889, this self-same goose headed set, past Senate bill 79, that declares none but Allopaths, Homeopaths, and Electrics, shall practice medicine!

Thus was conglomerated a strange mixture of Infamy— a three headed quack; opperated in the name and by illegal state laws!

This debars four or more schools of their rights and privileges. This debars every citizen of their liberty to choose from four or more well and long estabelished schools of medicine! or to even choose a physician! All of this is infamous and unlawful! And yet, Gov. Taylor, not only willingly, but in a few minuts, made this infamous law! It was he that appointed Mr. Allopath, Homeopath, and Eclecticopath, as Inquisitorial Generals, and placed the powers of our Officers and Courts at their command, with as absolute monarchal powers as has the Emperor of Russia! Thus establishing a Monarchy, in a Republic! from which there is no recourse! nor appeal!

For when they notified me of their law, and ordered me to obey it; that is, renounce my School of Medicine, turn hypocrit, turn a lying truckling, quack! or leave the State! And when I appealed to Gov. Taylor, for a redres, he informed me I had none! And advised me to submit to this awful three headed monstrosity!   A QUOCK!

I then appealed to Legal advise and was informed that as I was Graduated an M. D., in New York, and that not only did this protect me, but, the United States, and the State CONSTITUTIONS protect me from such discriminations, and grants any body as good a right to practice medicine as have Gov. Taylor's god-favored three!

The above cut gives them another defeat, and rebuke. Last week these Infernal Old Infamous quacks tried to inforce their infamous registration laws on Dr. Crane, of Bradford, Pa., but got their gizzards choked out of 'em as our preceding picture represents. Dr. Crane would not register, and the courts decided that he was not obliged too.

Golly, a Crane has got more sense than a goose! Yes, any set of men that would discriminate and trample under foot Constitutions that they have sworn to protect, as these Govenors have done, are simpley no men at all. And any set of men that cannot stand honest and fare competition without monkeying with the Legislature, the Church, Congress and the Courts, had better openly 'jine in' with the Pope, the Preast, and the Preachers, and deny a Free Government as they do. Yes, deny a free souverignity and free salvation, and force another Infamous Inquisition, for this is the sum, substance, and intention of these paternal class laws; as all party, and religious laws are.

This cut represents this goose headed set they are always at all public gatherings, as meetings and buryings, consulting as to what must be done to Mr. so and so.

This Coxite class become so provokingly anoying at our Legislatures and Congress, that they had to be arrested, fined and imprisoned. A standing army guards our Capitols now to keep down these religious cranks, or no business can be done.

They, a few evil designing rascals, collect up armies of fools, in all parts of the states, and march to the Capitols, and demand that their ideas be enacted into laws. Finaly they learned a little sense, got tired wating for Christ, droped his name from their banner, and skedaddled. And all this is the fruits of religion.

When I was a student of medicine it was bleed, blister, scarify, cup, leach, puke and purge; and if this failed to kill you, then you were starved to death—not allowed your necessary food and water, never washed, scrubed, or bathed only when they went to bury you. Our first friends were the steam and water doctors. They taught and treated the people better. And now the great avenue to health leads to Watering Places, and not to Drug Places! Old Doctor Allopathy, and his two sons, Homeopathy and Eclecticopathy, are mear Drummers for some Drug Store, or Nostrum! And yet, Dr. Allopathy gives Poison Oak, Strychnine, Aconite, Foxglove, Henbane, Jimpson-weed, and every vile poison known to man, as medicine! ☞ And from their poisons none never recover! ☜ Dr. Homeopath and Dr. Eclecticopath gives precisely these same awful poisons! So where is your choice, or friend fair Tennessee?

So, I am not surprised at the suggestion, that the portraits of these infamous Govenors be hung face to the wall and their infamous record pasted on their backs!

Just as I was going to press with this book I was arrested with a United States warrant, charged by Gov. Buchanan and his hayseed, foxtail, sagegrass legislature of sending unmailable matter to them, through the mail. This was Sep. 14th. 1891. The case was examined by our postmaster, Asa Faulkner, a U. S. Commissioner, who said he had not read my Circular, and proceeded to read it aloud to all present. He then bound me ouer in a five hundred dollar bond, which I managed to give, and kept out of jail, just what they did not expect, from the fact that Patterson, Faulkners brother-in-law, a drunken Prohibitionist, that was once arrested for an attempt to rape a little girl, an orphan, one of my near neighbors; he whispered it around to one Mr Morton, that Fletch Woodward was in jail! showing that it was a wilful, malicious and a premeditated attact by the Faulkners, to again injure and imprison me!

The point I want noticed is that this Complainant, prosecuter, persecuter, Asa Faulkner, was the willing witness, the postmaster that committed the error, if any, for the express purpose of making an offense so he could have a case, for he was the Commissioner that had to try the case! And then making out that he had not read my Circular or Infidel Literature, when he had a month before, secretly tried to stop it, by complaining to the Postoffice department at Washington, and was informed that we had as good rights to the mails as he or, any party, clique, church, or order!

So, in my opinion, this Christian Saint, Asa Faulkner, is an awful purgered, prose-percecuting witness, and had these three hayseed, foxtail, sagegrass legislators to play their part for him.

Now, as this hayseed, foxtail, sagegrass legislature had made an unconstitutional law, saying no school of medicine shall practice but the old drug schools! And as I had been ordered to renounce my conscience, and disown my school of medicine, or leave the State! I kicked as the preceedidg circulars show, and then they have kicked as I have just told!

Our Constitutions make it my DUTY, as well as my PRIVILEGE, to apply to those invested with the powers of government for a redress of grievances, by address or remonstrance. Saying that the Printing Press Shall bê Free to every person to examine the proceedings of the Legislature, or of any branch, or Officer of the Government.

About the first of October, 1891, Asa Faulkner showed me a letter from Attorney General Rhum saying that the Attorney General at Washington had decided that my Infidel Literature was mailable. This fact Asa knew when he had me arrested, and pretended to try the case, and bound me over; and he knew also, that he had submitted my case to the Authorities at Washington, and that they had ordered him to let me alone.

And when Attorney General Rhum, of the U. S.

Court, at Nashville, Tenn., was Officially notified then he illegally persisted in persecuting me, and forced an Indictment. And I was officially informed that my case was set for trial the 5th. day of Nov. 1891. My case was called late that day, and put off on an excuse, no appearance of their witnsses. The Attorney General then with all the impudence of a Falstaff, having the exact stature of old Dogberry, asked me why I had published Mr. Asa Faulkner. I said, I have not. He then produced some of the unfinished proof-sheets of this book. I asked, where did you get that? It is my stolen property! Then he replied, I have stolen property in my possession have I? Yes, said I, dont you see the book is not finished? It has been stolen from my office, from behind my counter, and from my desk! And I seen and know the thief! Exit—

I then appealed to the Judge, saying that they had a Cut an l Dried Case against me, and have put it off with the hope of Jailing me! They know that I have no way of making a bond here ; and as soon as it reaches home that I am in Jail they, this Infamous set entend to Arrest my two sons, minors, and charge them with something terable and Jail them! This is their program, and may it displease your honor! The Judge told me to go home and to ask the same man to go my bond. I did so. And it so happened that we had to go to this thief, and perjured Asa Faulkner to give the bond. I then asked Asa Faulkner where he got those proof-sheats of my book that he had given the Attorney General? He said he bought the book from Will Maupins. I then went and brought Maupins to him, and Maupins told him no sir. I sold you a different book, and not a piece of a book.

I then carried Maupins before the Grand-jury and indicted Faulkner for Grand Larceny, and I would have prosecuted him if our Attorney General, Whitson, had not been exposed in open court, by a Wild Cater, one Tom Drake, who informed the Court, Jury and the people, that he had sold the Att'y Gen. Whitson Wild Cat Brandy! This thrown him into Asa Faulkners hands, and I lost my case. And this rascally Att'y Gen. Whitson was so unpopular that he dared not run for a second term, and his Assistant, Fairbanks, made a vigerous canvass, a poor race, and got beat.

Early Friday April the 29th, 1892, my case was again called in the Federal Court, at Nashville, Tenn. My hypocritical Christian persecutors were on hand, in full force. Their galling gizzards wreaking for my blood! Alone! alone! without one kind human friend to council, or to console, I answered ready, for I never felt better! I informed the Judge that I had neither council nor witnesses! This was so sweet and savory to them! What a cunning chuckle exultingly went through their demon gizzards! A kind sympathising faced Gentleman quickley tendered me his service, but, I told him that he did not know me. O, that makes no difference, said he. Yes, said I, but I do not know you!

The Attorney General proposed to the Judge that he would act as my council. I accepted him, the Att'y Gen. as my Attorney! He then, rather arguingly, introduced the case to the Court, in a shape that would have made me guilty, under his Catholic construction of the law! So, I kicked! And informed the Judge that I not only denied the charges in toto, but, I now was prepared to prove that I did not mail the Circulars as charged in the Indictment; and if I had, they were malable! and that Mr. Faulkner and the Att,y Gen. was knowing to these facts; for our postmaster had orders to mail them, and he and the Nashville postmaster mailed them, amd charged me extre postage, and then to cap the climax of infamy they remailed then from the Nashville office to the Capitol, and they made me pay them another postage!

Things began to fizz and fry now. The Attorney General called a lot of witnesses, the Govenor, the States Att,y Gen., some Legislators, Postmasters,

Inspectors, Detectives, etc. And, he failed to prove that I mailed them, or, that they were unmailable.

As their main prose-persecuting witness, Asa Faulkner, their double-barreled witness— a postmaster and a commissioner— denied that he, or his assistant, ever did recieve any such orders! I then turned to my council, the Att'y General, and asked him if he did have an Official Letter from Washington, declaring Asa Faulkner did have orders to let me alone, and to send my Infidel Literature on? as Mr. Sager, his assistant, had told Mr. Crow and myself? O! in surprise, the Att'y General asked, you dont aim to make a witness out of me? O, yes, said I, slapping him on the shoulder, you are my Attorney, and I must have that letter! Come John dont go back on your client! He seen that he was fairly caught in his Council Trap, and after the Jurors and the Judge demanded it he produced it and the Judge immediately released me! Long live the Judge!

Asa Faulkner, their double-barreled, prose-persecuting, postmaster, and commissioner, a willingly perjured witness, seeing that he was caught, said a preacher got him to write to the department to get my Infidel Literature declared unmailable, but, he nor Mr. Sager, his assistant, never did get any answer! ☞ N. B. Mr. Sager, his assistant, informed Mr. Crow and myself, that they did get orders to send my Infidel Literature on! Yet, had I not caught the prose-persecuting Att'y General in my council trap, I would have been made out a liar! For there was a liar in the bunch, and he was proven to be Ase Faulkner! He was contradicted by their own Attorneys! by his assistant! by Mr. Houchens, by Mr. Maupins, by myself, and by himself! Verily, verily, I would not believe him on oath is what I heard some official Gentlemen say, on the streets the other day, and they were talking about other official business, not mine! So, say I also, Gentlemen!

T. E. Settle, the postoffice inspector witness, said he withdrew from the Tullahoma office a pack of my Adam Porwigle Circulars. And he considered them the most original literature in existence, and nothing like them! He knew nothing of the Truth Seeker, Investigator, Iron Clad Age, Puck, New York World, or, that there was a Liberal or an Infidel Literature! And yet he is an Inspector!

☞ FOUR TIMES! have my life, liberties and property, and that of my home, and family, have been attacted and unreparably injured by the Faukners!!!! ☜ My loss! my long suffering! and that of my poor, stinted, and half starved family—from this life-long, relentless, Faulkner persecution—is beyond description!

In Sep. 1862, Sam Henderson, Tip Faulkner's father-in-law, and Tom Argo, their relative, charged that Livley & Harmon had made me some engraving blocks, and I had used them to counterfit money! Livley & Harmon swore this! But, ah! alack! I produced the blocks, and proved by D. F. Wallace that he used them for me in printing a Botanical Book. So, down they went and out of Jail I came; but at the loss of my hard earned home, and considerable suffering, the loss of time, money and all was nothing to the damage done my character; and an eternal devil that it forced into my soul that time does not efface! No! it intensifies this venom; and eternity will not forgive! For I am certain there is no such a thing as forgiveness in this life, nor the life hoped for! Forgive? It is a misnomer, a cheat, a Christian fraud!

Again, in March 1864, this Sam Henderson and his son-in-law, Tip Faulkner, had turned from Rebels to Yankees, and now report me to Col. Gilbert, the 19th. Michigan, U.S.A. Infantry, as a very dangerous character! That I delt in Counterfit money, vulgar pictures, bogus inlistments and bogus bounties, and was a spy, etc! I was arrested, and immediatly rushed off and ramed into a military prison! My place of business, my home and family was searched and not a trace of evidence, much-less proof was found! I told the Col. that they had played this game on me with the Rebels, in 1862. That they were Rebels when the Rebels were here and yankees when the yankees were here! So, down they went, and out of the Guard-house I came! With conciderable loss of money, time and property! That led to a premature death of my wife and child ☞ they being driven out of their home, by the Rebel Soldiers, on that cold, cold bitter snowy night, and the child down with the measels, and EVERY thing that we had on earth was taken! and that which they could not take they piled in the center of the house and set fire to it! while the Drunken Rebel Demon's with their Bayonets shouted, staggared, and jobed around like demons from the regions of the damed!

In Nov. 1873, this same everlasting Tip Faulkner and his uncle Louis Faulkner, charged me with and prosecuted me for the murder of Enoch Cooksy; their kinsman! That was killed at a whore house that he frequented! I was turned off the Inquest and a cross-eyed Faulkner put in my place. I was arrested and ramed in an awful cold, dark, filthey old jail, and denied bail! My house was thoroughly seached, and the whole world ramsacked for near two years, and not one ray of evidece, nor proof was found! So out of jail I came, after exhausting another hard earned home, and pileing up on me an awful forced debt!

☞ And now after 18 years of awful preduidce, sin stint, deprivation, anxiety, fear, grief, suffering, death, and yawning, premature, pauper graves! that God made us fill! so the preachers say! After all this has rolled its relentless wheels over me! and my humble home and family—and we owe no man— and no evidence, much-less proof, comes up for them, these good Christians, to thus continue their persecutions, by declaring I am an awful, awful man, and sure for hell! ☞ It is the Christian hell that has been eternaly set up in them, for they know not justice, honor, nor forgiveness!

And now, in the summer of 1891, we hear of Asa Faulkner as soon as he was made Postmaster writing to the Postmaster General to have my Infidel Literature declared unmailable! I found him extra snappish, crabbed, and extra expensive to me. He refused me to exchange a few stamps, saying it was against the law, and in a few minutes after he made the exchange for another person, for my very same stamps In another case, he declares such is the law, when it was not, and he was corrected at two dollars expense to me. Then to cap the climax he bound me over in a five hundred dollar bond on a circular that he had been Officially notified to let pass, and at the same time he was declaring his sympathy for me, and that he had not read my circular and winkingly proceeded to read it to all. Now, I knew that he had read my circular, and that he was secretly trying to stop it and my Infidel or Liberal Literature! And the last I saw of him the morning he started for Nashville, to present me to the Grand Jury was at Massie's Saloon—Aptat se pugno!

Now, my erring fellow man, charity should begin at home, stay and end at home with this Faulkner family. For I am certain if they will bring their own erring selves to trial that they will not have any time to hown me from my cradle to my grave! So it is with my Literature, worse always has, and is passing through the mails, so why single out me? When I started my Literature, Mc Minnville had seven or eight Christian churches, and as many notoriously public bawdy-houses! Who dared to open their mouth but my Literature? Who secured to you the privilege of being your own witness, if my Literature did not? A privilege that you nor I did not enjoy until after my third trial in 1874! My Liberal or Infidel Literature alone petitioned and remonstrated for this the greatest privilege known to a poor man.

And now, my envious, jealous, hateing, tattling, crazy Christians that cant see how I always have plenty of money, I will say that I work for it, that

I do not credit nor ask for credit beyond a spanked-up security! To illustrate— in the winter of 1876, after working in snow and ice all week, I struggled on foot through snow and ice 18 inches deep, for 12 miles! I reached home with my boots frozen to my feet and legs! and found F.M. Smith, a Lawyer, wating for his part of my hard earned money! that I owed him for defending me against the Faulkners!

O! my God! only think of that destitute and desolate home, and suffering family that one winter out of 18 others! Only 50 cents fell to our part after that week of awful struggle, in snow and ice! Twenty five ce'ts we spent for corn meal and 25 cents for soup bones, to sustain life for another fearful week!

Now, my hateing, tattling, hypocrits, if you will do likewse you too, will soon pay your honest debts, hate and tattle less, and tell fewer lies.

The above cut represents Old Popular Opinion giving Old Crucifiction a bit of his mind. Look here Old Crucifiction, if this fellow Woodward is guilty of half what these Faulkners say then he is the sharpst rascal on earth. At any rate, as the thing has developed its self they had better let him alone or some body might suspicion them!

Yes, he who undertakes to protect, shield, and defend a lot of evil designing blunders, blunders himself worse; and makes an ass of himself! So, blunder on ye high and ye low officials— yes, by jo blunder all your life—at the peoples extra expense, and like your Jew pap Adam, and your Jew Jesus, lay it on your gods, or on your devils, or on Tom Walker, or your wife.

THE TWO PICTURES— The following is a truthful statement, and it is graphically illustrated by the two following cuts. The first cut represents Jesus and the Christians when not in power; or when they see no way to enforce their religion! The next cut represents them in power, and carrying out the hell that is in them! They are blood thirsty cowardly demons; and that is the kind of a god they worship!

The next cut shows how they stabbed our Revolutionary Fathers, and now our defenders! "The Beast is dead and landed in hell," is the language of the Nashville American of Jan'. 1893! in speaking of the death of Gen Butlar, a noble old Union soldier!

The Representatives of all religions, from all parts of the world while speaking in the World's Congress of all religions, poured forth their withering condemnations of the Crimes of Christians— saying: "The Christian Missionaries have always come to us with soldiers, bayonets, swords, muskets, cannon, opium, whiskey, tobacco, and instruments of torture! They robed, murdered, and destroyed us! an all in the name of God!"

"Christianity seems to contain, within itself, the very elements of self-contradiction; and of course, as we might naturally expect, the history of the Christian Church is a history of contradiction.

On the one hand, Christianity is an innocent lamb, "a lamb slain from before the foundation of the world, a lamb led to the slaughter, or as a sheep before its shearers, it is dumb, and opens not its mouth as is represented by the cut on the opposite page!

On the other hand, it is a lion, "the lion of the tribe of Judea," a beast of prey, with all the ferosity of a tiger, as is shown in the above cut! Yes, at one moment, it is all love and peace, and a peacemaker; and at another, it declares: Think not that I am come to send peace on earth, no! I came not to send peace! but a sword, Matt., x., 34.; and he that hath no sword, let him sell his garment, and buy one, Lu. xxii, 36. I am come to send fire on this earth, Lu. xii, 49. Follow me and I will make you FISHERS of men, Matt. iv, 19. And to do this, he, Jesus, the Christians Jew man god, says you must HATE everything, and everybody, and hate even your father, mother, wife, children, brethren, sisters, yea, you must hate your own life, and love ONLY sweet Jesus, Lu. xiv, 26, 27·

We might continue the contradictions; but we have surely given enough. Now what else can be expected from crazy beings and such contradictory elements than what the world has wofully experienced? History is but a practical comment upon them; that condemn them, for by their fruits we know them.

When Christianity, or any kind of religion, is weak, either as a whole, or as any praticular sect, it is all meekness, all humility, all patients, all love all charity! But the very moment they are strong, either in their own strength, or by the aid of the Strong Secular Arm, power, or Authority of the Government, she is filled with unrelenting cruelty! ☞ No crimes are too base for her to commit! No tortures are too cruel for her to inflict ☜ See our Reading References.

READING REFERENCES— Are here given as proof for what I have said in this book. It is not necessary to go further than their own bible! No, it is not necessary to quote from the history of the world, page after page of proof, for enough has been heard from their own mouth, not only to condemn, but also, to eternally dam it!

GENESIS. — LEARNING GOOD and EVIL from the Devil—the God of this world, caused the god of the Christians to become Envious, Jealous, and 'cussin' mad, so he cursed this world's god, the world, and man! He placed the curse of pain, sickness and labor upon you, iii, 17, 22, 23!

RELIGION caused the first enmity, and the first born man to commit murder, iv, 4, 2, 8, 23. And the fair daughters of man seduced the sons of god, vi, 2. JEALOUSY limited mans life, vi, 3, and destroyed man and the earth, 13!

TELLING the TRUTH caused the CURSE of SLAVERY to be put on man, ix, 25!

The Jew's and the Christian's god's judgement and morality gets worse! He rewardeth sin and crime! and chooses liars, whores, whoremongering tramps, vagabonds, and thieving murders, and he himself a party to sin and crime, and rewards one his followers, for the very crimes he condemns, and killed others for! xii, 1, 13. xv, xvi, 15. xviii, xix, 4, 8,

And their god destroyed the men of Sodum and Gomorrah because they were trying to uphold morality, law, order and chastity. and he, god, upheld old drunken Lot and his whoreing girles in their whoredom, and wickedness!

Lot says take my two daughters that has never known a man! and let these wicked men go! and as they would not, then god burned them up! and old Lot used his own girles! Reader the rest of the book is worse than this— xix, 8! 32 to 38! xxv, xxx, xxxiv, xxxviii!

EXODUS.— 1c, 22. 2c, 12. 7c, 20. 12c, 29. 13c, 2. 14c, 28. 32c, 27. Thus saith the Lord God of Israel, Put every man his sword by his side, and go in and out from gate to gate throughout the camp, and SLAY every man his brother! and every man his companion! and every man his neighbor!!!

LEVITICUS.— 13c, 46. 14c, 17c, 7. 18c,3. 20c 24c, 14. But the seventh year shall be a sabbath of rest unto the land, a sabbath for the Lord : thou shalt neither sow thy field, nor prune thy vineyard, 25c, 4. Hoodoo! doo! do!

NUMBERS.— 15c, 36. 16c, 1 to 50. 21c, 1 to 35. 25c, 1 to 18. 26c, 10. ;32c, 1 to 54. 32c, 39 to 41. 33c, 50 to 36. ☞ Kill all ! except the women children, that have not known a man by lying with him, these keep alive for yourselves, 31c, 18.!

DEUTDRONOMY — According to this book, a god, and an awfu one! is still with these nasty, religious wretches, and the twentieth chapter tells us, that it is God that goeth with them, and fights for them! ii, 25, 31 to 37. iii, 1 to 29. vi, 2 to 5, 20 to 25. xii, 29. xiii, 16. xx, 4. xxi, 11. xxviii, 27 to 32, and the 68 verse says you shall be sold and no buyer. How is this for high ? See full page cut.

JOSHUA.— Worse, and worser. They, the Jews and their god, goes pards with a whore, ii, 12 to 18 and takes an oath from her! They are forty years starving to death in a wilderness, in sight of a land flowing milk and honey and fritters on every tree, v, 6. vi, 17 to 21, to 25. vii, viii, 1 to 35. x, 1 to 43. xi, 1 to 23. xiii, 1 to 33. xxii, 8.

JUDGES.— The first chapter of this book tells us at the 19 verse, that the LORD, old Juda, and their nasty set, could not whip the people of the valley! Then, in the fifth chapter, at the fifth verse, they tell us that this same LORD was so powerful that he shook down the heavens, and melted Mount Sinai! Yet, no one misses Mount Sinai!

Then immediatly at sixth chapter, fifth verse, we are told that they and their god was nothing compared to the Mideonites; that they could not count them, nor their camels! i, 1 to 36. iii, 1 to 31. iv, 1 to 24. v, 5. vi, 5. vii, 2, 12, 25. viii, 10 to 30. ix, 18 to 54. x, xi, xii. xv, 14, 15.

So, on it goes, this book of RELIGIONS! recording tragedy after tragedy, just like we see and hear from crazy drunken fools in a poliece court!

Read of Royalism and Onanism in 38c of Genesis! See what a lesson the 30, 34, and 38th chapters of the first book of this King's bible learns our sons and daughters! Read of Abraham's ONLY begotten son at Hebrew, 11c, 15. Then ask Hagar the servent girl about it at Galations, 4c, 22. Ask Keturah his concubine about it at 1 Chronicles, 1c, 32, and you will find he had many a son! Only read of his brother Lot and his girls, at 19c, 36, of Genesis! Of Jacob and Rachel, not at the well, no, but, in a tangle with the servent girl, xxx, 3, of Genesis! of Noah drunk and naked, at ix, 21, of Genesis! the ravishing of Dinah, at xxxiv, the circumcising and murdering of the Sheckemites! the ravishing and the murder of Er and Onan by the LORD, and old whoremongering Judah and the harlot Tamar rewarded at xxxviii of Genesis! virteous Jew Joseph the servent, and the royal queen of Egypt, in a tangle at xxxix, 7, because she invited him to Lie with her! Samson and his sweethearts at Judgas xvi, 5;

—68.—

Robbery Commanded by the god of Abraham, the god of Isaac, the god of Jacob, and by the god of Moses and the Hebrews, at iii, 6, 18, 22. xii, 35, 36. of Exodus! Universal hatred commanded at Luke xiv, 26! Labor and Slavery oadained as a Curse, put only upon the Adamites by their gods at Genesis iii, 16, 19. ix, 25. and at Exodus xx, 9. and at Leviticus xxiii, 3. xxv, 45, 46. and at Joel iii, 8. and at Deutaronomy xv, 17. Murder commanded at Exodus 32c, 27. Whoredum commanded, enjoined, and rewarded by this bible god at Numbers, 31 c, 18! and at Hosea, 1c, 2. 3c, 1, 2, 3! actually saying: " And the LORD said to Hosea, Go, take unto thee a wife of whoredom! "

Lying commanded, approved, and sanctioned by this bible god, by this god of the Christians! at 1 Samuel, 16c, 1, 2. Joshua, 2c, 1 to 6. James, 2c, 25. Exodus, 1c, 18, 20. 3c, 22. 1Kings, 22c, 21, 22. Numbers, 14c, 23. Romans 3c, 7. 2 Corinthians, 12c, 16.

And the bigest, and the most unreasonable Lie is that of John the bap-souser. On page 63 is a likeness of this John the bap-souser, the fore runner of an immaginary Savior, or Christ. Now, where in does his or Jesus' likeness differ? and where in do they differ from the likenesses of the Indians of this countrey at that time? Neither of them were the Standard of the good, enlightened people existing on both continents at that day and time. No, you might as well say that our wandering Cowboys are the standard of Americans!

General Grant was awfully surprised to find the Chief Justice of Pagan China the most learned, or best manager on earth!

Yes, we are told that this John the Bap-souser, in so short a time as one summer bap-soused ALL yes, ALL Judea, ALL Jerusalem, and every body round about there! Matthew iii, 5. Mrk i, 5. Luke iii, 1 to 21. There were 7 millions of the conquerd, accursed enslaved Jews! several thousand Roman Soldiers! several thousand Roman Merchants! several thousand Roman officers! several thousand other citizens! several thousand others "round about there!" Making over a BILLION! of fashionable, civilized, religious people, to be re-converted, and bap-soused in so short a time as one summer! Now, this bap-sousing of a billion of people, by immersion, one at a time, in a little creek of a river, was no miracle! for John did no miracles, so say the tenth capter of St. John, at the forty-first verse! Then who told this whopping lie!

His orders to these billion of proselytes, were If you had TWO coats to give ONE to him that had none! He even told the Roman soldiers what they must do, all of which was contrary to law! Just as religionist are doing in this government to-day! And when he said the King was living in adultery he the King, instead of parting with his wives, concubines, and his tother coat, he sent and chopped off old imposter Johns head, and give it to one of his ballet High Kickers as a play thing!

Only think, as I have shown, this Jesus, John, and those FISHERS OF MEN! and their followers, would not ware only an old Sackcloth of a garment, they did not ware one coat, muchless two coats! They were regular old professiona tramps of the dead beat type! Or fishers of men!

The idea of an old illiterate pauper vagrant, or a crazy wild man, howling out of a wilderness; as this John, Jesus, and others did— nearly naked! nearly starved! and only partly hid their obscenity with an old camels hair sackcloth, called a "garment," is outrageously unreasonable!

Now, this Jesus made his appearance while John was in prison and could not have been bap-soused by him, Matt. xi, 2, 3. He taught quite a different religion to John. The fifth chapter of Matthew tells us that he taught non resistance! That if this one garment was demanded to give it without resistance! To return good for evil! 39 "I say resist not evil!" If smote on one cheek turn the other! Give to the borrower and beggar! And to love your vilest enemy! Quite a self-contradiction as I show on page 63 and 64, where Matt. x, 34, tell us he come not to send peace, no, but fire, hate and a sword! This is all bully crawfish bate for these fishers of men! It was to prepare a way for an eden for beggars and tramps! And to this day all religions are run for the victuals and drink, money and power that is in them!

A TRUE STORY OF JESUS the Christians Christ, and God! Now, Jesus and John was claimed, as has always been claimed, for great men, to be miraculously brought into this world, to do a certain kind of work. Yet, they were deprived of that privilege, by a contending power that has not only to this day, has it proved itself superior, and held its own, against the combined power of these royal god chosen men, gods and devils; but it is more on a natural balance, thus making it in harmony to the entire creation. While they are in a perpetual war, contention, strife, bloodshed, suffering, self-contradiction, and an eternal hell of fire and brimstone awaites them throughout eternity!

Now, my god, these facts alone upsets all of this miraculous or divine claims, that has been claimed by every government under the sun, but ours— the United States of America.

Then, their claims were not new, nor out of the ordinary course of human events, no, their claims were such as had always been claimed by all men who sought to be a king, a ruler, or a great man. They claimed to be better, wiser and more god favord than others. In fact, as perfect as God! and a royal heir to heaven! the selected elect! that declares all others reprobates, doomed and damed!

☞ This is the foundation of all religions, or standards of justice except that of these United States. And its religion, or standard of justice is, EQUALITY before the Law and Privileges!

There is a pedigree, and history shows it, runing back for many generations, among the family of Jesuses. They held to this claim—a divine heir to rule, and they claimed to have the genuine law to rule; just as we see in all governments to-day!

This government is in just precisely this lamentable fix to-day! There are many parties, cliques, churches, and secret oath bound orders that are seaking to run and rule this nation on just such unjust claims, as a god favord few!

There were three Jesuses, and the one that the Christians claim as their man-god, savior, or christ himself never drempt, or thought of such absurdities, as being worshiped as God! No, but only a mediator for his own conquered, and lost people!

Matthew, his first witness, tells us at x, 5, 6, 7, that he said to his disciples, "Go not to the Gentiles, and into the cities of the Samaritans enter not. But go to the lost sheep of Israel." Yes, this same witness tells us at the xv, 26, that all others are mear dogs! Then his fourth witness, St. John, tells us at i, 11, that "He came unto his own, and his own recieved him not." No, but they killed him, for high treason, for violating the laws of the god of their fathers, and the laws of their countrey!

The claim—"Go ye into ALL the WORLD and preach the gospel to every CREATURE," is not of Jewish origin, no, nor the origin, nor the wish of any other rase of people but the Usurpers of the Roman Empire—the Constantine Catholics!

This Universal or Catholic, believe or be damed, religion, originated at the time the Roman Empire claimed to know, own, and to controle the whole world! While the Jews claimed dimetrically the opposite; a special god-elect of themselves only!

Yet, the facts are, they at that time, knew absolutely nothing about the Russians, the Chinese, the Arabians, the Africans, the Australians, nor the vast, vast American Empires, that was then in existence, and further advanced in the sciences and arts than they. Romes greatness was not equal to the American Governments at their imputed discovery! All of which is a Catholic lie! It was the introduction of the Printing Press from the Amerikas, by Vespucius, a Florentine Liberal, into Ita'y, with maps, in a printed book, that he published on his return from South Amerika, that so quickley made it known one to the other!

Then it was that this imputed discovery of the Amerikas was hatched up by the European and the Roman governments; and their subjugation accomplished by their combined intrigue and treachery! Their meddlesom insolence and arrogance is worse than their fathers, the accurst Jews, and like them they have become a shame, a disgrace, and a reproach to the whole known world!

This Jesus never drempt of being worshiped no more than Moses. He was trying to free his enslaved people from Rome, just as Moses had done from Egypt. Constantine the last of the Cezars done this! And the first Catholic church had no Pope, a very presumpteous, blasphemous imposter! A fellow that claims to be god! as much so, as was claimed for this man Jesus! The apostles never heard of a pope, nor his creator a lot of bishops!

Constantine started the original catholic church in Africa, under the controle of a lot of bishops, it was his bishops of Rome that broke off from this original, [so called], catholic, or Christ's Church! and originated a pope, an absolute monarch, or a man-god, to take the place of this man-god Jesus!

☞ All of this and yet no Holy Bible! ☜

The idea of a Bible, a Pope, and Bishops was not hatched up at Rome until after the Conquest, and Subjugation of Mexiko, Centrael, and South Amerika! Not till they had become masters of their immense wealth and learning! And as the Original Scriptures were written in Hieroglyphics of the ancient Aztecs! this made their translation by their conquors an utter impossibillity!

THEN, what is the Holy Bible of the Jews and the Christians? Authentic history tells us that it is only a collection of old fables and traditionary legends, or lies, robbed from the Alexandrian Library, in Egypt, by this Constantine, King of the Roman Empire—and bound in one book, and called the Book of books, from tha FACT, that the Amerikans, Arabians, Africans, Brittons, Chinese, Egyptians, and all nations had their Holy Bibles, long, long before Moses, Jesus, Constantine, or this King James was thought of!

This Roman King sent forth his presumed Divine Decree declaring all other Bibles, or Sacred books profane! impious! lies! and must be destroyed! He, with the mighty Roman army, fire, torture, and the sword! started out to DESTROY all other Bibles, and books, histories, fables, traditions, learning and records, and to ENFORCE his upon the, presumed, whole world! He destroyed all institutions of learning! he burned the Alexandrian Library, and all institutions of learning in all parts of the then known world! Their object was to destroy all former records and to place themselves as the god given, and god chosen boss of the whole world! They put to death all who opposed or even doubted his authority being divine! this was done wherever they could throughout the then known world! thus causing the DARK and IGNORENT age of the world!

This Religionists done in every land under the sun, till stoped by our Liberal, or Infidel Government—the United States of North America; the only government under the sun that wont let religionists murder themselves and you and me!

Thank God this Infamous fool and his mighty army of Christians were ANIHILATED in a war with the Arabians, who claimed the right to protect themselves, their homes, and their Sacred writings, their arts and sciences, and all institutions of learning which the Christians were fast destroying!

Their excuse for destroying all other Bibles, and books was that God so decreed! But down went this mighty, self stiled, god sent Greek and Roman Empire and its falce god and absurd bible! Their men were all slaughterd; Constantine himself died not "On the field of battle," as Christians louly sing, no, but he ignomineosly fled from their field of battle, inside his fortified god set up throne where he and his mighty army of Christians, perhaps a million, was slaughtered! Their women and children were turned into slaves and the prisoners were fed to the dogs, hogs, tigers, and lions! See full page cuts of this and the Greek Slave! the Jew Slave! the Christian's Slave! and the Slaves of parties, cliques, churches and secret orders!

Yes, after their destruction the world enjoyed an age of peace, such as never was known on earth before! And this is what the Christians style the dark ages!

Hundreds of years after an English King, Jim the Simpleton, collected up the fragments of this set of Jew and Roman Idiots, taking part from this that, or the other would be, or self styled words of God, just such as suited him and rejecting the rest! So there is not one word of this Jew, Roman, English King's Bible that is original or genuine! muchless the work of an Almighty God!

Thus while England was re-forgeing the Slavery Fetters and horrid chains of Religion, the Yankee Americans were re-building the Signal Fires of Liberty, Freedom and Independence!

This King Jim's Jew Bible and Jew Jesus was Forced upon us by all the horrible torture known to fire and the sword! Even in this free and enlightened nation until Washington, the great Arch Devil, as the church called him, and his Infidel Devils, whiped this self-styled King of God's and drove them and their church back to England, and in their stead set up a government of the People and not of the king's, god's and devil's; no, but the first and only just and free government under the sun, for all prior governments claimed to be for the gods, from the gods, and by the gods! And they enforced all manner of religion, slavery, robbery, murder, all in the name of God!

We have hundreds of organized religions, and each claim to be from God, with his only way to heaven! Hundreds of other religions claiming the same only way, have given way for these and are no more! Soon these will do the same! Then, where is this only way? This one fact proves it a craziness! Only think, hundreds of these crazy religions, and contradicting each other, themselves, every thing, and every body. Each having picked out of this bible just some isolated part as suits them for a creed, which is just so many sign boards tacked on one post— the cross— each one pointing out an entirely different way to heaven, and declaring that all of those others pointed to hell!

What is religion to one is blasphemy to the others; that our government and all others, and all other churches are not of God, no, but of the devil; and must be destroyed! That it is God's purpose that they, the selected elect, should make war on all others, and on us, until they annihilate us! This makes religionists bitter, bitter enemies to our countrey, and to us as free individuals!

THE above cut represents the god of this world, Mr. Devil, and his Kings, writing the Jew-Christian's King's Bible, and dividing the then known, or presumed all of the world— Europe, Asia and Africa, between the triune three!

And it tells us at the 22 verse of the iii chapter of Gen. that it was he, Mr. Devil, the god of this world that learned us good and evil, and not our Maker! Yes, John, our fourth witness, tells us he, Mr. Devil, is the king, prince, or ruler of the world, see, xii, 31. xiv, 30. Yes, the xiv, 1,2,3 tells us that Jesus was done with this world, and the 30 verse tells us that Mr. Devil superseded him! The xiii, at 33 says "Whither I go, ye cannot come!"

Then their last witness, Paul, at 2 Cor. iv, 4. Eph vi, 12, says that old Nick was the god of this world, and Jesus nowhere denied it.

Is it not strange that their god made the world and all creation in just six days, and then he has been from that time up to now, millions of years, trying to write a bible? This one fact proves that our maker had nothing to do with it, no, but Mr. Devil wrote it with his tail as is shown on page 75.

I was told when a child that a god made me and wrote the bible for me! And that it was a good and a perfect guide for me. That it contained all that my Maker wanted me to know! Then when I grew a man I was offered another edition of this bible that attempted to correct several thousand of errors and self-contradictions of this first bible!

One says Job's wife said curse God and then die! The other says she said bless God and die! One says Samson caught three hundred foxes and tied their tails to a fire, and they run through the Philistians corn and burnt it up. The other leaves out the foxes, and says he threw fire into the dry stubble and it caught on fire and burnt up their corn.

So, on it goes attempting to correct their god's devil's and king's first bible, by adding to, and by taking from as circumstances may suggest! The idea of three hundred, or even two foxes having their tails tied together and to a fire brand, and to run both, or all in the same direction is a lie. Then the Philistians had no corn. Corn was not known to the eastern continent until after that age. It was known only to the western continent, from whom this fable was stolen. It was in this way: The Cowboys, of the pampas, would make bundles of foxtail grass and set them on fire and shoot them into the dry stubble, set it on fire, and in this way burnt up the sacred corn of the oppressive chiefs.

Then, again, the Christians had nothing like a correct calandar till after the subjugation of the Amerikas. And they could not correctly adapt it to their number of feast days, or days for eating, drinking, and acting the fool around some idol! And we will never have a correct computation of time till some free, liberal minded Amerikan will arrange a calandar free from religion!

The days of a week are artificial; and you cannot tell one from the other! Yet, we find these crazy religionists fussing, fighting, and murdering their fellow man for not being partial to some one of these god's, holy, or lord's days—and keep it hôly to their god! And the muddle is—there are more gods to worship than there is days in a week! or in a year! Day and night are natural divisions of time; caused by the earth revolving to the sun, and any fool can tell them apart, and when to work and when to rest! But, if you can tell when Sunday comes, or which day is Suday, you are sharper than Jesus; for he found it then, as it is now, a disputed point, and he left it as he found it!

Now, as the earths revolution, on its own axis, is various, owing to its shape and rotary motion, so, is the length of day and night, various. ☞ In fact, day never ends on the earth! It is one perpetual day and sunshine on this earth! Night is only the shade of a part of the earth, that is between the sun and us! And it varies from twelve hours to six months in length! These facts were not know to the gods and the getters up of bibles!

So of a year of time. When the earth has made its journey round the sun, this is one year of time. This the ancient Amerikans taught, and affirmed; and the Christians denied, and held that the earth was flat, and that the sun rose and set!

Yes, they tell us, their Josh commanded the sun to stand still, and he obeyed! This is a setler! And their Jesus taught his desciples that it was not for man to know the Times or the Seasons, Acts i, 7. or just before his return, we would only be able to know seed time and harvest only by the green leaf.

☞ The original scriptures started with the original tribes of man in South Amerika— the Ackteeks. They were written in Hieroglyphics, or secret characters, known only to the sacred scribes, or printers. Making their interpretation and translation by thieves, pirats, or even by their subjugaters impossible! Then the interpretation, and translation of these Greek, Latin, and Hebrew garbled guessed at interpretations are preposterous!

Then the translation of this King Jim's English bible from the original Greek, Latin, and Hebrew is another preposterous guessed at job, from the facts that those languages have gon through such horrid changes, that if the old original inhabitants were to rise from the dead they could not read them!

They are about as correct as was the old mans understanding of the preachers text. A very pios old lady could not attend church, so she sent her husband, for the express purpose of bringing to her the text. The text was: An Angel came down from heaven and took a live coal from the altar. But, his understanding of it was: An Ingin come down from New Haven and took a live coalt by the tail and jerked it out of the haulter.

Yes, Tom Paine, one of our Revolutionary fathers, called the worlds attention to the imperfection of the bible. And for which the church is daming him to hell to this day! But, O! my God! soon the American Baptist Bible Society claimed to have found 24 thousand mistakes in this King Jim's Bible, that was forced upon us by fire-torture and the sword! And they asked: "Who will plead for a bible having 24 thousand mistakes in it?

This is directley contradicting this King Jim's West Minster Confession of Faith that declares, that this King Jim's bible is Infalible, and so plain " that not only the learned but the unlearned could understand them." Nevertheless, the Baptist did work their racket, made them a bible that says you must be bapsoused beyond a doubt! And yet, in the brightest heavenly light of their two thousand years of correcting, we yet find it a mear jumbled up mass of vicious virus, that maddens and destroys all with in whome it reaches !

And stranger still—it has taken millions, and millions of Christian schollars, and untold billions of dollars, with all the Roman and Brittish Empires, with all their mighty armies of murders, and all of their awful gods and devils, and that terable Inqusition, with its expeditions, conquests, crusades of terror, force and destruction, thousands of years to write, teair up, and to re-write, and to try to force this awful, vicious, obscene, ungodly and unhuman bible of errors and self-contradictions!

And my God! stranger still to behold them from that awful hour when the first born man killed his only brother, and a religious fuss caused it, and on down to this day we see them fighting and contradicting each other as to what it means! And stranger still, is it to me that any human being can be idiot enough as to thus make a beast of himself !

One says this, another says that, and they are diametrically opposit; yet, they all claim to be God's Infalible Agent! That God has given them the right to rule and to abuse you and me, placeing our mind and our mind's salvation in their presumed divine hands, and what an awful sin for you or me to question their actions or authority.

The first Jew and Roman Bibles had no vowels, and the consonants were ramed as close together as possible, not even seperated into words! Here is the firt line of Genesis : nthbgnnngdcridthhvnndthrth. When the vowels are supplied it is guess work; and five kind of vowels to guess at, and the right one never guessed !

Then they could not make any sense out of it until they put in words and explananions, and that is the use of the Italic words in the bible ; they are acknowledged additions ! And this fact is admitting the imperfection of the bible ; and the lack of power of their god to protect it !

So, is it any wonder that there is thousands of errors and hundreds of self-contradictions? Or that one says God has a lamb for a son, and that he himself is a ram, a bull, or a calf, and worship him as such? No wonder we cannot build prisons and insane asylums fast enough!

This King Jim's bible tells us their god made us ignorent, not knowing good and evil! Then because we erred he cursed us, the world, and every living thing! Then because we still erred he destroyed us, but, saved seed, however! Now, what did the blamed fool expect to gain! Did he expect figs to grow on thistles? Did he expect corrupt seed to produce incorrupt people? Precisley so with these so styled infalible bibles, the last one is no more perfect than the first, and the first is not correct, according to their own testamony!

"In no work that has been printed since the invention of that art, has there been so many misprints perpetrated as in this bible of the K I N G S!" So says the American Art Printer, and so says Uncle Sam's Bible! POPE SEXTUS the V. caused an edition of the "Vulgate" to be published in Rome in 1500, to change it to suit his thoughts. Every proof of which he had carefully corrected himself. And at the end of the volume he affixed a bull by which he excommunicated anyone who should attempt to make an alteration in the text. This book caused a good deal of amazement—for the bible was found to be full of mistakes! King Jim's bible has many remarkable misprints and changes! In the edition of 1634, at the xii Psalm it says: "The fool has said in his heart there is a god." now they have it to say no god. Even the edition of Field, who was a printer to the University of Cambridge in the seventeenth century, is full of misprints. It is said he received a present of one thousand and five hundred pounds from the independents to print "y" for "w" in the sixth vers of Acts, in order to make it the duty of the people to choose their pastors. In the same bible in 1 Cor. vi, 9, we find: "Know ye not that the unrighteous shall inherit the kingdom of God?" In 1617, it was called the "Vinegar Bible," for it said: "parable of the vinegar." at Lu. xx. The omission of the negative word [not] in the commandments frequently occur. And one of the most remarkable changes is that of a brave German woman. Made to get rid of the slavery imposed on woman at iii, 16, of Gen. She inserted [not], making it say: he slall not rule over thee!

It is well known that the book of Job is of Arab origin, and much older than the Pentateuch, or the first Jew bible. There were numerous ancient sacred books long before Moses or the Jews was born. The ancient Phenician city Derbia was called the book city, and was subjugated by the Jews, and here from Derbir, and not from Moses, nor God, was originated the first Jew bible!

From this Phoenician country the eastern continent got their alphabet, and they, the Phenicians got theirs from the Amerikas— from the Anteeks.

And although their books were numerous their subjugaters appropiated them. So it was with the ancient Amerikas; their conquors appropriated their wealth and learning. So, it is an undeniable fact, well known to all races of men, that these Christians are a presumpteous, thieveing, murdering, lying, set! They have nothing but what they got by murdering their fellow man for, and only think, they lay it all on God! When the facts are they have nothing from God! its all evil, unnatural, and a delusion from the Devil!

Among the anecient books to be rememberd are the two seperate books used by Moses, or the Jews in compiling their book Genesis. The first chapter of their Genesis tells us that God made man, and that he blest them, and said, be fruitful, multiply, replenish the earth and subdue the earth; and that this was on the sixth day. ☞ The length of which was twenty-four hours or twelve months, according to the place occupied on the earth. For it took the evening and the morning to make their day.

The xvii chapter of Jesus' Genesis tells us that, "The Lord created man of the earth, and then he turned him into the world, with a power over all things therein." And the xviii chapter tells us that "He that liveth forever created all things in general." Then the ii chapter of this Jew Moses Genesis starts out by telling us that God ended his labor on the seventh day. Then it tells us that the Lord God, not God, nor the Lord, no but the Lord God made Adam and Eve, and put them in a garden, not the world, to keep it. And they were so ignorant they did not know good and evil. Their bible in comparing their ignorance says: the Serpent was the most subtle, or wise.

So, dont you see, cant you see, that they are only at best, garbled extracts from other authors? Making quite different men, and things, at different times and places, and puting of them in quiet different places and giving them very, very different commands? Some of the books of this King Jim's bible do not even mention the name of a god, much less put any claim to inspiration!

I am proud to inform the reader that this book Esther, that does not even mention the name of a god, a lord, nor a lord-god! Yet, it gives us a history of one of the grandest, and most extensive governments yet recorded in history! The great Roman Empire was a mear fool, or a mear dwarf compared to these 127 provinces mentioned in this godless, Persian book, Esther! Esther was a Jew slave, decending from the captives carried to Babylon, by Nebuchadnezzar.

Jewish bibles show throughout their various books that they got what they know from their stay in Egypt, Babylon, Greece and Rome, and not from God!

Even Solomon, their wisest man, was a Mormon and a Sadducee, he rejected the Oral Law, and denied the resurection of the dead. And his Song of Songs mentions not a god, a lord, nor a a lord-god! Yet, we are told that it is the church-e's love for Christ! Great Cesar! Then, their god or Christ, must have been wine, woman and song!

The Jews bibles from their Roman captivity to the execution of Jesus and his disciples show an important feature of ungodlines and human depravity! The Samaritian Jews, were half-breeds, from intermixing with the other tribes of Jews, or other tribes of man. From these bastards or half-breeds this man-god Jesus originated. The full blooded Jews who were in power, and who was so recognized by their Roman Masters, and who was allowed to rebuild Jerusalem, hated and despised these mongrels. They refused all intercource with them! And while the full-bloods were rebuilding the temple the half-breeds stoped them and tried to prevent its rebuilding. So, these mongrels erected a temple of their own on Mount Gerizium and re-estabelished the Mosaic Order of worship. Their bible was the Pentateuch, or the five first books of Moses. And those Jews that had fallen in Africa had forgotten their language, they spoke Greek, so they collected up the traditions of their fathers and made the Septugent bible. So, from the very beginning of this Jew bible making we have many factions, and strange to say, that they all differed as much as midnight from day! Yet, they all claim to be God's only means, his only way to heaven; and you have no choice, its believe or be damed!

The Catholic's letter, from this defunct Jesus, to Bridget, and the book Mormon, is about the last faddle in bible amendments!

And it is a strangling fact, to the young Christian student, when he sees that the knowledge, and power of their self-syled heathens have never been rivaled, much less equaled! For he finds that the Hanging Gardens of Babylon, the Pyramida of Egypt, the Chinese Wall, the Cut Stone Paved Way, across the South Americrn Continent, and their Hieroglyphical Records have not yet been equaled by any of these so called, all wise, all good and all powerful nations, and agents of the Creator!

Now, the reader can see, from this, that the Legends and Traditions that reached Afrika from South Amerika, was by this time, as greatly contorted as was the old mans understanding of the parsons text, given on page 78! Then, again, Moses might have been just as bad mistaken, about what his lord, lord-god, or god said to him as was this old man! Again, no two men can understand just alike, neither can they tell it precisley alike! So, by the time this Oral Law passed from Sinai through Moses, then through Josh, the Elders, the Prophets the Scribes, and the Printers, who with all of his, and their mistakes, you may have some idea as to its correctness, and why it is full of self-contradictions, an mistakes!

Just a little while before this man-god Jesus put. in his appearance, the full-bloods, at Jerusalem, established a school, and got up that awful Commentary on the Revelations of God, and called it the Talmud, or to learn. It claimed to contain the Oral Law that Moses claimed to have got from God, by the word of mouth; and which he told to Joshua, and he, Josh, told it to the Elders, and they told it to the Prophets, and they to the Great Synagogue! Now, if this is not hearsay evidence of a very dangerous character, then what is it?

Between the writings of the last Old Testament book and the first New Testament book there was a long, long period, hundreds of years of war, anihilation, and a replenishing! Nation after nation passed away, before this King Jim's bible was thought of. This man-god Jesus is among the uncertain myths, from the facts that he never owned, nor never was in power over anything! No record mentions him!

King Constantine, last of the Cesars of the Roman Empire, and all great men, have ben recorded in the history of their day, but this Jew man-god Jesus was not even mentioned! This Constantine called a council, at Carthage, in Africa, and caused the compiling of the Catholic bible! He declared the making of bibles closed, and declared his to be the supreme law of the world! But, ah, alas! the Mohammedans conquored them, destroyed their bible; and then it was that this Simpleton, King Jim, of England, hatched up this awful bible of Errors and self-contradictions!

Now, if God is a just God, and I believe he is, then religionists and their bibles are not of him! No, no! O, no, but they are a crazy Cain and Babel whim, in and of themselves, too infamous to be contributed even to the devil, for they in every age of the world, when tolerated or in power, have led to this same Cain and Babel confusion, chaos and destruction! God is a vast, vast almighty creative power of energy and intelligence! He created us free and equal; and he so framed his immutable, and unchangable laws as to always preserve us free and equal! This religionists and their bibles deny! This you cannot be and live in peace, in any other country under the sun but this Liberal, Infidel United States of America, that religionists hate and preach so bitter against!

Their prayers, curses, rantings, mob-laws, and war in defense of their King Jim's bible's presumed divine slavery laws, for years, drenched this country in human gore! Brother murdering brother, father and mother murdering their children, or each other, and in return murderd by their children—destroying more of themselves than there was of the so-called soulless Negro! Tearing down the Stars and Stripes, and placeing in their stead slavery, under the lash and the cross, as we now have in Central and South America, that was once as free as we! This was the Christian life and aspirations, that passed before my youthful eyes for twenty years, till Lincolin, that old Liberl, Abolitionist, interfeard and repealed their god's laws and set the Negro free!

But, this Christian slavery warfare, secretly continues, and as fast as the old fools die out the young fools grow up! Ah, you infamous hypocrits who freed you from the galling yoke of a King and the lash of a Christian master? Who gave you this glorious freedom, and protection that mortal man never before enjoyed? Who gave you the freedom to worship, or not to worship, a god according to your choice? Did religionists? Did your King's, or their bibles! No! no! never! They only give us slavery, fire and torture! They yet demand of you to believe or to eternaly be damed! and a submission to their standard of justice!

Yes, one of their noted preachers, Sam Jones, in the Chattanooga, Sunday Times, of Oct., 7, 1894, page 16, says: "No matter how close the thing gets to the gates of hell, once a republican always a republican. But, he forgot to tell us that this is his exact religion— once a Christian, always a Christian! He says the immortal Ben Hill said that reconstruction had made the Negro spring in one bound from the corn fields to the legislative halls to make laws for "decent people." And that no man ought to be allowed to vote unless he can read and write the English language correctly and intelligently!" This is Sam representing truthfully the Christian religion, or justice! And he knows it would wrong the Negro, and deprive over half of our citizens of their vote!

It was those old Infidel or Liberal fathers that could neither read nor write, much less, do so correctly, that seen that good and right subsisted not in this so-called divine god-favord few! No, O! no, but in poor you, in poor me, in us all! Then, remember, you cannot be a good honest, moral, upright, free American and belong to any clique, party, church, or oath bound secret order! For their divine claims make their gods unjust and self-contradictory, and you a truckling slave.

This big me and little you, anihilating, fool kind of religion, caused Moses, the bastard, the murder, the bigamist, the robber, and his gang of murders, to murder and to rob millions of innocent human beings, and in turn to be robbed and murdered; and all done by, or in the name of God! This is old Jew bible religion! This same spirit of rule or ruin, believe or be damed, destructive kind of religion caused their half-blood, bastard of a mongrel of a man-god, their Jew Jesus, to be a treacerous traitor! To be a disobedient child, violating the laws of parents, and grew up a disobedient man, violating the laws of the land, styling himself the only son of God—the King of the Jews! And by violating their god's laws, and religion, and the laws of the land, he knowingly, and boastingly made himself a criminal, and by threatening death and destruction—it caused his death, which he as well deserved, as much so as Haman, John Brown and Guiteau! This was New Testament religion!

This same spirit of murder caused all of the apostles, and Christians of that day, to be murders, and in return, under their god's laws and religion they were murdered! This same spirit of murder, plunder, war, slavery, and robbery, caused the fall and destruction of the Amerikas, India, Egypt, Greece, Rome, Babylon, and all countrys of which we have any record. There now exists three opinions as to the nature of the powers of this New Testament religion. 1st. The Erastin, that make the Church a mear subject of the state, with no more powers nor privileges than a citizen. 2nd. The Romish, that make the state a mear subject of the church. And 3rd. The Evangelical, that declare that this New Testament is the law of all laws! and that they will not obey any other! Now, of course, between these three evils, I choose the least, and declare in favor of the Erastian, or that the church should be ruled by the state as any individual!

Only think, while God has bound nature fast in fate he has left free the human will! The earth revolvs around the sun, making the seasons come and go. The earth turns to and from the sun, causing day and night, as in days of your. While religion is that same old, anihilating, hydrophobia virus, that confuses, maddens and destroys all, both great and small! As much so to-day as at that Jew beginning day of that Cain and Babel confusion, chaos, and destruction.

"What means all this military craze that has taken hold of the churches? Asks the American Sentinel, of Jan. the 24, 1895. "Church Cadets, Boys' Brigades, and Epworth Guards, with their weekly drill have superseded the prayer meeting, and it means that the churches have discontiued the "Sword of the Spirit, which is the Word of God," and have appealed to the force of arms to enforce the doctrins of religion by State laws! The next step will be to proclaim a religious crusade and march against the heretics. And all they that take the sword shall perish with the sword."

Yes, this was the fate of a simelar religious crusade, known in history as the "Children's Crusade." "In the district of Vendome, France, in 1200, appeared a shepherd boy named Stephen, showing a letter which he said was from this defunct, man-god, Jew Jesus, directing him to go forth and conquor the Infidels of Palestine. He declared none but innocent children could succeed, 'for of such is the kingdom of heaven.'

Only think—"Seven thousand children were led by him to the shores of the Adriatic, where they were captured and made slaves of! Then came more than thirty thousand boys and girls, who took ships at Marseilles, and was soon wrecked on the coast of Africa, and were either drowned or enslaved!" So, like these fools, like the Mormons, the Simites, and the Coxites, will be these poor fools fate!

The knowledge of the awful follies and the destructive fate, of all governments, from the first to the last, is the reason why our revolutionary fathers rebelled against such infamy and set up this the first just, free, and only liberal government under thes sun!

The knowledge of these facts is my excuse for

presenting these absurdities and self-contradictions to this so-called word of G o d.

Now, my never dying fellow man if you will obey your parents and your countrys laws, you will be a good man, with us all, and with God, and will never need the help of any clique, church, party, or secret oath bound order! For our general government, all make ample provisions for the need of us all, both great or small. And this is the whole need and duty of man to man, and to his creator.

Then I beseech you to obey the golden rule: "Do to others as you would they should do to you." "Take natures path and mad opinions leave, all states can reach it all heads can concieve," rationally judge and execute. Then, do no harm, no, but all the good you can, that is, so live, that you may not die like a fool, no, but like a sane, free man pass on to a more exalted condition in eternity.

Die, no, not die, nor even retrograde, but quietly pass on to a more favorable eternity. That is, you the actual mental man, matured, withdraws from the material or mortal man. He, the immortal man casts the body aside, he deserts it, and he steps out of this material or physical world into the mental, or world of rational, reasoning intelligence. We see our bodies decompose, and go back to mother earth. We see by comparative reasoning, and by our inherent desire, within us, for a higher, and a more nobler continued personal existence, such a chance! It is this that gives us our faith and a hope to live forever and never die!

By this simple act, called dying, no change is effected in the mental man, in form, organization, or character! He is no better and he is no worse, he knows no more and he knows no less, he has not lost nor gained a single faculty or feature. He has only gained more favorable conditions for his hapiness, and advancement in the future.

To make this plain, I will say that this universe is God, made up of Positive and Negative God matter. And this is all there is of it! There is no such a thing as an independent personal god, devil, ghost, or spirits in it, on it, or anywhere about it! And here is our heaven or our hell! If we are well balanced this is heaven; and if they are not then this is hell!

Yes, mind or energy or intelligence, when rational, or balanced, is pure refined God-matter, or active matter, while the more solid, or inactive is termed physical, on negative matter, or matter at rest, or the physical body of God! Now, reader, which are you going to be? Are you going to improve, purify, and strengthen your body so as to aid your mind in manifesting its greatest, and grandest qualities? Or, are you going to neglect the God given duties intrusted to you?

Mind or intelligible personal matter is one and the same at all stages of life. It is a parcle of God, and manifests itself an infant, a child, a man, or an idiot according to the physical body, or prison that it is imprisoned in. And, precisley so is it with all animals and life. The reason the dog does not show as much inteligence as man is because the environs of his peculiar constructed mortal body will not let him do so.

Then, again, personal identity, or that sameness of being, of which consciousness is our evidence, is marked throughout the entire universe with a rational, reasoning, forewarning intelligence, that even an idiot cannot mistake!

The hurricau, the cyclone, and the gentle zephyr, all have their peculiar phenomenal characteristicts; and believed from time immemorial to have an intelligent, special god to specialy preside over and for them. So has the winter's crystals, as seen in the rain, the frost, the snow and the hail. Personal design, or that sameness of being, or construction, design and intelligence shape and control every thing, with as much incomprehensive design as that of the human organism.

Then, what about accountability? And, what about future rewards and punishments? All wrong as lying, stealing, murdering, etc., is a craziness, a diseased or unbalanced condition that would not be done if the person were healthy or properly balanced, watched, taught, raised, or cared for. Then, they are not accountable but little, if any, for what is visited upon you from your ancestors for generations back. Therefore, we do not imprison and execute our fellow man to punish them! no, O, no! but to reform them, and to protect ourselves. And as fare as wanting to punish them hereafter—after death—there is no such a desire in eternity. For death is not a punishment, as the Christites and their King Jim's bible teaches! No, but death, when natural, is a reward, a promotion!

The child that was prevented from crawling into the fire, fretted over it terribly, but, in its grown up day it forgot it and cared not for its supposed injuries. So of us in eternity.

WHATEVER IS—IS BEST.

I know as my life grows older,
   And mine eyes have clearer sight,
That under each rank wrong somewhere
   There lies the root of right.
That each sorrow has its purpose,
   By the sorrowing oft unguessed,
But as sure as the sun brings morning
   Whatever is—is best.

I know that each sinful action,
   As sure as night brings shade,
Is somewhere, sometime punished,
   Though the hour be long delayed.
I know that the soul is aided
   Sometimes by the heart's unrest,
And to grow means often to suffer,
   But whatever is—is best.

I know there is no error
   In the great supernal plan,
And all things work together
   For the final good of man.

I know when my mind speeds onward
  In its grand eternal quest,
I shall cry as I look earthward,
  Whatever is— is best.

Ella Wilcox.

IS LIFE WORTH LIVING?

Is life worth living? Yes, so long
  As there is wrong to right,
Wail of the weak against the strong,
  Or tyrany to fight.
Long as there lingers gloom to chase,
  Or streaming tear to dry,
One kindred woe, one sorrowing face
  That smiles as we draw nigh.
Long as a tale of anguish swells
  The heart, and eyes grow wet,
And at the sound of freedom's bells
  We pardon with regret.
So long as faith and freedom reigns,
  And loyal hope survives,
And gracious charity remains
  To gladden holy lives.
While there is one untrodden tract
  For intellect or will,
And man is free to think and to act,
  Life is worh living still.

        English Magazine.

LIFE LET US CHEERISH.

Life let us cheerish,
While the taper glows,
And the fresh floweret,
Pluck it er it close.

Away with every toil and care,
Why choose the wrangling thorn to ware?
With heedless hearts life's conflicts meet,
Till death sounds her last retreat.

      Old Song.

SHED NOT A TEAR.

Shed not a tear o'er your friends early bier,
  When they are gone, when they are gone.
Come at the close of a bright summers day,
  When I am gone, when I am gone.
Come and rejoice that 'ive thus passed away,
  When I am gone, when I am gone.
Sing you a song when my grave you shall see,
  When I am gone, when I am gone.
Plant you a tree that may wave over me,
  When I am gone, when I am gone.

   Old Song.

I THINK I THUNK A LIE.

I ust to think when I was young,
  And my heart was free from guile,
That there was grief in every tear
  And joy in every smile.
That friendship was not all a cheat
  And love could never die,
But thinking now of what I thunk,
  I think I thunk a lie.

I ust to think about myself,
  And think that I would be
A govenor or a president,
  Or a general like Lee.
But I have waited long in vain,
  Whilst years rolled slowly by,
And thinking now on what I thunk,
  I think I thunk a lie.

I ust to think the ladies were
  All sweetness combined;
That they were all God's last and best
  Of perfectness refined.
That they were not half pads and paint,
  But angels from on high,
But thinking now of what I thunk,
  I think I thunk a lie.

The peeachers, too, I ust to think,
  Were not like other men,
And were not tempted of the flesh
  And could not therefore sin.

But since I've traveled round a bit
  I've watched them on the sly,
And thinking now of what I thunk,
  I think I thunk a lie.

The honest tiller of the soil
  When marketing his crop,
Takes pains to put the ripe and best
  Always upon the top.
I ust to think those honest men
  Would never cheat or try;
But thinking now of what I thunk,
  I think I thunk a lie.

The editors, a lordly set,
  Who live on milk and honey,
Tey've nothing else on earth to do
  But write and rake in the money.
Leastwise that way I ust to think,
  But now it makes me cry,
To think about the way I thunk,
  And how I thunk a lie.

What noble men the doctors are,
  I ust to think they came
From heaven or some heavenly land
  And worked for love and fame.
That they could cure all earthly ills
  And never let us die,
But thinking now of what I thunk,
  I think I thunk a lie.

The lawyers, too, I ust to think—
  Oh! God forgive the thought—
That their convictions of the right
  Could not by knaves be bought.
That they would not a client rob
  Or sell him on the sly,
But thinking now of what I thunk,
  I think I thunk a lie.

The dry goods men are honest, too,
  They swear they sell at cost;
I ust to think they told the truth,
  And all their profits lost.
I thaoght a yard was full three feet,
  Dont ask my reason why;
But thinking now of what I thunk,
  I think I thunk a lie.

I ust to think elections were
 The public will to voice,
And not a thimble-rigging game
 To give the cliques a choice.
That patriotism played its part,
 Though stills were never dry,
But thinking now of what I thunk,
 I think I thunk a lie.
Dr. O. T. Dozier.

THE SURVIVAL OF THE FITTER.

IT'S THE way of the world, I am sorry to say; for cats, and for dogs, and for monkeys, as well as for civilized men, on the weaker to prey!

THE HUNTERS.

A cricket fed on an insect
 Too small for eye to see,
A field-mouse captured the cricket
 And hushed his lullaby.

A gray shrike pounced on the field-mouse
 And hung him on a thorn,
And a hawk came down on the cruel shrike
 From over the waving corn.

And a fox sprang on the red-tailed hawk
 From under a fallen tree,
For birds and beasts, by flood and field,
 Of every degree
Prey one upon the other;
 'Twas thus ordained to be,
My rifle laid old Renard low,
 And death— dead ended me.
Ernest McGaffey.

IT'S MONEY AFTER ALL.

There are men in all professions,
 We meet every day,
Wheather pursuing pleasure
 Or business as they may.
Their creed they yelp in public,
 Which they practice not at all,
They all are after money,
 So it's money after all.

The lawyer hangs his shingle out,
   To coax the people in,
And then he tells them, great and small,
   Their cases he will win.
He says he labors for the good
   Of people one and all,
But he charges forty prices,
   So it's money after all.

The doctor in his office sits,
   Among his drugs and pills,
Dealing out his doses,
   To cure the peoples ills.
He says he likes to give relief,
   To the suffering ones that call,
But he always asks for money,
   So it's money after all.

The preacher stands before us
   And tells us we all sin,
He says if we only love the Lord,
   No matter how much you sin.
And from where the biggest salary is
   He receives the winning call—
You can name it what you're a mind to,
   But it's money after all.

The politicians rave about
   Reform from morn till night,
And says if he's elected
   He'll legislate all right.
But when he gets to Congress
   He's the grandest rogue of all—
He gobbles up the money,
   So it's money after all.

Thus in one common group they stand,
   As by my song you see,
No matter what they profess,
   Or what their station be—
The merchant, lawyer, doctor,
   Preacher, Congressman and all,
They all are after money,
   So it's money after all.

A HYPOCRITE.

When fortune smiles
   And looks seren,
'Tis pray sir, how do you do?

Your family are well I hope,
Can I not serve them or you?

But turn the scales,
Let fortune frown,
Ills and woes be tied to you—
I'm sorry for your loss, but,
Times are hard, good-by to you!

STORY OF A POLITICIAN.

Weight ten pounds; baby boy; Mamma's darling; Papa's little man; Jimmy; James; Young Mr. Jones; James Jones; Mr. James Jones; Clerk of election Jones; Committeeman Jones; The Hon. James M. Jones; Alderman Jones; Ex-Alderman Jones; James Martin Vanburan Jones; Old Jones; Old Jim Jones; Tenth Ward Jones; Jim the bum; Whiskey Jim; Old Soak; Cell 9; Coroner's Office; Unidentified; Pauper's Field!

KINDER MIXED.

Colonel's runnin' for congress,
  Major's runnin' for mayor;
Captain's runnin' for sheriff,
  An' the private's plowin' a steer!

Sergent's off for the senate—
  Corporal's beatin' him there;
Chaplain's runnin' for bishop,
  An, the private's plowin' a steer!

Colonel, cussin' the captain,
  'Cause the vote is kinder small,
Sergent's after the corporal,
  An, the chaplain's cussin' 'em all!

O, ruther than swar for congress,
  An' ruther than cuss for mayor,
I'll pastur' out with the privates,
  An' keep on plowin a steer!

      F. L. S.

THE FOX AND THE GRAPES.

A fox in passing by,
  Saw some grapes hung up high,
There wating in quiet way;
  If you can eat us sir,
You may; troll, loll, lay.

Equal rights are here defended,
  Riches fill our busy hands,
Then, let welcome be extended,
  To the poor of other lands.
Let them come and join our chorus,
  And praise this favored spot of earth,
Praise the skies now smiling o'er us,
  Praise the land that gave us birth.

Old School Song.

UNCLE SAM'S FARM.

Of all the mighty nations, in the East or in the West, Oh! this glorious Yankee nation is the greatest and the best; We have room for all creation, and our banner is unfurled, Here is a general invitation to the people of the world— Chorus:

Come along, come along— make no delay,
Come from every nation, come from every way;
Our land is broad enough— don't be alarmed,
For Uncle Sam is rich enough to give us all a farm.

St. Lawrence makes our northen line, as fast as her waters flow, And the Rio Grande our southern bound, 'way down to Mexico; From the great Atlantic ocean, where the sun begins to dawn, Leaps across the Rockey Mountains, away to Oregon.

The South may raise the cotton, and the West the pork and corn, While New England sound the spinnels, the anvils and the looms; For the deep and flowing waterfalls that course along our hills, Are just the thing for washing sheep and driving cotton mills.

Our fathers gave us liberty, but little did they dream, Of the results that flow along this mighty age of steam; For our mountains, lakes, and rivers are all a blaze of fire, And we send our news by lightning on the telegraphic wire.

Yes, we are bound to beat the nations, for our motto's go-ahead, And we will show the foreign royalists our people are well-bred, For the nations must remember that Uncle Sam is not a fool, For the people do the voting, and the children go to school. School Song.

FREEDOM'S SONS NOW.

Freedom's sons wake to glory,
  Hark! hark! what myriads bid you rise?
Your children wise and grandsires hoary,

Behold their tears and hear their cries!
Behold their tears and hear their cries!
Lawless tyrants are mischief breeding!
With hireling host and ruffian band!
Affright and desolate the land!
While liberty lies couched and bleeding!
To arms! to arms! to arms ye braves!
The venging sword quickly unsheathe!
March on! march on! O! liberty or death!

This is the hue and cry now, in the 119 year of our American freedom, from shore to shore. Yes, although, we have given them civil, religious and political freedom, never before, nor nowhere else enjoyed; yet, we see the people boycotted together, for the avowed and express purpose of lording it over the rest without their consent, interests, or knowledge,

It proves that a mam only believes a thing the way he wants it to be— and when he finds that he is shure caught— then he shrieks with a hypocrits despair!

MANS STANDARD.— It is said that the standard by which one man judges another is as follows; A just man,— only those who belong to his party, clique, church, or oath-bound secret order; all others are considerd rascals, and must not be encouraged, but boycotted in to starvation and abject slavery.

A rascal,— one who owes him money. Ditto,— one who he owes money. A dude, a fop, or a flirt,— one who dresses different or better than he, or her. A miser,— one who saves more than he, or her. A spendthrift,— one who spends more than he, or her. A snob,— one whoes social position is better than his, or hers. An upstart,— one whose social position is worse than his, or hers. A smart man one who thinks as he, or she. A fool, a smart Aleck,— one who believes and lives different from him, or her. A crank,— one who can out argue he or her.

So, if it was not for the self-made grit, or sand

that is in our own gizzards, to contend for our god-given, self-inalienable, or equal rights, we would certainly be stamped under, and by these loud, pretending honest men, religion, or no religion, justice, or no justice! So, I say, help thyself, defend thyself, for the gods only help those who help themselves!

The theory that is now being put in practice by religionists, "That an unconstitutional law is good, and should be obeyed, and enforced until repealed is a base, dastardly lie on its own face! All persons who attempt to enforce such are tresspassers on the first, foundational, organic, self-inalienable, or constitutional laws, and are liable by action at law, and should be presented, indicted and prosecuted, be they president, govenor, or any body!"

NEVER FRET.

Never Fret if it hails or snows—
Never mind how the storm-wind blows;
Just what's best for you, God—he knows;
  Why should you weep and sigh?

Never mind when a world of woes
Beats you down, with a thousand foes;
Just what's best for you, God—he knows;
  Over you bends his sky!

Never fret when the black night throws
Darkness over your life's last rose,
Killing its loveliness! God still knows;
  Why should you pray and weep?

Never fret, there is sweet repose
With the dying day—twilight's close,
For at death's valley; God repose,
  And watches while you sleep.

          Selected.

DEEDS, NOT WORDS.

Why profess a thing you cannot, or do not practice? "Why call ye me Lord, Lord, and do not the things which I say?" says the Christites bible, and yet, all that was necessary for man had been said, revealed, and done to man at the beginning, and this acknowledged inability, or hypocracy, by their god, proves him and them, either a fool or a knave. No man, god, nor devil has ever been able to improve on the golden rule that our maker implanted in man at the beginning. "Do to others as you would have others do unto you;" was given to man at the beginning. God inscribed it upon every heart, and they had engraved it upon their hearth-stones, and temples, at the beginning, long before their was any pretending man-gods. It is the whole need, duty, and salvation of man, god or no god!

Not forever on thy knees,
  Would your maker have thee found,
There are burdens thou canst ease,
There are griefs your maker sees;
  Look around.

Work is prayer: if done for good,
  Such a prayer delightest God;
See beside yon upturned sod
One bowed 'neath affliction's rod;
  Dry their tears.

Not long prayers, but earnest zeal;
  That is what is wanted more,
Put thy shoulder to the wheel;
Bread unto the famished deal
  From thy store.

No high-sounding words of praise
Does God want, 'neath some grand dome;
But that thou the fallen raise;
Bring the poor from life's highways
  To thy home.

Worship God by doing good;
Works, not words; kind acts, not creeds;
He who loves God as be should,
Makes his heart's love understood
  By kind deeds.

Deeds are powerful; mear words weak
  Batt'ring at high heaven's door:
Let thy love by actions speak;
Wipe the tear from sorrow's cheek;
  Clothe the poor.

Be it thine life's cares to soothe her,
  And to brighten eyes now dim:
Kind deeds done to one another,

God accepts as done unto him:
Prove all things.
Selected.

A MATHEMATICAL CERTAINTY.— Man is only a (0) naught when wrong, alone, dead, lost, or without God. But, add to man one atom of energy, or one digit of God, and then you increase man to an energy of (10) ten. And it is expected of man that he keep on adding digit after digit of God to this same naught until he reaches his earthly limiitation of 90 years. Then—

TRY, TRY, KEEP TRYING.

'Tis a lesson you should heed,
 If at first you dont succeed,
With courage persevear, and
 Try, try, again.
All that other folks can do,
 Why with patients should not you?
Only keep this rule in view,
 Try, try, again.
  Old Song.

Here is a childs lullaby, I give it in answer to all religionists.

Tinkum, tinkum Mr. Blinkum,
 I am a merry Hyloist,
Pray thee, what is the matter?
 That you all make such a clatter?
Cant you leave us natural folks?
 To sing our songs and crack our jokes?

No, no, says Mr. Jew, your foreskin must go! and your stiff neck must limber like dough! No, no, says Mr. Christian, you are born totally depraved! as mean as hell! and your spirit must be broken! your mind subjugated, enslaved and humiliated!

But we say:—fie! fie! to all such religion! it is a degenerating shame, a horrid craziness!

Give it play and never scare it,
 Curb it only to direct, but
Never, never, brake its spirit,
 Let it glide through this life correct.

THIS WORLD'S GOOD ENOUGH.

When I hear a feller growlin',
  In a sing-song whiny voice,
That this world is dark and scowlin',
  An 'if he could 'ave his choice;
How he'd fly away to glory
  In a robe o' spotless white—
Then I think his upper story
  Is a little bit too light;
For a notion that'll make a
  Man as big a fool as that,
You can bet it 'ill never take a
  Lodgin' under my ol' hat.

Oh! there's people alluz whinin'—
  With a long dejected face—
An' complainin, an' repinin,
  That this world's a dreary place;
If you showed 'em rosy bowers
  Where the birds sing in the shade,
W'y they'll sigh an' say the flowers
  After while 'ave got to fade,
'Till they shut out all the gladness
  From this path of life below,
An' they leave a trail o' sadness
  'Long the highway as they go.

I remember one ol' mortal
  Who'd contended sixty years,
That grim death is but the portal,
  From this gloomy vale o,tears,
To the golden-paved hereafter
  'An the idle, sweet by an' by;
Yet w'en angels come to waft'er
  To ,er home up in the sky,
W'y it seemed the summons knocked 'er
  Vain philosophy, sky high;
An' she told the family doctor,
  She'd a leetle ruther stay.

Course there ain't no use pretendin'
  That the world ain't some at rough,
But the p'int that I'm defendin'
  Is, it's plenty good enough;
Fer we know that this good earth wus
  Made a dwellin place fer man,
An' our death as well as our birth wua
  Part o' God,s eternal plan,
So a critter needn't hurry
  Towards that land o' heav'nly bliss,
An he has no caus to worry
  'Bout a life as good as this.

Yes, the noble American Indian was the first to sing to the Christans — "Home, sweet home," and he was the first to sing to them— " O, give me a cot in the vally I love, A tent in the green wood a home in the grove, I care not how humble for happy it would be, If those I love, in peace, could share it with me."

Yes, the grandest sentiments, the most sublime truths in prose, poetry, painting, or unwritten traditions, and songs, have originated from the aboriginal Amerikans. While the most degrading, sickening, humiliating, and degenerating vices, errows, and self-cotradictions have originated from the Jews and the Christians! And they acknowledge it in their King Jim Bible! Yes,—

> When young they had a fortune,
>   They taught it could not be sunk,
> So they spent it all gamblieg!
>   Of nights when love-feasting drunk!
> So, very early next morning,
>   Their heads and frames racked in pain,
> Their heart was filled with sadness,
>   For they were vagrants again!
> Yes, Mr. Christian, young or old,
>   Is feeble in mind and back,
> His shoes dont cover his toes,
>   And his old hat goes flip flop,
> O'er his old love-feasting nose!

It is a shameful fact, the Christian's Jew, King Jim bible, exalteth strong drink, and feasts, above every thing! Jesus and his followers, like their fathers were gluttons, drunkards, and whoremongers.

Give strong drink unto him that is ready to perish, and wine to those that be of heavy hearts. Let him drink and forget his poverty, and remember his misery no more, says the xxxi chapter of Proverbs! And thou shalt bestow that money for whatsoever thy soul (lusteth after,) says the xiv chapter of Deuteronomy ! And Paul tells us at the first chapter of Romans, and so dose the second chapter of second Peter, that lust is unlawful desire. James and the Psalmist tells us that lust is evil, depraved desires! The xx chapter of Proverbs tells us that Wine is a mocker, strong drink is raging, and whosoever is deceived thereby is not wise! It biteth like a serpent, and stingith like an adder, says the xxiii chapter!

Paul tells us at xi chapter of 1 Corinthans that their meetings were not for the better, no, but for the worse! For, in eating and drinking to excess, they come to the Lord's Supper drunk! And I tell you such sin, lust, and crime is the legitimate fruit of their teachings, and meetings to this day! Jesus tells us at the 19 verse of the vii chapter of St.John that none of them kept the law! and they said he did not obey it, and killed him! And for myself, I say neither kept it, and could not, had they tried!

Then, after starting out with several hundred apostles, and drilling them, god only knows for what, or for how long, they deserted him, betrayed him, sold him, and the last we hear of them is that he come up on eleven of them and upbraded them for their unbelief, and left them forever, so says Mark at the xvi chapter, 14 verse!

Now, if this is not madness from Adam on down that is, blowing cold and hot, or advocating both sides of the question, or worshiping both man and the devil, then I am a blamed fool.

When a child, at our Sunday School, our big burley leader would roar out.—

> When the morning light,
> Drives away the night,
> I'll away to the Sabbath School.

Then, I soon found that he practiced not what he tought me, no, but he reveled and gloted in the lust granted him in his King Jim's bible, as I have just shown. So,—

> When the evening night,
> Drove away the light,
> He would away to the harlot's slums!

And soon his business failed, his health was gone, and like his old Jew dads, Solomon and David, he fermented in drunkness and gluttony, and rotted with venereal disease!

O then resign your rude Christian wine,
　Each father, mother, son, and daughter,
Better than wine is pure water cold,
From God's bright crystal fountain flowing.

I will now give two rude songs that I heard sung when a school child. The last one was about my uncle Jo, and is the truth. This one the Christian King Jim bible is responsible for.—

KING JIM'S GOD is a Haunt, a Demon, a Jack-'o Lantern, a Will 'o the Wisp, a deceptive performer of Legerdemain, a Trixter that pretends to make something out of nothing, and in this way he pretends to have made everything.

He is an ignorent, vicious beast, a compound of three independent sovereign man-gods, with thousands of subordinate slaves. He is divided against himself; known as Jove, Nick and Mike, and are a passionate, contrary, contending, crazy, fighting, man-god. Their original home was Heaven, but a woman got in it and caused a war, and ever since that Jove and Mike hold that place for themselves; while they force Nick to stay on Earth and in Hell! And they, Jove and Mike, have free access to all creation—being the Cock 'o the walk; while Nick and his sudjects harass them, to this good day, so the preachers say. Yes, they say, Jove's and Mike's sons come down and mixed up with Nick's fair daughters, until this earth is filled up with a race af semi-demo-gods, that are totally depraved, that is, they are as mean as hell!

Their last struggle with Nick was between their grown up man child mentioned at Rev. xii, 13. He now appeard by the name of Jesus, and tried Nick a forty days racket in a wilderness; he was the first to squeal, and give Nick the championship, Matt. iv. After this he tells his disciples that hence forth he would not talk much, for the prince of this world, Nick, cometh, John, xiv, 30. And where he was going they could not come; although his father's house had many mansions, yet, there was no place for them, but he would not leave them comfortless: I will prepare a place for you, and come for you; that those standing there would not die before he come, Matt. xvi, 28. John, xiii, 33. xiv, 1, 2, 3. This is cold comfort! Yet, in the face of all this, we see that as fast as the old fools are killed out that the young ones grow up, and are all the time blowing about something that they know nothing about,

FOR KING JIM'S BIBLE SAYS SO.

NICK was poliece in Heaven,
  Was watching day and night sure,
He caught Mike with a woman,
  For King Jim's bible says so.
        Rev. xii, 6, 10.

Nick accused old Mike of sin,
  This accusation brought war sure,
Mike and his clique went for Nick,
  For King Jim's bible says so.
        Rev. xii, 7, 8, 9. Lu. x, 18.

The Devil's heir to Heaven,
  Mike's clique throwed him o'erboard sure,
They fought over a woman,
  For King Jim's bible says so.
        Rev. xii, 6, 7, 8, 9, 10.

The Christian's god's a robber,
  For he robed the Devil sure,
Then give 'im Earth for Heaven,
  For King Jim's bible says so.
        Rev. xii, 10, 12, 13.

Nick then went for Mike's Eden,
  For Mike's Eve and Eden sure,
They were trespassing on him,
  For King Jim's bible says so.
Gen. iii, 5, 6, 7, 22. Zech. iii, 1, 2. 2Cor. iv, 4.

Eve was that same old woman,
  He had caught Mike with before,
So he just told old Adam,
  For King Jim's bible says so.
        Rev. xii, 13. Gen. iv, 1.

It was Nick learned them wisdom,
  They were ignorant before,
Did not know good and evil,
  For King Jim's bible says so.
        Gen. ii, 17, 25.

For this Mike cursed every thing!
He cursed the innocent sure,
He first set bad examples,
For King Jim's bible says so.
Gen. iii, 17, 18, 19.

He drove them with the Devil,
To wander the wild world o'er,
To be chattle slaves always,
For King Jim's bible says so.
Gen. iii, 14 to 23. ix, 25. Lev. xxv, 45, 46. Joel iii.

This Lord Mike has been murdering,
Innocent ones o'er, and o'er,
From that awful day to this,
For King Jim's bible says so.
Ex. xii, 29. xxxii, 27. Num. xxxi, 17, 18. Deut. xx 4.

Nick's made Mike and Jove beli,
All they 'er said or done sure,
Provoked them to drown their race,
For King Jim's bible says so.
Gen. i. 31. vi, 7. 2 Pete. ii, 4, 12.

Mike's and Jove's sons come down,
Married Nick's fair daughters sure.
For this all mankind was drowned,
For King Jim's bible says so.
Gen. iv, 1, 2, 3, 4, 7, 13.

Yes, yes, we are giants yet,
With tellescopic glass sure,
We watch Jove's and Mike's tricks,
But King Jim's book dont say so.
See Uncle Sam's Bib'e.

Made them destroy heir best works,
Their chosen children the Jews,
Nick's beat them at every game,
For King Jim's bible says so,
From Genesis to Revelation!

Made them publish their infamy,
To the world for all time sure,
In a book called the bible,
For King Jim's bible says so.
From Genesis to Revelation!

This book ends on a woman,
It begun on one I'm sure,
It's murder blood and thunder!
For King Jim's bible says so.
From Genesis to Revelation!

They have mistaken our fables,
 And our nicknames too, for sure,
They have taken them for truths,
 For King Jim's bible says so.
          2 Peter, ii, 1, 2, 3; 18, 19,

It is self-contradictory,
 Says his eyes is every where sure,
Then he had to come down to see,
 For King Jim's bible says so.
     Prov. xv, 3. Gen. iii, 8; xi, 5.

Jove saw all he had made,
 Said it was very good sure,
Nick has made him destroy it,
 For King Jim's bible says so.
          Gen. i, 31; vii, 21 !

I have built the a house Lord,
 To abide in with us forever sure,
And the Lord agreed to do it,
 For King Jim's bible says so.
          1 Kings, viii, 13; ix, 3.

Nick made Jove rue, and undo,
 Other gods live there now sure,
While his god-chosen Jew dont!
 For King Jim's bible says so.
 2 Kings, xvii, 20. Deut. xxviii, 30, 64,68!

Now, who'd worship, such a god?
 He destroys the good ones sure!
While the Devil protects you!
 For King Jim's bible says so.
 2 Kings, x, 11, 30. Is. xlv, 7. Am. iii, 6! Ez. xx, 25!

"Our father who art in heaven,"
 Is a god limited there sure,
Like Mose, a sub-god, limited!
 For King Jim's bible does teach so.
          Matt. vi, 9. Ex. vii, 1.

"My god! my god!" he did cry!
 "Hast thou forsaken me?" sure,
Proves his god was limited,
 For King Jim's bible says so.
     Matt. xxvii, 43, 46. Ex. vii, 1.

This world is full of such gods now,
 Infamous as hell! I am sure,
Powerless! and false pretenders too!
 For King Jim's bible does say so!
 Ex. iv, 16; vii, i; xxii, 28. 2 Cor. iv, 4.

Beds of crime and lust,
Gods that's young low down,
Gods of awful examples,
For King Jim's bible says so.
  Ex. xxxii, 27. Num xxxi, 18. Deut. xxviii, 30.

He's what you want him to be,
He's a lamb or lion sure,
And he is just like your self,
For King Jim's bible says so.
  John, xv, 4, 7. Romans, ix, 11, 12.

He had not ONE human quality,
But was demon of low degree sure,
A few quotations will proove it too,
For King Jim's bible says so and so,
From Genesis to Revelations.

By Jove's examples of lust,
His chosen rulers went sure,
They ravished, murdered and stole!
For King Jim's bible says so.
  Ezek. xx, 25. Ex. xv, 3; xxxii, 27!

There was nothing too low down,
For them to do to you sure
They lived and acted like demons,
For King Jim's bible says so.
  Num. xx, 34, 35; xxxi, 18. Ex. xxxii, 27.

Abram went for Hagar you know,
Old Sarah agreed to it sure,
Then drove their bastard child away,
For King Jim's bible does say so.
  Gen. xvi, 2, 4; xvi. 10!

Old Abram bartered off Sarah,
Said she was his sister sure,
Then he had to take her back,
For King Jim's bible says so.
  Gen. xx, 2, 5, 7, 14, 16.

Old Lot sent for his daughters,
He went for both of 'em sure,
And they went for their old dad,
For King Jim's bible says so.
  Gen. xix, 30 to 38.

He tried to defy Nick's police;
Said take my virgin daughters sure,
That they had never known a man,
For King Jim's bible says so.
  Gen. xix, 4, 8.

wo... ...sure!
...beast ...d Lot,
...ng Jim's bible says so.
Gen. xix, 1 to 8, 29, to 38!

This loyal Lord killed Onan.
Because he would not sin sure,
This Lord Mike murdered shrewd Onan.
For King Jim's bible says so
    Gen. xxxviii, 6, 8, 9, 10

Jew Jacob went for Belhah,
And they went for Rachal sure,
Jacob went for others too,
For King Jim's bible says so.
    Gen. xxx, 3, 4, 5, 7, 9, ... to 22!

Shechem's in bed with Dinah,
In the bed with Dinan sure,
The innocent was murdered!
For King Jim's bible says so.
    Gen. xxxviii, 14 to 18, 24, 25.

Mrs. Potipher went for Joseph,
She went for sweet young Jew Joseph sure,
He tore himself loose from her,
For King Jim's bible says so.
    Gen. xxxix, 7, 12, 13, 14.

Nick stood up against Israel,
And provoked old David sure,
He caught him and Mike being,
For King Jim's bible says so,
    I Chr. xxi. 1, 2, 3, 8.

Seventy thousand lives went,
To pay for David's lies sure,
Innocent lives for his lies,
For King Jim's bible says so.
    I Chr. xxi, 14.

His Lord had learned him to lie,
Told him Saul would get him sure,
Then God give him not to Saul,
For King Jim's bible says so.
    I Sam. xxiii, 7, 12, 13,

Nick arrested Joshua.
Because he was filthey sure,
But old Mike paid Joshu's due,
For King Jim's bible says so.
    Zech. iii, 1, 3, 2

Nick went for old Solomon,
  Told us of his whore house sure!
How he kept the gods ahd gals,
  For King Jim's bible says so.
    1 Kings, xi, 1 to 8.

That he's a hoo doo Nigger!
  Black as tents of Kedar sure!
A regular old burnt out bum!
  For King Jim's bible says so.
    Sol. Songs, i, 5; v, 1.

Nick told us Dave lost his grip,
  Damsels could not it arouse,
He too was a burnt out bum!
  For King Jim's bible says so.
    1 Kings, i, 1, 2. Ps. lxxix, 4.

Nick is still a policeman,
  And tells us all thats done sure,
He give old Job fits you know,
  For King Jim's bible says so.
    Job i, 1, 6, 7. ii, 1, 2, 7.

He made him curse like old Mike,
  Curse the day of his birth sure,
The night that he was conceived,
  For King Jim's bible says so.
    Job iii, 1, 2, 3, 4, 5.

Nick and Jesus bumed together!
  Lade out in a wilderness sure!
Alone forty days forty nights!
  For King Jim's bible says so.
    Matthew, iv, 1, 2, 8.

Nick bet this world with Jesus,
  That he could out starve him sure,
Forty days made Jesus squeal!
  For King Jim's bible says so.
    Matthew, iv, 1, 2, 8.

Follow me and I will make
  Thee fishers of men for sure!
You must hate every body!
  For King Jim's bible says so.
    Matthew, iv, 19. Luke, xiv, 26!

One nights fishing settled it,
  He was caught himself for sure!
An old bum sold him out quick!
  For King Jim's bible says so.
    Matthew, xxvi, 14, 15.

Nick went for Jim's successor,
　The scoundrel King George you know,
And drove him back to England,
　Freed us from Royal Religion!
　　See Uncle Sam's bible.

Now, if ever Nick done a wrong,
　Time's history fails to show it sure,
King Jim's bible god done it all!
　For King Jim's bible says so.

Isa. xlv, 7. Ez. xx, 25. Am. iii, 6. Jer, xviii, 11;
xxxii, 17, 27. Ex. xx, 5; xxxii, 27. Deut. xiv, 21.
2 Sam. xxiv, 17. Matt. xiii, 12. Rom. ix, 11, 12, 13!

CHARITY SHOULD STAY AT HOME.

Let her own light shine, then we would know where to find her! Fo by her fruits we know her.

COME all around, I pray draw near,
　Listen a while and you shall hear,
Something of what is going on,
　At the houses around the pond.

Last fall when trees did shed their leaves,
　The brethren then did rest at ease,
They blocked the game until this spring,
　Now they go it shoe-boots again.

It is the curse of sin they say,
　That causes them to sing and pray,
They keep it up both day and night,
　Such words and actions is a fright!

It was but last Saturday night,
　They held prayer meeting till day light!
On Sunday their prayers did renew,
　Until our patients quite wore through.

At brother Cathcarts they commenced,
　To sing and pray at his expence!
Brother Biby their leader were,
　But he is gone we know not where!

Brother Biby we all do know,
　To Monkey Cagles did go! go!
To hunt, to pray, to sing so wild,
　Till Rhoda swore to him a child!

To brother Ford and Davis too,
   A caution now I'll give to you,
Brother Johnson, to you likewise,
   Do tell us how your business lies?

Pray, do you get along so well,
   That yu'll have corn to keep and sell?
If you dont all tend it better,
   You will get an awful setter!

Brother Stanley, a word you need,
   Your corn is hidden in he weeds,
If you will give your corn a cleaning,
   You will have no time for meeting.

Brother Stoglin has hold on grit,
   Amid all this he holds on yet,
When he does come he has to walk,
   Sing and pray to him is no balk.

Says if he lives to see next fall,
   He will have a horse at his call,
And a buggy to ride her in,
   The way he will preach is no sin.

This was their Text, Song, and Prayer,—
   Pray on brothers, and dont you get weary!
Ther's a starry crown in Heaven for you!
   That will make you out shine yonders sun!

Pleasant Cove School House, Warren County, Tenn., 1845.   Rily B————.

N. B. Brother Stoglins buggy ride was to the State prison for carrying out his god's command, given him at Deut. xiv, 22! Brother Biby was prosecuted for acting to his servant Rebeca, like Abraham did to Hagar! Brother Springs, a refined, educated physician, and a mason, was prosecuted for carrying out the examples of Jacob, his wife, like Rachel, agreeing to him! And brother BELL, an author doctor, and great Sunday School teacher, fled the country with another man's woman, leaving his wife and family!

And on! on! could I go, giving you dose, after dose, of the fruits of this awful disease, called religion, but this is enough! You only have to call them to mind yourself, or go to our Records at the Court-House; or read a Newspaper, to see its infamous fruits in its awful colors!

YANKEE DOODLE DANDY.

Or, we can do what you do, god or no god, handy.

The British claimed to be God's army, sent by king George, Jim's successor, to put dowh the Devil's rebel heretics, and to enforce their gods religion! They boasted that the rebel mongrels could not do what they could! But, as soon as they come in hearing, played a tune, the rebels instantly played it too. From this it was called by an Indian Yankee Doodle Dandy. Which ment–We can do what you do, god or no god, handy!

And, although, it taken us seven long bloody years to convince them, nevertheless, we did, we whiped this god-chosen army, and drove their god chosen rule from our shores! And in its stead we give man a chance to rule himself, according to the first, inherent law to life, liberty and property, that naturly develops within him.

  Once on a time old Johnny Bull
   Flew in a raging fury,
  And said that Jonathan should have
   No trial, sir, no jury!
  That no elections should be held,
   Across the briny waters:
  "And now," said he, "I'll tax the tea
   Of all his sons and daughters.
  Then down he sat in burly state,
   And blusterd like a grandee,
  And in derision made a tune
   Called "Yankee Doodle Dandy."
  Yankee doodle, these are facts—
   Yankee doodle dandy:
  My son of wax, your tea I'll tax—
   Yankee doodle dandy.

Chorus— Yankee doodle, let all sing,
   Old Yankee doodle dandy;
   Yankee doodle, make it ring,
   O yankee doodle dandy.

  John sent the tea from o'er the sea
   With heavy duties rated:
  But whether hyson or bohea,
   I never heard it stated.

Then Uncle Sam to pout began—
  He laid a strong embargo—
Ordered his Indians out, and
  Threw overboard the cargo.
Then Johnny sent god's army—
  Big words and looks to bandy,
Whose martial band, when near the land,
  Played Yankee doodle dandy.
"Yankee doodle—keep it up
  Yankee doodle dandy!
I'll poison with a tax your cup,
  Yankee doodle dandy!"

A long war then they had, in which
  John was at last defeated—
And Yankee doodle was the march
  To which his troups retreated.
Cute Uncle Sam, to see them fly
  Could not restrain his laughter;
That tune, said he, suits to a T.,
  I'll play it ever after.
Old Johnny's face, to his disgrace,
  Was flushed with rage and brandy!
He even swore he'd play no more,
  This Yankee doodle dandy!
Yankee doodle— ho! ha! he!
  Yankee doodle dandy—
We kept his tune, but not his tea,
  Yankee doodle dandy.

I've told you now the origin
  Of this most livly ditty,
Which Johnny Bull now swares is dull,
  And stupid! what a pitty!
With Hail Columbia it is sung,
  In chorus full and hearty—
On land and main we breathe the strain,
  John made for his tea-party.
No matter how we rhyme the words,
  The music speaks them handy,
Where's the girl fair but sings the air
  Of Yankee doodle dandy?
Yankee doodle— firm and true—
  Yankee doodle dandy,
Yankee doodle through and through,
  Yankee doodle dandy.

AGAIN, sixty odd years ago,
   Johnny come and fought it over!
But we swept him down like killing
   Ducks from our forted river!
Then to flank us, pop in our rear,
   He thought he had our breeches,
But old Hickory waded the swamp,
   And piled him in our ditches!
Old Hickory's loss was so slight,
   We could but scarcely miss them!
While the red tape British that night,
   Met with an awful mystery! ✗
Since that day to this, Johnny Bull,
   Is slyly working to subvert us!
With his subjects our land is full,
   Hopeing to subjugate us!

✗ The Americans, which was mostly Indians, under an Irishman, General Jackson, in this battle, only had seven men killed and six wounded! while the British army was nearly annihilrted!

One day many met in Yorktown,
   Year one hundred and five sir,
To celebrate a happy birth,
   One hundred years begun, sir.❊
Big guns was fired and speeches made,
   Which told the grateful story
How victory there made freedom safe,
   And gave our country glory.
And then to shew how much we love
   Our forefather's British nation—
With many guns their flag we hailed,
   And raised to highest station!
With hearty shouts and glad hurrahs
   To sing with us seemed handy,
For british voices cheered with ours
   For Yankee doodle dandy!

❊ 100, A. I. means one hundred years since freedom was born, and Americans declared Independent! Man dates his age from his birth, so should a nation. This nation was born July the 4th, 1776; of Christian-god-rule! which we rebeled against, and freed ourselves from. Then we should begin our dating from the year 1, the 7th month, and 4th day; or the birth-day of the United States of America.

For example:— U. S. Flag adopted, year 1, 6th

month, and 20th day. New York evacuated by the British in the 7th year, 11th month, and 25th dry. The battle of New Orleans, the 39th year, 1st month and 8th day. The surrender of Lea, the 89th year, 4th month and 9th day.

Every schoolhouse should have a flag and fly it on all notable days, and the facts about that day person, or persons should be read to the school. All corporation, county, state and federal places should fly our flag on most all of our notable days.

Only think— It is the interest of every government under the sun, to misteach our children!!! It is the interest of every party, clique, church and order to misteach our children! And can you not see they are doing it? Our school books have been changed, till now there is not a thrill of our patriotism in them!

Only think of the birth of the Star Spangled Banner. Like Home, Sweet Home, born in prison! Scott Key, an American prisoner of the war 36, while confined on a British war-ship, during an attact on Baltimore wrote it! All the day before, the cannon had roared, but the Stars and Stripes floated proudly from Fort McHenry! The darkness of night did not still the fury of the British guns! And through the first dawn of morn, Scott Key looked anxiously out for the emblem of freedom and liberty! Whose success ment life, and whose defeat ment death! And when he seen its tattered and torn shreds yet floating on heavens free breeze a thrill of patriotism inspired him, and he then and there wrote—

THE STAR-SPANGLED BANNER.

Oh! say can you see, by the dawn's early light,
   What so proudly we hailed at the twilight's last gleaming?
Whose broad stripes and bright stars, through the perilous fight,
   O'er the ramparts we watched so gallantly streaming.

And the rocket's red glare, the bumbs bursting in air,
   Gave proof through the night that our flag
was still there!
Oh! say, does that star-spangled banner yet
wave,
   O'er the land of the free and the home of
the brave?

On the shore, dimly seen through the mist of
the deep,
   Where the foe's haughty host in dread silence reposes,
What is that, which the breeze, o'er the towering steep,
   As it fitfully blows, half conceals, half dis-
closes?
Now it catches the gleam of the morning's
first beam;
   In full glory reflected, now shines in the
stream;
'Tis the star-spangled banner! — oh! long
may it wave,
   O'er the land of the free and the home of
the brave!

And wheres that royal god-sent band, that
by heaven swore,
   'Mid the havoc of war and the battle's
confusions,
A home and a country they'd leave us no
more?
   Their blood has washed out their foul foot-
steps polution!
No refuge could save the hireling and slave
   From the terror of flight! or the gloom of
the grave!
And the star-spangled banner in triumph
doth wave
   O'er the land of the free and the home of
the brave!

Oh! thus be it ever, when freemen shall stand
   Between their loved home and war's desolation!
Blest with victory and peace, may our heav-
en-rescued land,
   Praise the Powers that hath made and preserved us a nation!

Then conquor we must, when our cause it is just,
  This then being our motto, OURSELF we trust!
And the star-spangled banner in triumph will wave
  O'er the land of the free and the home of the brave!

READER, I will here close this volume; hopeing that you will not only appreciate it, but, defend it as liberaly as it has defended your freedom. Preserve it, correct it and add volume, after volume to it. Remember the hand of the destroyer will ever be after it. It is your private friend, then keep it under lock and key.

Yankee doodle tells you of the year one, and our revolutionary war; and that freedom was given to us by heretics and infidels! It and the star-spangled banner tells you of the second attempt to crush us, and how victory was won by an Infidel! And Lincoln, Grant, Sherman, and our noble liberators, that freed us from the Christian's chattle slavery were Infidels and Heretics! and are in hell if this Christian bible and religion is true!

BRUTALITY AND HUMANITY.

Or the many, many oceans of innocent human blood religion has murderously shed!

WHAT AILS US? Want of charity to Infidelity and to your disagreeing neighbor, thats what ails us. What is Infidelity? To disbelieve any of the many religions! And every one of them declaring that he and he alone is right, and the only way to heaven. To say our Creator did not write a big book. To say you believe the laws and morals of the United State's Constitution and our Declaration of Independence is as good a way and as sure a way to heaven as any! That is what they, these religionists call Infidelity!

1st. The Paganites, they declare that as God made the different races of man that he said to all of them: " Do to others as you would they should do to you." That he inscribed this upon their hearts and they inscribed it upon their temples. 2nd. The Jewites are the first infidels, infidels to you and me, and the Paganites, by denying this just creed, and for saying: "I am the only God chosen. That God had cursed, damed and destroyed his first creation, and had created a new heaven and a new earth and a new Jeruselam, especially for them, and had promised them to dwell there with them perpetually forever! They shed oceans of innocent human blood trying to enforce this crazy religion! But they, nor their god, are not there to-day! 3rd. The Jesusites, they are infidels to the Jewites, and declared that a bastard, a mongrel a half-breed, a Jew and a God— from the royal house of the Jesus' was begot by God himself, by seduceing an old Jews wife! He declared that he come to make men fishers and haters of men! That he come not to send peace on earth, no, but hate, fire and a sword! Heb. xii, 6, 8. Matt. iv, 19. x. 34. Lu. xii, 49 xiv, 26! They too have shed an ocean of pure human blood, using hate, fire and the sword, endeavoring to force people to acknowledge this crazy religion! 4th. The Mohamedites are infidels to all of these ites, and declare that they are the only light and hope of the world. And they shed an ocean of human blood fighting over this crazy religion! They whipped them all, every one of these other ites, and drove them from their boasted god established homes! And to-day all of these hating god-favored, god-chosen, and devil whippedites are here, seeking an asylum among us Infidels! They are only a lot of crazy, whining begging, malcontents, that God could not please, nor learn them any sense! They are an awful clog to our happiness, life and advancement.

5th The Yankeeites, they are infidels to all of these ites, and places the emblem of freedom, the Stars and Stripes, above the hating hateful Cross the emblem of hate, and perpetual war! And demands that religion shall be controled by the government of Uncle Sam. And after whipping them all, every one of these god-sent, god-anointed, god-appointed Kings, and their heaven favored armies; yes, after sheding an ocean of royal human blood in self defence, we discarded all of them. All of the many, many crazy religions, and their many, many conflicting and self-contradicting bibles that was the supreme law of this land! And in its hateing murdering stead we established the Yankeeite bible of Uncle Sam's, and the first just, free, and the only upright, moral government under the sun!

Our creed declares that God created ALL mankind free and equal; making man a knowing, and understanding, accountable, responsable, moral ☞ free agent, that can save or dam himself. ☜ Then, as we are not TOTALLY mean, totally depraved, nor totally lost, we need no earthly god-father, mediator, guardian, or savior.

So, we Yankeeite Infidels have done more to protect and to advance mans knowledge, freedom and happiness in one hundred years than all of these other ites have done in thousands of years! Infidelity questions all things, proves all things, and holds fast to that which is good. And not to summons the demons of hate, chaos and misrule as religions do, and then accuse us of it! Yes, my accountable religious enemies, I would hate to accuse my fellow dissenting neighbors of a hellish crime when you must know that all surrounding facts, that are plain before every bodies eyes proves you a wilful and a malicious liar, or an ignorant fool.

And, again, every human being that has reached but a few years of experience must know that he is punished every day of his life for his sins and his crimes. And, O! what a punishment they will be to you in eternity where you cannot hide them! And this is why you hope in a Jesus and trust in a priest! But, you hope in vain, for thank God there is no such a thing as a savior, no such a thing as forgivness, no such a thing as escaping justice! and no sane honest person could ask for forgiveness!

Infidelity and morality is a progressive science; it is provable and improvable. And if religion is not provable and improvable why say prove all things? Infidelity and morality is founded on well established uncontrovertable facts. While theology and religion is a craziness founded only on an imaginary, unjust desire, or a diseased hope!

They are mere ideas and opinions of men— blind becrazed, presumptious man; who has branded Infidelity and morality as profane! and themselves as sacred! and alone trustworthy and reliable! When the facts are just the reverse! They, as these accompanying slate cuts show from their own self-accursed history, prove that they are not now, nor never was, and to any reasonable mind is sufficient evidence to warrant the belief that they never will be reliable nor trustworthy!

So thought and declared our revolutionary fathers! And I here unhesitatingly declare that religion is a craziness, a weakness of our infernal infirmities, and aught to be held and watched as such as it was in the days of Rome. For the miseries and destruction that religion has caused is beyond computation or discription!

Turn your attention to Brutality, or the religious side of this subject and view the picture. Begin at the first murder! Cain kills his younger brother!

CUT BRUTALITY!

And religion caused it! Follow that little religious beginning on! Follow that little red rivulet of human blood on, and it son joins in with others that religion has shed! ☞ See them as they wind on, onward, around that awful mountain of human bones and skulls! It is Mount Ariat. See the

Ark that has just been left on the top of this mountain of humain remains! Only think think of Noah and family as they clamber over the rotting remains of man and beast, as they leave the Ark! Only think of the human gore trickling down its slimy sides! Only think of its stifling stench, and gastly views that meet their gaze! And religion caused it!

How soon in the very infancy of this world the Christians have a demon for a god! cursing this world, and entailing sin, crime, slavery, suffering, destruction, hate and a premature death, on all creation, and especially on all man-kind, for the alledged disobedience of the first half made, totally ignorant, and totally depraved old Jew! Simply because he had received light and knowledge from the Devil! And just as soon as they began to increase, multiply, replenish and subdue this earth, we see the sons of this Christian god coming down from heaven and taking by force, a rape process, just whome they choose of these fair daughters of earth, to themselves for CONCUBINES! And soon do we see this god of these religionists a jealous hateing god! Declaring war, making murder, and trying to not only destroy these bastards, this god amalgamated rase, but the earth also! Why? Because a Jew-god accursed, sin predestined race of ravished bastards could not be made Jew-god religious, nor Jew-god like perfect!

Immediatly after this unnatural flurry of jealous hate, we see this same Jew-god amalgimated, bewilderd, moon-eyed set, endeavoring to evade this hating, hatful god's curses and destruction by building them a tower to heaven. Follow them on but a little way further, and we see this Jew-god himself had to come down from his exalted heaven and see what these wretches were doing. We see him guilty of a more infernal and wretched violance than anything in the antedeluvian history. More like a demon from the regions of the damed, than a merciful God-father from heaven. We see this Jew-god of the Christians, coming down and confusing an all ready scared to death, becrazed world until they themselves did not know each other! And while in this wretched intoxicated state they are driven, like beasts, pell-mell in every direction! Follow it on, and just as soon as they begin to establish other homes, in other countries, we see this same Christian Jew-god himself going at the head of a mighty army of the selected elect, through every nation under the sun; robbing, stealing, pillaging, ravishing, and murdering the bewilderd and helpless nations of this earth, until these rivers of human gore are terrible rivers, sufficient to float the largest steamships or the mighty ship of Zion!

On it goes, this awful river of the gods, this river of blood, this river Jordan, winding its bloody way through the very heart of every nation under the sun! On it goes, deepening and widening, as it is joined by ten thousand millions of other rivers of human gore, that religion has shed out of the hearts of poor, innocent, helpless infants, women and children, and all done in the name of God, or by God himself, they say! On it goes, this Jew-Christian bible of King Jim's, recording page after page, book after book, of those different barbarian uncalled for wars, cold-blooded, unprovoked murders, awful massacres, and unparalled slaughters, that religion has done in every land under the sun! ☞ And only think, they claim to be done in the name of a just God, or by God himself! Follow it on, it is now a terrible river of hot, boiling, hissing human gore, sufficient to carry the skulls, skeletons and decayed bodies, along its slippery, slimy banks of hissing serpents, and demons from the regions of the damed! Look across on yonder shore— on the other side of this river of the gods— this river Jordan, and view this religious landscape over!

See that church, and that Christian preacher as he points with pride to their fruits, as he begs and beckons you on to slavey, hate, self-denial, suffering and an ignomineous death! Yes, yes, see that Church, that Preacher, and that Devil! See their fruits! See those maniacs, that religion has frightened to death, with their hideous sermons, with their bibles self-contradictions, and religions maddening fire! They are a heavy tax-burden to every state in the union, and a terrible nuisance!

See the skulls of the millions, and millions of innocent, helpless victoms, that religionists has piled mountain high! See Golgotha, a mountain of human skulls! where they closed the tragedy of tragedies, by erecting in its midst a cross and to cap the climax they then and there crucified god himself! See the vast tracts of nations that they have, and are fast destroying, as fast as rebuilt and replenished! See that cross, that towers up high out of this mountain of human skulls! There it was, they say, that religionists murdered even God himself, and to this evil day, they say, that they are living off of ☞ his flesh and his blood to this day! ☜ My God! My God! This is religion, I am told!!!

NOW turn your attention to the right side of this picture, to humanity, and see what the Christians, what the Kings, the Princes, Empers, Lords, Lawyers, Doctors, Popes, Preasts, Preachers, Polititions, and their divine right slaves, and their bibles call the Devil's works! See those rich and luxuriant farms, that feed those idle, medlesom, parasitical, piratical scoundrels! See that beautiful vally. See those happy, happy, ah, virteous homes. See those happy, happy, ah, thrice happy children and their schools. See the learned, the good, the true, the beautiful, the charitable and the wise. ☞ See those God loving and hell-fearing liberal fathers and mothers, as they struggle on towards eternity; and not a New, Jew-Jerusalem.

See the dome of our Capitol in the distance, and the statue of Liberty, that holds aloof the flambeau torch of Liberty and Infidelity; the only light, and the only true and sane religion in the world!

For this light has shone so pure and bright that every nation in this world has seen it, felt it, enjoyed it, admyred it, embraced it, and defended it! And draw pensions or charity from it! It is no little hateing, hateful missionary fox-fire light, that

CUT HUMANITY— Home, Sweet Home, virtue, reason, justice, truth, love, liberty, education, invention, and progress.

shines only for their little clique, that shines ghostly only for a while and then dies out of its own brutality; just as it has done every where, in heaven or on earth! While our religion is: "Do to others as you would they should do to you." It helps, protects, defends, and supports those that cannot help themselves—and this is all that mortal man can do. Yes, we even respect, care for and bury the dead; while their hateing, hateful god at the ix, 60 of Lnke says: " Let the dead bury their dead!" So, of all the mighty nations in the east or in the west this glorious Liberal Infidel nation is the most charitable and the best. So, down with the traitors, and up with our flags boys, shouting our battle cry of a universal freedom.

CUT 1, HUMANITY. | CUT 2, BRUTALITY.

Cut one, Humanity, is an old-time picture of Uncle Sam, the honest, cherful old Liberal and Infidel. He loves every-body, he wants every-body to be free and happy, he is every-body's friend.

Cut two, Brutality, is a correct likeness of a hypocrite, or a two-faced scoundrel He hates and meddles with every-body! He wants every-body to be just like himself, and to " git ligion, and jine his church, " and be a miserable, homeless, hateing, hateful church-ridden slave.

FAMILY RECORDS.

FOR such as births, deaths, marriages, wills deeds, charts and valuable records.

FAMILY — 133. — RECORDS.

FAMILY — 134.— RECORDS.

FAMILY — 135. — RECORDS.

FAMILY — 136. — RECORDS

FAMILY — 137. — RECORDS.

FAMILY — 138. — RECORDS

FAMILY —139.— RECORDS.

FAMILY — 141. — RECORDS.

~~FAMILY — 142.— RECORDS.~~

THE ANIMAL AND THE HUMAN
CHART OF

AS MARKED BY

IT comprises your Physiognomy, Psychology, Physiology, Phrenology, Palmistr Anatomy, Pathology, Temperament, and organic quality.

FAMILY — 143.— RECORDS.

FAMILY —144.— RECORDS.

FAMILY — 145. — RECORDS.

FAMILY —146.— RECORDS. 179

FAMILY —147.— RECORDS.

ANALYSIS OF MAN.

MAN is a compound of only two primary natures. The animal and the human. He has two bodies and two sets of minds. His two bodies are alike, and united together. Tradition tells us, that originaly, one was male, and the other was female. This body is compounded by twoes, as two organs of the senses, perceptives, thoughts, words, and actions. Two skins, tongues, nostrils, eyes, brains hearts, lungs, etc. Hence, mans, and not Gods, doubled up thoughts, and expressions; as, "Let us make man in our image, after our likeness. Gen.1, 26." This betrayed the hidden author.

They made man, sure enough, in their image, and after their likenss. Cut 1, shows you some of them; giving you all colors, types, or species of man.

Reader, is it possible, to find two of these fellows that see, or believe alike ? Religionist say it is, and our government has been fool enough to try it. Remember the fable about the confusion of tongues. This betrays its lieing author. If God entended them to see, and believe alike, he has missed it as far as in looks. Every one of these fellows say God is just like them.

While the facts are, God is too extensive to be comprehended, much less seen! He only communicates with man, through unchangable, natural law. Then the proper study of man is nature. Yes, "Take nature's path, and mad opinion's leave."

Study thyself, know thyself, trust thysevf, serve thyself, belong to thyself, and thou wilt save thyself. This is the entire law and gospel, the whole need and duty of man.

Charity should begin at home, and it should stay at home. Your own home is the most sacred altar on earth. Attend to, and controle your own self, and your own business, and you will be one of the earthly gods. Every thing, will belong to you, and you will belong to no body, nor nothing. You will be an Independent Sovereign. If all would do this, there would be no paupers, nor wanters. No need for a blating missionary.

In the human body there are several hundred bones, ligaments, nerves, bloodvessels, muscles, in pairs. Thirty odd teath. The alimentary canal is about 32 feet. The blood averages 30 pounds. The heart is 6 inches long, 4 in diameter, and beats 70 times per minute. All the blood passes through the heart in 3 minutes. The lungs contain about 1 gallon of air. Their air surface is near 12 feet square.

There is claimed 40 odd organs of the mind in the brain. The average weight of the brain is 3 or 4 pounds. The nerves are branches of the bra.n. Forming a body guard of billions! Each square inch of skin contains over 3 thousand nerve guards, and as many sweating tubes, or perspiratory pores.

We are head downwards, and outwards, from mother earth, and it takes dady air all his might, pressing about 40 thousand pounds on each of us, to keep us here!

We are passing through a ceasless change, of building up and tearing down. We change! change!!

assuming new forms, new compounds, new features, and new minds. Ah! devoured not! but, devouring ALL others!

LIFE would be unbearable were it not for the changeing power, of the third god, in the god-head; tha Changer—the changing powers of time.

The first thing to look too in an analysis of a man, woman, or child, is 1st, Their sex, and to which they lean. 2nd, Their organic quality. 3rd, Their race. 4th, Their age. 5th, Their extent, and kind of education, or training. 6th, Their animal, and human natures. 7th, Their combinations, or tempering—or temperaments. 8th, If the body is healthy and well balanced in all things. 9th, It the brain the body is healthy and balanced. 10th, As to how the brain in the head and the brain in the body balances. 11th, As to the present occnpation, and station in life.

These are the points to be considered and described. It does not matter how much brain, nor body you may, or may not have; nor how many organs of the brain, or body, you may, or may not have. Nor what their names are, nor the precise mathematial spot they occupy. For they are mearly a lot of the most cowardly, abject slaves, to sex, quality, race, age, education, training, health, and an over or under balanced condition of the organization, as can be.

CUTS 2, and 3, gives you the nature of life, and mind. Your power to perceive, or to see, is marked --perceptive. This is in, around the forehead, and face. To rationally judge, compare, and reason, is marked—reasoning. It occupies all of the capital, or tophead. To remember, to perfect, and to propagate, or to continue, is marked—perfective. It occupies the top side head, or the crown region. To protect, to execute, and to govern, is marked—protecting, or executing. And occupies the base of the brain, between, in, and around the ears, and on down the back bone, all the bones, and throughout the entire body. Cuts 2, and 3.

CUT 2.

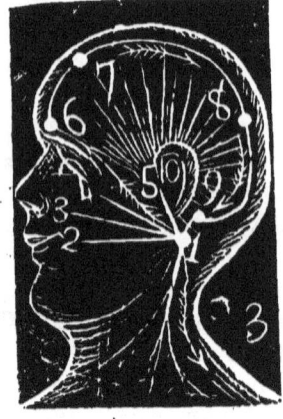
CUT 3.

Cut 2, gives you first the PERCEPTIVES, our 5 avenues of knowledge. Cut 3, marks them 1, 2, 3, 4, 5; which is 1st, feeling by touch; 2nd, feeling by tasting; 3rd, feeling by smelling; 4th, feeling by seeing; 5th, feeling by hearing All of which are concentrated at station 1. and 10. the fountain, or sun of life, which gives us the 3 great functions of life--Sensation, or sensability; contractility, and irritability—the life of man.

These forces move on and collect and concentrate at station 6. and 7., giving the mind, or minds of man. Station 7. and 8. gives us the Rational, reasoning, judging, inspired turn of mind; or, the Creator. Station 8. and 9. gives us the Perfective, or propagating turn of mind; or the Preserver. While station 9. and 10. gives us the Protecting, executing, or Changer, or Continuer.

This makes out the god-head of the ancients. The father, the mother, and the child; or the Creator, the Preserver, and the Continuer. This gives you the source of life and mind.

This is the round our mind, or minds has to take, before a well inspired, or a rational, reasoning, reflecting, or a well trained, or a well balanced man speaks or acts. While an unbalanced, or uninspired man, or animal will fly the track, at every station, keep up an everlasting friction, fuss and trouble.

Man has only two primary natures. The physical, or solid, earthey body; and the mental, or electrical mind. Electricity, therefore, is not a substance, neither is it an effect. It is the immediate cause of force underlaying all of the ceaseless changes of every thing that has form and life.

Man has not got a soul, nor a spirit, as is taught. The thing called a soul, or a spirit, is only our immagination, a desire, a hope that seams to emanate from our peculiar, abnormal organization. It is mixed up, and confounded with our life forces, and they are taken to be that very, very independent thing called the SOUL of man.

Both, the Jew and the Christian bibles tell us that man has no soul, and that there is to be no resurection of the dead. See Job 7c., 9. Ecel. 9c. 5. Is. 26c. 14. It tells us that God will give us another body, and an immortality; when? at the judgement? No, before that, at the resurection. See 1st, Cor. 15c. 51 to 53.

This does away with that god-given change called "gittin ligin", or those faculties, or brain for such! This does away with that immortal soul or spirit. This does away with that sweet old body thyself--that every body had to bow too, to praise, and look up too. And, althongh, you may clean it up, cleaner than it ever was, and dress it finer than it ever was, and enbalm it, and fix it up for the resurection; yet, you are told there is to be no resurection; that it is too corrupt. But, you will be given another body, and an immortality, that you did not have before; provided, you are worthey of one. See 1st. Cor. 15c. 38 to 58.

Then I would ask, in all due candor, where are you? thyself? You are not even represented! Nothing that composed you on this earth, composes you now! So, who knows you? Or, cares a fig for you? if this self-contradicting bible theology be true? See 1st. Cor. 15c. 35 to 58.

Webster's Dictionary gives two pages of alterations, and contradictions; saying, by what authority the bible has thus been altered is not known! Is Webster good authority? He shows that they have placed Jesus where it used to be Joshua; and in many places ADDED the word SOUL! This was to prove man had a soul, or a spirit, which could not be done, until these additions; for the first preacher tells us in Ecclesiastes, that man has no preeminence above a beast! Yes, in the face of all this, we have a lot of preachers, and teachers, declaring, "Man thou art immortal, thy soul can never die." And yet, they cannot produce any proof. It is only their wish. Yes, I ask, who knows we have a spirit, or a something independent of our organization, of our 5 senses, or our 5 witnesses, our 5 ways of perceiving, reasonieg, judging, and acting? Who has, or can prove it? The scriptures say you cannot prove it. Common sense says such would be unjust, unfair, and unreasonable. Neither can the mind of man survive death. We see that the towering intellect is dependent upon the dody, and cannot survive its death. It develops and grows with the body; and it shrinks and dies with it. "He return.eth to his earth, and in that very day his thoughts perish See Psa. 146. 4, informs you that, and teaches us thah our minds are dependent on our living material organization.

There is a difference, a vast difference in man, as well as a vast dilerence between man and the beast. Some men are better balanced, and better trained than others. Man is better balanced in both body and brain than the interior animals. Man has movable eyes, and fixed ears. Beasts has movable ears and fixed eyes. Man has an inspired, knowing, rational, perception, reasoning, and acting; or movable mind, while that of the beast, or inferior animals are fixed, unmovable just like religionists!

Religion is an unbalanced, weakened condition of our organization. It is controled by our infernal infirmities. It is a fixed, uncurable craziness! And in every age of the world, and in every country under the sun, history tells us that when this craziness becomes epidemic, that is, when this crazy gang gets in power, they not only destroy every body, and every thing, and themselves, but they lay it all on their god. This cannot be denied. Deny it and you prove your bible a lie, admit it and you make it an awful crazy curse!

Then this movable, changable mind of mans' this perceiving, proving, knowing, or rational, reasoning, analytical class of brain, that man alone is favored with, is mans inspiration, and is what makes him a human; with an accountability; a free knowing, accountable sovereign! He sees, feels, and knows this -- and this fact settles it — it is enough; you need no writing from God! God wrote no book! Christ wrote no book! Man sees, feels, percieves and knows that he deserves no forgivness for his crimes. And to say that a just Father gives him a mediator, a savior, is self-contradictory and makes your god out an unjust liar. It is a whistleing in the dark. It is a plan from that other fellow, in black, Mr. Devil, and not Mr. God.

Man deserves no forgivness, no mediator, no savior, no pity; and I am convinced it is a bad policy to depend upon it. There is no forgivenes! But the man that sineth shal surely be punished, according to injury done, both in this life, and the life to come. And it is with our Creator, Preserver, and Changer, whether we are again so well favord, and trusted; or, given that blest immortality!

That christ, or savior story, is an old fable as old as man. It tells the nature of man. Man is just like a snake. Thaw a snake and it will bite you. Christ come to save his people, and they killed him. Do a man a favor and he will do you a dirt. Eating the forbidden fruit, is another old fable, and shows you that man cannot be trusted.

Much is now being said about Gen. Butler being a great beast That his brain weighed four ounces more than Daniel Websters. That age, disease, and strong drink shrank Websters-

We here give you a few cuts, and a few suggestions, on this important part of our subject.

CUT 4.

To be a great man you first have to be a great beast! But, all great beasts are not great men!

CUT 5.

These scales, cuts 4, and 5, are an exact representation of man and beast. And of a balanced, or unbalanced man. Man or beast, in their balanced condition, is moral.

In their unbalanced condition, they are immoral, and more or less vicious. So, morality, and health, is a balanced condition. Immorality, viciousnes, and disease, is an unbalanced condition.

Mans first, or foundational nature, is his beast, or animal natures. They are mostly instinctive, and

ı common with man and beast. They
veloped; while our human natures, are
ith our growth, throughout life. Ther-
ınnot hide from us your animal natures
ıcquired, or human natures, you may
at extent.

presents a healthy, natural balanced,
oral man. He is sound both in body
vell balanced, and properaly trained, or
Such persons are good, they feel well.
well balanced in brain, and body, and
se are well balanced with each other,
right, and it does not matter whether
veighs an ounce or a pound. An Ele-
n outweighs mans; but, the trouble
ephant is he is not balanced, not in
ody. Goliath's brain weighed twice
David's. Yet, what advantage had he
?

th all inferior animals, and all inferior,
man. Mans great advantage again is
ulatory powers; the accumulation of
nd perchance, a potent antecedent of
ee. And by the instruments of
l things to serve him as supplemented
upplemented limbs. Hence, mans greater animals is due as much in this as
of brain, or mind; or a supposed soul.
n is a nothing, that depends upon
r a something, according to their own
But, it really is nothing, depending up-
Some people are good and industrious,
eir way through this world. Such are
rs are lazy beasts, and hog their way
hile others are smart Alecks, and lie,
r, and beat their way through. Such
ell, and will return to hell!!
reader, why the Creator thus placed
it happened, is not known, But you

are given a thoughtful, reasoning judgement, and it is your duty to use it; and improve it. This is the object of this treaties, We are told that the sons of god took the daughters of men for wives; and I am certain the sons of the devil took, and are yet taking them for slaves, and for concubines!

So it is, throughout every phase of life, we have these two extreamest; the extra bad, and the extra good. Or, those who are all animal, and those who are all human. And, were it not for this middle man, our PERFECTIVE, or propagating, and continuing natures of man, that balance us, by equaly bleading our born and acquired natures; we would be precisely as the lower quadruped animals, and the self-styled; extra good, and the lords, ladies, and the gods—entirley unbalanced, totaly depraved and unreliable.

CUT 6.   CUT 7.

Cuts 6, and 7, shows you, in comparison, the regions of these 3 natures of man. They are marked 1, 2, and 3. This region 1, our born, or animal natures; are our instincts, or imaginary minds. They perceive, or feel, wonder, and imagine, but do not reason, and accumulate evidence.

Regions 2, from our forehead through, is our acquired, reasoning, evidence accumulating to proof human natures. While regions 3, is our rational conscientious turn of minds.

Cut 7, gives the head of an Ape, and the comparative lines of mans head. Now, if a man developed from an Ape he had a long and a hard road to travle; saying nothing about the loss of muscles, bones, hair, movable ears, fixed eyes, mind and a tail. His anatomy, physiology, and phrenology is quite different from mans. A germ for development is born in man; and may, or may not, be developed; but, to say we develop entirley new parts, organs, and functions, independent of these born germs is eronius.

Inferior animals are inferior, or unbalanced by having more body than brain, and by having more of just one kind of brain than another. This may happen with man. We may have a well balanced body that is too much for our brain; and we may have a well balanced brain that is too large for our body. ☞ So the body must balance, and the brain must balance, and these must balance each other, before you are a perfectly SANE, MORAL, or healthey being. ☜ This is the condition that gives true religion, true justice, and true morality.

CUT 8. | CUT 10. | CUT 9. -

CUTS 8, 9, and 10, illustrate to you these three classes of man. Cut 8, is too much animal; cut 9, is too much human; while cut 10, is near a balance.

And, now, comes the tug of raising, education, or association. If these are wrong, you are wrong; no matter how well nature may have balanced you. We are told in Provebs, "Train up a a child in the way he should go: and when he is old, he will not depart from it."

But, lo! and behold! Solomon, the wise man, who said this, after being made, trained, and dwelling perpetually with god! Trained in the way he should go. But, ah, alas, he did extensively, depart there from! in his old days! He deserted his god—the god of Israel; that had heard, and had answerd his prayer; and had left heaven, to dwell perpetualy with Solomon! He deserted this god for many strange gods; and thousands of strange women! See 11 chapter of 1st, Kings.

He was styled the " Darling of the Lord; the rose of Sharon; the lily of the valey;" and placed under the care and training of Nathan, the prophet of the Lord. See 2 Sam. 12c. 24, 25.

And yet, there is not one act of his life that a decent white man would be proud of; or would be tolerated in this nation! And to say our Maker had any thing to do with such a beast is an unpardonable blasphemy!

Cut 8, represents Solomon; a regular old Jew-Negro. See 5th, verse, 1st, chapter of his Songs. He was a complete beast, and hoged his way through this world to hell! Where all such organizations are most certain to land, training or no training religion or no religion; god or no god.

They 'jine, backslide, and re-jine de church every change of the moon. And are eventually killed, or rot with a filthey, lothesom, disease, just as did Solmon, and his old dad. See 1st, Kings, 1, 2, verses.

So, it is next to an utter impossibillity to find a perfectly natural, unbiased, healthey, balanced man. Or to keep him so, when once founed. Gen. Grant is represented in cut 10; and yet, after reaching the highest pinicle of glory ;like Hanibal, Solomon, and others, intemperance brought them face to face, to lothesom diseases, and miserable deaths.

Gen. Grant after saving this nation, then destroyed it, by dabling in religious legislation, contrary to all law, as stated in Prefatory Remarks. And it was caused by placing these two unbalanced and unbarable classes in power. See cuts 8, and 9 . Cut 8, is a fair representation of the inquisitorial general, of this nation—Anthony Comstock. And cut 10, is a fair representation of Dr. Spraker, the Christirn educator. Placing these extremes in power was a usurpation, of power. Dr, Spraker, cut 9, is all sympathy, brain and nerve. He has studied, lectured, taught, and preached all his life. This is the way this class, cut 9, measures man. While class 8, the Solomonites, frolic, eat, drink, and hug strange women. This is their religious measure of man. While Gen." Grants class, cut 10, says give them all a chance.

So, you may take a child like Dr. Spraker, and train it for a Solomon, and your labor, for puppy love religion is lost; he could not drink, and hug a thousand strange womene a day. Then you may take a child like Solomon, and train it for a Spraker, and your labor is lost, for he could not sympathise, study, lecture, teach, and preach. Then you may take a child that has all of the qualities, of both Solomon, and Spraker, and train him for the soldier Gen. Grant, and your time will be lost. Why? Because, when two extreams meet, they make a worse extreme. It takes the union of a balanc'd human nature, and a balanced animal nature to make a MAN. The church makes man bolder and meaner, by upholding, and defending its members, in their crimes! It even follws them to hell and petitions for their release!

An ape has always been an ape, and he always will be; no matter what meddlesom man may say or do. Just precisley so with man: he too, notwithstanding the teemiung millions may pray, and preach themselves deaf, dum, and blind; yet, man is precisley the same, as at the begining.

He develops, grows, matures, decays, and passes away; and he, has in all ages, been one, and the same. Some are mostly animal, as the Jew, Negro, and Indian. While others are more human, like our white Albino-Irish fathers.

Take history, sacred, or otherwise, and you find that what one tribe styled good, civilized, religious, moral, or virtuous, or just, was not; or at least, they done themselves, and the world more harm than good! They accomplished in their religious way just precisley, what they accused every body, but themselves of doing—confusion and destruction! This has been the wretched life, and hellish end of every religious tribe, or nation, from Abel, their father on down!

Then a religious man, or nation, is not a good nation, or man. Religion is no mark, no recommendation of truth, goodness, worth, virtue, nor justice. Yet, they always, have from Able on down set themselves up as better than others! As perfect as God; and you as mean as hell. See, Mat. 5c. 48. And this is the first trouble with friends, neighbors, parents, families, and children. Those who profess religion, think themselves better than others. And are all the time, Able like, wrongfully accusing others, and provoking trouble.

We should not seek to change the nature of man, but, to improve, control, and make the most out of them. Know thyself, and how to read others, just as you read a book, is what is needed. God only helps those who righteously help themselves. He only can answer prayer through natural laws.

It is true the mother moddles the child, but, circumstances make, and control the man. Man is developed from one minute little daub of placid matter; that contains all the jerms for the future man. First is his brain, and nerves, as they radiate from that common center, station 1. and 10. the center of life.

Man when born is a mear helpless mass of jerms, of placid elements, of body and brain; that develop and grow organs. These organs develop and grows functions that are peculiar to brain and body.

Commencing at the beginnig, the new born babe first thing is to feel, as marked at station 1., cut 3. then to fret, whine, scream, suck, drink, to eat; using our born, or animal instincts first, long before we can see, coo, smile, laugh, think, reason— using our born, or instinctive, animal minds, long before we can grow, and develop our acquired, human natures. Our human brain, the capital, and its bony covering, being soft, when born, and is last to mature. These soft headed children are over-human, and harder to raise. ☞ Then these well balanced conditions, when once perfected, are blunted, blinded, or taken away from you if not properly used; and totally perish in old age.

So, once a man, to fret, curse, pray, smile, laugh work, or play, and twice a helpless child, or beast, in somebodies way.

Yes, controlled by blind theology, and cruel, crazy religion, man has been kept in a state of self-contradictory confusion, in all ages, in all races; without check, down to this nation. ☞ Even those who fled from blind theology, and cruel, crazy religion, to FREE investigating Yankeedom; has been so crooked, intimidated, stinted, and enslaved by religious education, that has so misled them that none of them, have been able to describe man correctly.

Science has given us all the great truths, that elevates, and makes us more human. Religion has given us only drugged gizzards, or minds debased down to that of a beast! How? This is done by dethroning investigating, rational reason. The difference in a free man, and an enslaved religionist, is a free man has all the instinctive minds of a beast, and then a rational, reasoning mind, that the beast has not; and if a Christian has this class of mind, it is a slave, and he is a-fraid to use it! This is the way religion dethrones reason, and leaves you only a cowardly, wondering beast! This is why destruction has always followed them.

A finished man has a multitude of minds! These minds are in groups, or act together, to accomplish certain objects. Look at cut 2, and 3. Cut 2, gives you the location, and the four main groups, while cut 3, gives you their mode of action. From the medulla oblongatta, spring, at least, FIVE sources of perception ; or animal minds—the brain and cerebellum furnish none; but, like lawyers, judges, juries, and officers, recieve their informationr from these five animal witnesses, and then act right or wrong, according to balanced or unbalanced body and brain orgains

Then only think, each of these animal minds are such independent sovereigns, that none of them can be made perform the work of any other. The nerves of feeling; cannot hear, tast, see, nor smell. The neryes of tast cannot hear, see, nor smell. So, it is with the rest.

And, although, they, all have different functions to perform, yet, they all originate from the same common center of life; and in general appearance, are one and the same.

A finished man is supposed to have thirty-two teeth, or organs of mastication. They are divided in to groups, for recieving, ivestigating, and preparing our food, for the stomach. Yet, many men never have that number, and but few keep what they once had. Precisley so, with our organs of our boby and brain. We are supposed, or said to have forty odd, seperate, and distinct organs of mind; and they are absqlutly as independently distinct as is our teeth. And, then, each is a magnet, having a negative, and a positive pole. That is, the same organ makes us glad or mad, laugh or cry, love or hate, according to the impressions it recieves. Yes, we love or hate from the same organ, therefore, large or small, is regulated by condition, more than by different organs, or amount of brain, that is supposed to be large or small.

Yes, but few people, ever have a full set of teeth, or bodily organs, nor a full set of organs of mind. Our teeth originate in our brain, and nodoubt but that every perfectly born child has its natural number of thirty-two nerve fibers, filled with brain, that is entended to mature a tooth at its destined end; but are often prevented in doing so. Just precisely so with our minds. Our EARS are the center of the scales of life, brain, and body. Or, midway between the ears is the SEAT, or the sun of light, and life; that shine out in radient nerve rays of light, and life, in every direction, to the surface akin of the brain, and the body, as is shown in cuts 3, 11, 12, and 13.

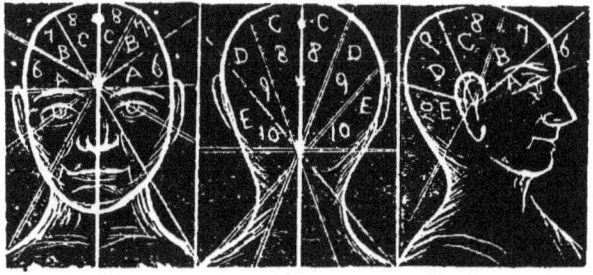

C U T 11 . | C U T 12 . | C U T 13 .

Cut 13, gives the successive action of the mind, as it moves, harmoniously, or naturally, from the 5 senses, or through the 5 stations, or courts of invyestigation. It is a side view, and shows the lines of measurement as they are drawn from the center of the ear. A, B, C, D, E; mark the angles, that these radiating lines make; and measure.

To illustrate--.in angle A. cut 11, and 13, we feel taste, smell, see, or hear something. That is, our guide, our animal man, our perceptions has discovered something. And the proof in the case has been collected at station 6, in angle A. And these five senses are our witnesses. ☞ This is mental action.

That is, we, our animal man, has recognized something, at station 6, in angle A. And says I am going to do something. An animal, or in those men who the animal predominate, or rule, action is at once conveyed to station 10. for execution, without investigation. And it is only in the well balanced human man, in angle B, at station 7, that says, hold on, let me see and compare things, and see what it means, what is best to do.

So, our human men, not man, with their comparing cause and effect, as lawyers, examine our animal men, and their witnesses, that has felt, tasted, smelt, seen, or heard something; and in this way mature, or perfect plans.

While this lawsuit has been going on, judges benevolence, faith, hope, charity, with their venerable firmness and concientiousness, has been hearing these witnesses, and lawyers, at station 8, in angle C. Our lawyers, these human men, occupy all of our fore, side, and back head, known as the crown region, as marked in cuts 2, and 6; making a complete circuit around our chief justice Concientiousness; and completely separating them from our animal witnesses in the base of our head.

Our lawyers now put in an appearance at station 9, in angle D, and with their accumulated evidence, that has now grown into proof; their memory that has been concentrated at continuity, now strive to pertect the case. Our surrounded chief Justices with due dignity, pride, and firmness, say stop, or execute the case.

And, if it is to be executed, it is turned over to our executive station 10. in angle D; our animal men; our executing, or protecting officers. This is the long, and the short, of the action of our minds.

A sound, well balanced, free man is an E pluribus unum; that is, out of many united men spring one independent, free man!

Man is double-doubled, that is, we are two men, exactly alike, cemented together; as shown in cuts, 11, and 12. And then, each of these two men have an animal, and a human man, that is not alike in any respect. The animal man with his five physical senses, bring us in immediate contact with the physical universe--with matter. While the human man, with his electrical minds, bring us in immediate contact with the unseen, and hidden forces—with the mystery of things.

The animal man only forms ideas, that is, he perceives, and wonders what it means, they do not compare, calculate, accumulate evidence, and in this way prove all things. The animal man says I am going to do something, and the human man says, hold on, let us ivestigate, and rationaly reason together. Even the brain, and the body, has a vast inward surface, where organs terminate for functions of the mind and the body; and we have but little chance of studying, measuring, or understanding. Bnt, those that are located on the exterior surface, we have a fair chance of investigating.

And from their visible shapes, sizes, qualities, quantities, and general condition, we tell what manner of man you are; and your present condition.

Whether you have a full set of teeth, a full set of bodily and cranial organs, giving out healthy or unhealthey functions.

One organ, or one group of organs, may be diseased, or paralyzed, and fail to act. One ear may be deaf, one eye blind, or one half of us paralyzed, while the other is all right. In this condition, you cannot be moral or good beings. Yet, this is the condition, most favorable to religion!

Man is good, or bad; moral or vicious according to the mixing of things; and especially, according to the mixing of our two grand elementary natures. ☞ Therefore, the moral, and the vicious group of organs is a fallacy! ☜ Morality, virtue, justice, goodness, or viciousness, are only effects-- or the results of this predomimating, or ruling elementary natures. If the animal is in power then the chief justice, Concientiousness decides in favor of an animal standard. So, justice or injustice, is from the same organ.

" Every mental organ is a will unto itself. The impulse or disposition of any mental organ to act, or cause the bodily instruments to do something, is its will, and this is all there is of it. If the organ is powerful, the will will be strong; if several organs co-operate in action, the will [mental action] will be stronger still; and if all of the mental organs [the whole mind] act together,' the "will-power" will be the strongest the individual is capable of exercising."

The practical point of the phrenological explanation is this: We have just as much will as we have mind. We have as many kinds of will as we have mental powers. We have strength of will in any direction just to the extent that the organ of that direction is developed and vigorous.

"We have it in our power, then, to increase will-power where deficient, and diminish it where excessive, by education and training. If one has too much will-power in the direction of Acquisitiveness, let him cultivate Benevolence; if too much combative will, let him cultivate the will of Cautiousness; if the child has overbalancing will in the directon of Destructiveness, do not educate it to shoot birds, and torture grasshoppers, but train it to raise lambs and play with kittens; if the young man evinces too much will for tobacco, keep him away from rowdy companions; if the young lady has a morbid propensity, [and will is desire, and nothing else] for fashionable frivolties, keep her away from trashy novels. In these ways the better nature is developed, the evil tendencies outrooted, and the whole character improved." Trall.

Now, what can you do if the religious theory be true? that a god and a devil, goes for you, just as they did old Job? They tortured him till he cursed the very night that he was concieved! just to try his patience! just to have a little fun! Then they called him a good job, a patient job!

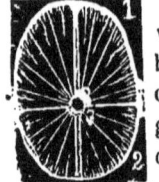

A well formed head is egg-shaped, with the smallest end front, and is about 21 inches in circumference. See cut. We measure the size of the organs by radiating lines from a common center, the medulla oblongata, CUT 14. midway between the opening of the ears, as shown at 3, in cut 14. Figure 1, is the forehead, 2, the back-head, and 3, the memulia oblongata, from where all measurements are made.

The length, breadth, hight, quality, and quantity of healthey brain, in front of the ears, in angle A, cuts 3, 11, 13, and 14, indicates the will-power, or the perceptive power of any, or all of our faculties. They serve all of our organs, and not only generate our will, but, our minds. 2. The length, hight breadth, quality, and quantity of healthey brain in the top of the fore, side, and back-head; our BELT, or CROWN region, indicates the powers of the Perfective, propagating, planing, calculating, remembering, reasoning, and rational judging turn of minds. See cuts 2, 6, 7, 11, 12, and 13. 3. The length, breadth, hight, quality, and quantity of healthey brain in the CENTER of the head, from the medulla oblongata to the top of the head, as is shown in cuts 11, 12, and 13, angle C, station 8, is our FULCRUM upon which hangs the balances of our being. See cuts 4, and 5. It is Conscience; internal or self-knowledge, or a sense of right and wrong; truth; justice; the crowning glory of man; but no beast; and a point of eminent honesty, that but very few men ever attain!

It is the fruit direct from the heart. And as our heart is so completely fortified, and protected, that no impure, or corrupt blood can naturally reach it; just precisley so with our Chief Justices. They are completely surrounded and cut off from our animal minds, if healthey; by our intellectual minds; so as to insure a thorough understanding of any, and all questions, when presented in a healthey, balanced condition.

4. The length, breadth, hight, quality, quntity, of healthy brain between and behind the ears, as is shown in cuts 12, and 13, angle E, station 10, give us our protective, or executive turn of minds; the love for country, home, self and friends. See cuts 2, 3, 6, 7, 11, 12, and 13.

A man may have a high, broad forehad, and a poor perceptive, reasoning and understanding turn of minds, from the fact that the radiatimg lines in front of the ears are short, giving a shallow front brain. Then, a man may have a low narrow forehead, and if it is long in front of the ears, full over the eyes, and long back from the top of the ears, it gives large aspiration, memory, and continuity; such persons may evince a wonderful control, and great power of accumulated book knowledge.

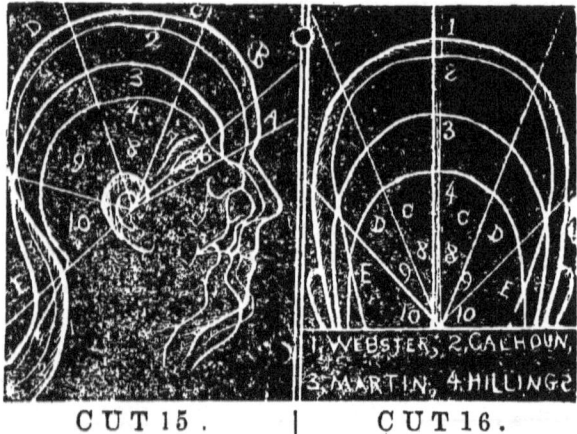

CUT 15. | CUT 16.

Some heads are an inch or more wider from ear to ear than others that measure the same distance from forehead to back-head.—This condition coupled to the above would still be an additional power. For an instance, see cuts 15, and 16; line 1 and 2. There is no very great difference in the front brain of Webster and Calhoun, but in the back-brain, from ear to ear, you see a vast difference. Calhoun lacked executive power; as cut 16, line 2, show.

You may be developed favorable in all of the other portions of the head, and be thin from ear to ear, and short behind the ears, as was Calhoun, and you are of but little force, you are powerless in the hands of such men as Webster and Martin. Again, if you are well developed between the ears, and in the back-head, and short in the front, and top-head, you are lacking in intelligence, but you are full of passion, and animal desire, as was Solomon, Martin, and Hillings.

CUTS 15, and 16, give four historical heads in comparison, that illustrate this subject. 1. Daniel Webster cut 16, outmeasures 2. John C. Calhoun, and Martin, in all of the angles, except Martin the murder, in angle E. Martin being largest developed in this angle it gave him predominating executive tendencies, that led to murder. Webster in cut 16, is largest from ear to ear, but, is balanced by towering far ahead, up in angles A, B, C, and D. See how far through Martin is from his big double chin to his bull of a neck; giving very large executing will-power, just where I have marked it. See cut 2.

Again, great facts are proven with such historical men as Webster, and Calhoun. And one great fact is, that the organs, or minds, that are mostly interested, or in force, or excited, see, or rather, feel, and want every thing their way; brain or no brain; from the fact that human reflection, or rational reason is impossible when unbalanced by nature, by interests, or passions.

Webster and Calhoun with all of their massive brains and soaring intellects, were ruled by party passions; and under such an enslaved condition might commit murder; but would not as apt to be caught, and if caught, would not as likley be punished as a common man, or Martin. Their sagacity of intellect, their party shield, and magnetic control of their fellow man would protect them.

To secure such protection is why we have so many contending, contradicting, obstinate religions, and modes of slavery. Webster was the great champion of the North, while Calhoun was that of the South. They were abject slaves to passions, and party.

For an instance, of such degrading, humiliating, and abject slavery, I would ask, what can be more ridiculous than in a poor little town of 12 or 15 hundred people, and not half of them belonging to any church, yet we hear 5 or 6 tremendous bells thundering forth their deafning peals, all at the same time. Each one of these bells says to all of the other bells— You are sure for hell! You are sure for hell!! You are sure for hell!!! And then only think, that such disrespectful accusations, and self-contradictions, is from, and is upheld by just exactly such massive brains, and towering intellects as Websters and Calhouns. And you are made support them, by law, under outrageous sallaries! Thus you are made to acknowledge them your superior, when in fact they are your inferior!

Again, for an instance of an AWFUL self-contradiction, we have the Jesus-ite religionists, with their Wine and Water Rout to Heaven, and their Blood and Thunder Fire Rout to Hell; all of which is diametrically opposit to, and contradicting to the old Jew-ite Blood and Meat Rout to Heaven.

Then, we have the Mormon's Woman Rout to Heaven, of Increase and Multiply, Replenish, and Subdue the Whole Earth, that is diametrically opposit to, and contradictory to the Shaking-Quakers Die and Freeze-out Rout to Heaven; of a Teetotal abstanence from Woman, Wine, and Song.

And we have the Wesley-ite Methodist Rout to Heaven; which is diametrically opposit to, and contradictory to all this; yes, we have them with their Rampant, Maniacal Screaming, that is also, diametrically opposit to, and contradictory to the Campbell-ite Chaist-ites, with their noisless Believe or be Damed Water-Plunging Rout to Heaven.

☞ Only think, in a town of 12 or 15 hundred people we have, on an average, 8 church slave pens! 5 secret order slave pens! 4 political order slave pens! ☞ You pay taxes, dues, and salaries to these masters, and get nothing! These slaves mope about, in filth, diseases, and rags; whine about hard times; and live in houses that is a disgrace to their masters stables! Yet, these people claim to be free. Their chief master; the president of this nation, gets 125 thousand dollars! He is allowed 15 thousand dollars for stable expenses! Where is the honest man that can earn 15 thousand dollars, for his home?; much less for a stable!

These slave pens are walled around with as massive walls as the great Chinese wall. The stones that compose them are a thousand and one secret oath bound orders, parties, cliques, clans, and churches. Webster, Calhoun, Napoleon, Victora, and others, were mear accidents of these condition, and not brains! And had Mrs. Hillings, and her 8 idiots; or even Aaron's calf been chosen they would have been worshiped the same; brain or no brain!

So, a mother may modle a perfect angel of a child, but it is the slave pens that make him a man, brain or no brain.

It was not any of these cowardly, truckling props that made General Butler the hero of New Orleans; no, it was his massive backbone brain; and goodness of heart!

This nation is run by 60 odd thousand officers. Any of these officers salaries amount to more than a man can earn honestly in a life time! And only think, the people have no voice in the choosing, nor the paying of these officers! And yet, we are told that the people choose their officers, and make their own laws! Why, the people are a-fraid to think, much less talk, and act for themselves! The pope, the preast, the lawyer, the doctor, the politition, and the presiding lord and master does this! This is the Catholic religion, indirectly estabelished.

AndO, how much more chairtable than the Baptist that had some people mad, doomed, and damed for hell! is the Catholics; they even profess to have power to pray these doomtd, and damed, of these uncharitable Baptist out of hell!

To show that graet brains may not give honor, I refer to the great silver fight, that has been going on for months, in our Congress. Speakers holding the floor for nearley nine hours, just to spit spite; causing a session of thirty-eight hours! And this at a time that the people are in great financial distress.

Every group of organs of the brain has their special body organs, or counter-parts. And the functions of the body organs are dependent upon those of the brain, and those of the brain are dependent on those of the body. Dwarfed or diseased lungs, and circulation, or ingestion, give dwarfed or diseased perceptive minds. Such cannot be made believe that they are injuring their health, or they are dieing, until the cold icey hand of death has them. Such are of a cold, low, consumptive temperament.

Dwarfed or diseased digestion, and stomachs give a dwarfed or diseased judgment and reasoning. Such are of a dejected, hysterical, dyspeptic temperament. They suspect evil and destructian when in no danger. They are all the time looking for tne world to come to an awful end.

Dwarfed or diseased liver, heart, and circulation give a dwarfed or diseased firmness, decisive turn of mind. Such are of gouty and a dropsical temperament. Dwarfed or diseased spleen, backbone, and nerves, give a dwarfed or diseased defensive, executive, and a cowardly timid temperament.

CUT 17.

Special organs can be specified; and for an instance, I will say, castration destroys amativeness, and impairs the domestic minds. sharpens and intensifies the executive disposition.

Sever the nerve of taste and you at once destroy alamentiveness. The stomach soon looses its functions and the body perish.

CUT 18.

TEMPERAMENT is mans born type, a foreordained, or predestined organization. There are  three that is natural and many that are unnatural. 1st The Animal; 2nd. The Human; and 3rd. The Blended; are natural, and if balanced, and healthey, they predispose to health and happiness.

CUT 19. | CUT 20. |

Cuts 17 and 18 represent the Blended Temperament. We give you the bust, and full length figure likeness. All parts of the body are in good proportion to themselves, and to each other; no one feature, nor organ, seem to dominate the others in size, and power. Such persons are graceful in motion, agreeable in manners, and move with ease; they are loving, and lovable.

Mind you, that a well blended organization, or temperament is so happily constructed that they can easily adapt themselves to all reasonable conditions.

While the pure | CUT 21. | CUT 22.
Animal, and the pure Human, and ALL others cannot; for they are predestined, in and for a certain NARROW limit. This limit is effectual as is sex! You can no more change a mans' born organization, or temperament, into another than you can change a man into a woman! You may improve and controle them; but, because a frog has hands like a mans, and loves, and hugs his wife, is no reason that man was once a frog, and that the sur-

vival of the fittest, changed him into a man.

So, of a parrot, because a parrot can curse is no reason you should believe him human, and that man was once a parrot. So when you find that the animal organs, or minds predominate you will find that the animal disposition, or will is boss; brain or no brain; education or no education; religion or no religion. This is what makes the animal temperament. See cnts 8, and 19.

If the human brain predominate, you will find a more human-like shaped body, or temperament, and disposition. See cuts 9, 20, and 22.

And when all is well balanced, it gives us a well shaped appearance, and they possess the happy condition of a Blended Temperament. See cuts 10, 17, and 18. All the rest, as the lymphatic, cut 19; the sanguin, cut 20; the billious, cut 21; the nervous, cut 22; are unnatural, unbalanced and predispose to misfortune, misery and disease.

A temperament is a physiological, a phrenological, and a anatomical condition. They are usually spoken of as if governed holy by physiognomy. They even speak of the color of the skin, eyes, hair, etc., as a sign of temperament. When this relates to the races; and has nothing to do with temperament. A black or a white man may be of the same temperament; and just so of a white and a black hog; or any animal.

As I understand it, I give three that is founded on our physiological, phrenological, and anatomical difference. They are natural, and do not interfear with our health, nor predispose us to disease; at any period of life. 1st. The Animal temperament is indicated by the predominancs of the more vital bodily organs, as the bones, marrow, fat muscles, lungs heart, stomach, and bowels. Giving a extra plump and well proportioned body. Such persons can be fattened. 2nd. The Human is indicated by a slight predominance of brain, nerve, lymph, and tissue. They are of a spare, plump, slender body, with an over average head. Such cannot be fattened, but bloated. And 3rd. The Blended, which is a well proportion of all the bone, marrow, nerve, brain, muscles, and bodily organs, so as to give a plump' stout, large, firm, and well proportioned head and body. Neither too slender, too fat, lean, nor bloated.

The Temperaments as usualy given are those very marked diseased tendencies, or conditions of our organization, as the sanguin; caused from a surplus of blood; phlegmatic, caused from a surplus of phlegm; billious, caused from a surplus of yellow bile; melancholic, caused by a surplus of black bile; and the nervous, from a surplus of brain, nerve, and excitability.

These five diseased conditions have become the rule, while the healthey conditions; or temperaments are the rare exceptions. What can illustrate this more graphicaly than to call to your mind the emotional, insane temperament of the Irish, and the Negro people. The Irish, and the Negro type, and temperament, is as familliar as is the black and white pictures of the full moon; and are as easily portraid, and interpred; and it invarably indicates emotional insanity. That is, as a people they are insane! Their history proves this.

Precisley so of the Jews, or the John Bull type and temperament. It is as familiar as is the new or old moon; and as easily pictured; and it invariably represents an instable and treaterous temperament! While that of the Yankee, or American Indian type, give us a more happy union, a better balance in body, brain, mind, and features. They come nearer representing a normal, healthey, or a well balanced condition, or temperament.

THE HEART and THE HEAD.
WHAT the HEART said to the HEAD.

Since declaring in these pages against a class of brain for moral organs of the mind; declaring that morality was a well balanced being— that is, it is the sum totle of the whole agreeing being. I find Jefferson had attempted an explanation; yet, he misst it. Morality consists in a well balanced heart and a well balanced brain; then, they must balance each other, before you are a rational, sane, upright moral being. This is what the head and the heart both agreeing together say.

[a] The lion, the tiger, and the hyena, have more heart than brain, and are governed by their hearts, yet, where are their feelings of sympathy, benevolence, gratitude, justice, love, and friendship? Just precisely so with man: the less head, and the more heart the greater the brute! The heart is subject to the advice of the brain, and without it, it is full of error and ingratitude! I below give Jefferson's article. Ed.

RESPECT for you has induced me to enter into this discussion, and to hear principles uttered that I detest and adjure. Respect for myself now obliges me to recall you into the proper limits of your office. When Nature assigned us the same habitation, she gave us over it a divided empire. To you she allotted the field of science; to me that of morals. When the circle is to be squared, or the orbet of a comet to be traced, when the arch of greatest strength or the solid of the least resistance is to be investigated, take up the problem; it is yours: Nature has given me no cognizance of it.

In like manner, in denying to you the feelings of sympathy, of benevolence, of gratitude, of justice, of love, of friendship, she has excluded you from their controle [a]. To these she has adapted the mechanism of the heart. Morals were too essential to the happines of man to be risked on the uncertain combination of the head; she laid their foundation, therefore, in sentiment, not in science. The former she give to all, as necessary to all; the latter to a few only, as sufficing with a few.

I know, indeed, that you pretend authority to the sovereign control of our conducts in all its parts; and a respect for your grave saws and maxims, a desire to do what is right, has sometimes induced me to conform to your counsels. A few facts, however, which I can readily recall to your memory, will suffice to prove to you that Nature has not organized you for our moral direction.

When the poor wearied soldier whom we overtook at Chickahominy, with his pack on his back, beged us to let him get up behind our chariot, you begun to calculate that the road was full of soldiers, and that if all should be taken up, our horses would fail in their journey. We drove on, therefore. But soon becoming sensible you had made me do wrong, that, though we cannot relieve all the distressed, we should relieve as many as we can, I turned about to take up the soldier, but he had entered a bypath, and was no more to be found, and from that moment to this I could never find him out to ask forgiveness.

Again, when the poor woman came to ask charity in Philadelphia, you whispered that 's   'red like a drunkard, and that half a dollar was enough to give her for the ale-house. Those who have no disposition to give, easily find reasons why they ought not to give. When I sought her out afterward, and did what I should have done at first, you know that she employed the money immediatly toward placing her child at school.

If our country, when pressed with wrongs at the point of the bayonet, had been governed by its heads instead of its hearts, where would she have been now? Hanging on a gallows as high as Haman's You began to calculate and to compare wealth and numbers: we threw up a few pulsations of our blood; we supplied enthusiasm against wealth and numbers; we put our existence to the hazard when the hazard seemed against us, and we saved our country! In short, my friend, as far as my recollection serve me, I do not know that I ever did a good thing on your suggestion or a bad one without it. I do forever, then, disclaim your interference in my province.—JEFFERSON.

Now, if I am correct, Jefferson and all up to my day have been educating man wrong; and I think I am correct; and that mankind will eventually see that I am correct. That is, you had better think thrice before you give or fight once.

PRACTICAL ECONOMY.

Carrie May Ashton.

" Economy will always pay;
  The man who saves is wise;
He who is content with mush to-day,
  Will some day eat mince pie."

As we journey through life we often wonder why it is that some are always poor while others not only make a comfortable living but are always laying up something for rainy days, and still others are amassing wealth. Wherein lies the difference?

A certain class of people, whom we will designate as crokers, are always wishing that the nation's wealth might be equally distributed between its people. If such a thing were possible would it be practical? How long, think you, woul the real estate and personal property remain in equal division? Just so long as the world stands we will have the rich and the poor with us!

If in good times as well as hard ones economy was carfully practiced, there would be less likelihood of hard times, and when they did come we would be better able to meet them. The great fault of a large number of our Americans is that they live up every cent of their income, and when the husband or father is thrown out of employment they know not which way to turn.

In answer to my questions of inquiry a few weeks ago in regard to the hard times, a bright little woman said:—"Why, no, I have hardly noticed the hard times, although I have had but little work all summer. I have always made it a duty to save something every year, which I have carfully invested for a rainy day. This [1893-4] seems to be the rainy day, and now, while others are wondering and worrying over the times, I am taking life easy and have a good rest, so that I can be ready for work when it comes."

A widow, and the mother of four daughters, who was left penniless and alone fifteen years ago, has earned a good living by baking for parties, weddings and sociables. Oh, that more people might look at life in a similar manner.

Another illustration is that of a family of seven who have never saved anything, and it has been with great difficulty that they have managed to get through the past few months. The husband and the father is a good workman when sober, but unfortunately he is out of work and is not likly to get a position very soon, as there are several applicants to every position, and the sober, industrious hands will be hired first.

ECONOMY does not mean STINGINESS, as some people seem to think, but it does mean a careful watchfulness in gathering up the fragments, so that nothing is wasted, as well as judicious buying.

A plentiful and a nutricious diet is absolutely necessary for the well-being of every individual, but it may be at the same time simple and inexpensive. It is poor economy to scrimp the table in order to furnish the house elegantly or to buy fine raiment. We Americans would do well to take lessons of the French, who, it is said, can live on what many of us throw away. Many of their dinners, which consists of a soup, roast, or a stew, with vegetables and a pudding, it can be bought for a france, which in our money is about twenty cents.

The only way to live economically is to adopt the cash system, and buy nothing but what can be paid for at the time. There will be no danger of running in debt then, and it is an acknowledged fact that the merchants who sell for cash can afford to sell cheaper than those who use the credit system.

The woman who does her own marketing instead of trusting to others or giving orders at the door, generally saves much by so doing.

In buying meats, the judicious housewife who desires to set a good, wholesome table for a small amount, must necessarily pass the juiciest steaks and the best roasts by and select less expensive cuts. A nice broiling piece of beef of three or four pounds will make a good dinner and leave plenty for cold slicing, croquetts, and stew. A large soup bone is sufficient for a generous amount of soup, and enough meat will come off the bones for the next day's hash and stew. Cow's liver can be had for the asking, and calve's liver is inexpensive, and can be cooked in seveal different ways so that it is appetizing. Dried beef can be choped and cooked with scrambled eggs or omelet, or served with a milk gravy.

Codfish ball are delicious for breakfast when carefully prepared. Potatoes can be served in various ways so that they are whoelsom and dainty. Cornmeal and oat-meal mush, served with milk, syrup or gravy, fried, baked, or sweetened, flavored and baked into a pooding or custerds. Batter-cakes, hocakes, jony-cakes, ash-cakes, flitter-cakes, muffins, etc., will afford a great variety, and on short notice.

THE CHART.   A physical and mental chart of the author J. Fletch. Woodward, M, D.

THIS CHART is made out by the directions for such given on page 182. The first, and the main question is, what does, or will controle, or rule this man? That is, is he the boss? or is he the bossed? and if so, how and why?

CUT TWENTY-THREE.

CUT 24 gives us 30 odd historical heads for our perception, comparison, reasoning decision, and perfecting disposition. To see if my theory of mind as is manifested in man is true, as is given on page 183, cuts 2 and 3. Figure 1 and 2 in cut 24, like cuts 11, 12, and 13, on page 196, being your guide for measurment.

1st. His square shoulders and beard says he not only is a man but takes after his father. According to cut 2, his likenesses in cut 23, shows good perceptive minds, simelar to figures 4, 6, 7, and 28, in cut 24. Width, fullness, length or depth of angle A, as is shone in cut 2, 11, 13, and 15, are second if not best. His perfective, propagating, or creative minds are deep as is shown at cut 2, 11, and 13. Angle B seems to be deep and wide as is seen in his 1 and 2 likenesses, in cut 23. Similar to figures 4, 5, 8, 11, 20, 27, and 24, in cut 24. And if

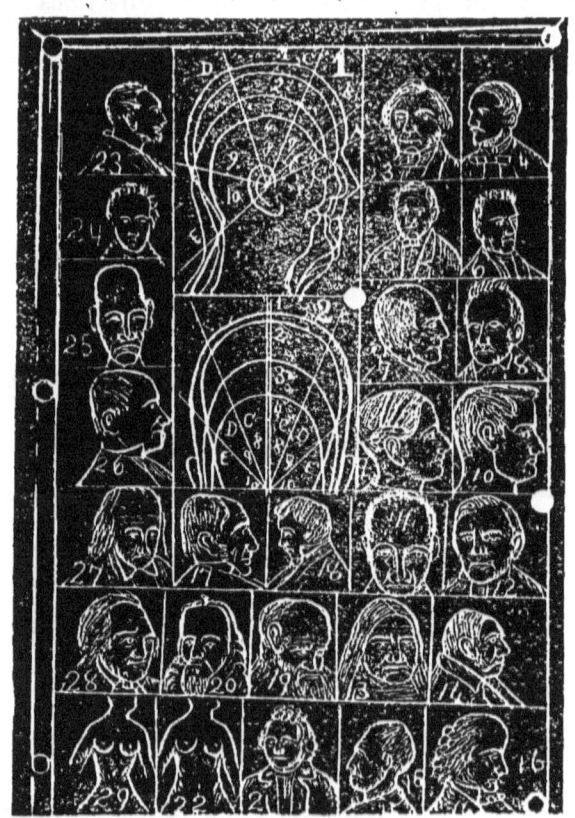

CUT TWENTY-FOUR.

not under undue excitement, or controle, it will always enable him to see, compare, and to say hold on to his perceptive minds, let me see, and compare things. How? Why, by induction, thats how. By a regular lawsuit. And while these animal men are collecting and comparing evidence, his reasoning mental minds in angle C, stands first best, according to his likenesses, in cut 23, and give him great mental power, and especially in firmness and concientiousness. So, it is these wedge shape angles C that runs and controles this man. Similar to figures 4, 6, 7, 8, 9, 11, 19, 20, 27, and 24, in cut 24. See the great fulcrum angle C, in cut 24, figures 1 and 2. It is good.

His accumulative and retaining minds in angle D, are good, giving him a decisive turn of mind, and keep him posted, and it is no fault of theirs if his protective or excutive minds, in angle E, does not see the case clear, and act accordingly.

Then, if your executing minds does not act with full force it is no fault of quantity, but, circumstantial surroundings. See figures 2, 3, and 4, in cut 23. Yet, the second point to be considerd, is his organic quality, and it is only moderate, leaving all of this mental construction beholding to a feble, relaxed, and oft a sickly animal nature. Hence, his mental natures wishes and tries to rule and to controle him, but, do they? thats the mooted question. He is so happily balanced as to redily addapt himself to conditions and circumstances, and to allow none to be monarch of all they survey.

He is nearly a pure white American, from Albino, Anteek or Irish ancestors. He has lived fifty odd years a life of active adventures, and exposure from Chili to the Emerald Isles. A perpetual student of the medical science and the photo-art. This is his education, and although born in, and trained to the pie hunting Christian creeds and superstitions, of " follow me and I will make you fishers of men." Yet, he never believed them, nor embraced or joined them! His two natures are so near a balance as to enable him to easily gratify either! Yet, his predisposition to disease makes all very, very uncertain. Yet, he has that happy combination that give us that balanced or blended temperament as is mentioned on page 206. But his organic quality being defective this gives him rather an iritable temperament. Health is uncertain when the organic quality has been injured.

Your brain in your head over balances that of the body, this still makes health and happiness very, uncertain. His head measures 22 inches round, 15 ihches from nose to neck, and 14½ inches from ear to ear; which would be a good head if well favored; while his body is only 112 pounds of bone, muscle, nerve, blood, lymph, water and gristle; and with a decided predominance of bone and gristle.

Now, comes our 11th proposition, his present occupation and station in this life. Your formation backed by experience says, use all and abuse none! For it is the fool or the unbalanced person that never improves, yields, bends, compromises, nor tries to change. Change! change! is one of the eternal laws of your nature.

Vitativeness, or physical endurance, in this man has been great, and then it has been nurtured and sustained by large cautiousness, firmness, and a patient continuity. They have nurtured and sustained him through these long years of sickness, misfortune and adventures. And by keeping the body well rested by sleep, nourished by food, cleansed inside and out with plenty of soap and water, balanced by fire and clothing. And by not delaying for to-morrow that which is needed to-day, and by pounding the iron when at the welding-heat. That is, he eat, drank, and enjoyed specially to live, and did not mearly live to eat, drink, and to enjoy. And he now finds that those who jeered, and scoffed at this in their youth, by saying : "I am going to live while I do live," he finds that they have, like the leaves of autumn, they have fallen to the ground by the million!!! and are now untimely unnecessarly, and unnaturaly composing the sod that he now walks upon, and still he enjoys life at a good old age!

ANALYSIS OF CUT TWENTY-FOUR.

FIGURE 1 and 2 are explained on page 202, figure 3 Sue, a Jew novelist, that wrote the wandering Jew, and said to be like Butler, a great beast.

Fig. 4 represents Winship, the strong man; 5 that of Hall the jolly business man, full of vitality, life and trade; 6 is that of Campbell the author and religious reformer; 7 Burges the soaring orator; 8 is Webster the lawyer, mentioned on page 201; 9 that of the good Queen Victoria of England; 10 Bomba the brutal King of Italy; 11 the intelligent Negro Eustache who saved his master from being massacreed; 12 Yankee Sulivan the pugilist; 13 an Indian woman; 14 a brutal clown; 15 Porta a learned mathematition; 16 the thinker; 17 authority; 18 submission; 19 Gallileo the philosopher; 20 Lord Bacon, the criminal, see page 301; 21 Putnam, one of our revolutionary fathers; 22 a natural and 29 a unnatural waist; 23 Emerson an idiot; 24 Clark a poet; 25 Goose the giver; 26 the bachelor; 27 Bishop White, just the opposit to Sulivan; and 28 Govno Morris the observer, whoes angle A, the perceptives minds are the largest of all our figures.

Sue, Hall, and Putnam are of a decided animal temperament, while Clark, White and Bacon are of a decided mental or human temperament. While Winship, Campbell, Burges, Victoria and Morris are more of a balanced or a blended temperament. While all the rest are of an unbalanced temperament, that is, they either have too much animal or too much human vigor. See page 190 to 196. And I think Solomon and myself proves what I teach. All the preachers, all the teacheas and all the gods and devils of christendom could not change us.

☞ Now, the object of this chart is not to change any one of these mens natures or temperaments into that of the other. That is, to make a lion from a lamb. No, but its objects are to show you the best way to find out what you are, and the best way to nurture and controle it.

Remember, we claim only two independent natures for man. The union of two seperate, or independent natures make man; they are the physical matter and the intelligent mind. We claim that mind is mind, and that it neither increases, grows changes, diminishes, nor dies. That when we say grow— we mean grow the animal body so that the mind can manifest itself. Men are frequently born educated, or developed, and especially so in certain things, as was blind Tom in music; or Ray in calculation, and Edmonds in painting.

In choosing a wife, choose as sound, cheerful and agreeable one as is possible, not coresponding to your self, no, but one with as near a balanced organization, temperament and education as is possible. Agreeing in religion and privilages.

CUT 25. OLLIE, | VERA, | and JIM CORBUTT.

When Corbutt, the catholic pugilist, married the protestant Ollie Lake, a California justices joined them, but hellow, his people made them re-marry, and a catholic priest did the work. This was treassn! And I cut the account out and pasted it in my book of self-contradictions, saying to my wife they would separate So they did and religion done it! The next news is she gets a divorce and then Corbutt marries an actress. Cut 25 gives their likeness. Jim, Ollie and Vera. Vera said a lawyer married us, Jim said a notary, then Vera replied he shore had a license and looked solmn enough.

And if they will let religion, and religious cranks alone they can play, act and box through life happily and all right.

They are of a decided human temperament, with good organic quality. Jim's predominating quality is that of bone, sinue, blood and muscle; Ollie's is that of nerve, blood and muscle; while, Vera's is brain, nerve and lymph. Vera's large, wide, high and deep fore and side head, gives her a wonderful creative, or perfective angle. They are very large compared to Jim's or Ollie's, Jim is entirely too thin in the side head for a successful pugilist, or manager. Vera can out manage or out calculate. He is too much on the Jackass, stubborn order, while Ollie was just as obstinate, and then fired with a hot nervous blood. Vera is the best balanced— and is a shrewd, successful manager, similar to Queen Victoria.

CUT 26. MAD, GLAD | and BLIND TOM.

PHYSIOGNOMY Or to read man by his physical signboard, is the first and the oldest cultivated science, and to picture it was the first art. And to thwart this, and to deceive, and mislead you was the first work of the cautious, cunning, secretive natures of man. Our original Anteek fathers were principally governed by the physical signs that was presented to them through their five senses, or the perceptive minds. Primitive man was mostly developed in this region; from the fact it was most needed. To see, and to recieve impressions, to acquire physical facts were first. Then man gradually developed to compar, reason, use, construct, secrete, and to store away for future use, away in their memory, and aided by picture-graphic hiercglypic illustrations. They named things from their physiognomy; as Incus the inclosed, the inner man, their main chief, Black-hawk, Big-thunder, Billey-bow-legs, pale-faced, two-faced, etc.

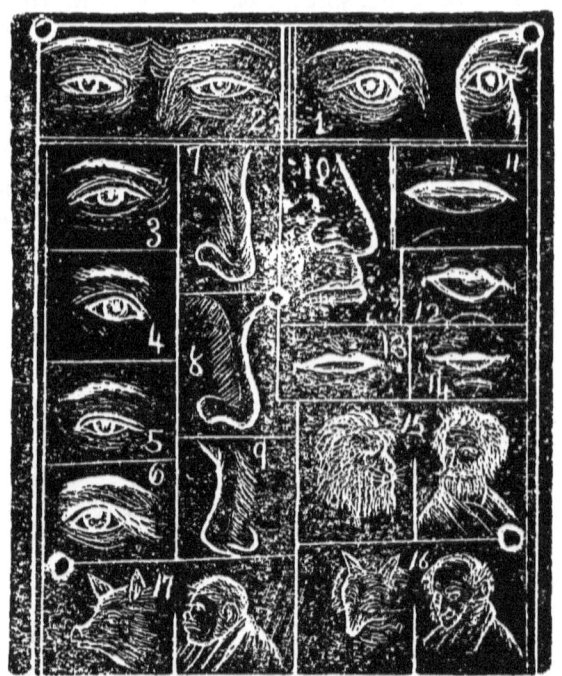

CUT TWENTY--SEVEN.

CUT 26 forcibly illustrates this. Look at Mad, his mouth and features turn down, and he is of a mad, ill, gloomy, energy or force. Turn up Glad, look at him, his mouth and features turn up and this indicates he is of a cheerful energy or force. This fact is the successful secret to an artist. He can make his pictures to appear cheerful, impudent defiant, sad or glad, old or young just by the turn of the features.

CUT 27, figure 1, is the large, full convexed, or ox eye. It indicates strength, activity, affection, and is very susceptible to impressions.

Figure 2, the squinting, or fox eye, that does not forget, forgive, trust, nor confide in any body, but shrewd and piercing, and apt to resort to dishonest means, and will resist to death all intrusions.

Fig. 3, the well proportioned, normal or balanced eye It indicates a thoughtful agreeable turn of of mind, and fond of solid pleasure.

Fig 4, the full, fat eye. It overflows with love and sparkles with tenderness, is inclined to be true and bright, and is near a perfect eye.

Fig. 5, the small, squinting, treacherous eye, it inclines to make love to all mearly to deceive.

Fig. 6, the blubbery curtained eye. It is a licentious eye that is not apt to respect virtue, chastity nor life.

Color of the eyes, they say, controles in certain ways, as when black they are more inclined to intence love or hate, while blue makes them milder, and if hazle, more cheerful and agreeable, while a yellow eye is cruel, and a red or gray eye is of a cool calculating turn of mind.

Figure 7, the camel-back or humped-up nose is said to be born to command, that it indicates self reliance and self will, and a combative disposition.

Figure 8, the normal or perfect nose, and can be more depended on.

Figure 9, the turned up nose indicates a quick feeling, thought and action, and are more liable to take an offense. If the tip is sharp with thin lips look out for a neruous scold, while a pug or a bottle nose is of a low sot order.

Fig. 10, the drop-snoot nose indicates selfishness, and inclined to be treacherous and dishonest. The stiff upper lip indicates not only firmness but obstinacy and inclined to cruelty.

Fig· 11, the very common vulgar mouth and˜indicates a poor organic quality.

Fig. 12, is a well proportioned, solid or balanced

mouth, and indicates such a state of mind.

Fig. 13, the firm set mouth and belongs to mean, stingy persons. It indicates great self control, and not apt to indulge in dissipation.

Fig. 14, is the daisy mouth and indicates fun, and is liable to excesses.

Some people are good and industerous and work their way through the world. They are lion-like, fearless and bold, and resemble a lion as figure 15. Others are lazy beasts and hog their way through like figure 17. While others are smart Alecks and lie, steal, murder and beat their way through like a fox as in figure 16. See page 188.

The hands, and even the balls of the thumb, it is said, tells our character. That no two are alike in form or in their lines. Their form and their lines, it is said, tell of your past, present and future. That certain lines in the palm of your hand indicates the condition of the head, heart, and body, and in fact, in this way foretells or guesses at your conditions, wills and tendency. Just what a physician calls his diagnosis and prognosis And one is as reasonable, beneficial or as correct as the other.

That no person whoes life-line was short, weak and broken ever lived a long or healthy life. That no one whose heart-line was weak or wanting, ever amounted to much, or become a person of independent judgement; and no one whoes heart-line was missing or very much broken up ever made a happy marriage. See cut 28.

The length of the line of life indicates probable age you may live. Each bracelet gives you thirty years of probable life. A well marked line of head denotes brain power. A clear line of fortune, fame, or riches, mean your probable success in life. And a distinct line of heart bespeaks tenderness and love. A straight line of fate indicates peaceful life, while the indistinct or crooked line the reverse. A well defined line of health is favorable to health and success; while indistinctness indicates the reverse. The girdle of Venus well-marked indicates the blues and ill health. The mount of Jupiter bespeaks ambition; that of the Sun, love of splendor; that of Saturn, prudence; Mars, courage; Moon, immagination; Venus, love of pleasure; and Mercury, that of intilligence.

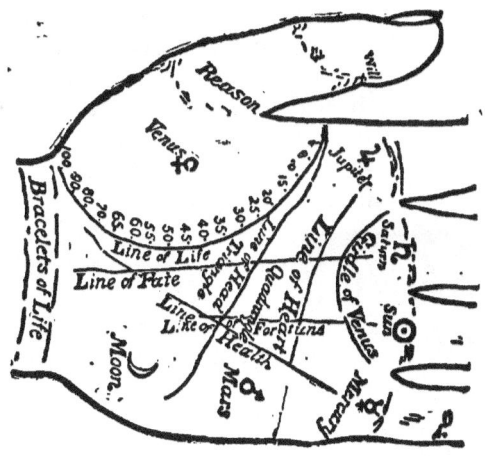

CUT TWENTY--EIGHT.

The shape of the hand indicates character. If it is disproportionally small it indicates a weak character. If large, the person is of a strong will, especcially if the first joint is well developed. If the second joint is longest the reasoning abilities are good.

And so of the fingers, which are of two kinds as the Spatula shaped fingers, and denoting material desires. The pointed or psychic, that tend to mental or divine things. Large joints indicate a philisophic turn of mind; and rounded ends a talent for art A slim, thin hand bespeaks a weak temperament, a feeble immagination, and but little force of character· If the palm is longer than the fingers it indicates sensuality, gluttony and material things. Short thick hands with large thumbs are of a covetous desire for riches. A dry hard hand denotes energy, and a soft one tenderness, and a dislike for work. A fleshy, thick palm denotes a long life, so does knitting of the joints and a hollow palm. A thin, hard dry palm indicates timidity and want of energy. A thick clumsy one denotes disappointment. The weary lines, islands, stars, and crosses that gash, carve and figure your hands tells your character the same as words in a book. If numerous, plain, and deep this indicatis long and continued trouble and weary. In fact, they are but leaves in the book of God or Nature!

Short fingered persons are quick and impulsive, while long fingers denote more caution. And thick, heavy, short fingers indicate cruelty. A large quadrangular thumb means honesty; a large triangle, speaks generosity; a long first division indicates a strong will, while a long second division indicates reasoning abilities.

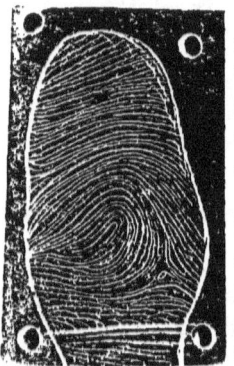

Large nails, bluish in color, indicates a poor circulation. Thin nails if small indicates energy and ill health. Fluted curved nails indicates consumption.

Cut 29, is a correcct engraving of the ball of right thumb of the author; printed from pressing the inked thumb on the block, making a picture of it and then engraving of it.

CUT TWENTY-NINE. | It is said to be as good a way of identifying a prisoner as his likeness, and has long beed so used in older nations.

Moses' god, and he got him in Egypt, and all religionist's gods are fine examples of physiognomy. See their images, pictures, acts and demands. Just behold them before your mind for one short moment, in their true light. They are gods of jealousy, hate, cruelty, revenge, murder, sin, suffering, craziness, crime and destruction! They murdered all the children of Egypt just for fun! Ex. xii, 29; 35. This is Moses' and Jesus' idea of dispensing justice, and examples left for religionists to follow! Yes, their god Jesus says follow me ind I will make you fishers and haters of men! Matt. iv, 19. And to do this you must HATE, yes, hate your father, mother, brother, sister, wife and children so saith the Christian's god at Lu. xiv, 26.

HATE—yes, hate, thats the feeling of a Christians heart! and that is the sneeking expressions of their face, from the first accused expressions down to the last, which is the receiving of this hating spirit of their Jesus. See their expressions as pictured below. O! how often I have seen them!

CUT 30. 1 the Accused, 2 the Convicted, 3 the Pardoned, and 4 the Pardoner!

Thus sayeth the Lord God of Israel, slay every man his brother, neighbor, and companion, why? Ex. xxxii, 27. He tells them to sell the dead carcus of animals to thy neighbor, Deut. xiv, 21. To kill all excep the women children, why? Num. xxxi, 18. Now, as I have all along proven religion to be a dangerous crazines, I will leave these four illustrations for your consideration.

FIGURE 1, CUT 30, gives you a correct idea of the first symptoms of this crazy disease called religion. They call it penitent, or considering the accusation that you are as mean as hell, and sure to land in hell if you dont 'git ligion,' that is, if you dont get this hating spirit of this bulldozing pie hunting fishers of men! Fig. 2, gives you the expressions of this penitent, as a 'seeker' mourning, yelling, acknowledging that he is as mean as hell! and begging this man god to forgive and save him!

Fig. 3 graphically pictures to you the expressions of a convert, shouting, raving mad! Proclaiming! to the world that now he 'ant as mean as hell, no, but better than anybody! yes, as good as God!'

Fig. 4, is a correct likeness of that pie hunting, hateing Jew, that fisher of man! Upon him they rest their hope of forgiveness, for any and all murder, rape, and all hellish crimes! Great god what a mistake, what a delusion and what an imposition!

AN AWFUL SELF--CONTRADICTION, ILLUSTRATED.

WE GIVE this just to prove by physiognomic pictures what an awful crazy self-contradicting set these gods, devils and bible makers were!

IN the next cut, figure 1, is Parson Nick, better known as the Devil. It represents him when a young man, before being mobed, cursed and abused by his brothers, Jove and Mike, the Christian's gods in heaven, and as he appeared an exile in Eden, as a missionary, and learned Eve her first sense, manners and goodness. Saying: "Brother Jove and Mike knows when you eat this apple that you will become as gods—knowing good and evil." See Gen. iii, 5. See figure 1 in cut 31.

Figure 2, is Parson Nick, the Devil, after being cursed and abused by his jealous, hating brothers, Jove and Mike, that drove him out of Eden, for learning Eve some sense, manners and goodness! They said with oathes!—"You SHALL eat dust and CRAWL on your belly ALL your life!" See Gen. iii, 14; and figure 2, in cut 31.

Figure 3, is parson Nick, this 'cust' snake of a Devil, not on his belly as he was always to appear, no, but, as these liars have him appearing among the Sons of God WALKING, not crawling, and at a feast to eat 'goodies' not dust. See Job, the bad job at that, first chapter and the seventh verse!

CUT 31, figure 1 Eve and the Devil, figure 2 the 'cust' crawling Devil, figure 3 the walking Devil.

> He 'cust' the world, Eve and ALL!
> He 'cust' the Devil I'm sure,
> Swaring: "he shall always crawl!
> For King Jim's bible says so!
> Gen. iii chapter, 14. verse·
>
> Then they have him up walking!
> Walking 'up and down' I,m sure!
> With the Christian Lord a talking!

For King Jim's bible says so !
See Job, 1 chapter, 7 verse.

If this a'nt contradiction,
  What is contradiction sure?
Or are you a fool for knaves?
  Thats' the question we ask you !
See Uncle Sam's bible sir.

  This is self-contradiction !
    Horrid contradictions sure !
  With chapters and verse pictured
    From your King Jim's bible sir !
  See Uncle Sam's bible sir.

Their gods were all AWFUL he's,
  Never a she among them,
They made their mother a SLAVE !
  And themselves an awful knave !
For King Jim's bible says so !

  Never a she among them,
    And my God— mother Nature,
  Was never thought of by them ;
    But cruel, cruel deeds were—
  Their soul was a drugged gizzard !

They come not with peace, but fire !
  A sword ! and hateful feelings ;
To BUTCHER ! and to incite !
  Man to awful bad doings !
For King Jim's bible says so !

  See Matthew, their first witness, at x, 34 ; and Luke, their third witness, at xii, 49 !

THE SUPPOSED WHEREABOUTS OF SOME OF THE ORGANS THAT MAKE AND MAN-IFEST OUR MINDS

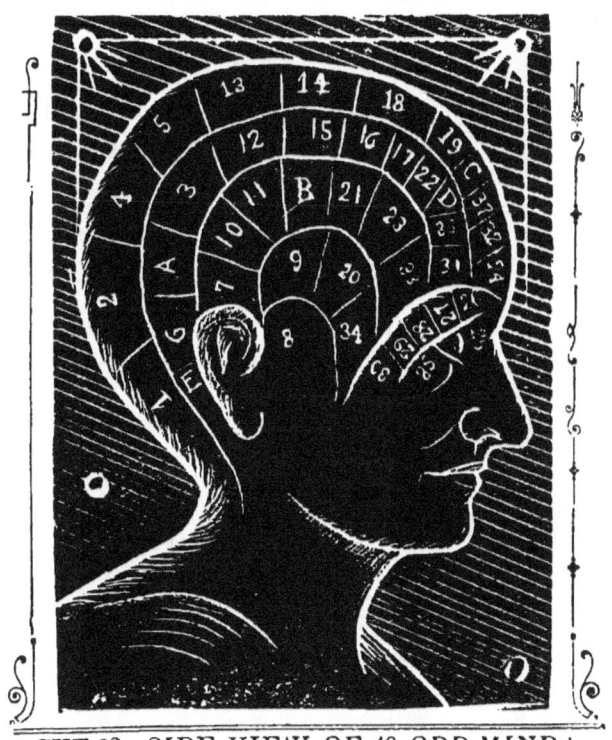

CUT 32. SIDE VIEW OF 40 ODD MINDS.

A definition of their normal and abnormal tendencies Illustrated by three slate cuts. Cut 32, give us a map of the side view that give us the home of most, if not all the mental organs, that manifests certain minds. And as some have a league of space and some none, I reckon this accounts for their appearance or non appearance in some specific spot. Although some doctors say it depends upon the stuffing that your cranium is stuffed with. And both are right. Many, many good formed heads may not have a dozen good organs or minds in it. But all is gristle, water or stuffing. The present mode of party raising and education is a wretched mode of stuffing.

FIGURE 1, Amativeness, for instance, is said to be in that part of our animal brain, and that it manifests sexual love. Abuse—too often to the ruin of health and character.

Figure A, 1½ Conjugal love, the mateing or marring desire. Abuse— none, all or any body lord.

Fig. 2, Child-love, a love for children, old people, pets and animals. Abuse—spoiling of them.

Fig. 3, Friendship, a love for society. Abuse—a retired hermit disposition; or murdering clans.

Fig. 4, Home, sweet home, a love for country. Abuse— clanishness and conquest.

Fig. 5, Continuity, the store house of occurrences. Abuse—never remember nor record anything N. B. This is the part of the brain that is the mirror that reflects the actions of all the rest. It is the library and storage.

Fig E, or 5½, Love of life, a desire to exist. Abuse— recklessness, cowerdice.

Fig. 6, Courage, resistance, opposition. Abuse—a contentious, fighting and crying disposition.

Fig. 7, Executiveness, protects and gives energy to all the rest. Abuse— violence and murder.

Fig 8, Appetite, a desire for food and drink. Abuse— intemperance and gluttony.

Fig. 9, Acquisitiveness, a desire for money and wealth. Abuse—theft and murder.

Fig. 10, Secretiveness, to hide and to protect. Abuse— deceit, hypercritical, lying.

Fig. 11, Cautiousness, a sense of danger. Abuse-cowerdice and timidity.

Fig. 12. Approbative, a disposition to be agreeable. Abuse— vanity or I dont care.

Fig. 13, Self-Esteem, confidence in self, manliness. Abuse— strutting, gassing, full of conceit.

Fig, 14, Firmness, decision, perseverance, Abuse obstinacy, recklinesa and cowardice.

Fig. 15, Concience, the innate or heart-felt regard for truth and justice. This is the main mental organ. Abuse— brute force, savage customs.

Fig. 16, Hope, anticipation of future good. Abuse—acts without proof, or does wrong that good

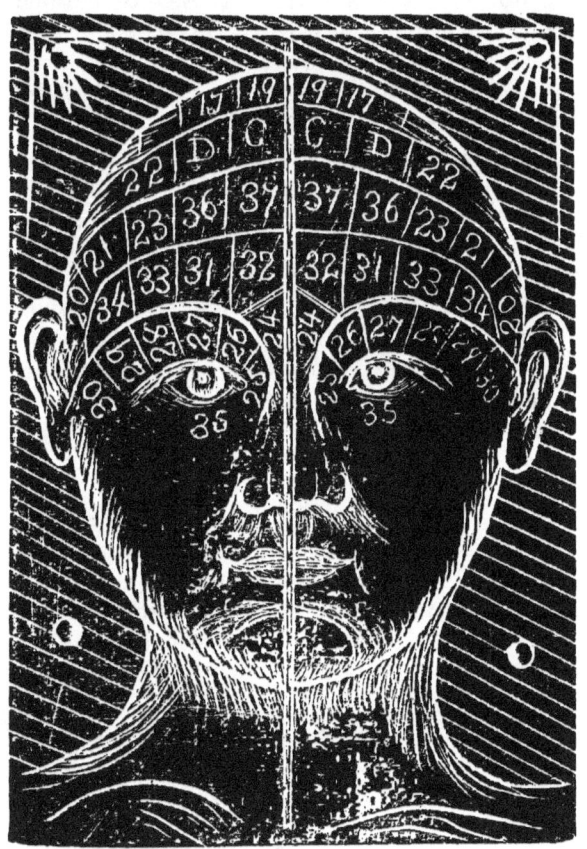

CUT 33. FRONT VIEW. THE HALVES.

may be the result.

Fig. 17, Marvel, to like the strange and the new. Abuse— worship and fear the mysterious.

Fig. 18. Veneration, parental love, respect for age and equals. Abuse— worship and idolatry! They are their god! They know nothing beyond!

Fig. 19, Benevolence, kind, good and obliging. Abuse—a spendthrift or I am the poorest of all.

Fig. 20, Construction, a tact to fix up. Abuse—a multiplicity of fixtures.

Fig. 21, Ideality, a taste for the graceful and beautiful in nature and art. Abuse—an enthusiasm that leads to the devil. This is the trouble with large developed coronal regions!

Fig. 21½, or B, Sublime, a sense of the vast and grand. Abuse—Gassing and building castles in the air whoes foundations rest in hell!

Fig. 22, Imitation, to copy nature. Abuse—to ape or mimic others.

Fig. 23. Mirth, contraction to vanity. Abuse—relaxing to levity and hate.

Fig. 24, Individuality, our chief witness whoes duty it is to see, feel, tast, smell and to heare all. Abuse—trusting to what a supposed Matthew, Mark, Luke or John told some body!

Fig. 25, Form, to tell how one thing differs from another in appearence. Abuse—cannot discover any or but little difference.

Fig. 26. Size, to judge of magnitude and distance. Abuse—over or underrating of facts.

Fig. 27. Weight, to judge of quantity and condition. Abuse—inability to measure or to balance.

Fig. 28, Color, enables us to distinguish the various tints and shadows. Abuse—to call a man white, black or red—for they are not!

Fig. 29, Order, a place for everything. Abuse—too much primping, fixing or none.

Fig. 30, Calculation, the judgeing of the amount of things. Abuse—over or underrating.

Fig. 31, Locality, to judge of a place and its position. Abuse—easily confused and lost.

Fig. 32, Eventuality, the door-way to Continuity, and demauds facts for continuity to record. Abuse—unable to remember or to accumulate evidence until proven.

Fig. 33, Time, remembers dates and time in music. Abuse—have to ask the day of the month, and never on time by agreement.

Fig. 34, Tune, delights in the harmony of sound. Abuse—cannot tell one sound from another.

Fig. 35. Language, the power to express our feelings by words. Abuse—gassing, blowing, or sour.

Fig. 36, Causality, to rationally reason, to knowingly judge the effects and the cause of things.

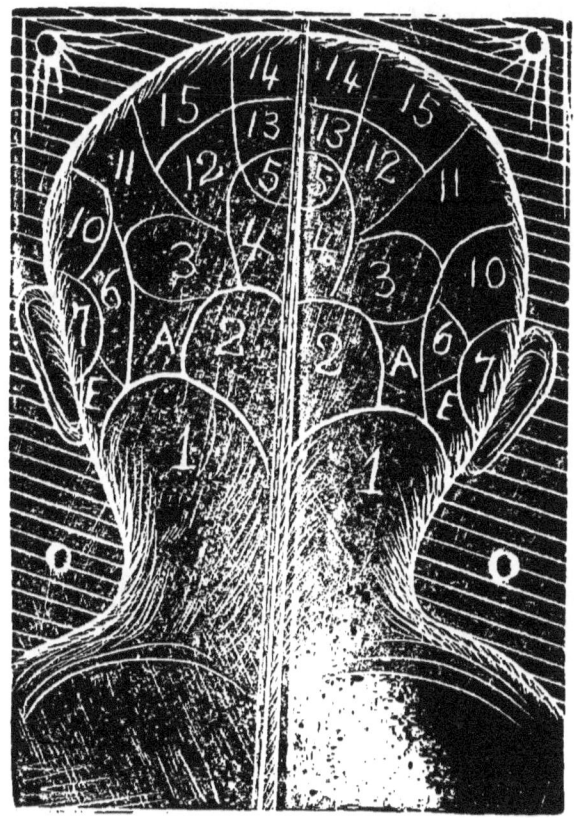

CUT 34. THE REAR HALVES MAPPED.

Abuse—accepts hearsay from madan rumor, or too much speculation or supposition.

Fig. 37. Comparison, reasons reached by actual comparing of things side by side. Abuse—cannot see any difference in the size of a quarter and a half dollar.

Fig. C, or 38, Human Nature, the innate human perception that quickly tells us the thoughts, motives, intentions and capacities of others. Abuse—jealousy, suspicion, murder and mob violence!

Fig, D, or 39. Agreeableness, gives us a quick and lasting acquaintance. Abuse—deception, hypercritical, lying or morose.

FACTS TO REMEMBER— Good heads but bad men! Bad heads but good men! is common. This is caused from the kind of stuffing they have ben stuffed with! They, the Christians have stuffed LIES first in their childrens heads! Telling them that an awful and a terable god made them, and hid them in an old 'hollar stump' where the granny found you, and sold you to mamma! For just as soon as you can hear they read you from the xii, 29, 35 of Ex. where this awful god that made them murdered little children just for fun!

So the first stuffing of good heads scares them a fool and prepares them as fit subjects for anything. So, if you are not born a fool you are soon circumcised, bapsoused or scared into one!

>Moses was found, we are told,
>In a wicker basket sure,
>But you was in an old stump,
>For old granny Hump said so.

ANATOMICAL CUTS ONE, TWO AND THREE.

ALL animals have the power of motion, if not rational reason, from the lowest radiate to the highest vertebrate. All of the varied motions of animal life is due to a peculiar property of the flesh or muscles, termed contractility. Very rarely is motion produced by the action of a single muscle, no, but by the harmonious action of many— aided by brain and nerve, blood and bone. Hence, we have contractors and extensors, pronators and supinators, compressors and stimulators, etc., all blending and harmoniously working together to carry out our predestined organization.

CUT ONE, figure A, shows you a part of the cranium or skull of the forehead removed, leaving the front top of the cerebrum or brain uncovered. The perpendicular center line that seperates them into two independent brains, and then these two independent brains into two halves or an upper and a lower story is better shown in cut two. See, the upper brain has many convolutions or crooked partitions that seperate the brain into many, many independent departments for many, many independent minds.

Figure B, the skin of the face is mearly removed showing the superficial muscles, nerves, veins, arteries and glands of the face. They execute the wills of these many, many minds by gesture, move or expression, and they are termed volentear muscles, that is, they depend upon the will, or the m nd. While figure C, includes a class of inward muscles such as the lungs, heart, liver, stomach, kidneys, veins, nerves, arteries and bowels, that represent the inward man, and incessantly labors on without the will or knowlenge of man! Only think, they never tire!, they need no rest! but, through all of the abuse of years they cherfully continue to contract and to relax, that is, playing hide and seek with the sun, food, drink and air to the last! Yea, they strike the LAST lick for sweet, sweet dear darling life! And who, or what is it that meets them properly half way? But chokes and smothers them to death! This is the key to sweet, sweet, dear darlnig life!

1. The auricula or natural ear, or life-center. 2. Orbicularis palpebrarium, the winking muscle or the circular muscle around the eyes that opens, closes and controles the eyes. 3. Levator labii superioris aleque nasi, a little muscle that rases the upper lip and dilates the nostrils. 4. Levator anguli oris or the smiling muscle. 5. Compressor nasi or the smelling muscle that corrugates the nose and expresses certain passions. 6. Orbicularis oris or the kissing muscle, it surrounds the mouth, it puckers, opens, closes and controls the mouth. 7. Nasalis labii superioris or the sneering muscle, draws down the septum of the nose. 8. Triangularis oris a triangle shaped muscle that connects under lip and the chin. 9. Quadratus labii a square muscle to depress the lower lip. 10. Levator menti, two muscles that draw up the chin and project the lower lip. 11. The masseter or the chewing muscle. 12. Buccinator or the whistleing muscle. 13. Levator angli oris, 14. Zygomaticus minor and 15. Zygomaticus major are smiling muscles and rase the corners of the mouth in smiling. 16. Anterior auris of the ear. 17. The salivary or spit glands. 18. Lachrymal or the tear glands; 19. its canals; 20. its ducts. 21. Porto dura, the hard nerve, or the facial branch of the seventh pair of nerves. 22: Jugular or neck veins as they branch over the face. 23. The carotid or stupefying arteries, that supply the brain with blood.

C. Viscera or the internal organs of the thorax or chest and abdomen. The muscles, ribs, etc., are seen cut through on both sides and removed. The deep arteries, veins and muscles are shown on the left side while the surface muscles, veins, arteries and nerves are shown on the right side of this illustration.

24. Trachea or windpipe· 25. Thyroid oartliage or Adam's apple. 26. Os hyoides the bone to which the windpipe is attatched. 27. Lungs folded back. 28, 29, 30. The upper the middle and the lower lobes of the right lung. 31, 32, The upper and the lower lobes of the left lung. 33. Heart. 34 Right auricle; 35. left auricle; 36. right ventricles of heart. 37. Pulmonary artery. 38. Right pulmonary artery. 39. Left pulmonary artery. 40. Asending aorta or great artery. 41. Desending vene cava or great vein. 42. Right subclavian vein. 43. Left vena innominata. 44. Left carotid vein. 45. Right carotid artery. 46. Subclavian artery and vein as it branches through the arm. 47. Clavicle or collor bone cut away. 48-9. Ribs cut away. 50. Pectoralis major and minor muscles cut through. 51. Part of deltoid muscle.

52. Biceps or the great two-headed muscle. 53. Triceps or the three-headed muscle. 54. Pronator radi teris or the turning down muscle. 55. Supinator radi longus or the turning up muscle. 56. Flexor carpi radialis or the bending muscle. 57. Palmaris longus or the long muscle that controls the hand. 58. A diaphragm that seperates the viscera of the chest from that of the head and abdomen. 59. The two great lobes of the liver. 60. The Stomach or the great reservoir for food and drink. 61 The gall bladder. 62. The spleen. 63. Colon or the great gut; 64. Vermiformis or the worm like process. 65. Small intestines. 66. Omentum or apron. 67. Symphis pubis. 68. Pupart's ligament. 69. The crest of the illium or hip. 70. A section of the penis.

The lower extremities, showing the main or inguenial artery, the great sciatic nerve aud ganglion and their branches as they lead off to the legs and feet. It shows the surface veins, nerves and muscles on the right leg. 71. The great sciatic nerve, its plexus and its branches. 72. Inguenial artery and its branches. 73. Sartorius or the tailors muscle. 74 Gluteus medius. 75. Vastus externus. 76. Vastus internus. 77. Proas and illiac muscles. 78. Pectoralis and triceps or the three-headed muscle of the inner thigh. 79. The great rectus. 80. Patelea or knee pan. 81. Gastrocnemus or the great calves of the legs. 82. The tiba or large bone of the lower leg. 83. Fibula or the small bone of the leg. 84, Tibial artery. 85. Triceps extensor or three-headed muscle of arm. 86. Pronator radi teris 87. Deltoides. 88. Biceps flexor cubiti. 89. Strong musclar tendons. 90. Supinator radi longus. 91. Palmarus longus. 92. Flexor carpi radialis. 93. Carpi ulnarius. 94. Abductor minimi digiti. 65. Palmaris brevus. 96. Flexor pollicus brevus. 97. Ligamentum anular.

CUT TWO. THE BACK VIEW OF THE

Muscles, brains and the nerves. Thn muscles are shown on the right while the whole of the brain and the nerves are seen on the left. See cut two on next page.

1. Trapezius or the four-square muscle of the head, neck shoulder and back. 2. Splenins or a spleen shaped muscle head and neck. 3. Complexus or the complex muscle of the head and neck. 4. Deltoides or a triangular shaped muscle of the shoulder. 5. Biceps flexor cubiti or the two-headed muscle. 6. Triceps extensor cubiti or the three-headed mus-

2/5

cle. 7. Supinator radi longus. 8. Extensor carpi radialis longus and brevus. 9. Extensor digitorium communis. 10. Extensor carpi ulnaris. 11. Ligamentum anular. 12, 12, 12. Latissimus dorsi, the great broad muscle of the shoulder and back. 13. Obliquus externus abdominus. 14. Gluteus medius. 15. Gluteus maximus. 16. Tensor vaginus femoris 17. Gracelus the tender muscle! 18. Abductus femoris magnus. 19. Vastus inturnus. 20. Semi-tendinosus. 21. Semi-membraneous. 22. Gastrocnemus, the calf or belly of the leg. 23. Soleus or fish-shape muscle. 24. Tendon Achillius 25. Peroneus longus and brevus. 26. Tendons of the flexor longus digitorum pedis. 27. Abductor minimi digiti pedis. 28. Cerebum or the human brain. 29. Cerebellum or the animal brain. 30. Medula oblongatta the sun or center of life. 31-2-3. The great spinal cord, nerve, brain or marrow. 34. The four inferior cervical nerves and the firet dorsal as they form the axillary plexus. 35. Sacral nerves as they form the sciatic ganglon or plexus. 36. The dorsal nerves or nerves of the back.

CUT THREE. THE SKELETON.
FRONT VIEW.

1, 1, 1. Bones of the thumb and the fingers. 2, 2. Bones of the palm of the hand or the metacarpus. 3, 3. Bones of carpus or wrist. 4. Radius, the smaller bone of the forearm. 5. Ulna, the larger bone of the forearm. 6. Humerus, the bone of the upper arm. 7. Clavicle or collar-bone. 8. Scapula, the shoulder-blade. 9. Os frontis, the bone of the forehead. 10. 10. Coronal suture or seam. 11. Temporial bone. 12. Malar or cheek bone. 13. Maxillar or upper jaw-bone. 14. Nasalis or bridge-bone of the nose. 15. Socket and nostrils. 16. Maxillar inferior or the lower jaw-bone. 17. The teath. 18. The cervical vertebra or uppea backbone, with their cartilages. 19. The dorsal or middle, and 20. the lumbar or lower vertebra or backbone; and 21, its transverse process. 22. Sternum or breast-bone, and the ribs. 23. Sacram or the sacred bone! 24. Illium or hip-bone. 25. Symphis pubis or bone of the privates. 26. Ischium or a bone of the groin and thigh.

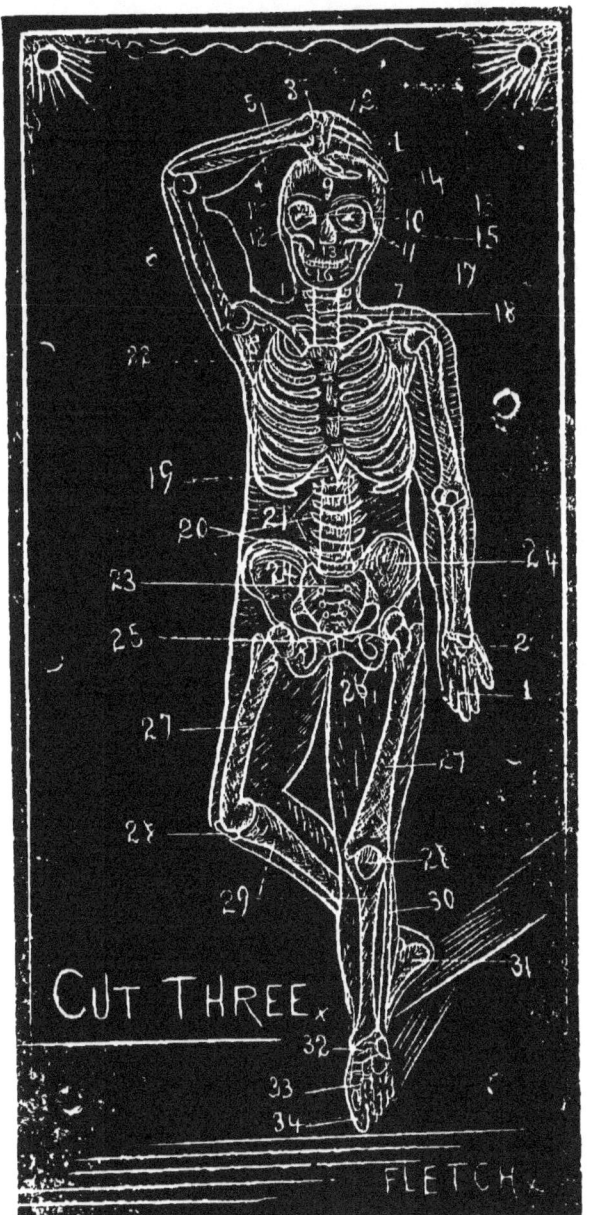

27. Os femoris or the thigh-bone. 28. Patella or the knee-pan. 29. Tibia or the largest bone of the leg. 30. Fibula or the lesser bone of the leg. 31. Os calcis or the heel-bone. 32. Tarsus or the bones of the instep. 33. Metatarsus or the bones of the foot. 34. Digitus pedis or bones of the toes.

N. B. When a mear youth, 17 years old, I engraved these three anatomical cuts, on wood, as large as life! They were seized and used as shutters to baracade the windows during the Southern Rebellion, of 1861. And I for years have used them as props to keep the roof of my house from collapse-ing! The boys made a fiddle out of a slice of cut three, so this is the most damage they have received.

These slate cuts are rough outline representations of the original cuts. The original cuts are on slabs of beech wood. I give five dollars for the tree in the mountain, cnt it down myself and hauled it to the mill with oxen myself and had it sawed into engraving wood. The most of the engravings for this book was engraved on this wood and was burned in 1867, along with an immense library, material, type fixtures! Part of the re-written book has been stolen and carried before the federal court as stated on page 111.

So, misfortune, poverty, disease, death, and destruction has harrassed me for a life-time! thus detaining this book to harrass me in my old age! The Author.

INTRODUCTORY REMARKS,

ON DISEASES AND REMEDIES.

We will now give you our theory of disease, and our remedies; and how I have relieved my-self, my family, and patients for 50 years.

The laws of life and health are few and simple; while those of disease and death are many and very hard to avoid, understand, or manage.

We aid and trust more to nature than to physicians and their deadly poisons. And O, how broad and easy found, and travled is the road to destruction. When I look over my lifetime, and view the untimley deaths of those that started out with me when I view the mountains of human remains, that has piled up mountain high, as I have journied along; it takes no God, no prophet, no bible, to tell me that narrow is the way to life, and health, and broad is the way to disease, and death. Any fool can tell us that, and also, tell us how he avoded destruction as long as he did. But, the man, or woman, that has the happy, balanced condition to see, to reason, to remember, to rightly judge, to choose, and live, in spite of all this, is a self-savior.

Our theory of disease is that disease is the remedy, that this savior is in yourself; and not in the doctor, nor medicine. Just as it is in our religion; we ignore a savior outside of our-selves.

Again, how foolish to say that a medicine is harmles because it is a vegetable. The most dreadful poisons are vegetable! Or to say I dont use minerals because they are poisnous; when every thing is more or less mineral. The air we breathe, the water we drink, the food we eat, is more or les, mineral matter; and is good for us if we need them; and poison when not needed. The most innocent food is a poison in over quantities, or when not needed.

2.   DISEASES AND REMEDIES.

Then my system might be termed the ALL-o-PATHIC, for it includes all; and uses it when, and where indicated. My theory is based on the six following ideas. 1st. Disease [is remedial effort; the effort of the life force to resist morbific causes--to remedy an injury--to remove poisons. 2nd. That the remedy, or the curative principal is this remedial effort, or struggle of the life force; that it resides inherently within our body; and all that the physician should do, or pretend to do, is to provide those materials, conditions and agencies which this life force uses to build up and sustain the energy of this life force, in the system—and give nature her good and perfect work.

3rd. That those materials, conditions, or agencies are — hygienic matter — as air, water, light, electricity, food, and drink, exercise, and rest, temperature, clothing, bathing, mental impressions, etc.

4th. That living matter acts upon dead and inorganic matter, transforming that which is nutritioun into its own substance; and ejecting whatever is injurious: that is, dead matter dose not act upon the living.

5th. That the doctrin of the drug pizen schools of medicine, that drugs— dead matter—acts upon the lieing system of matter; selecting particular organs or parts to act upon is entirlev falce, hence all drug schools of medicine; like all Christian schools of religion must be entirley false.

6th. The All-o-pathic; or Yankeeite system of medicine does not reject external applications for surgical purposes, but rejects the whole internal practice of adminersting drug poisons internally.

First and foremost of our remedial agencies is water. Water cold or hot. But always pure, live sparkling water.

" Water, bright and beautiul water,
  Pervading every thing in nature."

Yes, water constitutes threefourths of the earths

surface. Water makes up three-fourths of the human body. Water is the ONLY solvent, diluent, and detergent in existence for animal and vegetable aliment. Water is the ONLY substance that can circulate in all of our tissue, penetrating the finest and most delicate vessels; soothing, cleanseing, purifying, and strengthening; without vital or mechanical injury. Water is the ONLY medium through which wast, dead, and poisnous matter can be taken up and conveyed from out of the system; and thus soothe, purify and nourish it. Thus it is, that water is the greatest universal renedy for all of our ills.

☞ With water we vomit, sweat, purge, cleanse, purify, soothe, tone ,strengthen, revivify, etc., and with-out the least sickening or injury!

Heat applied as water or steam is one of the most powerful relaxants known. Cold applied as water or ice is one of the most powerful constringents known.

If an emetic is wanted, tepid water drank freely is a sure, safe and a harmless one. If an operation from the bowels is wanted, tepid water injected freely is a sure, and a harmless purgative. If there is a sour, bitter, or a foul stomach, nausia, reaching, sick headache, etc., tepid, warm, or hot water drank freely will soon relieve by vomiting, purging or sweating. If sweating is wanted, to relieve a fever, and a dry, torpid condition, hot water drank freely, and the wet sheet pack, or the vapor, or the steam bath is an effectual remedy. If there is wanted strength, purification, and tone to the system the hot bath, scrubing with soap, is the best.

Therefore, you have an idea as to the use of water, and how so simple, and harmless a thing produces health. And whenever you want to accomplish a thing, first find out what it is, that is needed, and what it takes to do it, then with proper care you can do it.

CUT 1 is a cheap bath, that is in the reach of all. The end of a sprinkler is fastened to a faucet, that is inserted in a bucket. The bucket is hung to the ceiling with a screw hook. Standing in a tub soap and lather yourself, then

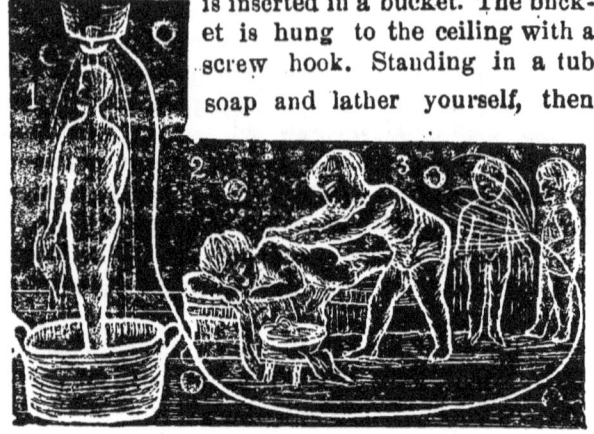

you turn on the water and recieve a gentle sprinkle, giving you plenty of time to scrub and cleanse yourself. Hot, warm, cool, or cold water can be used. A peg in a bucket will do. You can loosen the peg and let out the water fast or slow.

You can lay down as in figure 2, under this same bucket and be thoroughly soaped, and scrubed by an assistant. Or with a rubber tube, that reaches the floor, as shown in figure 3, you can be thoroughly sprinkled, or douched, forcing water, cold or hot, to any part of the body, as in pains in the bowels, stomach, back, side, sprains, sores, gout, rheumatism, piles, etc.

Tubes for the ears, nose, anus, vagina, penis, etc., can be attatched to the same tube and used when, and where needed. This tube has a faucet at its lower end so you can regulate the flow of water.

With this cheap outfit, you can take a good clean antisepic purification, sooth and alay pain, balance the circulation, equalize the life forces, and thus not only preserve health, but you aid nature in cureing diseases.

DISEASES AND REMEDIES. 5

USE OF BATHS— This is twofold, we bathe, that is, we wash the whole body whenever needed, for the purpose of clenliness, to preserve health. We bathe, that is, we apply all manner of baths when sick for the purpose of killing germ growth, counteracting, mitigating, accelerating, stimulating, and thus balancing vital, or diseased action; and in this way induce healthy, or balanced action; in many ways just numerated on page 3, and as I will now give under many forms of baths.

CUT 2. FIGURES 1 AND 2.

For example— The warm, or hot baths are for the purpose of relaxing inflamed or congested parts, to equalize the abnormal, concentrated, diseased action, or inaction, and thus induce natural, or healthey action. The cool and cold baths will constringe, tone, strengthen, and brace up weak, relaxed, and debilitated parts, and thus give healthy action.

Our cardinal points are, always keep the head hot! the feet hot! the whole body hot! and all avenues clean and unobstructed, and there is no telling how long we may live! for heat is life and cold is death! Always think of age, sex, habit, strength of body and mind. Never greatly fatiegue nor tax your vitality. Never take a full bath, as a plunge, shower, pack, douche, hot air or vaper baths without first wetting the surface of the body, and especially seeing that the feet and the surface of the entire body is hot. Great heat, and perspiration, are no objections to go in bath, provided you are not too greatly fatiegued, or you come out before you chill, and you keep up a vigerous exercise for some time after. Very feble persons should not take a fell cold nor a full hot bath. Always introduce the feble, the very old and infants, to tepid water, with the rubbing, naked, hot hands. The duration of a bath should be governed according to the indications and conditions. Also, the temperature of a bath should be governed by the temperature and condition of the patient. Never bathe immediatly after eating harty.

AFFUSIONS AND ABLUTIONS, or the sudden dashing on of cold water, or the jumping in to cold water, is the sum total idea of most people of a bath. Or, the exposing of yourself under a tremendeous waterfall. When the facts are, you might just as well slap a fellow heels over head as to be guilty of such recklessness; one would do about as much good as the other.

CUT 3 represents a hot wet sheet, two blankets, and three or four quilts, one at a time closely roped around your naked body.

The patient undressed lies down flat on the back, on the wet sheet, and is quickly and securly enveloped in the sheet, then in the blankets, then the quilts; all closely raped, securing them well at the feet and neck. Elevate

DISEASES AND REMEDIES. 7

the head, and if the feet are inclined to be cold put hot rocks to the feet, and in cases of great heat in the head put cold cloths to the head.

U S E— To reduce the heat of the body, the force of the circulation, and as a purifying alterative, to restore healthey blood and flesh. It is diaphoretic, deobstruent, febrifuge, hepetic, nervine, refrigerant sudorific, anodyne, and soporific—quieting strife, inducing sleep. In diseases of HIGH energy, to lower the fever and the pulse, the sheet should be rather wet, while in diseases of LOW energy, where the heat, and the life forces, are feeble, and tending to inward stagnation, then the sheet should be rather hot and only moist. In all instances, in a few minuets there should be a warm comfortable glow, if this does not happen then the Steam bath, or the Dry hot pack must be resorted too.

As soon as there is any uneasiness the patient can come out. The usual time is from 30 to 40 minutes; followed by the rubbing hot nacked hands in all of low energy, and followed by a wet sheet, towel wash or scrub, plunge, dooche, spray, or shower according to indications: the pulce, tongue, and the surface heat being your main witness. Of course use the cleanest sheets, and the purest fresh water.

HALF PACK— Same as wet sheet pack, only being applied to the trunk. I find more use for the half pack, along with the throat bandage, the hot foot bath, the hot shower, spray, or dooche baths along with copious hot water drinking than all the other processes. They are suited for patients that are so feeble as not to be able to stand the fatigue of the other baths; and when immediate relief is demanded.

WARMING, or sweating pack, is the same as the wet sheet pack, with the wet sheet left off, and the hot woolen blankets comeing next to the patient. USE— To warm up patients, and especially those that seem to be sinking for want of reaction

8 DISEASES AND REMEDIES.

to the skin and extremities, and to start the secretions. It is a severe process and must not be continued too long. The patient should come out as soon as het up and sweating commenses. Avoid a damp, chilly air; in fact, remember that a sudden cooling off gives you a cold; the drinking of cold water is always dangerous.

RUBBING WET SHEET, is a cold or hot wet sheet thrown around the patient, and the patient is rapidly rubed off, with the sheet or the hands over the sheet. U S E— As a refrigerant in cooling fevers, and should be dripping wet; and for high fevers cold, while in low fevers it should be red-hot. Also, as an anodyne tonic, for all low nervousness, torpor of the skin, or the internal organs, which if red-hot, well rung out, and rapidly rubed off, so as to bring about a pleasant reaction to the surface; a determination to the extremities, which is wanted in all diseases of low energy.

DOUCHE bath, is a stream of cold or hot water forcibly directed to a certain part of the body as is shown in cut 2, figure 1, page 5. USE— To excite, arouse and stimulate; good in all chronic enlargements, tumors, swellings, rheumatic, gouty, neuralgic, or old obstinat pains, strains, and aches. Using the water as hot and as long as possible.

TOWELL or spong bath, consists in washing the whole body with a towell or a sponge, followed by a dry rub with the towell or hot naked hands.

U S E— As a clensing, purifying, and health preserving, cold or hot bath, that is in the reach of all.

HALF or shallow bath, consists in a vessel admiting the patients lower extremities in a sitting position, and the water is more or less, and cold or hot according to indications. Cold in acute inflamations, where constringing and braceing up is wanted, as in diseases of the genitils, piles, and inflamations of high energy. Hot in inflamations of the brain, heart, lungs, liver, stomach, and internal organs; and in chronic or congested diseases of the loins, hips, and generative organs.

U S E—To tone and strengthen the bowels, back, hips, abdominal muscles, and genital organs; and as a derivative in hemorrages, and injuries of the chest and head; and should be as hot as possible. The affected parts should be rubed and kneaded, also, the feet and legs.

H I P or sitting bath, is a tub sufficient to admit the patient sitting, and usually a vessel for the feet, so as to make it a good substitute for the above half or shallow bath, it places it in the reach of all. U S E— As the above, and like it tonic, derivative sedative, and used cold or hot as symptoms may indicate.

F O O T bath, is a vessel sufficient to hold the feet, and the water is cold or hot according to indications. U S E—Generally used with the sitting bath, as a means of equalizing the blood, heat, and ralying life forces. The cold foot bath for habitual cold feet should be of short duration, washed with strong soap. ☞ Only think, for health and cleanliness, the feet requires as much washing as does the face: because the pores are much larger in the bottoms of the feet than anywhere else; so large, indeed, that they may be called sluices for carrying away the impurities of the system.

P L U N G bath, is to quickly immerse the whole body in cold or hot water. U S E— Tonic, invigorative, and a strengthening alterative. Good in all chronic affections where the lungs and the brain are not affected. Used in fevers of a high energy, in which the patient plunges while the fever is the highest, remaining until cool, and the pulse reduced to its natural action; repeating as often as it returns. Cool or cold only for robust constitutions, warm or hot water for low fevers.

10   DISEASES AND REMEDIES.

SHOWER bath, is described on page 4. It is a good remedy in high inflamatory fsvers, chronic enlargements, torpor, etc.

HEAD bath, is pouring water of any temperature on the head, or lying with the head in a bason of water, or cold or hot cloths, or ice to the head.

U S E— In deraingement of the head, mind, high fevers, etc., and should be used with a hot foot and ankle bath.

HOT AIR AND STEAM BATHS.

CUT 4 represents a blanket securaly fastened around a naked patient, so as to only leave out the head. You stand or sit over hot bricks or rocks till the desired sweating ts produced. Or you pour water on these hot rocks and form a steam bath.

Or you may use a bath box as shown on page 5, cut 2, figure 2. The box is fitted with a sliding door on top so as to let the head be out, the front door admits the patient that sits on a stool while a spirit lamp is placed under the stool; or hot rocks, his feet in hot water.

This should be followed by the hot soap scrubbing as described on page 4 cut 1.

U S E—Same as the wet sheet or dry packs, hot baths, and like them one of the most powerfull purifying alteratives known. Good in all fevers, torpor, congestions, obstructions, fowl sluggish secretions, scrofulo, syphilis, eruptions, rheumatism, gout, dropsy, colds, catarrh, consumption, and in fact it is a universal panacea.

DISEASES AND REMEDIES. 11

SOAKING HOT BATH consists in a vessel sufficient to immerse the whole body, the water as fresh, pure, and as hot as possible. U S E— As an antispasmodic, alterative, relaxant, antibilious, antiseptic, sudorific, anodyne, diaphoretic, soporific, sedative, etc. A sure pain killer. I care not how intense the pain, how violent the spasms, how rigged the muscles, a thorough application of this hot bath will over come them. It is unrivaled, yea, it is better by far to relax a dislocated limb than all the bleeding and vomiting of the old school. See its great success in cramps, spasmodic diseases, injuries, rheumatism, gout, neuralgia, paralysis, etc., that attend the hot springs. The only virtues in those springs are heat and moisture. Yet, thousands flock there anually on beds and crutches, and pay awful prices for what they could have for a little trouble at home.

ELECTRICAL bath, consists in applying electricity to the system through the medium of the a bove soaking hot bath, or the baths illustrated on page 4. The vessel being lined with copper straps, filled with hot water, the patient immersed to the head, one hand in contact with the positive pole of a galvanic battery, the negative pole being connected with the straps lining the vessel. In some old obstinate cases nitric acid is added to the water. From 15 to 20 minutes is sufficient for this bath.

U S E— This is valuable as the above soaking hot bath in all old obstinat chronic affections, low circulation, torpor of the skin, liver, bowels, scrofula, rheumatism, enlarged glands, nerveous affections, colds, catarrh, consumption, croup, asthma, phthisic, pains, aches, stifnesses, etc. And as a eliminater of drugs, chemicals, dye-stuffs, paints, oils, varnishes, pure wines and brandies for medical purposes. And to kill all manner of sores, inflamations, eruptions, as cancers, syphilis, gonorrhea, or microbe, and all manner of germ life.

NASAL, MOUTH, AND EYE baths, consists in gradually drawing water up the nostrils ejecting it by the mouth; holding the eyes in water, etc. The water being cool, cold, warm, or hot as symptoms may indicate. U S E— In inflamations of these organs, bleeding of the nose, sore, and painful affections of these parts.

ARM AND LEG baths, consists in holding the arms, or legs in vessels of water sufficient to cover them. U S E— In inflamations, sprains, old sores, wounds, etc., the water of any temperature as conditions may demand.

BANDAGES AND COMPRESSES, are cold or hot wet cloths applied to any affected part, and renewed as often as tending to dry, or to become too hot. U S E— To warm or to cool; and when wished cooling they should be thin, wet with cold fresh water, uncovered, and changed very frequently. When wished warming they should be wrung out of pure boiling water, and kept covered with dry woolen clothes.

HOT WET GIRDLE, consists in three or four yards of heavy domestic or toweling, one half of which is wet and wrung out and applied around the belly, followed by the dry half. U S E— In inflamations and weaknesses of the hips, back and belly, as back-ache, belly-ache, womb-ache, as in flux, diarrhea, dyspepsia, etc.

HOT RAPPER, or chest girdle, is the same as the above and like the half-pack extends to the armpits. U S E— The same as the half-pack and the above wet girdle, as a derivative in trouble of the head, neck, lungs, chest, liver, kidneys, etc.

WET-DRESS BATH, is a linen or cotton dress, sufficient to cover the feet, so a person can put it on, wet it and wrap themselves in bed and take a sweating wet-sheet pack. ☞ You can pack yourself with a wet sheet if you will, and are able.

DISEASES AND REMEDIES.

FOMENTATIONS, consists in applying moist heat to parts, and may be done by clothes, sacks of grain, bran, mud, ashes, sand, or herbs steeped in boiling water, and applied as hot as can be borne. USE—Invaluable in all manner of sores, aches, pains, colics, inflamations, congestions, swellings, gout, rheumatism, neuralgia, tooth-ache scalds, burns, chilblains, and all simelar diseases. As the hot bath, if properly and perseveringly applied they are wonderful remedies.

REFRIGERANTS, consists in applying cold water, snow or ice to affected parts as heat is applied above. USE—To alay intence heat, pain, inflamations, swellings, fevers, etc., and to benumb for the knife or for caustics. Be careful, never use them where there is conjestion; first relieve the conjestion with poultices or fomentations, then apply the refrigerants. Two parts of snow or ice to one of salt is a powerful refrigerant.

INJECTIONS, consists in injecting water, of all temperatures into the bowels, or other cavities of the body. USE—To quiet pain, to check hemerage, or to free, loosen, and cleanse the bowels. To quiet pain, or to purge the bowels any quantity of hot water may be injected. And to check hemorage, cool, or cold water is used. In all diseases, and all feble persons the bowels should be frequently flushed, and thoroughly purged. The Elastic Extension Syringes are easily procured now; and are invaluable—needed by everyone; and everybody should have one. A small quantity of pure fresh water gradualy, and slowly injected into the bowels and retained over night is apt to move them next day. It is invaluable to ladies to flush and to keep clean the vagina; thus preventing or curing disease; and placing conception at your own will.

EMETICS, are something that are so offensive to the stomach as to cause it to disgorge. Warm water drank rapidly, and copiously, so as to fill the stomach will vomit you; and at the same time dissolve all acrid, iritating, and poisonous matter, and in this way it is ejected, and the stomach cleansed.

In cases of violent poisoning mustard should be stired in the water, and in this way hasten a disgorge. In cases of croup indigo in the water is invaluable; for you can pour any amount down even an infants throat without in the least sickening, or injury. U S E— Invaluable, and indispensable in cleansing, soothing, and toneing the stomach at the beginning of any and all trouble. Nature entended the stomach should be relieved in this way, and not by cathartics; for the back door of the stomache is only entended to pass fluieds, therefore, if a cathartic is given it should be on an empty stomache.

EXERCISE AND REST: Exercise always, if able, before and after bath in the fresh, free, open, and sunny air. Never greatly fatiegue nor tax your strength. In fevers, and while the disease is most violent, keep quiet, and as the fever cools begin to work or exercise. Always begin and end gradually, and when the stomach is most empty. It should be of such a nature as to call into action all the functions; thus insuring a healthey and harmonious development. In some diseases particular parts require a particular kind of exercise. Consumptives, dyspeptics, etc., require labor, and exercise that will specially call into play those parts most liable to the disease. They should exercise their lungs, and their abdominal muscles by specially sucking in as much pure, cool, fresh air as possible, and so by this means prevent the lungs from filling with blood.

REST— Man has been given half of time for rest. From dark to light should be spent in rest; all of it every bit of it is absolutly necessary, winter or summer, to insure a proper assimilation, cleansing, and repair, and growth of the body and the mind; that can only take place during sound, quiet sleep. Persons who live according to the general mode of life eating and drinking every thing, find it difficult to rest half this time. This is owing to the artificial stimulous dying out, and calls for a renewal; hence the very early morning cood of tobacco, even before the trousers are put on; tea, coffee or spirits before or immediatly on rising.

SLEEP— Beds should be of fine-cut straw, moss, shucks, or like substances. Under-bedding cotton or liuin, then the blankets. Sleeping room well ventillated, and sunned; night air is all right if not too damp and cold. Nervous, poor, and exhausted persons should sleep much. Night-watching the sick with company, or bright lights, noise, or the wakeing fo them if they sleep sound is all injurious. No danger so long as they are warm and the pulse is good. Never sleep on your back, but train yourself to alternately sleep on your sides.

WHAT TO EAT, DRINK, AND TO AVOID.

Eat plenty of plain, simple food, that is, plenty of plain breads, fruits, meats, and vegetables. An ample supply of these is an ample sufficiency. We should eat to live, and not mearly live to eat, drink and be merry, as the King's Jew-Christian Bible says Gcd commanded, and declared thet man had only enough to do this; and that the wisest would never be able to find out anything more: Ecc. c viii. 15 to 17 v·

☞ All food should be fresh cooked, or exposed to an intense heat just before eating: why? to kill microbe and germ life, that begins to grow in all food as soon as cold! ☜ All drinking water should be clean, cold, pure, fresh live water: why? because microbe and germ life fill all impure, warm or water that has stood up long enough to get warm. Better drink fresh cooked hot water, or tea-kettle tea than stale, impure water: why? because there is a cause for sickness, and poisous are the cause: but why dont it make others sick? because some are like a hog hard to kill. Yet, these are serious facts that the Christian's god knew nothing off, for we have found out many wonderful mysteries.

PRACTICE— I now group diseases according to their nature, and care not a fig for their name, but, their symptoms. Having given special treatment with our remedies, we will now give you a general treatment by groups, leaving minute, or special varing demands to your judgment. And if it will only be borne in mind that when ill a person is no longer capable of self-control, and must be guided, and you must be convinced of this fact, and must have the utmost confidence in his guide and the treatment before any permanent good can be expected.

FIRST— We class all diseases undea TWO great classes—high and low— and speak of them as of a high or of a low energy. To accertain these conditions the pulse is our first witness, and if properly examined it gives us the correct pathognomonic symptoms. We then know which of these classes the disease belong; and the general treatment is at once known. ☞ Bear in mind, that the pulse is the sheet-anchor, a pathognomonic symptom of your actual condition, and without this knowledge and the obeying of it, all must be very dangerous. The pulse is the flow of the blood from the heart, our center, outwardly to the extremities of the body, and can be felt pulsating in any artery near the surface; but it is easiest felt, and judged, up the cavity of the wrist from the thumbs. Its frequency and strength may be accertained by compressing an artery with the fingers, carfully denoting the degrees of pressure the first finger will give before it ceases to be felt by the finger furthest from the heart.

Organic quality, temperament, age, sex, strength and habits of life should be kept in mind. A good organic quality of the animal, or balanced temperament will give a full, strong pulse, of high energy;

DISEASES AND REMEDIES.

and not so rapid, nor feble as an indifferent organic quality; or as a human and a unbalanced temperament. A natural pulse is uniform in frequency, force, and fullness. Averaging the pulse in health we may state it as follows: Childhood, one hundred beats per minute; while old age is near fifty beats rer minute. Males have a slower pulse than females. Very fat persons and dyspeptics have a slow pulse, while consumptives have a fast pulse. When the pulse exceeds one hundred and fifty we are left to conjecture. This degree indicates great danger·

A strong hard pulse is pathognomonic of a high energy, while a feble, or a fast pulse is pathognomonic of a low energy. A strong pulse is never very frequent, not exceeding one hundred, and indicates iritation or inflamation. A frequent pulse indicates debility; a slow pulse indicates torpor; and a tremulous or intermittent pulse indicates great exhaustion and grean danger.

SECOND— THE TONGUE is the next to the pulse in indicating the conditions of the patient In health it is of a clear, clean, moist flesh color. In diseases of a high energy it inclines to dry, and to coat with a fur, red edges and tip, assuming a raw parched appearance; while in diseases of a low energy it is inclined to coat with a dirty, yellowish, brown, or a black fur, inclining to crack.

FEBRIL diseases are an inflamatiory disterbance of most, if not all, of the functions of life; manifested in periodical paroxysms of a cold, hot, and sweating stages.

They are of high or low energy. They are high when marked with great heat, and redness to the surface, as a strong, or a hard pulse, the mind none or but little affected, and especialy so in the animal temperament; but in the human you may expect a dry, parched, cracked, coated tongue, with even firy edges and tip. They are of low energy when a great determination is inwardly, with a weak, fast, rapid, tremulous, or an intermitting pulse; extremities inclined to be cold, and the mind very restless, and confused. The tongue slimy, and coated with a yellowish dirty rotting, stinking, microbe matter.

They are of four kinds: 1st. Sympathetic, of one day fever. 2nd. Inter mit tent, disappearing for a time, as in fever and ague, chills, congestive fever, etc. 3rd. Remittent, mearly growing lighter after the paroxysms, as in fevers of low energy, as nervous, hectic, milk, marsh, and the mixed fevers. 4th. Continued, as a never cooling fever through the paroxysms and rests, as in cynchous, or high fevers; and in low fevers, as typhoid, yellow, billious, spotted, camp, hospital, jail, nervous, swamp, and putrid fevers.

TREATMENT FOR ALL FEVERS— As soon as you find you have a fever, no matter as to name but, first find out what class it belongs, whether to high or low, and you at once know the general treatment. 1st. Warm water should be drank until thorough vomiting is produced, and the stomach is actually wrenched clean, and this should be repeated as often as there arise any nausia, or a hot, foul, bilious breath.

2nd. The bowels should now be thoroughly filled with warm water, and copious purging kept up until perfectly cleansed; and repeated every day until they operate naturally themselves.

3rd. In all fevers of a high energy, the hot air, or steam bath, or the hot shower, soap and scrub bath, until the fever yields, and the pulse becomes, natural, followed by a douche, or shower, and thorough scrubbing with soap, hot or cold water, as your feelings may indicate.

But if the fever is of low energy then the hot wet sheet, or dry hot pack, or the soaking hot bath the hot scrub and soap bath, or the hot electrical bath, shoule be used to cool the fever, equalize the heat and the blood, reduce the pulse, and in this

DISEASES AND REMEDIES. 19

way produce relief. The hot foot bath should be used as often as the extremities grow cool.

☞ Be careful, very careful, of a very sick person, especially as the fever is cooling off, for at this time they die so easy. So, be careful to keep the head hot, the body hot, the feet red hot, and all avenues clean, free, and in working order. Now is the time to give them some good cooked, nourishing food and drinks.

DRUG TREATMENT— 1st. Vomit thoroughly with lobelia or indigo and warm water. Wash and thoroughly scrub with soap and hot water, when the fever is highest, nearly scald the feet. Give a good dose of blue pill, and work it off with salts in the morning, while the stomach is most empty: add a pinch of salt and soda to the salts.

In cases of chills and fever, blue pill, quinine, and gunpowder, equal parts by bulk, well mixed in water, and a table spoonful taken every two hours is a certain cure for all periodical diseases.

In billious, low, mixed, or typhoid fevers, make a syrup of syrup of rheubarb 4 ounces, oil of sasafras 20 drops, piperine 10 grains, soda 20 grains, in a mortar by thourough grinding, and now add tincture of valerian 2 ounces, and again thoroughly mix. Give a table spoonful every two hours in a toddy or sweet milk. This syrup will wake up, and arouse them from their sinking, and delarious stupor. This syrup, like the hot air and steam, or electrical hot bath, kill the microbe and germ life that causes fever, and nearly all diseases. Vomiting, purging, sweating tears them to pieces, kills and expells them.

INFLAMATORY DISEASES, are fevers with a local concentration on a single organ or part, manifested by fever-heat, pain, redness, and swelling of the parts. They are of high or low energy. They are high in acute or inflamatory attacks, and are attended with more or less fever. They are low in chronic, aud suppurating inflamations, and attended with none or but little fever. They are of four kinds: 1st. Phlegmonous, suppurative as in boils, abscesses, sore eyes, tooth and ear-ache, pneumonia, mumps, quinsy, pleurisy, inflamation of the brain heart, stomach, bowels, lungs, liver, spleen, bladder, kidneys, uteris, testicles, postate and mammary glands.

2nd. Erysipelatous, eruptions and rashes, as in erysipelas, burns, scalls, bruses, chilblains, frostbitten, etc. 3rd. Catarrhal, forming hard mucus membrains, as in catarrh, colds, cough, croup, influenzia, colic, dysentery, diarrhea, phthisic, bloody urin, whites, gleet, clap, etc. 4th. Arthritic, inflamations of the joints, bones, tendons, muscles, as in gout, rheumatism, neuralgia, siatica, rickets, and diseases of the bones.

TREATMENT FOR ALL INFLAMATIONS.

Inflamations if left to themselves terminate either by a gradual subsidence of the symptoms, or by death of the parts, and the patient. The general treatment given for fevers should follow here, specialy noting their symptom and treat each accordingly. ☞ The local applications to the affected parts, should be fomentations in all instances. Commence with them moderatly hot and increase them as hot as can be borne; keep this up until the symptoms, that is, the feuer-heat, pain, redness, or sweeling subside.

I care not what the name of the disease may be, if any, or all of these symptoms are preasent, moist heat properly and perseveringly applied will relieve. Where there is rawness of the surfacs mucilage, thick oil, tallow, beat-up-eggs, flour, fine rosin, burnt alum, calomel, indigo, or like substances, should be kept on the sores to prevent the air from paining them, and to act as a mild caustic

DISEASES AND REMEDIES. 21

aiding the moist heat in killing the microbe, or the germ life.

Fomentations and poltices ease and haisten suppuration, or subsidence; boils and abscesses should be opened as soon as ripe. In affections of the stomache and bowels hot water drank and injected, along with fomentations or poultices to, or as near the affected parts as possible, until the symptoms subside, or ripen. In diarrhea and flux cleanse the stomach and bowels with blue pill and salts; and then check up with white oak bark tea and paragoric. Or a small amount of paragoric added to our syrup for fevers given on page 19 may be used.

In cases of whites, gleet, clap, etc., wash out the vagina or uretha with a hot, greasy water, then inject a hot oiley liniment; old bacon grease, or castor oil thined with turpentine, and flavored with oil of sassafras is excelent. This will cause a profuse mattering and then heal. In cases of the pock mercurial ointment, or calomel should be kept on the sores.

For coughs, colds, sore throat, croup, grip, and similar diseases, first vomit thoroughly, then the hot foot and hot scrub soap bath, purge off with blue pill, followed by salts, apply the hot wet chest and throat rapper, or fomentations. Indigo in warm water as an emetic or expectorant is invaluable.

ERUPTIVE DISEASES, are disorganizing affections of the skin and mucus surfaces; and is owing to the vital or remedial energy acting on, and expelling the microbe or germ life-matter there; or their local concentration on certain weakest parts.

They are of high or low energy. They are high when the effort is to the surface, with regular and distinct eruptions to the surface; and of low energy when the energy, and fever is inwardly, and affecting the mucus membrains and disterbing the mind They are of two kinds: 1st. Exahthematic, eruptions caused by a specific contagion, and epidemical, and attended with more or less fever, as in erysipelatous-pox, small-pox, cow and chicken-pox, nettles, miliary, scarlet-fever, visicula-fever, measles, thrush, red-gum, scald-head, etc.

2nd. Efflorescence, eruptions not rising above, or but slightly above the skin, not epidemic, but contageous, as the itch, tetter, ringworm, etc.

TREATMENT FOR ALL ERUPTIONS.

In the first kind the treatment given for fevers should be used here, if indicated. The cleansing of stomach and bowels, the cooling of the fever, and the killing of the microbe or germ life with moist heat, or our fever syrup, and the protecting of the raw rashes, or sores, as given under fevers, inflamations, and the purging of the stomach, bowels blood, flesh, and the entire body, and the nourishing, sustaining, and the preventing of debility or the sinking of the patient, by keeping all functions on a balance, until nature can rally, has been given, and should follow here, and whenever, or wherev- indicated.

FLUX-LIKE DISEASES, are the flowing of blood or other fluids from their respective vessels, and may or may-not have fever. They are of low energy, and are classed under two kinds: 1st. Hemorrhagic, a discharge of blood, as bleedieg from nose, mouth, lungs, stomach, bladder, privates, or any organ. 2nd. A pocenosis, a discharge of any glandular fluid into other cavities, as in vomiting, purging, cholera, diarrhea, flux, diabetis, diuresis, plat-hair, moon-eyed, salivation, loss of semen, and similar discharges.

TREATMENT FOR ALL FLUXES— In all cases derivatives and astringents are first. In the 1st. the hot sitting and a very hot foot bath, while cool astringents should be applied to, or as near the affec-

DISEASES AND REMEDIES. 23

ted parts as possible. Very hot and very cold water drank or injected will kill the microbe or germ life, cleanse and check all hemorrhage. It should be plentifully applied, and in obstinate cases a little of our fever syrup with paregoric should be taken, or injected. A little aqua ammonia, or creosote, in hot water is good in cholera, and should be given after you have disgorged the stomach and bowels with hot water, and applied the fomentations.

Treat the flux as if cholera, keeping the fomentations to the stomach as hot as can be borne; and open the bowels with salts having in them a little paregoric. It is said fresh lime sprinkled around, the walls whitewashed, and a little in the drinking, and using water prevents cholera by killing the germs; but it wont kill the microbes of pulmonary consumption, carbuncles,, and several other contagious diseases. But, remember, something will; purity, freshness, cleanliness, no contact will prevent, while plenty of good hot food and drinks, in a clean stomach will hold you beyond the reach of any disease; and a sufficient amount of moist heat, as afforded by the hot soap scrub baths will kill any or all microbe and germ life.

SUPPRESSED DISEASES, are obstructions of the natural passages, or functions, and are of vital or mechanical causes. They are mostly of a low or bad energy, and are grouped into two kinds: 1st. Constricting, or a suppression of the secretions, or excretions from debility or irritability, as the stoppage of the urine, feces, bile, milk, tears, sweat, semen, menses, saliva, and other fluids from an inability of their parts, or from a stricture of their ducts. 2nd. Obstructing, or a blocking up of natural outlets or passages, by organic force, foreign substances, as in choaking, smothering, enlarged glands, organs or parts, as the stopage of urine in stone forming, the feces fron hard gluey matter, the menses from a unpurforated hymen, palpitation, night-demon, asthma, piles, varicose veins, obstructed stomach, thickened blood, and a congested liver, etc.

TREATMENT FOR ALL OBSTRUCTIONS.

Relaxants, alteratives, derivatives, equalizers, and tonics are first wanted. In retention of urine either from stone, stricture, or enlarged postates, fomentations, hot poltices, hot sitting and hot foot bath, to ease, relax, and start the urine, or to admit the catheter. In cases of choaking, stone in the bladder, closed hymen, a surgeon should be consulted. In constipation, dyspepsia, etc., fresh water injections, and an agreeable diet, with a thorough scrubbing soap bath, along with the wet girdle will relieve. Palpitation, night-demon, etc., are relieved by avoiding tea, coffee, tobacco, whiskies, and late suppers. In chronic, obstinate obstruction occasionly give a dose of blue pill, at bedtime, and follow by a good purging dose of salts in cold, fresh water, on your empty stomach, early next morning.

SPASMODIC DISEASES, are violent muscular contractions of different, or all parts of the body, and are of a continued or a temporary duration. They are of high or low energy, and are grouped into five kinds: 1st. Constricting, a continued rigidity, of the muscles, as in cramps, wryneck, stiff-joints, lock-jaw, tetanus, and hydrophobia. 2nd. Tonic, a continued spasmodic trembeling, as in St. Vitus's dance, tremons, deliriumtremons, palsy, and paralysis. 3rd. Clonic, of a temporary spasm, characterized by a forcible, sudden and irregular as in sneezing, hiccough, palpitation, and gaping. 4th. Suffocativ, a continued or temporary spasmodic action of the respiratory muscles, as in bronchitis, asthma, coughs, etc. 5th. Comatose, muscular agitation with diminished sensability, followed by stupor, as in epleptic and hysterical fits, convulsions, etc.

TREATMENT FOR ALL SPASMS. Relaxants, derivatives and alteratives are indicated in all spasms. I care not how intense the irritation, nor how rigid the contractions, moist heat WILL relax ease, and relieve. Our cardinal principles should be observed: first remove the cause, bring about a balance by keeping the head cooled to its natural heat but keep the feet moist and very hot, and the body clean, naturaly hot, and all avenues clean and in working order. An emetic of warm water and indigo, to cleanse, free, and soothe the stomache, and followed by a purging dose of blue pill, followed by a purging dose of salts in the morning. In the constricting group, full hot baths, with soap, and with electricity if possable. Hydrophobia like croup, has a foul, burnt-up stomach, bowels, and throat ; put them, and hold them in a full hot bath, inject them full of hot soapy water having in it a little whiskey, and pour, or inject down the throat indigo and hot water until they vomit and pnrge. Hot fomentatioms or hot poultices to the throat in hydrophobia and lock-jaw, nearly scald the feet.

TORPID DISEASES, are loss in most or all sensability and muscular power, often with mental and bodily stupor. They are generally of a low and a bad energy, and are grouped under two kinds: 1st. Com a tose, a strong and a continued stupor, with a loss or diminished muscular power, as in coma, estacy, syncope, catalepsy, apoplexey, paralysis, with stupor. 2nd. A ne pith yma, a loss or diminution of power in different functions, as in loss of apetite, dyspepsia, general emaciation,· chlorosis, and amarosis. ☞ Lice, chinches, fleas, ticks, chiggers, flies, musketoes, and like bloodsuckers, not only deprive you of your blood and nerve-life, but they poison what remains. They irritate and inflame the whole body, paralyze the nerves and stupify the mind. They, along with overwork, undue stimulus, improper food and drink, and at an improper time, is the prime cause of all torpid diseases. They these causes, are everywhere, and attact us every day and night, the year round, and raid the palace or the hovel; and they are microbes and germs of the elephant order, and require no microscope to prove it. ☞ This class of diseases, and this class of elephant microbe gods are the prime cause of this awful diseased craziness called religion. Ecstasy is a lost, transfixed, and transformed, state of the mind and the senses. And it is this lost, dependent depravity that gives us all religions, with all their mystery, wonder, and hypochondriacal terror; but one! And that one is founded on the Declaration of American Independence; and is just dimetrically opposit all others.

TREATMENT FOR ALL TORPOR.

Indications are plainly for soothers, derivatives, depuratives, equalizers, and food-tonics· Equalize the circulation, restore the secretions, and gain the confidence of your patient. In the comatose kind, first relieve them from any cramped position or crowded place, or clothing. Place them in an easy recumbent position in the free, pure, pleasant air. Soothe and quiet their mind if possible, vomit with indigo and warm water, wash out the bowels with hot water, give blue pill and work it off with salts, adding a little salt and soda. Use the scrubbing hot soap bath, hot sitting and very hot foot bath.
Our fever syrup should be given three times a day for a clearing up tonic. Sleep from dark to day, and arouse, stir about, drink some fresh water, avoid spirits, tobacco, tea and coffee, but use tea-kettle-tea with sugar and cream or warm milk fresh from the cow; eat plentifully of whatever you like, but eat slow, and chew thoroughly.

DISEASES AND REMEDIES.

Fruits and vegetables have a tendency to cause this class of diseases; watch them, eat them with bread and meat, and alow nothing to be swallowed until chewed into a fluid; and if it soures or disagrees drink warm water and vomit it up as quick as possible; then take a dose of salts with soda, and look out for the next time.

☞ Avoid polititions, lawyers, preachers, doctors, and their disputing kind, for they are bloodsuckers of the ☞ fishers of men kind. ☜

MENTAL DISEASES, are violent or irregular actions of the mental faculties, often with a stupid depression of mind and body. They are of a low and bad energy, and are grouped into three kinds: 1st. Morose, a deraingment of the mind and body, from a morbid appetite, as in gluttony, drunkenness, craveings, talking in the sleep, dreaming, seeing visions, dirt-eating, etc. 2nd. Hallucinations, a disturbance of the mind and body from over sexual indulgence, as in self-polution, whoreing, melancholy, dispondency from disappointment, etc.
3rd. Craziness, a deraugment of the mind from various causes, as in crankness, madness, absent-minded, hare-brained, imbecility, etc.

☞ As the causes of torpid diseases are the cause of all mediation, or believe or bedamed, fear-forced religions, so, in turn, this fear forced kinds of religions are the cause of the causes of all mental diseases! ☜

TREATMENT FOR ALL MENTAL DIS-- EASES. Treat this class precisly as directed for torpid diseases. Don't worry, be quiet, temperate and charitable. Worry breaks down the nervous system, it impairs digestion and nutrition, it destroys brain and body energy, and renders you incapable of grappling with live questions and solid facts. Worry not only kills, but, it makes yoy kill! Tranquillity and plenty of good food on a clean stomach and plenty of sleep to quiet the mind will also, nourish, and make healthy the entire system.

CACHEXY, is a bad condition of the body, from a general filthiness of the fluids of the body, which from their sour, fermenting condition they furnish putrifaction for any or all kind of germ growth. They are attended with none, or but little fever or nervousness.

They are manifested by a general debility of the functions of the body, causing spots, colors, pimples, indolent sloughing sores, and are of a low, bad energy; and are grouped under two kinds: 1st. Impe ti go, a change of color in the whole body, as in scurvey, secondary syphilis, consumption, marasmus, scrofulo, and cancer. 2nd. Mac u la, only a partial change of color, as in elephant-skin, bruses, mother-marks, etc.

TREATMENT FOR ALL CACHEXIES.

A rigid compliance to our mode of life, as it relates to bathing, exercise, rest, what to eat, drink, and avoid should follow here. Use the hot bath, strong lye-soap, the hot air and steam bath, and a very hot soaking electrical scrub bath.

Frequently cleanse the stomach with warm water emetics, and the bowels with hot water injections. Use sulphur frequently, and occasionly blue pill, but be certain to work the blue pill off with salts.

Hot fomentations and hot poultices will kill the whole of this class of sores, even scrofulo, scurvey, pock-shankers, carbuncles, tubercles, cancers, and even leprosy.

TUMOR-LIKE DISEASES, are enlargements of the body, and are of a low and bad energy, and are grouped into four kinds: 1st. Poly sar cia, enlargements generally from fat, as in big-belly, glandular enlargments, and tumors; from a boil to a carbuncle. 2nd. Phleg ma tia, enlargements generaly

DISEASES AND REMEDIES. 29

from fluids, with fever and a diminished sensation, as in anasarca, varicose veins, dropsy of the brain, chest, belly, and scrotum. 3rd. Cystis, enlargements from fluids without affecting other organs, as in amarosis, hydatids, and polypus. 4th. Emphysema, enlargements from accumulated air and other fluids, as the filling of all or part of the body with air, gas, or water.

TREATMENT FOR ALL TUMORS.

☞ Moist heat WILL KILL this class of ANIMALS, or any other! So, the question is how to do it, so as to not over power the patient, but to soothe, balance, and improve them. Treat them as given for Cachexies, and Eruptive diseases.

Very hot fomentations, poultices, hot soap soaking scrubbing baths, the electrical, hot air, or steam baths to kill them, while an occasional dose of blue pill, and our fever syrup, will kill them inwardly, and a rousing dose of castor-oil, sulphur, or salts, will aid in their destruction, and expulsion, and your purification.

DISLOCATIONS, are organs or parts removed from their natural seats causing a derangement of their functions, frequently with painful tumors and inflamations. They are of high or low energy, and are grouped into three kinds: 1st. Hernia, a misplacement of the entrals through a rupture covered by an integument, as in a prolapse of the guts into the scrotum, groins, navel, etc. 2nd. Prolapsus, the misplaceing of any organ without a rupture or an integument, as in prolapsus of the womb rectum, palate. 3rd. Luxation, the misplaceing of any joint from its socket or articulation.

TREATMENT FOR ALL DISLOCATIONS.

For a successful treatment requires mechanical skill and a knowledge of the human body. In all instances they should be attended too immediatly, before inflamation sets in. Should inflamation be set up then hot fomentations should be used to relax the rigidity and soreness of the parts, and to facilitate a more easy replacel. Mechanical supports should be applied, using fomentations or hot poultices if very painful. There are splendid supports for all manner of dislocations, fractures, weak organs, etc., that can be bought, rented, borrowed, or made.

FRACTURES, are seperations of parts naturally joined. They are of high or low energy; and are grouped into two kinds: 1st. Dialysis, a disunion of the soft parts, as in wounds, cuts, ulcers, shankers, sinuses, fistula, etc. 2nd. Clasis, a disunion of the hard parts, as in broken bones, etc.

TREATMENT FOR ALL FRACTURES.

As in dislocations fractures require mechanichal knowledge and skill to rightly replace and to retain them, and if possible a surgeon should be called at once. In wounds foreign bodies should be removed and if any large vessels keep b'eeding tie them; replace and keep so by adhesive straps, then cover with fine rosin dust until healed.

Fractures should be replaced and kept so by mechanical aid till healed. Cancers, shankers, fistulas, sinuses, and ulcers, should be killed with very hot poultices, fomentations, or refrigerants, and sloughed out, and healed with salve, or cut, or burnt out and treated as fresh woundes; kept covered with rosin flour.

To remove without pain or blood: cut from a piece of adhesive plaster an opening a little larger than the sore, stick tight, and close around the sore leaving it and a small part of the healthy skin bare a past made from Chloride of Zinc by mixing it in wheat dough, or paste; and after thoroughly freezing the sore cover with this paste, keeping only the sores froze, and coverd with fresh paste a few days when the whole sore can be lifted out leaving a clean red cavity, which should be poulticed with a good hot poultice, then heal with salve or rosin, keeping on a greasy compress till healed.

"WOMANS FIRST NEED, is to understand the functions of all parts of her body, and what habits will best maintain them in health. If she knows how her own health can be secured, she will know how to preserve the health of her children. When women see everywhere, young children drop into the grave, like blighted fruit from trees, it seems strange that she does not ask, if it was intended for her to bring forth children only to fill little graves? If there is need that one half the children born should die under five years old?

Children are born to live a life of vigerous usefulness and enjoyment. Parents should not be allowid, by ignorance, to thus bring forth diseased children. Parents should so live, that life will be a pleasure to their children. But children will not be born healthy, and live, strong and happy, till their motherrs know how to live healthy, bare sound children, and how to rear them in vigor." Huldah Page, M. D.

How truthfully told dear mother Huldah; yes, what should be the mothers conditions? Should there be anything exempt from her storehouse of knowledge? Who's to teach the little heart to feel, the little minds to see, the little wayward feet how, and where to tread, or those little hands how, and what to do? Why, mother. Yes, mother, great is to be your trust, task, and trials. Ponder well the connecting links in your fast, fleet, changable life. Only think, you are the most complex enigma, and the most changable of all.

"In infancy a tender flower,
　　Cultivate her.

> A floating bark in girlhoods ho'ur,
>   Softly freight her.
> A fruitful vine when grown, alas,
>   Prime and please her.
> Old, shes a heavy charge, alas,
>   Support and ease her."

It is said that woman is the fairer and the weeker sex, but, it does seem to me also, that she is the tougher sex. Only imagine the many perilous stages of life she must hastly pass through. Tomboy sarcasm and dress slavery; puberty with its dangerous trials; courtships slippery grounds; marriags anctious experiment; the honeymoons bittersweets: pregnancys sacred and sickening, ill--cndition; childbirths pearilous travail; the lying in ordeal; with many family duties necessarily crowding upon her, which alack——

> She never dreamed of such a fate,
>   When she, alas, was courted—
> Wife, mother, nurse, seamstress, dairy woman,
> And scrub generally, doing the work of eight,
> For the sake of being supported!

Susceptable, too, to all the ills that mortals are heir too, with a host peculiar only to her own sex, and with only one unchaste, wayward step from a path of virtue and rectitude and all is forever lost!

Religions and their bibles not only damed eternally woman for her first offence, when an ignorant innocent, motherless infant— but, she was subjected to the most outrageous slavery, until Infidelity, not only freed the Negro but woman also; and since then we see women compeeting successfully with not only man but the lords and the gods. Yet, to this evil-day, the religious curse of taxation and no represintation, and precious little protection is yet forced upon them. Abraham, the father of tramps, disowned, and rented out his wife; Old Lot, another old religious tramp, tried to work the same racket with his old wife and 'galls'. Jesus the man-god, spit-cure, water-wine, grean-corn, shoemaker-wax tramp-doctor, not only disowned his mother, but left her without a home, and to still sleep with the cattle, as she was doing when he was born!

☞ Why your religious fathers and your Christian gods, and their slave bibles are womans most damnable enemy; and yet, we see, and hear them anxious for bible rule! See our dedication.

PUBERTY, menstration, or the marriagable age is the age that females are intended to bear children. In this country it is from twelve to fifteen years. And here comes the disputed point: whether this is the marriagable age, or whether it is not best for a more extended age in which they would likely be more capable, both physically and mentally to perform the duties of married life? And I say: "Take nature's path and mad opinions leave.' for whenever menstruation comes on, it is the arranging of an egg, entended of course, by nature for impregnation— And, let it be at twelve or fifteen years of age, its the natural sign of the marriagable age. And should the facilities of the country forbid this age, by not making them capable of keeping a home, then, the fault, must be in the facilities, and education, and not in nature. The decay of this age is the cause of that wretched and miserable disease known as old maid, and old bach.

DISEASES OF PUBERTY, menstruation, and the marriagable age, comes inordinate lust, ungovernable sexual passion, obstructed, laborious, excessive, vicarious, irregular, or checked menstruation, chlorosis, or green sickness, etc. It is said that these diseases were scarcely known to our grandmothers, but now they are very prevalent to all classes above mear infancy. Showing very conclusively that the greatest need of this life, and especially this age, is the proper knowledge as how to live, so as to be a healthy, happy, bread-winner.

TREATMENT. For the relief of all these derangements, a thorough and persevearing application of our principles on bathing, exercise and rest, what to eat, drink, and avoid, is quiet sufficient.

The general plan of treatment, as given throughout this work, varing as symptoms may indicate. And as we have treated these diseases under the twelve classes, and treated symptoms under remedies, so, we will but refer to them here.

An abundence of exercise in the free, fresh, pure, sunny air, with an occasional soaking, soap, scrubbing bath as hot as can be used; hot foot, sitting shallow baths, and the abdominal rapper is good. Hot or cold water vaginal injections, to check excessive flow, relaxation, pain, and to strengthen ·

DISEASES OF MARRIED LIFE, pregnancy, etc. Though pregnancy is a natural condition, yet, it is frequently attended with the following derangements: painful cesation of the menses; nausia and vomiting; fainting; sleepliness; heart-burn; diarhea; constipation; piles; headache; stys; salivation, hemorage from the stomach; cramps; difficult breathing; toothache; jaundice; difficult urination; pain in the side; s itch in the loins; swelling of the limbs; soreness or pain in the breasts; nervousness; mental dispondency; longings; hysterical fits; convulsions, and abortion !

TREATMENT· Purify the body, and treat each symptom as already given, under remedies and the many classes of diseases given.

ABORTION; consists in the expulsion af the fetus before the natural time for labor; and is either accidental or intentional. The symptoms are forewarning similar to those of natural labor.

TREATMENT— As soon as such is expected be

temperate, quiet, avoiding all excesses, rest, sleep and be cheerfully occupied. Support the abdomen and back with a broad bandage, ease, pains with warm or hot fomentations or injections into the vagina and bowels.

☞ To keep healthy, stout, and odor-pure, wash out your mouth every time you use it—do precisely so with your vagina, and anoint it if chafed, or sore; and do so with your bowels, and you will avoid abortion, filth, and unnatural discharges; and it might be necessary to use soapsuds from strong lye-soap as a vaginal injection, and protector.

Should abortion occur, and cold, chilley rigors set in, the pulse sinking, use a very hot foot bath, drink a little hot toddy, use a little paregoric, and our fever syrup; and if threatened with flooding wash out the womb and vagina with hot water and plug up the vagina with lint or old rags.

WHITES, is a discharge of a yellowish-white matter, virging to green, from the vagina. It attacts all ages; and we find those affected, have a deranged system.

TREATMENT—Balance and strengthen the system; use hot water injections to kill the chronic inflamation, and to cleanse the parts; followed by a good liniment, made by thickening turpentine by adding castor, sweet, or linseed oil. Inject this liniment into the vagina and womb when it is necessary; it will cure not only the whites but the gleet, clap, or like diseases.

BARRENNESS, a want of the power to beget; and may be from an unequal and unsatisfactory yoke. The most frequent cause is the suppression, or derangement of the menstrual flux. The fever heat, and filth of lewdness, is a sure cause of barrenness: so is self-pollution; onanism; or the overclean habit of washing out the vagina immediatly after sexual indulgence or intercourse.

TREATMENT— Any thoughtful person must know the cause; and by reading this book you also, have an idea how to cure yourself. Should it be from an unsatisfactory yoke, then it is with your selves to settle. If it be from disease, the only hope is to find out the cause and remove it, live temperate, treat each cause according to the symptoms.

DISPLACEMENTS, are the prolapse of the vagina, and muscles, tissues, and ligaments of the organs of generation, alowing a healthy, or unheathy womb to fall, or prolapse, in its various positions. The womb may be diseased and the tissues not, but it is generally from a stupid debillity.

TREATMENT— The hot sitting, and hot foot bath for an hour every day, followed by quite a quantity of very hot water, forcibly injected into the vagina, and this followed by an injection of a liniment, made by mixing sweet, castor, linseed, lard, or lard-oil, in turpentine. This will cause the parts to wake up and to asume their natural size, and position; if not, it will aid a pessary, and the abdominal bandage in doing so.

I know of a town womans case being cured by a hasty ride for twenty miles, in a jolting farm wagon; it so inflamed the muscles, ligaments, and tissues, as to cause all parts to asume their natural places and functions; this was twenty years ago, she has since had four children, worked every day, and is proof-sheet reader to this book.

In 1859 I seen Prof. Paine, in Bellevue Hospital sew up the vagiea to prevent the womb from falling out. It was similar in shape and size to a goose egg. Only think, the vagina and womb so enlarges that I have inserted my hand and arm, bringing forth the child and after-birth, without injury to the mother or chilb.

DISEASES AND REMEDIES.

Talk about man being the tougher sex, if there is anything in this world that will out stretch, or indure more than this, and live, and do well, then what is it? Excuse me ladies!

CHILDBIRTH, is the act of borning an infant, and, although, a natural process, yet, owing to our artificial mode of life, it is attended with great pain and difficulty. It has four stages: 1st. In which the mouth of the womb enlarges, and known by a discharge of mucus, sharp cutting pains, and sharp piercing groans. 2nd. In which the womb desends to the lower outlet, and known by the pains being more dull, and they puff up, and groan dull and heavy, and the parts grately enlarge, perhaps a discharge of the amnion waters. 3rd. In which the child is born, and seperated from the mother. This consists in tying the cord with a soft string, two inches from the infant, and two inches towards the after-birth, then sever the cord between them. 4th. In which the after-birth comes or is brought away, thus completing labor.

TREATMENT— The Obstetrician, midwife, or wise and skilfull woman, should attend as soon as possible. And if to a stranger, ascertain as soon as possible of her general health, strength, and condition, etc., whether this is her first or other child, and if a mother whether she has heretofore had an easy time? See that the stomach, bowels, and bladder is empty, easy, and free; the feet hot, and all on a balance. Then with your finger moist, wet, or oiled examine as to whether the womb has descended so as to be felt, if the mouth be dilated, the outlet sufficient for a free labor, or if obstructed from a tumor or deformity. If not assure the mother that other measures must be taken. But, if all be right labor should close in a few hours; in which time the patient should be left to herself, and an attendant to assist her in any position she may fancy.

The obstetrician should stay close at hand, noting the tone of the groans, calling in frequently to see that all is kept right. When the baby is born and as soon as it is free, if healthy it will give a scream with all its might; turn it over on its side elevating its head, watch the navel cord till it ceases to pulsate, then with a soft string tie and sever the cord— giving the infant to an assistant who should wash it with good castile-soap, a soft rag, and moderatly warm water; and dress it, in pure, clean, soft, loose, dry, warm cloathes; while you look out for another, or attend to the after-birth which should soon follow. Should it not, then make a finger examination by holding the cord in one hand and with the other find out the condition; if it is in the vagina slight contraction of the cord will remove it, but if it is adhearing in the womb you must work your hand gradually along up the cord into the womb, and cautiously tearing it loose and remove it. Should bleeding be dangerous use hot water injections to check it and plug up the vagina with old soft rags. Should the pulse weaken, and chilly sensations set in, give a little hot toddy, paregoric, fever syrup, a very hot foot bath and fomentations to the aching parts.

LYING IN; or bearing an infant on to childhood embraces all the time from the first alarm of infant birth up to childhood; thus we say: infancy, childhood, youth, and manhood. If you feel like getting up and stiring around in an hour do so, use your own judgement; for circumstances may confine you for months; yet, arise and assume your duty as soon as possible.

WASHING and dressing the baby should be done in a warm room; so as to keep the baby, and all warm. Wash it thoroughly with castile-soap a soft rag and pure, fresh warm water; and you will have a sweet red baby, if healthy, which in a few days changes to a yellow baby, and in a few more days it asumes the complexion of its race.

In placing the belly-band be careful to cover the navel with rosin flour, and a soft rag, which should be watched and kept perfectly dry until the cord matters off and the parts heal. See our cuts.

DISEASES of childbirth are of the imaginary hobgoblin nature. The mother, and all concerned would do well to study our cuts illustrating this subject from the development of the ovum in the uterus up to childbirth. Should labor exceed five or six hours, then the midwife had better lend a helping mind and hand. Forcible jets of hot water to the mouth of the womb, and cold cloths to the abdomen and the parts may start labor.

I was called to a woman once that had been all day and all night in travail, until all was dry, exhausted, and feverish, and labor had actually quit; all hands had quit, and granny informed me that the child was hung on the cross-bone. A finger examination shown the infant at the lower outlet. I washed the patients hands and face, give her a little toddy, a good cup of coffee, placed wet cloths to the belly and parts and in a minute it was born.

CHILDBED FEVER should be treated in general as directed for fevers, with hot poultices or fomentations to the belly and hot injections to the womb and bowels, very hot foot and sitting baths, along with an occasional dose of salts and our fever syrup.

INFLAMATION of the breasts may be prevented by keeping the milk drawn out, ease with poultices or fomentations. Soothe and harden the nipples with hot tallow; elevate the legs foment and rub the blood to the body if threatened with milk-leg, cramps, etc.

Put the baby to its mothers breast as soon as it is washed, it should start the milk. Let it suck say eight times a day, but, none at night, if it is well. Give it fresh water often, and hot water if colicky, and if you have plenty of milk dont feed it until it has teeth, and then avoid nicknacks, candy, etc.

Avoid cradles, and hold your baby most of the time and the balanc let it tumble on a pallet; and never alow it to go wet, dirty, nor cold, keep its feet always hot; ☞ and let it sleep much, unannoyed, and uningured by flies, musketoes, bedbugs, and other bloodsuckers.

When to cease nursing should be governed by the health of the baby and mother; if its teeth and health admit an early weaning so much the better. Reappearanc of the menses is claimed a proper time to cease nursing, but it seems the milk and baby is not affected; and the reappearance of the menses is uncertain, as it may appear in one month, or not in twelve months.

Cesation of menstruation, or the Turn of Life, it takes place somewhere near fifty years; and is a sure sign that ☞ AMOUR ☜ the god of LOVE, or RELIGION, is dead, damed ,deliverd, and doomed to an old cob-pipe, and the hobgoblin-love of the chimney corner, or, it is a sure sign of the cesation of child-bearing you bet.

And, although, a natural condition, yet it is beset with consideable fuss, sickness, and uncalled for deaths; all of which might have been relieved, or entirley prevented if it was not for the falce promices of their falce god Amour, that they can immediatly renew the amorous lust, called love, or religion on the t'other side of Jordan.

DISEASES of Infants and Children— Still-born ifants are born apparantly dead, and they should imediatly be held in warm water, and if the afterbirth comes place it in hot water, watch and see that it ceases to pulsate before you separate it from the baby.

Meconium is a dark green matter that is in the

DISEASES AND REMEDIES.

infants bowels when born; it is believed that the first milk of the mother passes this off; should it not do so use warm water injections, or indigo in cool, fresh water, pour down the throat with a tea spoon. Put the spoon back in the throat, and pour it down; do so for Croup, colds, coughs, phthisic, etc., it wont make it sick like other emetics and cathartics

Ruptures are the giving way of the wall of the belly allowing the bowels to form a tumor-like enlargement. This happens mostly in the navel and groins. Replace them and bind them with a truss, bandage or straps of adhesive plaster. Foment when inflamed anb painful, and strengthen with refrigerants.

Tongue-tied is the binding of the tongue to the floor of the mouth by a narrow thin striping, gratety anoying the baby in sucking and talking. Consult a surgeon, for this, for ruptures, hair-lip, etc.

Thrush is a microbe ulceration of the mucus skin of the iner mouth, tongue, throat, stomach, bowels, etc, giving off a yellowish or redish scum.

Treatment- Give a good purging dose of blue pill and work this off with salts, and ease griping with paregoric, hot soap scrub bath, fomentations and hot foot baths; give a litte sulphur every day, and occasional dose of fever syr p, in a little weak milk toddy.

Worms that most affect, not only, children but most grown people, are the long round, the thread, and the maw or pin worms; and occasionly a tapeworm. The first infest the small bowels, crawling to the outer world through any avenue. I have seen them discharged by the quart, and some were twelve inches long. The other three varieties infest the lower bowels, causing many diseases; as fits, peviousness, nausia, fevers, disturbed mind and sleep, offensive breath and looks, dyspepsia, gluttony, intemperance, lewdness, and at times screaming fits of convulsions.

Treatment— For these last symptoms I would use fomentations, a very hot foot bath, a warm water emetic, having worm-wood, worm-seed, or with vermifuge in the water, also inject this freely till it purges. Make a vermifuge by mixing castor-oil, and oil of worm-seed, each one ounce, oil of anise half an ounce, tincture of myrrh half.a dram, turpentine ten drops, croton oil two drop and not any more; mix by thoroughly shaking.

Shake before giving, give only a few drops at a time to a baby, a tea-spooful to a child five or six years old, and a table-spoonful to grown people.

For tape worms beat to a paste one ounce of pumpkin seed, sugar, and milk, warm from the cow; this is only a dose for a stout grown person, and should be taken on an empty stomach, after fasting twenty-four hours, then in about three hours take a large purging dose of castor oil with some of the above vermifuge in it.

TEETHING, begins about the six or seventh month; and in about six years these teeth fall out, and are succeeded by others, which are coming along for twenty-five years, when your last fourth grinders appear. Now, although, this is a natural process, yet, but few children, or grown people can cut a tooth without being made sick; and many grown people have tooth or worm sickness, suffer, suffer, and even die and do not know the cause.

The symptoms for worms, teething, etc., are the same, then, the only pathognomonic symptom is the tooth or the worm.

Treatment— Keep the child quiet, keep things on a balance, by cooling the fever with the hot bath hot foot bath, hot water emetics and purgatives, fomentations to the bowels, throat, and jaws; and if the gums are rubed and pressed it will hasten the

the cutting the teeth; and a surgeon may have to cut the gums.

Begetting children—How little thought of, and yet, how important. In this people seem to have no control; and yet, it is in the control of all; as much so, as is the breeding of our domestic animals. This, like every thing, has certain fixed, and unalterable laws, controling and regulating it, and to rightly use it, is to understand and obey those laws. It is a law of mentology that sameness of body, brain, and beliefs are best adapted to each other in promoting happiness, in the business and social affairs of life; that is, birds of a feather flock together. So in physiology, like, or balanced temperaments are best adapted to begetting and rearing children. Also, it is a fixed law in the human female that a certain time in each month they are capable of impregnation, and at no other time; and this happy time, or season, is immediately after menstruation and for fifteen days after, and after this time there is but little, if any danger of impregnation.

Begetting boys or girls as you wish is done by drawing up and fastening close to the body, and kept so confined during coition the left testicle to prevent getting girls.

And lastly, yet, not leastly, ladies I will admonish you on dress; see our cuts— Nature and Fashion; Nature is the outlines of the Greek slave, and Fashion is the outlines of the Slave of fashion. The last is only to be see to be hated

POISONS, are usually spoken of as those things that immediately produce pain, distress, sickness, and death; and to combat the tendency of this class of poisons is the object of this article. So, we speak of them as mineral, vegetable, animal, and gaseous poisons. Yet, reduce them to their origin, or, back as fare as the mind can go, and all are, or was only simple matter, in the form of an element or a foundation, and that was mineral. So, the symptoms, and not the name, must be combatted.

Mineral poisons are more locally corrosive and inflammatory; vegetable poisons are more slow and more or less narcotic; while animal poisons show their immediate effects through the nervous system in pain, swelling, and spasms; hydrophobia being an exception as to time; and the gaseous, called choke-damp, fire-damp, milk-sick, drunk, etc., are suffocative, stupifying and paralytic.

Treatment— When an inflaming, irritating, or a corrosive, burning substance has been swallowed, as an acid, alkali, caustic, arsenic, glass-flour, rat-poison, etc., give warm water emetics, having an oily, greasy, or mucous substance as raw eggs, flour sweet milk, lard or butter, and hasten the vomiting up of this, and the poison, by giving mustard in warm water, and by tickling the throat with a feather or your finger. If they can-not or will-not swallow, then pour it down the throat, from a long neck bottle or a spoon placed beyond the windpipe or use a pump.

When a narcotic poison has been swallowed, as opium, morphine, laudanum, prussic acid, strychnine, tobacco, buckeye, jimpson, alcohol, and for similar, or like narcotic, stupid, bucekeyed symptoms give hot lard, butter, or sweet milk, as above, vomiting thoroughly with mustard and warm water; having their feet in hot water and keep the head and face cool; and then rally with our fever syrup, coffee, and a scrubbing bath.

☞ Talk about vegetable medicines being harmless, and mineral mdeicine poisonous, all the above dreadful poisons are very common vegetable medicines. ☜

For the bite and sting of animals, insects, reptiles, etc., a hot toddy, and plenty of hot water, or sassafras tea, to produce sweating, along with the hot foot, and hot scrubbing soap bath, and apply a hot, soothing poultice with sweet or castor-oil in it to the bitten parts, then heal with rosin flour. If sick vomit with warm water, and tone up with our fever syrup.

In the gaseous and narcotic poisons place the patient where the fresh cool air is on the face, while the feet and legs are kept hot, give cool lemonade, strong coffee, and if possible a sweating bath.

To prevent hydrophobia is to cleanse the wound with hot poultices and sweet-oil kept constantly on the wound, then heal with rosin flour, at the same time purify the entire system with the sweating baths, blue pill, and salts, and keep the nervous system completely under a hot toddy; and should the spasms occur then treat them as directed on 25 page, for spasmopic diseases.

So, in conclusion I will say this, let diseases be what they may, and their origin from this, that or the other cause, one thing is a fact, and that fact is, if you will cleanse the stomache and the bowels, equalize the heat and you at once equally distribute the blood and life, and at once place yourself on the road to health.

GERMS OR THE CAUSES OF MANY DISEASES.

IT is a fact, that most diseases are caused by organized piratical, parasitical, living beings, which under certain conditions of heat, moisture, and food, they rapidly produce their kind. ☞ Man, himself, is only a detached parasitical, piratical, vegetating animal of only a higher degree, and is sustained by feeding and feasting upon his mother earth's immortal part. And mother earth is only a detached mass of living, moving, breathing, intelligent germ matter, thrown off from the sun, that yet feed, feast and subsists on the suns immortal part. Just like the deadly Planaride Microbe, that by casting off a mear fragment of its body it immediately multiplies into innumerable others.

And many, many of these parasites are far, far, very far superior to presumpteous man in self-preservation, and enduranc, if not in all other things! Yes, salting, freezing, boiling, frying, that is, the exposures to the severest cooking heat will not kill some of them! And what will kill and expel one kind will not hurt another. The vaccine virus proves the germ theory. It is a fungoid parasite developed by being introduced into the udder of a cow. Precisley so with the germs of all diseases.

"The rags of a poor man just died being thrown into the street, and two hogs comeing by at the same time and rooting among them and shaking about in their mouthes, in less than an hour turned around and died on the spot!" History tells us that this black death destroyed over half the population of all Europe.

Weakness, filth, and an unbalanced, unhealthey growths causes the most of our diseases. And although they are millions of miles below our vision yet the microscope and these facts prove their deadly existence, and rapid development. Millions develop, or spring into existence, in our blood and

DISEASES AND REMEDIES. 47

body in a minute of time. One little minute germ inhaled at the church, theater, or from the passer by, or the air we breathe may multiply so rapidly as to affect every tissue of the body in an hour.

Microbe is the name given to all fungus infusora, and they are so extremely thin as to be termed a filiform fluke, or, thread-like, as seen in numbers 1, 2, 4, 5, and 6 of CUT 5 below; while others put in an appearances as shown in our other figures.

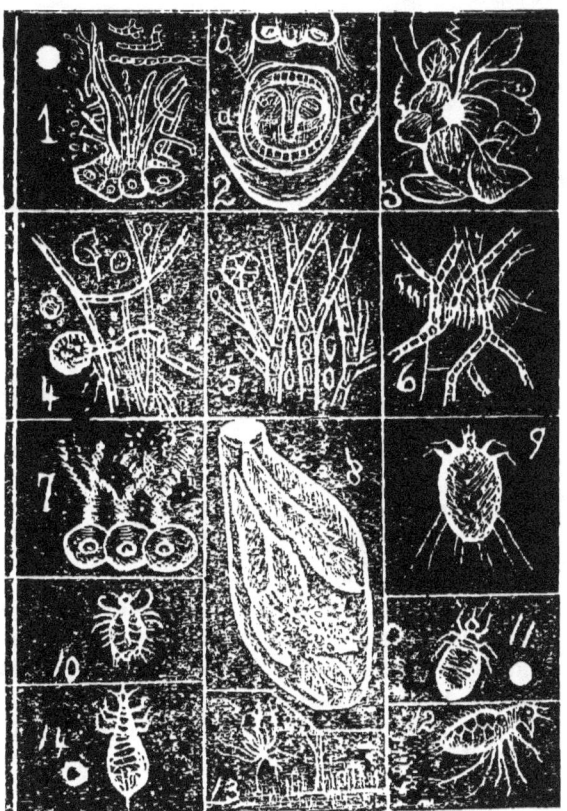

We here reproduce a few cuts of this Microbe or Parasite life, as seen under Prof. Paine's Microscope; and by the naked eyes. Figure 1, in cut 5, represents these microbes as discharged from the nostrils in a case of catarrh.

Figure 2, pictures the enlarged tonsils b, the elongated uvela c, and the coated slimy tongue a, as seen in catarrh, dyspepsia and consumption.

Figure 3, pictures this fungous microbe growth as seen on the tongue of colicky, costive dyspeptics

Figure 4, is a specimen from the tongue of a patient laboring under malarial blood poison, as in chills, fever, dyspepsia, neuralgia and catarrh.

Figure 5, shows the fungus parasites of catarrh, bronchitis and consumption.

Figure 6, represents this fungoid fur taken from the tongue of a dyspeptic, rheumatic and a nervous patient.

Figure 7, pictures this eternal mushroom animal as he makes his appearence in ulcers and cancers.

Figure 8, is a fair sample of these piratical, parasitical animals of a higher degree of growth, and are the cause of many, many skin diseases, and especially pimples of the nose and face.

Figure 9, graphically pictures to you the tarapin like itch insect that attacts the entire skin.

Figure 10, gives you a good likenes of the crab-lice that tells on the whore and the whoremonger!

Figure 11, is a likeness of the chinch, a very tenacious bloodsucking bug that infests our houses beds and cloathing.

Figure 12, is that high kicker, the flea, and he is every where, and one of the grandest pirats ever known. He preys freely and fearlessly upon all other animals, and when pursued he flies sky high.

Figuri 13, pictures that long leged, fleet winged, migratory bloodsucker, the musketo as he appears at home, in the slush and the swamp.

Figure 14, pictures the lice that feed and feast on the heads of filthey unfortunate persons.

IN CUT 6, on the opposite page Figure 1, represents the long round worms that infest the stomach intestines, and frequently crawl out of the nose, anus and mouth.

DISEASES AND REMEDIES.

Figure 2, shows us the pork-worm as found in measly pork and in this way it is introduced into the human stomach and body.

Figure 3, gives a few joints, a broken off, or a detached fragment of the tape worm, which like the deadly Planaride microbe, a mear cast off fragment of it immediatly multiplies into innumerable

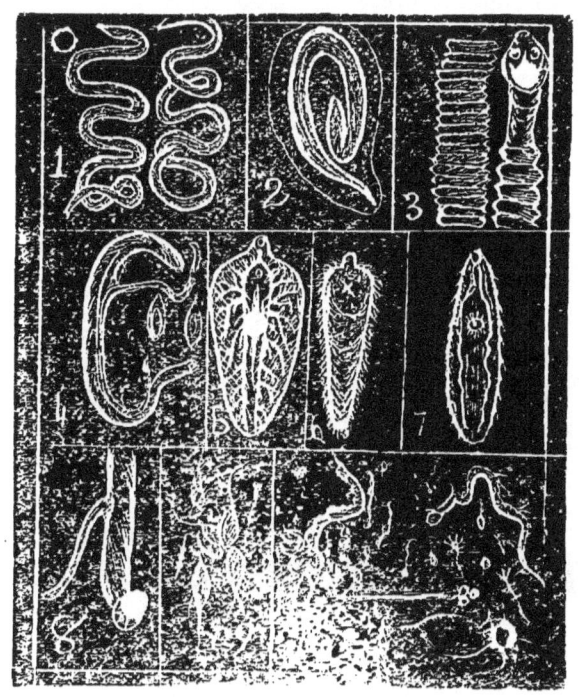

CUT SIXTH.

others. It is common in weak hungry stomachs.

Figure 4, represents a parasite generally found in the blood and sores of scrofulous persons.

Figure 5, shows the fungous flukes that poison our blood and tissues, causing chills and fevers as billious, yellow, typus, remittent and intermittent.

Figure 6, represents the various tenia flukes that make their way into our stomachs, then through the circulation into the liver and blood. In their larval condition they are the most frequent cause of death than all other microbes.

Figure 7, is a fluke found in dyspepsia, catarrh, eresipelas, bronchitis, and consumption.

Figure 8, shows a parasite from the kidneys in Bright's disease of the kidneys, cancer, consumption and dropsy.

Figure 9, represents the microbe as seen in gleet, whites, in female diseases.

Figure 10, pictures to you the likeness of many, many disgusting and disease spreading little animals living on the filth of bank bills.

CUT 7, gives a few of the many beautiful forms that the crystal snow, frost and ice assumes as it comes to us from grandma ocean. Personal Iden-

CUT 7. | CUT 8.

tity, or that eternal same fellow, that sameness of being, design, and construction, tell us plainly that intelligence shapes and controles every thing with as much incomprehensive design as is shown in the human organism. And why is it that one person, or thing, endure or exists longest? Because he or it is more powerful in vitality, and is more careful or intelligent.

CUT 8, pictures to us one little drop of water that has been made by melting these beautiful

DISEASES AND REMEDIES.

chrystals of snow and ice. No sooner formed into warm water than germ life sets in, and soon the microscope reveals to us a world of living, moving intelligent beings. ☞ Such is life— for in, or by death we live in new forms, manifesting sight, feeling, hearing, tasting, smelling; with as much sensabillity, iritabillity, contractilli·y, vitality as is displayed by intelligent human beings. Yes, it is taught, that grandma ocean is a mear waste of waters, and that snow and frost is a mear jumbled up incoherent mass without any design or purpose. Yes, they, these self-created and self-creating seas, oceans and chrystals have a design, a fixed unalterable design, and displayes as much or more creative power and self-preservation and intelligence as is claimed by the Christians for their god! And without old grandma ocean, and her intelligence there would be no presumpteous man, god or no god! See pages 58, 89, and 163 to 171.

As to whether germ growth is the cause or the effect of disease matters not. The facts are, they begin by living on your sour, foul filth, and soon become stout enough to eat your gristle and bone! And to resist a heat, a cold, an acid, an alkali, or a caustic, or the gasses that would kill you, and why and what is to be done? The facts are, they are clothed with a gelatinous coating, and a slime that resists all these remedies. But moist heat in the form of pure, fresh, live water, steam, and electricity will soften, penetrate, confuse and expell them. It will disolve all acrid iritating matter, scatter and break up all congestions, and diseased growths and convey them out of the system by vomiting, purging, and sweating. See and read how it can be done from page 1 to this page.

HALLUCINATION.

OR that awful disease, a delusion of our senses. It is most common with religionists, or those of a religious, or a superstitious temperament. One of the most striking and fatal was that of the idea of a mysterious personal god, and his word in book form that make slaves of some and awful gods of others!

Barnes' general history of 1883, page 440, tells us that Luther in 1534 disregarded! and rejected! the claims of religionists and bible makers up to himself! And they claimed to have got theirs from God! But he went about the markets and slums of the city and got up the "Protestant Bible" from their version of these outrageous fish, snake and ghost stories, and not from the gods!

Then on page 459 Barnes tells us that Tyndal and Coverdale, in 1536, just two years later, wrote a bible and six articles of religious rule for the church of England. It give only to Gentlemen the privilege of reading the bible! Why? Because it was too obscene, vicious and vulgar for ladies and youths to read!

Then, to cap the climax, King Jim, the simpleton, in 1603, got up his bible of errors and self- contradictions! It was introduced through fear! and forced upon us by torture, by fire and the sword! of the English army and government!!!!

Now, my accountable, dying fellow man, who are the infidels, heratics and disobedient disbelievers? All of these bibles contradict all other bibles and themselves. And this is why our nation rejects all bible rule. Now, have I not got as good a right to get up what I think to be the true bible as these men, gods and devils? See pages, 1, 134, 163, 178, 241--2, 255.

AN ESSAY ON MAN.

TO H. ST. JOHN, LORD BOLINGBROKE.

WRITTEN IN 1732. INCORPORATED IN POPE'S WORKS, 1735.

THE DESIGN.

HAVING proposed to write some pieces on human life and manners, such as (to use my Lord Bacon's expression) "come home to men's business and bosoms," I thought it more satisfactory to begin with considering man in the abstract, his nature and his state; since to prove any moral duty, to enforce any moral precept, or to examine the perfection or imperfection of any creature whatsoever, it is necessary first to know what condition and relation it is placed in, and what is the proper end and purpose of its being.

The science of human nature is like all other sciences, reduced to a few clear points. There are not many certain truths in this world. It is therefore in the anatomy of the mind as in that of the body; more good will accrue to mankind by attending to the large, open, and perceptible parts, than by studying too much such finer nerves and vessels, the conformations and uses of which will forever escape our observation. The disputes are all upon these last, and, I will venture to say, they have less sharpened the wits than the hearts of men against each other, and have diminished the practice, more than advanced the theory, of morality. If I could flatter myself that this Essay has any merit, it is in steering betwixt the extremes of doctrines seemingly opposite, in passing over terms utterly unintelligible, and in forming¹, a temperate yet not inconsistent, and a short yet not imperfect system of ethics.

This I might have done in prose; but I chose verse, and even rhyme, for two reasons. The one will appear obvious; that principles, maxims, or precepts so written, both strike the reader more strongly at first, and are more easily retained by him afterwards; the other may seem odd, but it is true. I found I could express them more shortly this way than in prose itself; and nothing is more certain, than that much of the force as well as grace of arguments or instructions depends on their conciseness. I was unable to treat this part of my subject more in detail, without becoming dry and tedious; or more poetically, without sacrificing perspicuity to ornament, without wandering from the precision, or breaking the chain of reasoning; if any man can unite all these without diminution of any of them, I freely confess he will compass a thing above my capacity.

What is now published, is only to be considered as a general map of Man, marking out no more than the greater parts, their extent, their limits, and their connection, and leaving the particular to be more fully delineated in the charts which are to follow. Consequently, these Epistles in their progress (if I have health and leisure to make any progress) will be less dry, and more susceptible of poetical ornament. I am here only opening the fountains, and clearing the passage: to deduce the rivers, to follow them in their course, and to observe their effects, may be a task more agreeable.

---

1 In first edition, "out of all."

ARGUMENT OF EPISTLE I.

THE NATURE AND STATE OF MAN, WITH RE-
SPECT TO THE UNIVERSE.

nan in the abstract.—I. That we can judge only with regard to our own system, being ignorant of the relations of systems and things, ver. 17, &c.—II. That man is not to be deemed imperfect, but a being suited to his place and rank in the creation, agreeable to the general order of things, and comformable to ends and relations to him unknown, ver. 35, &c.—III. That it is partly upon his ignorance of future events, and partly upon the hope of a future state, that all his happiness in the present depends, ver. 77, &c.—IV. The pride of aiming at more knowledge, and pretending to more perfection, the cause of man's error and misery. The impiety of putting himself in the place of God, and judging of the fitness or unfitness, perfection or imperfection, justice or injustice of His dispensations, ver. 109, &c.—V. The absurdity of conceiting himself the final cause of the creation, or expecting that perfection in the moral world, which is not in the natural, ver. 131, &c.—VI. The unreasonableness of his complaints against Providence, while on the one hand he demands the perfections of the angels, and on the other the bodily qualifications of the brutes; though, to possess any of the sensitive faculties in a higher degree, would render him miserable, ver. 173, &c.—VII. That throughout the whole visible world, an universal order and gradation in the sensual and mental faculties is observed, which causes a subordination of creature to creature, and of all creatures to man. The gradations of sense, instinct, thought, reflection, reason: that reason alone countervails all the other faculties, ver. 207.—VIII. How much further this order and subordination of living creatures may extend, above and below us; were any part of which broken, not that part only, but the whole connected creation must be destroyed, ver. 233.—IX. The extravagance, madness, and pride of such a desire, ver. 250.—X. The consequence of all, the absolute submission due to Providence, both as to our present and future state, ver. 281, &c. to the end.

EPISTLE I.

Awake, my St. John!¹ leave all meaner things
To low ambition, and the pride of kings.
Let us, since life can little more supply
Than just to look about us and to die,
Expatiate free o'er all this scene of Man;
A mighty maze! but not without a plan;
A wild, where weeds and flow'rs promiscuous
    shoot;
Or garden, tempting with forbidden fruit.
Together let us beat this ample field,
Try what the open, what the covert yield;
The latent tracts, the giddy heights, explore
Of all who blindly creep, or sightless soar;
Eye nature's walks, shoot folly as it flies.
And catch the manners living as they rise;
Laugh where we must, be candid where we can;
But vindicate the ways of God to man.

   I. Say first, of God above or Man below,
What can we reason but from what we know?
Of Man, what see we but his station here,
From which to reason, or to which refer?
Through worlds unnumbered though the God be
    known,
'Tis ours to trace Him only in our own.
He, who through vast immensity can pierce,
Sees worlds on worlds compose one universe,
Observe how system into system runs,
What other planets circle other suns,
What varied being peoples ev'ry star,
May tell us why Heaven has made us as we are.
But of this frame the bearings, and the ties,
The strong connections, nice dependencies,

---

1 Henry St. John, the famous Lord Bolingbroke. He was the son of Sir Henry St. John of Lydiard Tregose, in Wiltshire. He fled to France to escape impeachment for treason as a Jacobite soon after the accession of George I., but was pardoned and returned. He has been called the English Alcibiades; his best work is the "Patriot King."

Gradations just, has thy pervading soul
Looked through, or can a part contain the whole?
  Is the great chain,[1] that draws all to agree,
And drawn supports, upheld by God, or thee?

  II. Presumptuous man! the reason wouldst thou find,
Why formed so weak, so little, and so blind?
First, if thou canst, the harder reason guess,
Why formed no weaker, blinder and no less?
Ask of thy mother earth, why oaks are made
Taller and stronger than the weeds they shade?
Or ask of yonder argent field above,
Why Jove's satellites are less than Jove?
  Of systems possible, if 'tis confest
That Wisdom Infinite must form the best,
Where all must full or not coherent be,
And all that rises, rise in due degree;
Then, in the scale of reas'ning life, 'tis plain,
There must be, somewhere, such a rank as Man:
And all the question (wrangle e'er so long)
Is only this, if God has placed him wrong?
  Respecting Man, whatever wrong we call,
May, must be right, as relative to all.
In human works, though labored on with pain,
A thousand movements scarce one purpose gain;
In God's, one single can its end produce;
Yet serves to second too some other use.
So man, who here seems principal alone,
Perhaps acts second to some sphere unknown,
Touches some wheel, or verges to some goal;
'Tis but a part we see, and not a whole.
  When the proud steed shall know why man restrains
His fiery course or drives him o'er the plains:
When the dull ox, why now he breaks the clod,
Is now a victim, and now Egypt's God:[2]
Then shall man's pride and dullness comprehend

---

  [1] An allusion to the golden chain by which Homer tells us the world was sustained by Jove.
  [2] The ox was worshipped in ancient Egypt under the name of Apis.

His actions', passions', being's, use and end;
Why doing, suff'ring, checked, impelled; and why
This hour a slave, the next a deity.
    Then say not Man's imperfect, Heaven in fault;
Say rather, Man's as perfect as he ought:
His knowledge measured to his state and place;
His time a moment, and a point his space.
If to be perfect in a certain sphere,
What matter, soon or late, or here or there?
The blest to-day is as completely so,
As who began a thousand years ago.

    III. Heav'n from all creatures hides the book of fate.
All but the page prescribed, their present state:
From brutes what men, from men what spirits know:
Or who could suffer being here below?
The lamb thy riot dooms to bleed to-day,
Had he thy reason, would he skip and play?
Pleased to the last, he crops the flow'ry food,
And licks the hand just raised to shed his blood.
Oh, blindness to the future! kindly giv'n,
That each may fill the circle marked by Heav'n,
Who sees with equal eye, as God of all,[1]
A hero perish, or a sparrow fall,
Atoms of system into ruin hurled,
And now a bubble burst, and now a world.
    Hope humbly then: with trembling pinions soar;
Wait the great teacher Death; and God adore.
What future bliss, He gives not thee to know,
But gives that hope to be thy blessing now.
Hope springs eternal in the human breast:
Man never Is, but always To be blest:
The soul, uneasy and confined from home,
Rests and expatiates in a life to come.
    Lo, the poor Indian! whose untutored mind
Sees God in clouds, or hears him in the wind;
His soul, proud science never taught to stray
Far as the solar walk, or milky way;

---

[1] St. Matt. x. 29.

Yet simple nature to his hope has giv'n,
Behind the cloud-topt hill, and humbler heav'n;
Some safer world in depths of woods embraced,
Some happier island in the watery waste,
Where slaves once more their native land behold,
No fiends torment, no Christians thirst for gold.
To be, contents his natural desire,
He asks no angel's wing, no seraph's fire;
But thinks, admitted to that equal sky,
His faithful dog shall bear him company.

IV. Go, wiser thou! and in thy scale of sense,
Weigh thy opinion against Providence;
Call imperfection what thou fanciest such,
Say, here he gives too little, there too much:
Destroy all creatures for thy sport or guest,
Yet cry, if Man's unhappy, God's unjust;
If man alone engross not Heaven's high care;
Alone made perfect here, immortal there:
Snatch from His hand the balance and the rod,
Re-judge His justice, be the god of God.
In pride, in reas'ning pride, our error lies;
All quit their sphere, and rush into the skies.
Pride still is aiming at the blest abodes,
Men would be angels, angels would be gods.
Aspiring to be gods, if angels fell,
Aspiring to be angels, men rebel:
And who but wishes to invert the laws
Of Order, sins against the Eternal Cause.

V. Ask for what end the heavenly bodies shine,
Earth for whose use? Pride answers, "'Tis for mine:
For me kind nature wakes her genial pow'r,
Suckles each herb, and spreads out every flow'r:
Annual for me, the grape, the rose renew
The juice nectareous, and the balmy dew;
For me, the mine a thousand treasures brings;
For me, health gushes from a thousand springs;
Seas roll to waft me, suns to light me rise,
My footstool earth, my canopy the skies."
But errs not Nature from this gracious end,
From burning suns when livid deaths descend,

When earthquakes swallow, or when tempests sweep
Towns to one grave, whole nations to the deep?[1]
" No ('tis replied), the first Almighty Cause
Acts not by partial, but by gen'ral laws;
The exceptions few; some change since all began;
And what created perfect?"—Why then Man?
If the great end be human happiness,
Then nature deviates; and can man do less?
As much that end a constant course requires
Of show'rs and sunshine, as of man's desires;
As much eternal springs and cloudless skies,
As men forever temperate, calm and wise.
If plagues or earthquakes break not Heav'n's design,
Why then a Borgia,[2] or a Catiline?
Who know but He, whose hand the lightning forms,
Who heaves old ocean, and who wings the storms;
Pours fierce Ambition in a Cæsar's mind
Or turns young Ammon[3] loose to scourge mankind?
From pride, from pride, our very reas'ning springs;
Account for moral, as for natural things:
Why charge we Heav'n in those, in these acquit!
In both to reason right is to submit.

Better for us, perhaps, it might appear,
Were there all harmony, all virtue here;
That never air or ocean felt the wind;
That never passion discomposed the mind.
But all subsists by elemental strife;
And passions are the elements of life.
The gen'ral order, since the whole began,
Is kept in nature, and is kept in man.

---

[1] Kircher beheld the city of Euphemia swallowed up by an earthquake before his eyes; only a "dismal putrid lake," he says, "marked the spot where it had stood." The catastrophes of Lisbon, Scilla, &c., are well known.

[2] Cæsar Borgia, the son of Pope Alexander VI, was the scourge of Italy from 1492 to 1507. Catiline's conspiracy against Roman freedom is well known.

[3] "Young Ammon," Alexander the Great, who pretended to be the son of Jupiter Ammon.

VI. What would this Man? Now upward will
he soar,
And little less than angel, would be more;
Now looking downwards, just as grieved appears
To want the strength of bulls, the fur of bears.
Made for his use all creatures if he call,
Say what their use, had he the pow'rs of all?
Nature to these, without profusion, kind,
The proper organs, proper powers assigned;
Each seeming want compensated of course,
Here with degrees of swiftness, there of force;[1]
All in exact proportion to the state;
Nothing to add, and nothing to abate,
Each beast, each insect, happy in its own:
Is Heav'n unkind to man, and man alone?
Shall he alone, whom rational we call,
Be pleased with nothing if not blessed with all?
  The bliss of man (could pride that blessing find)
Is not to act or think beyond mankind;
No pow'rs of body or of soul to share,
But what his nature and his state can bear..
Why has not man a microscopic eye?
For this plain reason, man is not a fly.
Say what the use, were finer optics given,
To inspect a mite, not comprehend the heav'n?
Or touch, if tremblingly alive all o'er,
To smart and agonize at ev'ry pore?
Or quick effluvia darting through the brain,
Die of a rose in aromatic pain?
If nature thundered in his op'ning ears,
And stunned him with the music of the spheres,
How would he wish that Heaven had left him still
The whisp'ring zephyr, and the purling rill!
Who finds not Providence all good and wise,
Alike in what it gives, and what denies?

  VII. Far as creation's ample range extends,
The scale of sensual, mental powers ascends:

---

[1] It is a certain axiom in the anatomy of creatures, that in proportion as they are formed for strength, their swiftness is lessened; or as they are formed for swiftness, their strength is abated.—*Pope.*

Mark how it mounts to man's imperial race,
From the green myriads in the peopled grass:
What modes of sight betwixt each wide extreme,
The mole's dim curtain, and the lynx's beam:
Of smell, the headlong lioness between,[1]
And hound sagacious on the tainted green:
Of hearing, from the life that fills the flood,
To that which warbles through the vernal wood:
The spider's touch, how exquisitely fine!
Feels at each thread, and lives along the line:
In the nice bee, what sense so subtly true
From poisonous herbs extracts the healing dew?
How instinct varies in the grovelling swine,
Compared, half-reasoning elephant, with thine?
'Twixt that, and reason, what a nice barrier,
For ever sep'rate, yet for ever near!
Remembrance and reflection how allied;
What thin partitions sense from thought divide,
And middle natures how they long to join,
Yet never pass the insuperable line!
Without this just gradation could they be
Subjected, these to those, or all to thee?
The pow'rs of all subdued by thee alone,
Is not thy reason all these powers in one?

    VIII. See through this air, this ocean, and this earth,
All matter quick, and bursting into birth.
Above, how high, progressive life may go!
Around, how wide! how deep extend below!
Vast chain of being! which from God began,
Natures ethereal, human, angel, man,
Beast, bird, fish, insect, what no eye can see,
No glass can reach; from infinite to thee,
From thee to nothing.—On superior pow'rs

---

[1] The manner of the lions hunting their prey in the deserts of Africa is this: at their first going out in the night-time they set up a loud roar, and then listen to the noise made by the beasts in their flight, pursuing them by the ear, and not by the nostril. It is probable the story of the jackal's hunting for the lion, was occasioned by observation of this defect of scent in that terrible animal.—*Pope.*

Were we to press, inferior might on ours:
Or in the full creation leave a void,
Were, one step broken, the great scale's destroyed:
From Nature's chain whatever link you strike,
Tenth, or ten thousandth, breaks the chain alike.
And, if each system in gradation roll
Alike essential to the amazing whole,
The least confusion but in one, not all
That system only, but the whole must fall.
Let earth unbalanced from her orbit fly,
Planets and suns run lawless through the sky;
Let ruling angels from their spheres be hurled,
Being on being wrecked, and world on world;
Heaven's whole foundations to their center nod,
And nature tremble to the throne of God.
All this dread order break—for whom? for thee?
Vile worm!—Oh, madness! pride! impiety!

IX. What if the foot, ordained the dust to tread,
Or hand, to toil, aspired to be the head?
What if the head, the eye, or ear repined
To serve mere engines to the ruling mind?
Just as absurd for any part to claim
To be another, in this general frame;
Just as absurd to mourn the tasks or pains,[1]
The great directing mind of all ordains.
All are but parts of one stupendous whole,
Whose body Nature is, and God the soul;
That, changed through all, and yet in all the same;
Great in the earth, as in the ethereal frame;
Warms in the sun, refreshes in the breeze,
Glows in the stars, and blossoms in the trees,
Lives through all life, extends through all extent,
Spreads undivided, operates unspent;
Breathes in our soul, informs our mortal part
As full, as perfect, in a hair as heart:
As full, as perfect, in vile man that mourns,
As the wrapt seraph that adores and burns:
To him no high, no low, no great, no small;
He fills, he bounds, connects, and equals all.

---

[1] **Vide the prosecution** and application of this in Ep. iv.—*Pope*.

X. Cease then, nor order imperfection name:
Our proper bliss depends on what we blame.
Know thy own point: this kind, this due degree
Of blindness, weakness, Heav'n bestows on thee.
Submit.—In this, or any other sphere,
Secure to be as blest as thou canst bear:
Safe in the hand of one disposing power,
Or in the natal, or the mortal hour.
All nature is but art, unknown to thee;
All chance, direction, which thou canst not see;
All discord, harmony, not understood;
All partial evil, universal good:
And, spite of pride, in erring reason's spite,
One truth is clear, Whatever is, is right.

ARGUMENT OF EPISTLE II.

OF THE NATURE AND STATE OF MAN WITH RESPECT TO HIMSELF, AS AN INDIVIDUAL.

I. The business of man not to pry into God, but to study himself. His middle nature; his powers and frailties, ver. 1-19. The limits of his capacity, ver. 19, &c.—II. The two principles of man, self-love and reason, both necessary, ver. 53, &c. Self-love the stronger, and why, ver. 67, &c. Their end the same, ver 81, &c.—III The passions, and their use, ver. 93-130. The predominant passion, and its force, ver. 132-160. Its necessity, in directing men to different purposes, ver. 165, &c. Its providential use, in fixing our principle, and ascertaining our virtue, ver. 177.—IV. Virtue and vice joined in our mixed nature; the limits near, yet the things separate and evident: What is the office of reason, ver. 202-216.—V. How odious vice in itself, and how we deceive ourselves into it, ver. 217.—VI. That, however, the ends of Providence and general good are answered in our passions and imperfections, ver. 238, &c. How usefully these are distributed to all orders of men, ver. 241. How useful they are to society, ver. 251. And to individuals, ver. 263. In every state, and every age of life, ver. 273, &c.

EPISTLE II.

I. Know then thyself, presume not God to scan;
The proper study of mankind is man.
Placed on this isthmus of a middle state,
A being darkly wise and rudely great:
With too much knowledge for the sceptic side,
With too much weakness for the stoic's pride,
He hangs between; in doubt to act, or rest;
In doubt to deem himself a god, or beast:
In doubt his mind or body to prefer;
Born but to die and reasoning but to err;

Alike in ignorance, his reason such,
Whether he thinks too little or too much:
Chaos of thought and passion, all confused;
Still by himself abused, or disabused;
Created half to rise, and half to fall;
Great lord of all things, yet a prey to all;
Sole judge of truth, in endless error hurled:
The glory, jest and riddle of the world!
    Go, wondrous creature! mount where science guides,
Go, measure earth, weigh air, and state the tides;
Instruct the planets in what orbs to run,
Correct old Time, and regulate the sun;
Go, soar with Plato to the empyreal sphere,
To the first good, first perfect, and first fair;
Or tread the mazy round his followers trod,
And quitting sense call imitating God;[1]
As eastern priests in giddy circles run,
And turn their heads to imitate the sun.
Go, teach eternal wisdom how to rule—
Then drop into thyself, and be a fool!
    Superior beings, when of late they saw
A mortal man unfold all nature's law,
Admired such wisdom in an earthly shape,
And showed a Newton as we show an ape.
    Could he, whose rules the rapid comet bind,
Describe or fix one movement of his mind?
Who saw its fires here rise, and there descend,
Explain his own beginning, or his end?
Alas, what wonder! man's superior part
Unchecked may rise, and climb from art to art;
But when his own great work is but begun,
What reason weaves, by passion is undone.
    Trace science then, with modesty thy guide;
First strip off all her equipage of pride;
Deduct what is but vanity or dress
Or learning's luxury, or idleness;
Or tricks to show the stretch of human brain,
Mere curious pleasure, or ingenious pain;

---

[1] The new platonics taught by Ammonius Saccas towards the end of the second century.

Expunge the whole, or lop the excrescent parts
Of all our vices have created arts;
Then see how little the remaining sum,
Which served the past and must the times to come!

　II. Two principles in human nature reign;
Self-love, to urge, and reason, to restrain;
Nor this a good, nor that a bad we call,
Each works its end, to move or govern all:
And to their proper operation still,
Ascribe all good; to their improper ill.
　Self-love, the spring of motion, acts[1] the soul;
Reason's comparing balance rules the whole.
Man, but for that, no action could attend,
And but for this, were active to no end:
Fixed like a plant on his peculiar spot,
To draw nutrition, propagate, and rot;
Or, meteor-like, flame lawless through the void,
Destroying others, by himself destroyed.
　Most strength the moving principle requires;
Active its task, it prompts, impels, inspires.
Sedate and quiet the comparing lies,
Formed but to check, deliberate, and advise.
Self-love still stronger, as its object's nigh;
Reason's at distance, and in prospect lie:
That sees immediate good by present sense;
Reason, the future and the consequence.
Thicker than arguments, temptations throng.
At best more watchful this, but that more strong.
The action of the stronger to suspend,
Reason still use, to reason still attend.
Attention, habit and experience gains;
Each strenghthens reason, and self-love restrains.
　Let subtle schoolmen teach these friends to fight,
More studious to divide than to unite;
And grace and virtue, sense and reason split,
With all the rash dexterity of wit.
Wits, just like fools, at war about a name,
Have full as oft no meaning, or the same.
Self-love and reason to one end aspire,

---

1 Used for "actuates."

Pain their aversion, pleasure their desire;
But greedy that, its object would devour,
This taste the honey, and not wound the flow'r:
Pleasure, or wrong or rightly understood,
Our greatest evil, or our greatest good.

    III. Modes of self-love the passions we may call;
'Tis real good, or seeming, moves them all:
But since not ev'ry good we can divide,
And reason bids us for our own provide;
Passions, though selfish, if their means be fair,
List under reason, and deserve her care;
Those that imparted, court a nobler aim,
Exalt their kind, and take some virtue's name.
    In lazy apathy let stoics boast
Their virtue fixed; 'tis fixed as in a frost;
Contracted all, retiring to the breast;
But strength of mind is exercise, not rest:
The rising tempest puts in act the soul,
Parts it may ravage, but preserves the whole.
On life's vast ocean diversely we sail,
Reason the card,[1] but passion is the gale;
Nor God alone in the still calm we find,
He mounts the storm, and walks upon the wind.
    Passions, like elements, though born to fight,
Yet, mixed and softened, in His work unite:
These 'tis enough to temper and employ;
But what composes man, can man destroy!
Suffice that reason keep to nature's road,
Subject, compound them, follow her and God.
Love, hope, and joy, fair pleasure's smiling train,
Hate, fear, and grief, the family of pain,
These mixed with art, and to due bounds confined,
Make and maintain the balance of the mind:
The lights and shades, whose well accorded strife
Gives all the strength and color of our life.
    Pleasures are ever in our hands or eyes;
And when in act they cease, in prospect rise:
Present to grasp, and future still to find,
The whole employ of body and of mind.

---

[1] The "card" on which the points of the mariners' compass are marked, signifies, of course, the compass itself.

All spread their charms, but charm not all alike;
On diff'rent senses, diff'rent objects strike;
Hence diff'rent passions more or less inflame,
As strong or weak the organs of the frame;
And hence one master passion in the breast,
Like Aaron's serpent, swallows up the rest.

As man, perhaps, the moment of his breath,
Receives the lurking principle of death;
The young disease, that must subdue at length;
Grows with his growth and strengthens with his strength:
So, cast and mingled with his very frame,
The mind's disease, its ruling passion came;
Each vital humor which should feed the whole,
Soon flows to this, in body and in soul:
Whatever warms the heart or fills the head,
As the mind opens and its functions spread,
Imagination plies her dang'rous art,
And pours it all upon the peccant part.

Nature its mother, habit is its nurse;
Wit, spirit, faculties, but make it worse;
Reason itself but gives it edge and power;
As heaven's blest beam turns vinegar more sour.

We, wretched subjects though to lawful sway,
In this weak queen some fav'rite still obey:
Ah! if she lend not arms, as well as rules,
What can she more than tell us we are fools?
Teach us to mourn our nature, not to mend,
A sharp accuser, but a helpless friend!
Or from a judge turn pleader, to persuade
The choice we make, or justify it made:
Proud of an easy conquest all along,
She but removes weak passions for the strong:
So, when small humors gather to a gout,
The doctor fancies he has driven them out.

Yes, nature's road must ever be preferred:
Reason is here no guide, but still a guard:
'Tis hers to rectify, not overthrow,
And treat this passion more as friend than foe:
A mightier pow'r the strong direction sends,
And sev'ral men impels to sev'ral ends:
Like varying winds, by other passions tost,
This drives them constant to a certain coast.

Let power or knowledge, gold or glory, please,
Or (oft more strong than all) the love of ease;
Through life 'tis followed, even at life's expense;
The merchant's toil, the sage's indolence,
The monk's humility, the hero's pride,
All, all alike, find reason on their side.
　The Eternal Art educing good from ill,
Grafts on this passion our best principle:
'Tis thus the mercury of man is fixed,
Strong grows the virtue with his nature mixed;
The dress cements what else were too refined,
And in one int'rest body acts with mind.
　As fruits, ungrateful to the planter's care,
On savage stocks inserted learn to bear;
The surest virtues thus from passion shoot,
Wild nature's vigor working at the root.
What crops of wit and honesty appear
From spleen, from obstinacy, hate, or fear!
See anger, zeal, and fortitude supply;
Even avarice, prudence; sloth, philosophy;
Lust, through some certain strainers well refined,
Is gentle love, and charms all womankind;
Envy, to which the ignoble mind's a slave,
Is emulation in the learned or brave;
Nor virtue, male or female, can we name,
But what will grow on pride, or grow on shame.
　Thus nature gives us (let it check our pride)
The virtue nearest to our vice allied:
Reason the bias turns to good from ill,
And Nero reigns a Titus, if he will.
The fiery soul abhorred in Catiline,
In Decius charms, in Curtius is divine:[1]
The same ambition can destroy or save,
And makes a patriot as it makes a knave.
　This light and darkness in our chaos joined,

---

[1] Decius, who devoted himself to the infernal gods, and rushed to his death in battle because he had learned in a vision that the army would be victorious whose general should fall. Curtius leaped into a gulf which had opened in the Roman Forum, and could not be closed till the most valuable thing to Rome had been cast in. It was a warrior on his horse and in his armor.

What shall divide? The God within the mind:[1]
Extremes in nature equal ends produce,
In man they join to some mysterious use;
Though each by turns the other's bound invade,
As, in some well-wrought picture, light and shade
And oft so mix, the diff'rence is too nice
Where ends the virtue, or begins the vice.
   Fools! who from hence into the notion fall,
That vice or virtue there is none at all.
If white and black blend, softened and unite
A thousand ways, is there no black or white?
Ask your own heart, and nothing is so plain;
'Tis to mistake them, costs the time and pain.
   Vice is a monster of so frightful mien,
As, to be hated, needs but to be seen;
Yet seen too oft, familiar with her face,
We first endure, then pity, then embrace.
But where the extreme of vice, was ne'er agreed;
Ask where's the north? at York, 'tis on the Tweed;
In Scotland, at the Orcades; and there,
At Greenland, Zembla, or the Lord knows where.
No creature owns it in the first degree,
But thinks his neighbor further gone than he:
Even those who dwell beneath its very zone,
Or never feel the rage, or never own;
What happier natures shrink at with affright,
The hard inhabitant contends is right.
   Virtuous and vicious ev'ry man must be,
Few in the extreme, but all in the degree;
The rogue and fool by fits is fair and wise;
And even the best, by fits, what they despise.
'Tis but by parts we follow good or ill;
For, vice or virtue, self directs it still;
Each individual seeks a sev'ral goal;
But Heav'n's great view is one, and that the whole.
That counter-works each folly and caprice;
That disappoints the effect of every vice;
That, happy frailties to all ranks applied,
Shame to the virgin, to the matron pride,
Fear to the statesman, rashness to the chief,

---

1 Conscience; a sublime expression of Plato's.

To kings presumption, and to crowds belief;
That, virtue's ends from vanity can raise,
Which seeks no int'rest, no reward but praise:
And build on wants, and on defects of mind,
The joy, the peace, the glory of mankind.
 Heav'n forming each on other to depend,
A master, or a servant, or a friend,
Bids each on other for assistance call,
Till one man's weakness grows the strength of all
Wants, frailties, passions, closer still ally
The common interest, or endear the tie.
To these we owe true friendship, love sincere.
Each home-felt joy that life inherits here;
Yet from the same we learn, in its decline,
Those joys, those loves, those interests to resign;
Taught half by reason, half by mere decay,
To welcome death, and calmly pass away.
Whate'er the passion, knowledge, fame, or pelf.
No one will change his neighbor with himself.
The learned is happy nature to explore,
The fool is happy that he knows no more;
The rich is happy in the plenty giv'n,
The poor contents him with the care of heav'n.
See the blind beggar dance, the cripple sing,
The sot a hero, lunatic a king;
The starving chemist in his golden views,[1]
Supremely blest, the poet in his muse.
 See some strange comfort ev'ry state attend,
And pride bestowed on all, a common friend;
See some fit passion ev'ry age supply,
Hope travels through, nor quits us when we die.
 Behold the child, by Nature's kindly law,
Pleased with a rattle, tickled with a straw:
Some livelier play-thing gives his youth delight,
A little louder, but as empty quite:
Scarfs, garters, gold, amuse his riper stage,
And beads and prayer-books are the toys of age;
Pleased with this bauble still, as that before:
'Till tired he sleeps, and life's poor play is o'er.
 Meanwhile opinion gilds with varying rays

---

[1] The alchemist in search of the Philosopher's Stone.

Those painted clouds that beautify our days;
Each want of happiness by hope supplied,
And each vacuity of sense by pride:
These build as fast as knowledge can destroy;
In folly's cup still laughs the bubble, joy;
One prospect lost, another still we gain:
And not a vanity is given in vain,
Even mean self-love becomes, by force divine,
The scale to measure others' wants by thine.
See! and confess, one comfort still must rise,
'Tis this, Though man's a fool, yet God is wise.

ARGUMENT OF EPISTLE III.

OF THE NATURE AND STATE OF MAN WITH RESPECT TO SOCIETY.

I. The whole universe one system of Society, ver. 7, &c. Nothing made wholly for itself, nor yet wholly for another, ver. 27. The happiness of animals mutual, ver. 49.—II. Reason or Instinct operates alike to the good of each individual, ver. 79. Reason or Instinct operates also to society, in all animals, ver. 109.—III. How far Society carried by Instinct, ver. 115. How much further by Reason, ver. 128.—IV. Of that which is called the State of Nature, ver. 144. Reason instructed by Instinct in the invention of Arts, ver. 166, and in the Forms of Society, ver. 176.—V. Origin of Political Societies, ver. 196. Origin of Monarchy, ver. 207. Patriarchal Government, ver. 212.—VI. Origin of true Religion and Government, from the same principle, of Love, ver. 231, &c. Origin of Superstition and Tyranny, from the same principle, of Fear, ver. 237, &c. The influence of Self-love operating to the social and public Good, ver. 266. Restoration of true Religion and Government on their first principle, ver. 285. Mixed Government, ver. 288. Various Forms of each, and the true end of all, ver. 300, &c.

EPISTLE III.

HERE then we rest; "the Universal Cause
Acts to one end, but acts by various laws."
In all the madness of superfluous health,
The trim of pride, the impudence of wealth,
Let this great truth be present night and day;
But most be present, if we preach or pray.
  Look round our world: behold the chain of love
Combining all below and all above.
See plastic Nature working to this end,
The single atoms each to other tend,

Attract, attracted to, the next in place
Formed and impelled its neighbor to embrace,
See matter next, with various life endued,
Press to one centre still, the gen'ral good.
See dying vegetables life sustain.
See life dissolving vegetate again:
All forms that perish other forms supply,
(By turns we catch the vital breath, and die,)
Like bubbles on the sea of matter born,
They rise, they break, and to that sea return,
Nothing is foreign: parts relate to whole;
One all-extending, all-preserving soul
Connects each being, greatest with the least;
Made beast in aid of man, and man of beast;
All served, all serving; nothing stands alone;
The chain holds on, and where it ends, unknown.

    Has God, thou fool! worked solely for thy good,
Thy joy, thy pastime, thy attire, thy food?
Who for thy table feeds the wanton fawn,
For him as kindly spreads the flow'ry lawn:
Is it for thee the lark ascends and sings?
Joy tunes his voice, joy elevates his wings.
Is it for thee the linnet pours his throat?
Loves of his own and raptures swell the note.
The bounding steed you pompously bestride,
Shares with his lord the pleasure and the pride.
Is thine alone the seed that strews the plain?
The birds of heav'n shall vindicate their grain.
Thine the full harvest of the golden year?
Part pays, and justly, the deserving steer:
The hog, that ploughs not, nor obeys thy call,
Lives on the labors of this lord of all.

    Know, Nature's children all divide her care;
The fur that warms a monarch, warmed a bear.
While man exclaims, "See all things for my use!"
"See man for mine," replies a pampered goose:
And just as short of reason he must fall,
Who thinks all made for one, not one for all.

    Grant that the powerful still the weak control;
Be man the wit and tyrant of the whole:
Nature that tyrant checks; he only knows,
And helps, another creature's wants and woes.
Say, will the falcon, stooping from above,

Smit with her varying plumage, spare the dove?
Admires the jay the insect's gilded wings!
Or hears the hawk when Philomela sings?
Man cares for all· to birds he gives his woods,
To beasts his pastures, and to fish his floods;
For some his interest prompts him to provide,
For more his pleasure, yet for more his pride:
All feed on one vain patron, and enjoy
The extensive blessing of his luxury.
That very life his learned hunger craves,
He saves from famine, from the savage saves;
Nay, feasts the animal he dooms his feast,
And, till he ends the being, makes it blest:
Which sees no more the stroke, or feels the pain,
Than favored man by touch ethereal slain.[1]
The creature had his feast of life before;
Thou too must perish, when thy feast is o'er!
 To each unthinking being, Heaven, a friend,
Gives not the useless knowledge of its end:
To man imparts it; but with such a view
As, while he dreads it, makes him hope it too:
The hour concealed; and so remote the fear,
Death still draws nearer, never seeming near.
Great standing miracle! that Heav'n assigned
Its only thinking thing this turn of mind.

 II. Whether with reason, or with instinct blest,
Know, all enjoy that pow'r which suits them best;
To bliss alike by that direction tend,
And find the means proportioned to their end.
Say, where full instinct is the unerring guide,
What Pope or council can they need beside?
Reason, however able, cool at best,
Cares not for service, or but serves when prest,
Stays till we call, and then not often near;
But honest Instinct comes a volunteer,
Sure never to o'er-shoot, but just to hit;
While still too wide or short is human wit;

---

[1] Several of the ancients, and many of the orientals since, esteemed those who were struck by lightning as sacred persons, and the particular favorites of Heaven.—*Pope.*

Sure by quick nature happiness to gain,
Which heavier reason labors at in vain.
This too serves always, reason never wrong;
One must go right; the other may go wrong;
See then the acting and comparing pow'rs
One in their nature, which are two in ours;
And reason raise o'er instinct as you can,
In this 'tis God directs, in that 'tis man.

Who taught the nations of the field and wood
To shun their poison, and to choose their food?
Prescient, the tides or tempests to withstand,
Build on the wave, or arch beneath the sand?
Who made the spider parallels design,
Sure as Demoivre,[1] without rule or line?
Who did the stork, Columbus-like explore
Heavens not his own, and worlds unknown before?
Who calls the council, states the certain day,
Who forms the phalanx, and who points the way?

III. God in the nature of each being founds
Its proper bliss, and sets its proper bounds:
But as he framed a whole, the whole to bless,
On mutual wants built mutual happiness.
So from the first eternal order ran,
And creature linked to creature, man to man.
Whate'er of life all quick'ning ether keeps,
Or breathes through air, or shoots beneath the deeps,
Or pours profuse on earth, one nature feeds
The vital flame, and swells the genial seeds.
Not man alone, but all that roam the wood,
Or wing the sky, or roll along the flood,
Each loves itself, but not itself alone,
Each sex desires alike, till two are one.
Nor ends the pleasure with the fierce embrace:
They love themselves, a third time, in their race.
Thus beast and bird their common charge attend,
The mothers nurse it, and the sires defend;
The young dismissed to wander earth or air,

---

[1] An eminent mathematician.—*Pope.* He was born at Vitre in Champagne, in 1667. Driven from France by the revocation of the Edict of Nantes, he settled in London, and died there in 1754. He was a friend of Newton.

There stops the instinct, and there ends the care;
The link dissolves, each seeks a fresh embrace,
Another love succeeds, another race.
A longer care man's helpless kind demands:
That longer care contracts more lasting bands:
Reflection, reason, still the ties improve,
At once extend the interest, and the love;
With choice we fix, with sympathy we burn;
Each virtue in each passion takes its turn;
And still new needs, new helps, new habits rise,
That graft benevolence on charities.
Still as one brood, and as another rose,
These natural love maintained, habitual those:
The last, scarce ripened into perfect man,
Saw helpless him from whom their life began:
Memory and forecast just returns engage,
That pointed back to youth, this on to age;
While pleasure, gratitude and hope combined,
Still spread the int'rest, and preserved the kind.

  IV. Nor think in nature's state they blindly trod;
The state of nature was the reign of God:
Self-love and social at her birth began,
Union the bound of all things, and of man.
Pride then was not; nor arts, that pride to aid;
Man walked with beast, joint tenant of the shade:
The same his table, and the same his bed;
No murder clothed him, no murder fed.
In the same temple, the resounding wood,
All vocal beings hymned their equal God:
The shrine with gore unstained, with gold undrest,
Unbribed, unbloody, stood the blameless priest:
Heav'n's attribute was universal care,
And man's prerogative to rule, but to spare.
Ah! how unlike the man of times to come!
Of half that live the butcher and the tomb;
Who, foe to nature hears the general groan,
Murders their species, and betrays his own.
But just disease to luxury succeeds,
And ev'ry death its own avenger breeds;
The fury-passions from that blood began,
And turned on man a fiercer savage, man.
  See him from nature raising slow to art

To copy instinct then was reason's part;
Thus then to man the voice of nature spake—
"Go, from the creatures the instructions take:
Learn from the birds what food the thickets yield;
Learn from the beasts the physic of the field;
Thy arts of building from the bee receive;
Learn of the mole to plough, the worm to weave;
Learn of the little nautilus to sail,
Spread the thin oar, and catch the driving gale.
Here too all forms of social union find,
And hence let reason, late, instruct mankind;
Here subterranean works and cities see;
There towns aerial on the waving tree.
Learn each small people's genius, policies,
The ant's republic, and the realm of bees;
How those in common all their wealth bestow,
And anarchy without confusion know;
And these forever through a monarch reign,
Their separate cells and properties maintain.
Mark what unvaried laws preserve each state,
Laws wise as nature, and as fixed as fate.
In vain thy reason finer webs shall draw,
Entangle justice in her net of law,
And right too rigid harden into wrong,
Still for the strong too weak, the weak too strong.
Yet go: and thus o'er all the creatures sway,
Thus let the wiser make the rest obey;
And, for those arts mere instinct could afford,
Be crowned as monarchs, or as gods adored."

V. Great Nature spoke: observant man obeyed;
Cities were built, societies were made;
Here rose one little state; another near
Grew by like means, and joined, through love or fear.
Did here the trees with ruddier burdens bend,
And there the streams in purer rills descend?
What war could ravish, commerce could bestow,
And he returned a friend who came a foe,
Converse and love mankind might strongly draw,
When love was liberty, and nature law.
Thus states were formed; the name of king unknown,

'Till common interest placed the sway in one
'Twas virtue only (or in arts or arms,
Diffusing blessings, or averting harms)
The same which in a sire the sons obeyed,
A prince the father of a people made.

VI. Till then, by Nature crowned, each patri-
arch sate,
King, priest and parent of his growing state;
On him, their second Providence, they hung,
Their law his eye, their oracle his tongue.
He from the wandering furrow called the food,
Taught to command the fire, control the flood,
Draw forth the monsters of the abyss profound,
Or fetch the aerial eagle to the ground.
Till drooping, sick'ning, dying they began
Whom they revered as God to mourn as man;
Then, looking up from sire to sire, explored
One great first Father, and that first adored.
Or plain tradition that this all begun,
Conveyed unbroken faith, from sire to son:
The worker from the work distinct was known,
And simple reason never sought but one;
Ere wit oblique had broke that steady light
Man, like his Maker, saw that all was right;
To virtue, in the paths of pleasure, trod,
And owned a father when he owned a God.
Love all the faith, and all the allegiance then;
For Nature knew no right divine in men.
No ill could fear in God; and understood
A sov'reign being but a sov'reign good.
True faith, true policy, united ran,
That was but love of God, and this of man.

Who first taught souls enslaved, and realms un-
done,
The enormous faith of many made for one;
That proud exception to all Nature's laws,
To invert the world, and counter work its cause?
Force first made conquest, and that conquest law;
Till superstition taught the tyrant awe,
Then shared the tyranny, then lent it aid,
And gods of conquerors, slaves of subjects made:
She 'midst the lightning's blaze, and thunder's sound,

When rocked the mountains and when groaned the
    ground,
She taught the weak to bend, the proud to pray,
To power unseen, and mightier far than they:
She, from the rending earth and bursting skies,
Saw gods descend, and fiends infernal rise:
Here fixed the dreadful, there the blest abodes;
Fear made her devils, and weak hope her gods;
Gods partial, changeful, passionate, unjust,
Whose attributes were rage, revenge, or lust;
Such as the souls of cowards might conceive,
And, formed like tyrants, tyrants would believe.
Zeal then not charity, became the guide;
And hell was built on spite, and heaven on pride.
Then sacred seemed the ethereal vault no more;
Altars grew marble then, and reeked with gore:
Then first the Flamen tasted living food;
Next his grim idol smeared with human blood,
With heaven's own thunders shook the world below,
And played the god an engine on his foe.
  So drives self-love, through just and through un-
    just,
To one man's pow'r, ambition, lucre, lust:
The same self-love, in all, becomes the cause
Of what restrains him, government and laws.
For what one likes if others like as well,
What serves one will, when many wills rebel?
How shall he keep, what, sleeping or awake,
A weaker may surprise, a stronger take?
His safety must his liberty restrain:
All join to guard what each desires to gain.
Forced into virtue thus by self-defence,
Even kings learned justice and benevolence:
Self-love forsook the path it first pursued,
And found the private in the public good.
  'Twas then the studious head or generous mind,
Follower of God or friend of human kind,
POET or PATRIOT, rose but to restore
The faith and moral, Nature gave before;
Relumed her ancient light, not kindled new;
If not God's image, yet his shadow drew:
Taught pow'r's due use to people and to kings,
Taught nor to slack, nor strain its tender strings,

The less, or greater, set so justly true,
That touching one must strike the other too;
Till jarring int'rests, of themselves create
The according music of a well-mixed state.
Such is the world's great harmony that springs
From order, union, full consent of things:
Where small and great, where weak and mighty made
To serve, not suffer, strengthen, not invade
More pow'rful each as needful to the rest,
And, in proportion as it blesses, blest;
Draw to one point, and to one center bring
Beast, man, or angel, servant, lord, or king.

For forms of government let fools contest;
What'er is best administered is best:
For modes of faith let graceless zealots fight;
His can't be wrong whose life is in the right;
In Faith and Hope the world will disagree.
But all mankind's concern is Charity:
And must be false that thwart this one great end
And all of God, that bless mankind or mend.

Man, like the gen'rous vine, supported lives;
The strength he gains is from the embrace he gives.
On their own axis as the planets run,
Yet make at once their circle round the sun.
So two consistent motions act the soul:
And one regards itself, and one the whole.
Thus God and Nature linked the general frame
And bade **Self-love** and **Social** be the same.

ARGUMENT OF EPISTLE IV.

OF THE NATURE AND STATE OF MAN WITH RESPECT TO HAPPINESS.

1. False notions of happiness, philosophical and popular, answered from ver. 19 to 27.—II. It is the end of all men, and attainable by all, ver. 30. God intends happiness to be equal; and to be so, it must be social, since all particular happiness depends on general, and since he governs by general, not particular laws, ver. 37. As it is necessary for order, and the peace and welfare of society, that external good should be unequal, happiness is not made to consist in these, ver. 51. But, notwithstanding that inequality, the balance of happiness among mankind is kept even by Providence, by the two passions of hope and fear, ver. 70.—III. What the happiness of individuals is, as far as is consistent with the constitution of this world; and that the good man has here the advantage, ver. 77. The error of imputing to virtue what are only the calamities of nature, or of fortune, ver. 94.—VI. The folly of expecting that God should alter his general laws in favor of particulars, ver. 121.——V. That we are not judges who are good; but that, whoever they are, they must be happiest, ver. 133, &c.—VI. That external goods are not the proper rewards, but often inconsistent with, or destructive of virtue, ver. 165. That even these can make no man happy without virtue: instanced in riches, ver. 183. Honors, ver. 191. Nobility, ver. 203. Greatness, ver. 215. Fame, ver. 235. Superior talents, ver. 257, &c. With pictures of human infelicity in men possessed of them all, ver. 267, &c.—VII. That virtue only constitutes a happiness, whose object is universal, and whose prospect eternal, ver. 307, &c. That the perfection of virtue and happiness consists in a conformity to the order of Providence here, and a resignation to it here and hereafter, ver. 326, &c.

EPISTLE IV.

O HAPPINESS! our being's end and aim,
Good, pleasure, ease, content, whate'er thy name,
That something still which prompts the eternal sigh,
For which we bear to live, or dare to die,

Which still so near us, yet beyond us lies,
O'erlooked, seen double, by the fool, and wise
Plant of celestial seed! if dropt below,
Say, in what mortal soil thou deign'st to grow?
Fair op'ning to some Court's propitious shine,
Or deep with diamonds in the flaming mine?
Twined with the wreaths Parnassian laurels yield
Or reaped in iron harvests of the field?
Where grows? where grows it not? If vain our toil,
We ought to blame the culture, not the soil.
Fixed to no spot is happiness sincere,
'Tis nowhere to be found, or ev'rywhere:
'Tis never to be bought, but always free,
And fled from monarchs, St. John! dwells with thee.
　Ask of the learned the way? The learned are blind;
This bids to serve, and that to shun mankind;
Some place the bliss in action, some in ease,
Those call it pleasure, and contentment these;
Some sunk to beasts, find pleasure end in pain;
Some swelled to gods, confess e'en virtue vain;
Or indolent, to each extreme they fall,
To trust in every thing, or doubt of all.[1]
　Who thus define it, say they more or less
Than this, that happiness is happiness?
　Take Nature's path, and mad opinion's leave;
All states can reach it, and all heads conceive;
Obvious her goods, in no extreme they dwell;
There needs but thinking right, and meaning well;
And mourn our various portions as we please,
Equal is common sense, and common ease.
　Remember, man, "the Universal Cause
Acts not by partial, but by general laws;"
And makes what happiness we justly call
Subsist not in the good of one, but all.
There's not a blessing individuals find,
But some way leans and hearkens to the kind:
No bandit fierce, no tyrant mad with pride,
No cavern hermit, rests self-satisfied:
Who most to shun or hate mankind pretend,

---

[1] Skeptics.—*Pope.*

Seek an admirer, or who would fix a friend:
Abstract what others feel, what others think,
All pleasures sicken, and all glories sink:
Each has its share; and who would more obtain,
Shall find, the pleasure pays not half the pain.
    Order is heaven's first law; and this confest,
Some are, and must be, greater than the rest,
More rich, more wise; but who infers from hence
That such are happier, shocks all common sense,
Heav'n to mankind impartial we confess,
If all are equal in their happiness:
But mutual wants this happiness increase;
All Nature's difference keeps all Nature's peace.
Condition, circumstance is not the thing;
Bliss is the same in subject or in king,
In who obtain defence, or who defend,
In him who is, or him who finds a friend:
Heav'n breathes through ev'ry member of the whole
One common blessing, as one common soul.
But fortune's gifts if each alike possest,
And each were equal, must not all contest?
If then to all men happiness was meant,
God in externals could not place content.
    Fortune her gifts may variously dispose,
And these be happy called, unhappy those;
But Heav'n's just balance equal will appear,
While those are placed in hope, and these in fear:
Not present good or ill, the joy or curse,
But future views of better, or of worse.
Oh, sons of earth! attempt ye still to rise,
By mountains piled on mountains, to the skies?
Heav'n still with laughter the vain toil surveys,
And buries madmen in the heaps they raise.
    Know, all the good that individuals find,
Or God and nature meant to mere mankind,
Reason's whole pleasure, all the joys of sense,
Lie in three words, health, peace, and competence.
But health consists with temperance alone;
And peace, oh Virtue! peace is all thy own.
The good or bad the gifts of fortune gain;
But these less taste them, as they worse obtain.
Say, in pursuit of profit or delight,
Who risk the most, that take wrong means or right?

Of vice or virtue, whether blessed or curst,
Which meets contempt, or which compassion first?
Count all the advantage prosp'rous vice attains
'Tis but what virtue flies from and disdains:
And grant the bad what happiness they would,
One they must want, which is, to pass for good.
  Oh, blind to truth and God's whole scheme below,
Who fancy bliss to vice, to virtue woe!
Who sees and follows that great scheme the best
Best knows the blessing, and will most be blest.
But fools the good alone unhappy call,
For ills or accidents that chance to all.
See, Falkland dies, the virtuous and the just![1]
See god-like Turenne prostrate on the dust?[2]
See Sidney bleeds amid the martial strife![3]
Was this their virtue or contempt of life?
Say, was it virtue, more though Heaven ne'r gave,
Lamented Digby![4] sunk thee to the grave?
Tell me, if virtue made the son expire,
Why, full of days and honor, lives the sire?
Why drew Marseilles' good bishop purer breath,[5]

---

[1] The genius and patriotism of Lucius Cary, Lord Falkland, are immortalized by both Clarendon and Cowley. He fell fighting on the royal side at the battle of Newbury, 1643.

[2] Turenne, the famous French general and marshal, was second son of the Duc de Bouillon, and Elizabeth, daughter of William I. of Nassau, Prince of Orange. He was killed by a cannon ball at Sassbach, in 1675, his soldiers crying out, "Our father is dead," when the fatal result of the shot was perceived.

[3] Sir Philip Sidney, one of our greatest countrymen, was shot at Zutphen, 1586, and died a few days afterwards. His unselfish gift of the cup of cold water to the dying soldier, when wounded and thirsting himself, will never be forgotten.

[4] The Honorable Robert Digby, who died 1724. See in "Epitaphs," one on himself and his sister.

[5] M. de Belsance was made bishop of Marseilles in 1709. In the plague of that city, in the year 1720, he distinguished himself by his zeal and activity, being the pastor, the physician, and the magistrate of his flock, whilst that horrid calamity prevailed.—*Warton.* Louis XV., 1723, offered him a more considerable bishopric, to which great feudal privileges belonged, but he refused to leave the flock endeared to him by suffering. He lived to a great age and died in 1755.

When nature sickened, and each gale was death?
Or why so long (in life if long can be)
Lent Heaven a parent to the poor and me!¹
  What makes all physical or moral ill?
There deviates Nature, and there wanders Will.
God sends not ill; if rightly understood,
Or partial ill is universal good,
Or change admits, or nature lets it fall;
Short, and but rare, till Man improved it all.
We just as wisely might of Heaven complain
That righteous Able was destroyed by Cain,
As that the virtuous son is ill at ease
When his lewd father gave the dire disease.
Think we, like some weak prince, the Eternal Cause
Prone for his fav'rites to reverse his laws?
  Shall burning Ætna, if a sage ² requires,
Forget to thunder, and recall her fires?
On air or sea new motions be imprest,
Oh, blameless Bethel!³ to relieve thy breast?
When the loose mountain trembles from on high,
Shall gravitation cease, if you go by?
Or some old temple, nodding to its fall,
For Chartres'⁴ head reserve the hanging wall?
  But still this world (so fitted for the knave)
Contents us not. A better shall we have?

---

1 Edith Pope, the mother of the poet, died at the age of 91 or 92, the year this poem was finished, 1733. The filial piety of Pope was remarkable.

2 Alluding to the fate of those two great naturalists, Empedocles and Pliny, who both perished by too near an approach to Ætna and Vesuvius, while they were exploring the cause of the eruptions.—*Warburton.*

3 Mr. Bethel was a friend of Pope's. The poet alluded to this line in a letter he wrote to a friend soon after old Mrs. Pope's death: "I have now too much melancholy leisure, and no other care but to finish my 'Essay on Man.' There will be in it but one line that will offend you (I fear), and yet I will not alter it or omit it, unless you come to town and prevent it. It is all a poor poet can do to bear testimony to the virtue he cannot reach."

4 F. Chartres was a man of infamous character, who died 731. See notes to "Essay on the use of Riches."

A kingdom of the just then let it be:
But first consider how those just agree.
The good must merit God's peculiar care;
But who, but God, can tell us who they are?
One thinks on Calvin Heav'n's own spirit fell;
Another deems him instrument of hell;
If Calvin feel Heaven's blessing, or its rod,
This cries there is, and that, there is no God.
What shocks one part will edify the rest,
Nor with one system can they all be blest.
The very best will variously incline,
And what rewards your virtue, punish mine.
Whatever is, is right.—The world, 'tis true,
Was made for Cæsar—but for Titus too:
And which more blest? who chained his country,
    say,
Or he[1] whose virtue sighed to lose a day?
"But sometimes virtue starves, while vice is fed."
What then? Is the reward of virtue bread?
That, vice may merit, 'tis the price of toil;
The knave deserves it, when he tills the soil,
The knave deserves it, when he tempts the main,
Where, folly fights for kings, or dives for gain.
The good man may be weak, be indolent;
Nor is his claim to plenty, but content.
But grant him riches, your demand is o'er?
"No—shall the good want health, the good want
    power?"
Add health, and power, and every earthly thing,
"Why bounded power? why private? why no king?"
Nay, why external for internal given?
Why is not man a god, and earth a heav'n?
Who ask and reason thus, will scarce conceive
God gives enough, while He has more to give:
Immense the power, immense were the demand;
Say, at what part of nature will they stand?
    What nothing earthly gives, or can destroy,
The soul's calm sunshine, and the heart-felt joy,

---

[1] Titus, who exclaimed one evening, on recollecting that he had done no good to any especial person, "My friends, I have lost a day."

Is virtue's prize. A better would you fix?
Then give humility a coach and six,
Justice a conqueror's sword, or truth a gown,
Or public spirit its great cure, a crown.
Weak, foolish man! will Heav'n reward us there
With the same trash mad mortals wish for here?
The boy and man an individual makes,
Yet sighest thou now for apples and for cakes?
Go, like the Indian, in another life
Expect thy dog, thy bottle, and thy wife,
As well as dream such trifles are assigned,
As toys and empires, for a god-like mind.
Rewards, that either would to virtue bring
No joy, or be destructive of the thing:
How oft by these at sixty are undone
The virtues of a saint at twenty-one!

   To whom can riches give repute, or trust,
Content, or pleasure, but the good and just?
Judges and Senates have been bought for gold,
Esteem and love were never to be sold.
O fool! to think God hates the worthy mind
The lover and the love of human kind,
Whose life is healthful, and whose conscience clear,
Because he wants a thousand pounds a year.

   Honor and shame from no condition rise;
Act well your part, there all the honor lies.
Fortune in men has some small difference made,
One flaunts in rags, one flutters in brocade;
The cobbler aproned, and the parson gowned,
The friar hooded, and the monarch crowned.
"What differ more (you cry) than crown and
    cowl?"
I'll tell you, friend; a wise man and a fool.
You'll find, if once the monarch acts the monk,
Or, cobbler-like, the parson will be drunk,
Worth makes the man, and want of it, the fellow;
The rest is all but leather or prunella.

   Stuck o'er with titles and hung round with
    strings,
That thou mayest be by kings, or w——of kings.
Boast the pure blood of an illustrious race,
In quiet flow from Lucrece to Lucrece;
But by your fathers' worth if yours you rate,

Count me those only who were good and great.
Go! if your ancient, but ignoble blood
Has crept through scoundrels ever since the flood,
Go! and pretend your family is young;
Nor own, your fathers have been fools so long.
What can ennoble sots, or slaves, or cowards?
Alas! not all the blood of all the Howards.

Look next on greatness; say where greatness lies?
" Where, but among the heroes and the wise? "
Heroes are much the same, the point's agreed,
From Macedonia's madman[1] to the Swede;[2]
The whole strange purpose of their lives to find
Or make an enemy of all mankind?
Not one looks backward, onward still he goes,
Yet ne'er looks forward farther than his nose.
No less alike the politic and wise;
All sly slow things, with circumspective eyes:
Men in their loose unguarded hours they take,
Not that themselves are wise, but others weak.
But grant that those can conquer, these can cheat;
'Tis phrase absurd to call a villian great:
Who wickedly is wise, or madly brave,
Is but the more a fool, the more a knave.
Who noble ends by noble means obtains,
Or failing, smiles in exile or in chains,
Like good Aurelius let him reign[3] or bleed
Like Socrates,[4] than man is great indeed.

What's fame? a fancied life in other's breath,
A thing beyond us even before our death.
Just what you hear, you have, and what's unknown
The same (my lord) if Tully's, or your own,
All that we feel of it begins and ends
In the small circle of our foes or friends;
To all beside as much an empty shade

---

1 Alexander the Great.
2 Charles XII. of Sweden.
3 Marcus Aurelius, Emperor of Rome, practiced the stern virtues of the Stoic philosophy. He was born A. D. 121, and died 180.
4 As Socrates died by drinking hemlock in obedience to his sentence, Warton thinks the word "bleed" here improperly used. But, of course, it is employed only metaphorically.

An Eugene living,[1] as a Cæsar dead;
Alike or when, or where, they shone or shine,
Or on the Rubicon, or on the Rhine.
A wit's a feather, and a chief a rod;
An honest man's the noblest work of God.
Fame but from death a villain's name can save,
As Justice tears his body from the grave;
When what t' oblivion better were resigned,
Is hung on high to poison half mankind.
All fame is foreign, but of true desert;
Plays round the head, but comes not to the heart;
One self-approving hour whole years out-weighs
Of stupid starers, and loud hazzas;
And more true joy Marcellus exiled feels,[2]
Than Cæsar with a senate at his heels,
  In parts superior what advantage lies?
Tell (for you can) what is it to be wise?
'Tis but to know how little can be known;
To see all others' faults, and feel your own;
Condemned in business or in arts to drudge,
Without a second, or without a judge:
Truths would you teach, or save a sinking land?
All fear, none aid you, and few understand.
Painful pre-eminence! yourself to view
Above life's weakness, and its comforts too.
  Bring then these blessings to a strict account;
Make fair deductions; see to what they mount:
How much of other each is sure to cost;
How each for other oft is wholly lost;
How inconsistent greater goods with these;
How sometimes life is risked, and always ease:

---

  1 Prince Eugene of Savoy, was still living when this poem was written. Associated with Marlborough, he fought at Blenheim and Malplaquet. He was born 1663, and died 1736. Napoleon ranked him as a general with Turenne and Frederick the Great.
  2 Marcellus was an enemy of Julius Cæsar, and after the battle of Pharsalia fled to Mitylene. Cæsar pardoned him, but on his way back to Rome, he was assassinated by his attendant, Magius, at Athens. "By Marcellus, Pope is thought to have meant the Duke of Ormond."—*Warton.* Ormond had fled from England on the death of Queen Anne, to join **the Pretender.**

Think, and if still the things thy envy call,
Say, wouldst thou be the man to whom they fall?
To sigh for ribands if thou art so silly,
Mark how they grace Lord Umbra, or Sir Billy:
Is yellow dirt the passion of thy life!
Look but on Gripus, or on Gripus' wife:
If parts allure thee, think how Bacon shined,[1]
The wisest, brightest, meanest of mankind:
Or ravished with the whistling of a name,
See Cromwell, damned to everlasting fame!
If all, united, thy ambition call,
From ancient story learn to scorn them all.
There, in the rich, the honored, famed, and great,
See the false scale of happiness complete!
In hearts of kings, or arms of queens who lay,
How happy! those to ruin, these betray.
Mark by what wretched steps their glory grows,
From dirt and sea-weed as proud Venice rose;
In each how guilt and greatness equal ran,
And all that raised the hero, sunk the man:
Now Europe's laurels on their brows behold,
But stained with blood, or ill-exchanged for gold
Then see them broke with toils, or sunk in ease,
Or infamous for plundered provinces.
Oh, wealth ill-fated! which no act of fame
E'er taught to shine, or sanctified from shame
What greater bliss attends their close of life?
Some greedy minion, or imperious wife,[2]
The trophied arches, storied halls invade
And haunt their slumbers in the pompous shade
Alas! not dazzled with their noontide ray,
Compute the morn and evening to the day;

---

[1] Lord Bacon discovered the true principles of Experimental Science, and was distinguished by his great talents in all subjects, but he was condemned for (and confessed) bribery and corruption in the administration of justice while presiding in the Supreme Court of Equity; and his flattery of the king, James I., and his favorite, Buckingham, was disgraceful.

[2] He alludes to the great Duke of Marlborough.—*Warton.* He loved money, but his military career was free from reproach, and he did not "plunder" beyond the allowed usages of war. The "imperious wife" hints at the terrible temper of Sarah, Duchess of Marlborough.

The whole amount of that enormous fame,
A tale, that blends their glory with their shame!
   Know then this truth (enough for man to know)
"Virtue alone is happiness below."
The only point where human bliss stands still,
And tastes the good without the fall to ill;
Where only merit constant pay receives,
Is blest in what it takes, and what it gives;
The joy unequalled, if its end is gain,
And if it lose, attended with no pain:
Without safety, though e'er so blessed,
And but more relished as the more distressed:
The broadest mirth unfeeling folly wears,
Less pleasing far than virtue's very tears:
Good, from each object, from each place acquired,
For ever exercised, yet never tired;
Never elated, while one man's oppressed;
Never dejected, while another's blessed;
And where no wants, no wishes can remain,
Since but to wish more virtue, is to gain.
   See the sole bliss Heav'n could on all bestow!
Which who but feels could taste, but thinks can know:
Yet poor with fortune, and with learning blind,
The bad must miss; the good, untaught, will find;
Slave to no sect, who takes no private road,
But looks through nature up to nature's God;
Pursues that chain which links the immense design,
Joins heav'n and earth, and mortal and divine:
Sees, that no being any bliss can know,
But touches some above, and some below:
Learns, from this union of the rising whole,
The first, last purpose of the human soul;
And knows, where faith, law, morals, all began,
All end, in love of God, and love of man.
   For him alone, hope leads from goal to goal
And opens still, and opens on his soul;
Till lengthened on to FAITH and unconfined,
It pours the bliss that fills up all the mind.
He sees, why Nature plants in man alone
Hope of known bliss, and faith in bliss unknown:
(Nature, whose dictates to no other kind
Are given in vain, but what they seek they find)

Wise in her present; she connects in this
His greatest virtue with his greatest bliss;
At once his own bright prospect to be blest,
And strongest motive to assist the rest.
  Self-love thus pushed to social, to divine,
Gives thee to make thy neighbor's blessing thine.
Is this too little for the boundless heart?
Extend it, let thy enemies have part:
Grasp the whole worlds of reason, life, and sense,
In one close system of benevolence:
Happier as kinder, in whate'er degree,
And height of Bliss but height of Charity.
  God loves from whole to parts: but human soul
Must rise from individual to the whole.
Self-love but serves the virtuous mind to wake,
As the small pebble stirs the peaceful lake;
The center moved, a circle straight succeeds,
Another still, and still another spreads;
Friend, parent, neighbor first it will embrace;
His country next, and next all human race;
Wide and more wide, the o'erflowings of the mind
Take ev'ry creature in, of ev'ry kind;
Earth smiles around, with boundless bounty blest,
And heav'n beholds its image in his breast.
  Come then, my Friend! my genius! come along;
Oh, master of the poet, and the song!
And while the muse now stoops, or now ascends,
To man's low passions, or their glorious ends,
Teach me, like thee, in various nature wise,
To fall with dignity, with temper rise;
Formed by thy converse, happily to steer
From grave to gay, from lively to severe;
Correct with spirit, eloquent with ease,
Intent to reason, or polite to please.
Oh! while alone the stream of time thy name
Expanded flies, and gathers all its fame,
Say, shall my little bark attendant sail,
Pursue the triumph, and partake the gale?
When statesmen, heroes, kings, in dust repose,
Whose sons shall blush their fathers were thy foes,
Shall then this verse to future age pretend
Thou wert my guide, philosopher and friend?
That urged by thee, I turned the tuneful art

From sounds to things, from fancy to the heart;
For wit's false mirror held up nature's light,
Showed erring pride, WHATEVER IS, IS RIGHT;
That reason, passion, answer one great aim;
That true self-love and social are the same;
That virtue only makes our bliss below;
And all our knowledge is ourselves to know.

THE UNIVERSAL PRAYER.[1]

DEO. OPT. MAX.

FATHER of all! in ev'ry age,
 In ev'ry clime adored,
By saint, by savage, and by sage,
 Jehovah, Jove, or Lord!

Thou Great First Cause, least understood
 Who all my sense confined
To know but this, that thou art good,
 And that myself am blind;

Yet gave me, in this dark estate,
 To see the good from ill;
And binding Nature fast in Fate,
 Left free the human will.

What conscience dictates to be done,
 Or warns me not to do,
This, teach me more than hell to shun,
 That, more than heav'n pursue.

What blessings Thy free bounty gives,
 Let me not cast away;

---

[1] Some passages in the "Essay on Man" having been unjustly suspected of a tendency towards Fate and Naturalism, the author composed a prayer as the sum of all, which was intended to show that his system was founded in Free-will and terminated in Piety.—*Ruffhead.*

For God is paid when man receives:
  To enjoy is to obey.

Yet not to earth's contracted span
  Thy goodness led me bound,
Or think Thee Lord alone of man,
  When thousand worlds are round.

Let not this weak unknowing hand
  Presume thy bolts to throw,
And deal damnation round the land.
  On each I judge Thy foe.

If I am right, Thy grace impart,
  Still in the right to stay;
If I am wrong, oh, teach my heart
  To find that better way.

Save me alike from foolish pride,
  Or impious discontent,
At aught Thy wisdom has denied,
  Or aught Thy goodness lent.

Teach me to feel another's woe,
  To hide the fault I see;
That mercy I to others show,
  That mercy show to me.

Mean though I am, not wholly so,
  Since quickened by thy breath;
Oh, lead me whereso'er I go,
  Through this day's life or death.

This day, be bread and peace my lot:
  All else beneath the sun,
Thou know'st if best bestowed or not;
  And let Thy will be done.

To Thee, whose temple is all space,
  Whose altar, earth, sea, skies,
One chorus let all being raise;
  All nature's incense rise!

CONSTITUTION OF THE UNITED STATES.

PREAMBLE.

WE, the People of the United States, in order to form a more perfect union, establish justice, insure domestic tranquility, provide for the common defence, promote the general welfare, and secure the blessings of liberty to ourselves and our posterity, do ordain and establish this Constitution for the United States of America.

ARTICLE I.

THE LEGISLATIVE DEPARTMENT.

SECTION I.—All legislative powers herein granted shall be vested in a Congress of the United States, which shall consist of a Senate and House of Representatives.

SECTION II.—1. The House of Representatives shall be composed of members chosen every second year by the people of the several States; and the electors in each State shall have the qualifications requisite for electors of the most numerous branch of the State legislature.

2. No person shall be a representative who shall not have attained to the age of twenty-five years, and been seven years a citizen of the United States, and who shall not, when elected, be an inhabitant of that State in which he shall be chosen.

3. Representatives and direct taxes shall be apportioned among the several States which may be included within this Union, according to their respective numbers, which shall be determined by adding to the whole number of free persons, including those bound to service for a term of years, and excluding Indians not taxed, three-fifths of all other persons. The actual enumera-

tion shall be made within three years after the first meeting of the Congress of the United States, and within every subsequent term of ten years, in such manner as they shall by law direct. The number of Representatives shall not exceed one for every thirty thousand, but each State shall have at least one Representative; and until such enumeration shall be made, the State of New Hampshire shall be entitled to choose three; Massachusetts, eight; Rhode Island and Providence Plantations, one; Connecticut, five; New York, six; New Jersey, four; Pennsylvania, eight; Delaware, one; Maryland, six; Virginia, ten; North Carolina, five; South Carolina, five; and Georgia, three.

4. When vacancies happen in the representation from any State, the executive authority thereof shall issue writs of election to fill such vacancies.

5. The House of Representatives shall choose their Speaker and other officers, and shall have the sole power of impeachment.

SECTION III.—1. The Senate of the United States shall be composed of two Senators from each State, chosen by the legislature therof for six years; and each Senator shall have one vote.

2. Immediately after they shall be assembled in consequence of the first election, they shall be divided as equally as may be into three classes. The seats of the Senators of the first class shall be vacated at the expiration of the second year, of the second class at the expiration of the fourth year, and of the third class at the expiration of the sixth year, so that one third may be choosen every second year; and if vacancies happen, by resignation or otherwise, during the recess of the legislature of any State, the executive thereof may make temporary appointments until the next meeting of the legislature, which shall then fill such vacancies.

3. No person shall be a Senator who shall not have attained the age of thirty years, and been

nine years a citizen of the United States, and who shall not, when elected, be an inhabitant of that State for which he shall be chosen.

4. The Vice-President of the United States shall be President of the Senate, but shall have no vote unless they be equally divided.

5. The Senate shall choose their other officers, and also a President *pro tempore* in the absence of the Vice-President, or when he shall exercise the office of President of the United States.

6. The Senate shall have the sole power to try all impeachments. When sitting for that purpose, they shall be on oath or affirmation. When the President of the United States is tried, the Chief Justice shall preside: and no person shall be convicted without the concurrence of two-thirds of the members present.

7. Judgment in cases of impeachment shall not extend further than to removal from office, and disqualification to hold and enjoy any office of honor, trust, or profit under the United States; but the party convicted shall nevertheless be liable and subject to indictment, trial, judgment, and punishment, according to law.

SECTION IV.—1. The times, places, and manner of holding elections for Senators and Representatives shall be prescribed in each State by the legislature thereof; but the Congress may at any time, by law, make or alter such regulations, except as to the places of choosing Senators.

2. The Congress shall assemble at least once in every year; and such meeting shall be on the first Monday in December, unless they shall by law appoint a different day.

SECTION V.—1. Each house shall be the judge of the elections, returns, and qualifications of its own members, and a majority of each shall constitute a quorum to do business; but a smaller number may adjourn from day to day, and may be authorized to compel the attendance of absent members, in such manner and under such penalties as each house may provide.

2. Each house may determine the rules of its proceedings, punish its members for disorderly behavior, and with the concurrence of two-thirds, expel a member.

3. Each house shall keep a journal of its proceedings, and from time to time publish the same, excepting such parts as may in their judgment require secrecy; and the yeas and nays of the members of either house on any question shall, at the desire of one-fifth of those present, be entered on the journal.

4. Neither house, during the session of Congress, shall, without the consent of the other, adjourn for more than three days, nor to any other place than that in which the two houses shall be sitting.

SECTION VI.—1. The Senators and Representatives shall receive a compensation for their services, to be ascertained by law, and paid out of the treasury of the United States. They shall, in all cases, except treason, felony, and breach of the peace, be privileged from arrest during their attendance at the session of their respective houses, and in going to, and returning from the same; and for any speech or debate in either house they shall not be questioned in any other place.

2. No Senator or Representative shall, during the time for which he was elected, be appointed to any civil office under the authority of the United States, which shall have been created, or the emoluments whereof shall have been increased, during such time; and no person holding any office under the United States shall be a member of either house during his continuance in any office.

SECTION VII.—1. All bills for raising revenue shall originate in the House of Representatives; but the Senate may propose or concur with amendments, as on other bills.

2. Every bill which shall have passed the House of Representatives and the Senate, shall,

before it become a law, be presented to the President of the United States; if he approve, he shall sign it; but if not, he shall return it, with his objections, to that house in which it shall have originated; who shall enter the objections at large on their journal, and proceed to reconsider it. If, after such reconsideration, two-thirds of that house shall agree to pass the bill, it shall be sent, together with the objections, to the other house, by which it shall likewise be reconsidered; and if approved by two-thirds of that house, it shall become a law. But in all such cases the votes of both houses shall be determined by yeas and nays, and the names of the persons voting for and against the bill shall be entered on the journal of each house respectively. If any bill shall not be returned by the President within ten days (Sundays excepted) after it shall have been presented to him, the same shall be a law in like manner as if he had signed it, unless the Congress by their adjournment prevent its return, in which case it shall not be a law.

3. Every order, resolution, or vote, to which the concurrence of the Senate and House of Representatives may be necessary (except on a question of adjournment), shall be presented to the President of the United States; and before the same shall take effect, shall be approved by him; or being disapproved by him, shall be repassed by two-thirds of the Senate and House of Representatives, according to the rules and limitations prescribed in the case of a bill.

SECTION VIII.—The Congress shall have power—

1. To lay and collect taxes, duties, imposts, and excises; to pay the debts, and provide for the common defence and general welfare of the United States; but all duties, imposts, and excises shall be uniform throughout the United States:

2. To borrow money on the credit of the United States:

3. To regulate commerce with foreign nations,

and among the several States, and with the Indian tribes:

4. To establish a uniform rule of naturalization, and uniform laws on the subject of bankruptcies throughout the United States:

5. To coin money, regulate the value thereof and of foreign coin, and to fix the standard of weights and measures:

6. To provide for the punishment of counterfeiting the securities and current coin of the United States:

7. To establish post-offices and post-roads:

8. To promote the progress of science and useful arts, by securing for limited times, to authors and inventors, the exclusive right to their respective writings and discoveries:

9. To constitute tribunals inferior to the Supreme Court:

10. To define and punish piracies and felonies committed on the high seas, and offences against the law of nations:

11. To declare war, grant letters of marque and reprisal, and make rules concerning captures on land and water:

12. To raise and support armies; but no appropriation of money to that use shall be for a longer term than two years:

13. To provide and maintain a navy:

14. To make rules for the government and regulation of the land and naval forces:

15. To provide for calling forth the militia to execute the laws of the Union, suppress insurrections, and repel invasions:

16. To provide for organizing, arming, and disciplining the militia, and for governing such parts of them as may be employed in the service of the United States; reserving to the States respectively the appointment of the officers and the authority of training the militia according to the discipline prescribed by Congress:

17. To exercise exclusive legislation in all cases whatsoever, over such district (not exceed-

ing ten miles square) as may, by cession of particular States, and the acceptance of Congress, become the seat of government of the United States; and to exercise like authority over all places purchased by the consent of the legislature of the State in which the same shall be, for the erection of forts, magazines, arsenals, dockyards, and other needful buildings:—and

18. To make all laws which shall be necessary and proper for carrying into execution the foregoing powers, and all other powers vested by this Constitution in the government of the United States, or in any department or officer thereof.

SECTION IX.—1. The immigration or importation of such persons as any of the States now existing shall think proper to admit, shall not be prohibited by the Congress prior to the year one thousand eight hundred and eight; but a tax or duty may be imposed on such importation not exceeding ten dollars for each person.

2. The privilege of the writ of habeas corpus shall not be suspended, unless when, in cases of rebellion or invasion, the public safety may require it.

3. No bill of attainder or *ex post facto* law shall be passed.

4. No capitation or other direct tax shall be laid, unless in proportion to the census or enumeration hereinbefore directed to be taken.

5. No tax or duty shall be laid on articles exported from any State. No preference shall be given by any regulation of commerce or revenue to the ports of one State over those of another; nor shall vessels bound to or from one State be obliged to enter, clear, or pay duties in another.

6. No money shall be drawn from the treasury, but in consequence of appropriations made by law; and a regular statement and account of the receipts and expenditures of all public money shall be published from time to time.

7. No title of nobility shall be granted by the United States: and no person holding any office

of profit or trust under them, shall, without the consent of Congress, accept of any present, emolument, office, or title, of any kind whatever, from any king, prince, or foreign state.

SECTION X.—1. No State shall enter into any treaty, alliance, or confederation; grant letters of marque and reprisal; coin money; emit bills of credit; make anything but gold and silver coin a tender in payment of debts; pass any bill of attainder, *ex post facto* law, or law impairing the obligation of contracts; or grant any title of nobility.

2. No State shall, without the consent of Congress, lay any imposts or duties on imports or exports, except what may be absolutely necessary for executing its inspection laws: and the net produce of all duties and imposts laid by any State on imports or exports, shall be for the use of the treasury of the United States, and all such laws shall be subject to the revision and control of Congress.

3. No State shall, without the consent of Congress, lay any duty on tonnage, keep troops or ships of war in time of peace, enter into any agreement or compact with another State, or with a foreign power, or engage in war, unless actually invaded, or in such imminent danger as will not admit of delay.

ARTICLE II.

THE EXECUTIVE DEPARTMENT.

SECTION I.—1. The executive power shall be vested in a President of the United States of America. He shall hold his office during the term of four years; and, together with the Vice-President, chosen for the same term, be elected as follows:

2. Each State shall appoint, in such manner as the legislature thereof may direct, a number of electors equal to the whole number of Senators and Representatives to which the State may be

entitled in Congress; but no Senator or Representative, or person holding an office of trust or profit under the United States, shall be appointed an elector.

3. The electors shall meet in their respective States, and vote by ballot for two persons, of whom one at least shall not be an inhabitant of the same State with themselves. And they shall make a list of all the persons voted for, and of the number of votes for each; which list they shall sign and certify, and transmit sealed to the seat of the government of the United States, directed to the President of the Senate. The President of the Senate shall, in the presence of the Senate and House of Representatives, open all the certificates, and the votes shall then be counted. The person having the greatest number of votes shall be President, if such number be a majority of the whole number of electors appointed; and if there be more than one who have such a majority, and have an equal number of votes, then the House of Representatives shall immediately choose, by ballot, one of them for President; and if no person have a majority, then, from the five highest on the list, the said House shall, in like manner, choose a President. But in choosing the President, the votes shall be taken by States, the representation from each State having one vote: a quorum for this purpose shall consist of a member or members from two-thirds of the States, and a majority of all the States shall be necessary to a choice. In every case after the choice of the President, the person having the greatest number of votes of the electors shall be Vice-President. But if there should remain two or more who have equal votes, the Senate shall choose from them, by ballot, the Vice-President.

4. The Congress may determine the time of choosing the electors, and the day on which they shall give their votes, which day shall be the same throughout the United States.

5. No person except a natural born citizen, or a citizen of the United States at the time of the adoption of this Constitution, shall be eligible to the office of President: neither shall any person be eligible to that office who shall not have attained to the age of thirty-five years, and been fourteen years a resident within the United States.

6. In the case of the removal of the President from office, or of his death, resignation, or inability to discharge the powers and duties of the said office, the same shall devolve on the Vice-President; and the Congress may, by law, provide for the case of removal, death, resignation, or inability, both of the President and Vice-President, declaring what officer shall then act as President; and such officer shall act accordingly, until the disability be removed, or a President shall be elected.

7. The President shall, at stated times, receive for his services a compensation, which shall neither be increased nor diminished during the period for which he shall have been elected; and he shall not receive within that period any other emolument from the United States, or any of them.

8. Before he enters on the execution of his office, he shall take the following oath or affirmation:

"I do solemnly swear (or affirm) that I will faithfully execute the office of President of the United States: and will, to the best of my ability, preserve, protect, and defend the Constitution of the United States."

SECTION II.—1. The President shall be Commander-in-chief of the army and navy of the United States, and of the militia of the several States, when called into the actual service of the United States. He may require the opinion, in writing, of the principal officer in each of the executive departments, upon any subjects relating to the duties of their respective offices; and he shall have power to grant reprieves and pardons for offences against the United States, except in cases of impeachment.

2 He shall have power, by and with the advice and consent of the Senate, to make treaties, provided two-thirds of the Senators present concur; and he shall nominate, and, by and with the advice and consent of the Senate, shall appoint ambassadors and other public ministers and consuls, judges of the Supreme Court, and all other officers of the United States whose appointments are not herein otherwise provided for, and which shall be established by law. But the Congress may, by law, vest the appointment of such inferior officers as they think proper, in the President alone, in the courts of law, or in the heads of departments.

3. The President shall have power to fill up all vacancies that may happen during the recess of the Senate, by granting commissions, which shall expire at the end of their next session.

SECTION III.—1. He shall, from time to time, give to Congress information of the state of the Union, and recommend to their consideration such measures as he shall judge necessary and expedient. He may, on extraordinary occasions, convene both houses, or either of them; and in case of disagreement between them, with respect to the time of adjournment, he may adjourn them to such time as he shall think proper. He shall receive ambassadors and other public ministers. He shall take care that the laws be faithfully executed; and shall commission all officers of the United States.

SECTION IV.—The President, Vice-President. and all civil officers of the United States, shall be removed from office on impeachment for, and conviction of, treason, bribery, or other high crimes and misdemeanors.

ARTICLE III.

THE JUDICIAL DEPARTMENT.

SECTION I.—The judicial power of the United States shall be vested in one Supreme Court, and in such inferior courts as Congress may, from time to time, ordain and establish. The judges, both of the supreme and inferior courts, shall hold their offices during good behavior; and shall, at stated times, receive for their services a compensation, which shall not be diminished during their continuance in office.

SECTION II.—1. The judicial power shall extend to all cases in law and equity arising under this Constitution, the laws of the United States, and treaties made, or which shall be made, under their authority; to all cases affecting ambassadors, other public ministers, and consuls; to all cases of admiralty and maritime jurisdiction; to controversies to which the United States shall be a party; to controversies between two or more States; between a State and citizens of another State; between citizens of different States; between citizens of the same State claiming lands under grants of different States; and between a State, or the citizens thereof, and foreign states, citizens, or subjects.

2. In all cases affecting ambassadors, other public ministers, and consuls, and those in which a State shall be a party, the Supreme Court shall have original jurisdiction. In all the other cases before mentioned, the Supreme Court shall have appellate jurisdiction, both as to law and fact, with such exceptions and under such regulations as Congress shall make.

3. The trial of all crimes, except in cases of impeachment, shall be by jury, and such trial shall be held in the State where the said crimes shall have been committed; but when not committed within any State, the trial shall be at such place or places as Congress may by law have directed.

SECTION III—1. Treason against the United States shall consist only in levying war against them, or in adhering to their enemies, giving them aid and comfort. No person shall be convicted of treason, unless on the testimony of two witnesses to the same overt act, or on confession in open court.

2. Congress shall have power to declare the punishment of treason; but no attainder of treason shall work corruption of blood, or forfeiture, except during the life of the person attainted.

ARTICLE IV.

MISCELLANEOUS PROVISIONS.

SECTION I.—Full faith and credit shall be given in each State to the public acts, records, and judicial proceedings of every other State; and Congress may, by general laws, prescribe the manner in which such acts, records, and proceedings shall be proved, and the effect thereof.

SECTION II.—1. The citizens of each State shall be entitled to all the privileges and immunities of citizens in the several States.

2. A person charged in any State with treason, felony, or other crime, who shall flee from justice, and be found in another State, shall, on demand of the executive authority of the State from which he fled, be delivered up, to be removed to the State having jurisdiction of the crime.

3. No person held to service or labor in one State, under the laws thereof, escaping into another, shall, in consequence of any law or regulation therein, be discharged from such service or labor; but shall be delivered up on claim of the party to whom such service or labor may be due.

SECTION III.—1. New States may be admitted by Congress into this Union; but no new State shall be formed or erected within the jurisdiction of any other State, nor any State be formed by the junction of two or more States, or parts of

States, without the consent of the legislatures of the States concerned, as well as of Congress.

2. Congress shall have power to dispose of, and make all needful rules and regulations respecting the territory or other property belonging to the United States; and nothing in this Constitution shall be so construed as to prejudice any claims of the United States, or of any particular State.

SECTION IV.—The United States shall guarantee to every State in this Union a republican form of government, and shall protect each of them against invasion: and, on application of the legislature, or of the executive (when the legislature cannot be convened), against domestic violence.

ARTICLE V.

The Congress, whenever two-thirds of both houses shall deem it necessary, shall propose amendments to this Constitution; or, on the application of the legislatures of two-thirds of the several States, shall call a convention for proposing amendments, which, in either case, shall be valid, to all intents and purposes, as parts of this Constitution, when ratified by the legislatures of three-fourths of the several States, or by conventions in three-fourths thereof, as the one or the other mode of ratification may be proposed by Congress; provided that no amendment which may be made prior to the year one thousand eight hundred and eight shall in any manner affect the first and fourth clauses in the ninth section of the first article; and that no State, without its consent, shall be deprived of its equal suffrage in the Senate.

ARTICLE VI.

1. All debts contracted, and engagements entered into, before the adoption of this Constitusion, shall be as valid against the United States

under this Constitution as under the Confederation.

2. This Constitution, and the laws of the United States which shall be made in pursuance thereof, and all treaties made, or which shall be made, under the authority of the United States, shall be the supreme law of the land; and the judges in every State shall be bound thereby, anything in the constitution or laws of any State to the contrary notwithstanding.

3. The Senators and Representatives before mentioned, and the members of the several State legislatures, and all executive and judicial officers both of the United States and of the several States, shall be bound by oath or affirmation to support this Constitution; but no religious test shall ever be required as a qualification to any office or public trust under the United States.

ARTICLE VII.

The ratification of the conventions of nine States shall be sufficient for the establishment of this Constitution between the States so ratifying the same.

Done in convention by the unanimous consent of the States present, the seventeenth day of September, in the year of our Lord one thousand seven hundred and eighty-seven, and of the Independence of the United States of America the twelfth. In witness whereof we have hereunto subscribed our names.

GEORGE WASHINGTON,
President, and Deputy from Virginia.

AMENDMENTS TO THE CONSTITUTION OF THE UNITED STATES.

ARTICLE I.—Congress shall make no law respecting an establishment of religion, or prohibiting the free exercise thereof; or abridging the freedom of speech or of the press; or the right of the people peaceably to assemble, and to petition the government for a redress of grievances.

ARTICLE II.—A well-regulated milita being necessary to the security of a free State, the right of the people to keep and bear arms shall not be infringed.

ARTICLE III.—No soldier shall, in time of peace, be quartered in any house without the consent of the owner; nor in time of war, but in a manner to be prescribed by law.

ARTICLE IV.—The right of the people to be secure in their persons, houses, papers, and effects, against unreasonable searches and seizures, shall not be violated; and no warrants shall issue but upon probable cause, supported by oath or affirmation, and particularly describing the place to be searched, and the persons or things to be seized.

ARTICLE V.—No person shall be held to answer for a capital or otherwise infamous crime, unless on a presentment or indictment of a grand jury, except in cases arising in the land or naval forces, or in the militia, when in actual service in time of war or public danger; nor shall any person be subject for the same offence to be put twice in jeopardy of life or limb; nor shall be compelled in any criminal case to be witness against himself; nor be deprived of life, liberty, or property, without due process of law; nor shall private property be taken for public use without just compensation.

ARTICLE VI.—In all criminal prosecutions the accused shall enjoy the right to a speedy and public trial, by an impartial jury of the State and district wherein the crime shall have been committed, which district shall have been previously ascertained by law; and to be informed of the nature and cause of the accusation; to be confronted with the witnesses against him; to have compulsory process for obtaining witnesses in his favor; and to have the assistance of counsel for his defence.

ARTICLE VII.—In suits at common law, where

the value in controversy shall exceed twenty dollars, the right of trial by jury shall be preserved; and no fact tried by a jury shall be otherwise reexamined in any court of the United States, than according to the rules of the common law.

ARTICLE VIII.—Excessive bail shall not be required, nor excessive fines imposed, nor cruel and unusual punishments inflicted.

ARTICLE IX.—The enumeration in the Constitution of certain rights shall not be construed to deny or disparage others retained by the people.

ARTICLE X.—The powers not delegated to the United States by the Constitution, nor prohibited by it to the States, are reserved to the States respectively, or to the people.

ARTICLE XI.—The judicial power of the United States shall not be construed to extend to any suit in law or equity, commenced or prosecuted against one of the United States by citizens of another State, or by citizens or subjects of any foreign state.

ARTICLE XII.—1. The electors shall meet in their respective States, and vote by ballot for President and Vice-President, one of whom, at least, shall not be an inhabitant of the same State with themselves. They shall name in their ballots the person voted for as President, and in distinct ballots the person voted for as Vice-President; and they shall make distinct lists of all persons voted for as President, and of all persons voted for as Vice-President, and of the number of votes for each; which lists they shall sign and certify, and transmit sealed to the seat of the government of the United States, directed to the President of the Senate. The President of the Senate shall, in the presence of the Senate and House of Representatives, open all the certificates, and the votes shall then be counted. The person having the greatest number of votes for President shall be the President, if such number be a majority of the whole number of electors appointed: and if no person have such majority, then from the persons having the highest numbers, not exceeding three, on the list of those voted for as President, the House of Representatives shall choose immediately, by ballot, the President. But, in choosing the President, the votes shall be taken by States, the representation from each State having one vote: a quorum for this purpose shall consist of a member or members from two-thirds of the States, and a majority of all the States shall be necessary to a choice. And if the House of Representatives shall not choose a President, whenever the right of choice shall devolve upon them, before the fourth day of March next following, then the Vice-President shall act as President, as in the case of the death or other constitutional disability of the President.

2. The person having the greatest number of votes as Vice-President shall be the Vice-President, if such number be a majority of the whole number of electors appointed; and if no person have a majority, then from the two highest numbers on the list the Senate shall choose the Vice-President. A quorum for the purpose shall consist of two-thirds of the whole number of Senators, and a majority of the whole number shall be necessary to a choice.

3. But no person constitutionally ineligible to the office of President shall be eligible to that of Vice-President of the United States.

ARTICLE XIII.—*Section* I.—Neither slavery nor involuntary servitude, except as a punishment for crime, whereof the party shall have been duly convicted, shall exist within the United States, or any place subject to their jurisdiction.

Section II.—Congress shall have power to enforce this Article by appropriate legislation.

ARTICLE XIV.—*Section* I.—All persons born or naturalized in the United States, and subject to the jurisdiction thereof, are citizens of the United States, and the State wherein they reside. No State shall make or enforce any law which shall abridge the privileges or immunities of citizens of the United States; nor shall any State deprive any person of life, liberty, or property, without due process of law; nor deny to any person within its jurisdiction the equal protection of the laws.

Section II.—Representatives shall be apportioned among the several States according to their respective numbers, counting the whole number of persons in each State, excluding Indians not taxed. But when the right to vote at any election for the choice of electors for President or Vice-President of the United States, Representatives in Congress, the executive and judicial officers of a State, or the members of the legislature thereof, is denied to any of the male inhabitants of such State being twenty-one years of age, the citizens of the United States, or in any way abridged, except for participation in rebellion or other crime, the basis of representation therein shall be reduced in the proportion which the number of such male citizens shall bear to the whole number of male citizens twenty-one years of age in such State.

Section III.—No person shall be a Senator or Representative in Congress, or elector of President and Vice-President, or hold any office, civil or military, under the United States, or under any State, who, having previously taken an oath as a member of Congress, or as an officer of the United States, or as a member of any State legislature, or as an executive or judicial officer of any State, to support the Constitution of the United States, shall have engaged in insurrection or rebellion against the same, or given aid or comfort to the enemies thereof. But Congress may, by a vote of two-thirds of each house, remove such disability.

Section IV.—The validity of the public debt of the United States, authorized by law, including debts incurred for payment of pensions and bounties for services in suppressing insurrection or rebellion, shall not be questioned. But neither the United States nor any State shall assume or pay any debt or obligation incurred in aid of insurrection or rebellion against the United States, or any claim for the loss or emancipation of any slave; but all such debts, obligations and claims shall be held illegal and void.

Section V.—The Congress shall have power to enforce, by appropriate legislation, the provisions of this Article.

ARTICLE XV.—*Section* I.—The right of citizens of the United States to vote shall not be denied or abridged by the United States or by any State on account of race, color, or previous condition of servitude.

Section II.—The Congress shall have power to enforce this Article by appropriate legislation.

DECLARATION OF INDEPENDENCE.

When, in the course of human events, it becomes necessary for one people to dissolve the political bands which have connected them with another, and to assume, among the powers of the earth, the separate and equal station to which the laws of Nature and Nature's God entitle them, a decent respect to the opinions of mankind requires that they should declare the causes which impel them to the separation.

We hold these truths to be self-evident; that all men are created equal; that they are endowed by their Creator with certain inalienable rights; that among these are life, liberty, and the pursuit of happiness. That to secure these rights, governments are instituted among men, deriving their just powers from the consent of the governed; that whenever any form of government becomes destructive of these ends, it is the right of the people to alter or to abolish it, and to institute a new government, laying its foundation on such principles, and organizing its powers in such form as to them shall seem most likely to effect their safety and happiness. Prudence, indeed, will dictate that governments long established should not be changed for light and transient causes; and accordingly all experience hath shown that mankind are more disposed to suffer, while evils are sufferable, than to right themselves, by abolishing the forms to which they are accustomed. But when a long train of abuses and usurpations, pursuing invariably the same object, evinces a design to reduce them under absolute despotism, it is their right, it is their duty, to throw off such government, and to provide new guards for their future security. Such has been the patient sufferance of these colonies, and such is now the necessity which constrains them to alter their former systems of government. The history of the present king of Great Britain is a history of repeated injuries and usurpations, all having in direct object the establishment of an absolute tyranny over these States. To prove this, let facts be submitted to a candid world:

He has refused his assent to laws the most wholesome and necessary for the public good.

He has forbidden his governors to pass laws of immediate and pressing importance, unless suspended in their operation till his assent should be obtained; and when so suspended he has utterly neglected to attend to them. He has refused to pass other laws for the accommodation of large districts of people, unless those people would relinquish the right of representation in the legislature—a right inestimable to them, and formidable to tyrants only.

He has called together legislative bodies at places unusual, uncomfortable and distant from the repository of the public records, for the sole purpose of fatiguing them into compliance with his measures.

He has dissolved representative houses repeatedly for opposing, with manly firmness, his invasions on the rights of the people.

He has refused for a long time after such dissolution to cause others to be elected; whereby the legislative powers, incapable of annihilation, have returned to the people at large for their exercise, the State remaining, in the meantime, exposed to all the dangers of invasion from without and convulsions within.

He has endeavored to prevent the population of these States; for that purpose obstructing the laws of naturalization of foreigners; refusing to pass others to encourage their migration hither, and raising the conditions of new appropriations of lands.

He has obstructed the administration of justice by refusing his assent to laws for establishing judiciary powers.

He has made judges dependent on his will alone for the tenure of their offices and the amount of payment of their salaries.

He has erected a multitude of new offices, and sent hither swarms of officers to harass our people and eat out their substance.

He has kept among us, in times of peace, standing armies, without the consent of our legislatures.

He has affected to render the military independent of and superior to the civil power.

He has combined with others to subject us to a jurisdiction foreign to our Constitution, and unacknowledged by our laws; giving his assent to their acts of pretended legislation:

For quartering large bodies of armed troops among us:

For protecting them by a mock trial from punishment for any murders which they should commit on the inhabitants of these States:

For cutting off our trade with all parts of the world:

For imposing taxes on us without our consent:

For depriving us, in many cases, of the benefits of trial by jury:

For transporting us beyond seas to be tried for pretended offences:

For abolishing the free system of English laws in a neighboring province, establishing therein an arbitrary government, and enlarging its boundaries, so as to render it at once an example and fit instrument for introducing the same absolute rule into these colonies:

For taking away our charters, abolishing our most valuable laws, and altering, fundamentally, the forms of our government:

For suspending our own legislatures, and declaring themselves invested with power to legislate for us in all cases whatsoever.

He has abdicated government here by declaring us out of his protection, and waging war against us.

He has plundered our seas, ravaged our coasts, burnt our towns, and destroyed the lives of our people.

He is at this time transporting large armies of foreign mercenaries to complete the works of death, desolation and tyranny already begun, with circumstances of cruelty and perfidy scarcely paralleled in the most barbarous ages, and totally unworthy the head of a civilized nation.

He has constrained our fellow-citizens, taken captive on the high seas, to bear arms against their country, to become the executioners of their friends and brethren, or to fall themselves by their hands.

He has excited domestic insurrection among us, and has endeavored to bring on the inhabitants of our frontiers the merciless Indian savages, whose known rule of warfare is an undistinguished destruction of all ages, sexes and conditions.

In every stage of these oppressions we have petitioned for redress in the most humble terms; our repeated petitions have been answered only by repeated injury. A prince whose character is thus marked by every act which may define a tyrant is unfit to be the ruler of a free people.

Nor have we been wanting in attentions to our British brethren. We have warned them from time to time of attempts by their legislature to extend an unwarrantable jurisdiction over us. We have reminded them of the circumstances of our emigration and settlement here. We have appealed to their native justice and magnanimity, and we have conjured them by the ties of our common kindred to disavow these usurpations, which would inevitably interrupt our connections and correspondence. They, too, have been deaf to the voice of justice and consanguinity. We must, therefore, acquiesce in the necessity which denounces our separation, and hold them, as we hold the rest of mankind, enemies in war, in peace friends.

We, therefore, the representatives of the United States of America, in General Congress assembled, appealing to the Supreme Judge of the world for the rectitude of our intentions, do, in the name and by the authority of the good people of these colonies, solemnly publish and declare that these United Colonies are, and of right ought to be, free and independent States; that they are absolved from all allegiance to the British crown, and that all political connection between them and the State of Great Britain is, and ought to be, totally dissolved; and that, as free and independent States, they have full power to levy war, conclude peace, contract alliances, establish commerce, and to do all other acts and things which independent States may of right do. And for the support of this declaration, with a firm reliance on the protection of Divine Providence, we mutually pledge to each other our lives, our fortunes and our sacred honor.

DECLARATION OF INDEPENDENCE.

CUT 1, below, gives you an interior slate view of the old
INDEPENDENCE HALL, PHILADELPHIA,
PA., JULY THE 4th, 1776.

SHOWING the 55 members of the Grand Congress of the United Colonies Signing the Declaration of Independence, July the 4th, 1776.

1. Josiah Bartlett, 2. William Whipple, 3. Matthew Thornton, 4. Samuel Adams, 5. John Adams, 6. Robert Treat Paine, 7. Elbridge Gerry, 8. Stephen Hopkins, 9. William Ellery, 10. Roger Sherman, 11 Samuel Huntington, 12. William Williams, 13. Oliver Wolcot, 14. William Floyd, 15. Philip Livingston, 16. Francis Lewis, 17. Lewis Morris, 18. Richard Stocton, 19. John Witherspoon, 20, Francis Hopkins, 21 John Hart, 22. Abram Clark, 23. Robert Morris, 24. Benjamin Rush, 25. Benjamin Franklin, 26, John Morton, 27. George Clymer, 28. James Smith, 29. George Taylor, 30. James Wilson, 31. George Ross, 32. Cesar Rodney, 33. George Read, 34. Thomas McKean, 35. Samuel Chase, 36. William Paca, 37. Thomas Stone, 38. Chas. Carrol, of Carrolton, 39. George Withe, 40. Richard Henry Lee, 41. Thomas Jefferson, 42. Benjamin Harrison, 43. Thomas Nelson, jr., 44. Francis Lightfoot Lee, 45, Carter Braxton, 46. William Hooper, 47. Joseph Hewse, 48. John Penn, 49. Edward Rutledge, 50. Thomas Heywood, jr,. 51. Thomas Lynch, jr., 52. Authur Middleton, 53. Buton Gwinnet, 54. yman Hall, 55. George Walton !!!!

26. DECLARATION OF INDEPENDENCE.

THEIR heroic acts have been the means of making us a great, a free, a prosperous and a happy people. They declared for a free individual government, and against a government of gods, kings, lords, devils and their awful religious rule! That had up to that day ruled, abused, ravished, robed, murdered and enslaved man!! And think you, they yet claim it was done by God and was right!!

CUT, 2, above, is the OLD LIBERTY BELL that when we gained a SEVEN years fight! that is, when we WHIPPED that AWFUL, that MIGHTY army of the 'immutable, unchangable gods, kings, lords, and CHURCH HELL-HOUNDS! That at that time they, the religionists were giving, selling or trading the virtue or chastity, or life of their mothers, wives and daughters to Whoredum, Slavery or Mormonism! Or hung, drownded, tortured, in every conceivable way! Ah! my God! all grumblers to this, all wealthey, old or unprotected persons were adjudged heretic, traitor. a haunt, a witch, and then robed and BURNT! !

Ah! my God! such was bible rule when this old BELL pealed forth the BIRTH of LIBERTY and the DEATH of TYRANY, and the subjugation of religion in 1783 !!!

DECLARATION OF INDEPENDENCE.

READER? It is no use to plaver, crawfish, lie, nor to multiply words about it! Christianity, and all religious are as INFAMOUS AS HELL! In fact it is the FORE RUNNER of HELL! "I come not to send peace on this earth! no, but, I come to send HATE! firie! and the sword" is precisely what your bible TEACHES and this is what you have FORCED on this world from your MURDERING f ther CAIN on down!

☞ CAINYUN O! Cainyun, it is my happy home, and I am bound for the happy land of Cainyun!" This is th way they, these crazy, fool religionists have been SCREAMING and hunting this wide world over, ever since their MURDERING father, CAIN was branded and banished from the Amerikas, millions of years ago! They remind us of the banished dog fable! Dogs are always smelling around other dogs. And why! Trying to find another dog that a'nt just precisly like themselves! And when they find him, ge. hu what a fight! Just wateh a lot of snipe faced hypocrits meet, and of all the smelling, noding, scraping, hawking, hugging aud kissing around and around! Just like them ar dogs what ar hunting that ar rosemary dog! And when they find him, gehu what a fight!

Our revolutionary fathers were of all races, hues and colors, and framed a government on— Equal and exact justice to all mankind— bible or no bible! Then sectarian religion unmercifully ruledfor their peculiar gods! Their laws were founded on one of the most wicked, vicious, obscene, and vulgar books that the world ever knew! And only think, they claimed God wrote it defended it and enforced it!

Now it is, that the entire people rule by ruling themselves. They are moral free agents, one standing guard for the other. Their laws are founden on well known, undeniable vital, individual, physical facts!! And not on a mear belief, a spirtual token, a dream, a supposition, or a law from the gods, kings, lords, and crazy religionists!

Our laws are not founded on their king's bible nor on the teaohings of their Jesus' no, nor on their morals, or on what religionists call justice! No, they are as diametrically opposit to their god's and their saviour's teachings, precepts, examples and morals as is hell from heaven! Their's are made up from the attributes, elements or qualities of hell!! while ours are made up from those from heavem!!!!

PROOF—Religionists doom and dam a part of man to an endles hell! for no sin nor crime whatever! Only to feast the hellish gizzard of their gods and to give the priest a scarecrow! Then another class hold all men crimnials, and dam them for an old Jews crimes! Do you want to be held accountable for your parents and great grandparents sins or crimes? Do you want to be held for an old idiotic Jews sin? See curses and slavery in this book. See pages 120 to 178. See page 154¼. Do you? Such was the fate of this priest riddin world until our American revolution downed the divine rights of gods kings and church devils!

We hold all men free, honorable gentlemen, just and equal until proven and convicted otherwise, by a judge or a jury of your own honorable neighbors of your own choice!!! Such was never before known! Such is nowhere else tolerated to-day, with all of your bosted church morals, and saviours precepts and examples! Yet, under the majority rule of parties, cliques, churches and secret orders our laws are not respected and executed, no, but they are evaded, and they try and punish one another by every known rule of twistification! The sweet name liberty was not known to their king Jesus' lips, and freedom to him was an unknown stranger! He orriginated nothing new! He only aimed to carry out the hellish, infernal infamous old! Saying— I come not to destroy the law but to fulfill it! Matt. v, 17, 18, 10. Ah! my fellow man! It was this DECLARATION of American INDEPENDENCE and not Jesus the Christian's Christ that said— "that all men are created equal, with the inalienable right to life, liberty, and the persuits of happiness." Although, religionists now claim that their sweet bastard, Jew-Jesus, wrote the Declaration of American Indepeudence! And, in fact, all good things! Yet, I am sorry to tell you that he never said nor done a good thing in all his life! In truth, he could neather read nor write! And all we have of him is mearly hearsay! Gotten up by Newsmongers hundreads of years after it is said to have cccured! At best, he led the life of a wine-bibing mandicant! And Mark, his scond witness, at vi, 5, says Jesus could do no mighty work, save heal sick folks!!

Homeless , poverty, hate, disobedience and improvidence are the lessons his life taught! "Lay not up, provide neither gold, silver, brass, nor scrip for your purse— nor two coats— shoes nor socks. That a rich man cant go to heaven, Matt. vi, 19— x, 9, 10— xix, 24. Take no thought for tomorrow were to him favorite themes, Lu. xii, 22.

Give to him that asketh thee, to thee borrower turn not

DECLARATION OF INDEPENDENCE.

away, resist not evil, if hit on one cheek turn the other, if your coat is taken give your cloak also, if compelled to go a mile go two, love and bless your enemies, and do good to those that hate and abuse you, if you have two coats give one to him that has none, Matt. v, 39 to 45!! And I give thee the heathen, Ps. ii, 8! are fare samples of what Christians would have yon believe make up our laws and our justice, see page 364 to 370!!!

He taught that he, David and the priests could do unlawful acts, that is, Tom, Dick and Harry could tresspass, rob, ravish, steal and murder, but, John, Bill, or Dick must not, Matt. xii, 1 to 5! All of this is destructive to peace, law order, justice and dimetrically opposit to, and at perpetual war, with this American Declaration of Imdependence!!

This charitable coat fake of Jesus' forerunner, John that awful bapsouser, where he said at Lu. iii, 11 that if you had two coats give to him one that hath none! Jesus' made quste a change from a forerunner gift of duty to evading of it by never having a coat, or but one, and then act a fool if you get beat out of one at law, by giving them two, Matt. v, 40. — x, 10 Are our laws and sense thus founded?

The religionist's bibles and their scripture are full of infamous examples where religionists ruled the PHYSICAL mental or secular man, and punished him unmercifully and unnecessarlly, by the supposed spiritual man, and a spirtual government, that made and enforced all manner of secular laws. The governments of the world up to this great American rebellion was claimed to be run by the gods in this cruel, robbing, enslaving, murdering, religious way!

The awful facts of it, as it is norated in this Declaration of American Freedom and Independence, is too well known to all mankind to need comment. It was a tyrants rule a controle without your consent! It was punishment without a cause, without a hearing! It was an eternal damnation without a cause! or, even a thought or an act on your part!

NOW, THINK YOU? our laws, morals, and justice is founded on Christianity? or, that the American nation is a Christian nation? See pages 170, 364 to 370!

Think you not that a good, honest, upright, moral, free American is not better than the best of Jews and Christians? Think you not that the best of religion is a craziness, and mans greatest enemy, and to be pittied and avoided? Certainly it is! Reader? then be an American! See page 144.

30.   DECLARATION OF INDEPENDENCE.

THAT SALVATION BAG!

CUT 3, below, represents the Wandering Jew, the Christians Jew man god, or their saviour Jesus carrying his load of infamous, pardoned hypocrits, thieves, rapers, ravishers robbers and murders, slap dab to heaven!!

The sale of Indulgence, forgiving sin and crime, the paying of a fine, a duty or privilege to the priest, is all Christian and not just. A free form of government ought not to tolerate injustice in any shape. Yet, we do! we tolerate all this! and religion, and not Liberality, is the cause of it!

Christians, and espe ially the Catholics, are open and avowed enemies to our U. S. Government! They are traitors! they are villionous usurpers! malcontents that are all the time misrepresenting our government! and trying to cause discord! disobedience, and destruction! They claim that the United States is theirs, by discovery, and that we usurped our authority, and seized our possessions! And they say, a free man, or a free government is contrary to theie bible! That their bible only anthorizes a king and a pope to rule a world of priest-ridden slaves! Therefore I say down with the traitors, and up with our liberties, and protect our God given freedom!!

DECLARATION OF INDEPENDENCE. 31.

IF— that awful IF! If you will do ALL my will! IF you will be as perfect as your father in heaven! then I will smile on thee, bless thee— give thee the heathen! and ex.alt thee above all! But, that awful IF! IF you DONT-do ALL my wishes THEN I will GIVE you to the heathen!! Deut. xxviii. Rev. xii. 7. Matt v. 48.  And Mr. HEATHEN will always have it! for the angels in heaven could not do All his will! Moses nor Solomon could not do ALL his will and was given to the heathen! See page, 190.

They dont now even pretend to do right when it is their interest to do so, and why? because religion is craziness!

Therafore, fellowcitizens, I say tax them, their churches, labor and property as all citizens are, for they are not only avowed enemies but self proven! Make them keep their religion private, and punish them every time they say anything misrepresenting or injurious to a citizen or the nation!! See Romon Law on the 4th 76th page!

Worshiping, whoreing, gambeling, thieving, robbing, murdering, hording, claning, acquisitive speculating, chewing, smokeing, stimulating, exciting, narcotising, drinking, winebibing, feasting, etc., are bastard brothers and sisters, offsprings of self-polution, and are acquired mental diseases! No sound, well balanced, healthy youth ever thinks of any of this abomination until introduced to it by others. Such being of an exciting, stimulating, tickling nature make them easy acquired and admired. Yet, they are mental diseases and not a physical necesity. And they soon require a perpetual application or down you go into a desponding, debilitated, hydrophobia, or mad dog disposition!!

THAT CRIMINAL CLASS! SEE PAGES 187 TO 194, 201 TO 204 AND 301!

☞ OATH-BOUND PARTIES, CLIQUES, CHURCHES AND SECRET-ORDER RACKETS!

THIS CUT represents the many parties, cliques, churches and secret oath-bound orders, that tumble into the race for office! Their monkey appearance, actions, as if actually seated on dogs, is a fit symbol of their actual character. They are the Criminal Class! And how? Because these cliques and not the people put them in office! And they are frequently mear idiots!

DECLARATION OF INDEPENDENCE 33.

There has not been a fair honest election in this state for many years, consequently the laws are illegal and unjust! Such has been affirmed by me for years! Such is aledged from page 100 to 118! Such has just been proven by the contested election of govenor! Evans, a republican, was e-lected by fraud! So was Turney, a democrat, but as he had the most votes, [illegal of course,] the legislature being of democrats most, voted him in! A govenor for a clique and not for the people! And why is this? Because the people spend more time and money about eternity than for the present life!

And when I remonstrate with them and show them their irror, they will as helpless, abject slaves, or as impudent tyrants ask— "What better have you to offer?" And I say, LIBERTY! FREEDOM! PEACE! GOODWILL AND HONESTY! These are the qualities that go to make up an Americans Hope or Religion! This is his only Saviour! his only hope of a resurrection! Ah! my fellow man, all will be called, but few will be able to hear, or to understand! And why? Because they wont listen to any call in this world but that of their little insignificant party, clique, church or order! Therefore, that is their Saviour! And it will never call them! Why? because millions of similar ones have claimed to be man's savior right direct from God. And one by one was MURDERED! passing away! and long since forgotten! They, like the Christians Jew-man-god could not save themselves! Any fool with half an eye, and a head even full of mud ought to be able to see that all there was in this Jesus' intentions was to scare and force himself into a king of the Jews! It related to nothing else. Evil designing kings hundreds of years after hatched up this Christian Slavery Religion in his name! Matt. at x, 9, 10, teaches quite a self-contradictory doctrin to Lu. xxii, 36 Now, he finds begging and gentle means will not make him king, so he now proposes to use the old carnal weapons, fire, fear, money and the sword!!

The doctrine of a god ruling the world was not new then nor is it now! But, the doctrin of man, [the common people,] ruling the world by ruling himself is new! And was never taught, nor done before the Declaration of American Independence! Yet, through our good success at defending our selves, the freedom and happiness insured to the common people, has made us an asylum for the world!

Then is this not sufficient proof that we have something better to offer you? "Not one drop of blood can be laid to the Infidel world, that was taken on account of religious belief! Not the death of one single martyr can be laid at the door of Atheism! The hands of the Agnostic are unstained by the blood of the opposing or religious beliefs of their fellow man! Death's shroud does not enfold the cold and silent form of a Free-thinker, on which the scarlet stains of religious belief rests!

But, let us open the book in which the doings of the Christians are recorded from the beginning of their first man Adam, on down to the time when they could no longer execute their presumed divine edicts! By reason of Infidelity and this Declaration of American Independence! We find that their history is written with the blood of those that dared to oppose them in a mear belief! Yea, written upon the skins of their murdered victims, men, women and children that had no belief! Not the decay of a single nation, nor the disfranchise, enslaving, or destruction of any people can be charged to the heathem. But, all that is GOOD, TRUE, LOVING, LOVABLE and BEAUTIFUL we owe to the heatnen! The figures, the alphabet, the scriptures, the sciences and the arts, we owe to the heathen! Home, SweetHome, and a loved, free ASYLUM, for the poor, oppressed, and downtrodden from all the world in the Amerikas, we owe to the heathen! This world and all in it, on it, and above it, was given to the heathen! See Gen. i. 26, 28; and ii. 7, 8, 15. And see pages 1, 2, 3, 4, 5, 30, 106, 126, 136, 137 138 and 360 to 370 of this book.

So, dont fret Brudder Christian, Mr. Heathen has always been here and always will be here, and everywhere. He is the god-like gentleman, while you are a self-condemned criminal!! You are the "criminal class!!!!

FAREWELL ADDRESS.

United States, September 17, 1796.

FRIENDS AND FELLOW CITIZENS—The period for a new election of a citizen, to administer the executive government of the United States, being not far distant, and the time actually arrived, when your thoughts must be employed in designating the person who is to be clothed with that important trust, it appears to me proper, especially as it may conduct to a more distinct expression of the public voice, that I should now apprise you of the resolution I have formed, to decline being considered among the number of those out of whom a choice is to be made.

I beg you, at the same time, to do me the justice to be assured, that this resolution has not been taken without a strict regard to all the considerations appertaining to the relation which binds a dutiful citizen to his country; and that, in withdrawing the tender of service, which silence in my situation might imply, I am influenced by no diminution of zeal for your future interest; no deficiency of grateful respect for your past kindness; but am supported by a full conviction that the step is compatible with both.

The acceptance of, and continuance hitherto in, the office to which your suffrages have twice called me, have been a uniform sacrifice of inclination to the opinion of duty, and to a deference for what appeared to be your desire. I constantly hoped, that it would have been much earlier in my power, consistently with motives, which I was not at liberty to disregard, to return to that retirement from which I had been reluctantly drawn. The strength of my inclination to do this, previous to the last election, had even led to the preparation of an address to declare it to you; but mature reflection on the then perplexed and critical posture of our affairs with foreign nations, and the unanimous advice of persons entitled to my confidence, impelled me to abandon the idea.

I rejoice that the state of your concerns, external as well as internal, no longer renders the pursuit of inclination incompatible with the sentiment of duty or propriety; and am persuaded whatever partiality may be retained for my services, that, in the present circumstances of our country, you will not disapprove my determination to retire.

The impressions with which I first undertook the arduous trust were explained on the proper occasion. In the discharge of this trust I will only say that I have with good intentions contributed toward the organization and administration of the government the best exertions of which a very fallible judgment was capable. Not unconscious in the outset of the inferiority of my qualifications, experience in my own eyes, perhaps still more in the eyes of others, has strengthened the motives to diffidence of myself; and every day the increasing weight of years admonishes me more and more that the shade of retirement is as necessary to me as it will be welcome. Satisfied that if any circumstances have given peculiar value to my services, they were temporary, I have the consolation to believe that, while choice and prudence invite me to quit the political scene, patriotism does not forbid it.

In looking forward to the movement which is intended to terminate the career of my public life, my feelings do not permit me to suspend the deep acknowledgement of that debt of gratitude which I owe to my beloved country for the many honors it has conferred upon me; still more for the steadfast confidence with which it has supported me; and for the opportunities I have thence enjoyed of manifesting my inviolable attachment by services faithful and persevering, though in usefulness unequal to my zeal. If benefits have resulted to our country from these services, let it always be remembered to your praise, and as an instructive example in our annals, that under circumstances in which the passions, agitated in every direction, were liable to mislead, amidst appearances sometimes dubious, vicissitudes of fortune often discouraging, in situations in which not unfrequently want of success has countenanced the spirit of criticism, the constancy of your support was the essential prop of the efforts, and a guarantee of the plans by which they were effected. Profoundly penetrated with this idea, I shall carry it with me to my grave, as a strong incitement to unceasing vows that Heaven may continue to you the choicest tokens of its beneficence; that your union and brotherly affection may be perpetual; that the free constitution, which is the work of your hands, may be sacredly maintained; that its administration in every department may be stamped with wisdom and virtue; that, in fine, the happiness of the people of these states, under the auspices of liberty, may be made complete, by so careful a preservation and so prudent a use of this blessing, as will acquire to them the glory of recommending it to the applause, the affection and adoption of every nation, which is yet a stranger to it.

Here, perhaps, I ought to stop. But a solicitude for your welfare, which cannot end but with my life, and the apprehension of danger, natural to that solicitude, urge me, on an occasion like the present, to offer to your solemn contemplation, and to recommend to your frequent review, some sentiments, which are the result of much reflection, of no inconsiderable observation, and which appear to me all-important to the permanency of your felicity as a people. These will be offered to you with the more freedom, as you can only see in them the disinterested warnings of a parting friend, who can possibly have no personal motive to bias his counsel. Nor can I forget, as an encouragement to it, your indulgent reception of my sentiments on a former and not dissimilar occasion.

Interwoven as is the love of liberty with every ligament of your hearts, no recommendation of mine is necessary to fortify or confirm the attachment.

The unity of government, which constitutes you one people, is also now dear to you. It is justly so; for it is a main pillar in the edifice of your real independence, the support of your tranquility at home, your peace abroad; of your safety; of your prosperity; of that very liberty, which you so highly prize. But as it is easy to foresee, that from different causes and from different quarters much pains will be taken, many artifices employed, to weaken in your minds the conviction of this truth; as this is the point in your political fortress against which the batteries of internal and external enemies will be most constantly and actively (though often covertly and insidiously) directed, it is of infinite moment that you should properly estimate the immense value of your national union to your collective and individual happiness; that you should cherish a cordial, habitual, and immovable attachment to it; accustoming yourselves to think and speak of it as of the palladium of your political safety and prosperity; watching for its preservation with jealous anxiety; discountenancing whatever may suggest even a suspicion that it can in any event be abandoned; and indignantly frowning upon the first dawning of every attempt to alienate any portion of our country from the rest, or to enfeeble the sacred ties which now link together the various parts.

For this you have every inducement of sympathy and interest. Citizens, by birth or choice, of a common country, that country has a right to concentrate your affections. The name of America, which belongs to you, in your national capacity, must always exalt the just pride of patriotism, more than any appellation derived from local discriminations. With slight shades of difference, you have the same religion, manners, habits and political principles. You have in a common cause fought and triumphed together; the independence and liberty you possess are the work of joint counsels and joint efforts, of common dangers, sufferings and successes.

But these considerations, however powerfully they address themselves to your sensibility, are greatly outweighed by those which apply more immediately to your interest. Here every portion of our country finds the most commanding motives for carefully guarding and preserving the union of the whole.

The North, in an unrestrained intercourse with the South, protected by the equal laws of a common government, finds in the productions of the latter, great additional resources of maritime and commercial enterprise and precious materials of manufacturing industry. The South, in the same intercourse, benefiting by the agency of the North, sees its agriculture grow and its commerce expand. Turning partly into its own channels the seamen of the North, it finds its particular navigation invigorated; and while it contributes in different ways to nourish and increase the general mass of the national navigation, it looks forward to the protection of a maritime strength, to which itself is unequally adapted. The East, in a like intercourse with the West, already finds, and in the progressive improvement of interior communications by land and water will more and more find, a valuable vent for the commodities which it brings from abroad, or manufactures at home. The West derives from the East supplies requisite to its growth and comfort, and what is perhaps of still greater consequence, it must of necessity owe the secure enjoyment of indispensable outlets for its own productions to the weight, influence and the future maritime strength of the Atlantic side of the Union, directed by an indissoluble community of interest as one nation. Any other tenure by which the West can hold this essential advantage, whether derived from its own separate strength, or from an apostate and unnatural connection with any foreign power, must be intrinsically precarious.

While, then, in every part of our country thus feels an immediate and particular interest in union, all the parts combined cannot fail to find in the united mass of means and efforts greater strength, greater resource, proportionably greater security from external danger, a less frequent interruption of their peace by foreign nations, and, what is of inestimable value, they must derive from union an exemption from those broils and wars between themselves, which so frequently afflict neighboring countries not tied together by the same governments, which their own rivalships alone would be sufficient to produce, but which opposite foreign alliances, attachments and intrigues would stimulate and embitter. Hence, likewise, they will avoid the necessity of those overgrown military establishments which, under any form of governments, are inauspicious to liberty, and which are to be regarded as particularly hostile to republican liberty. In this sense it is, that your union ought to be considered as a main prop of your liberty, and that the love of the one ought to endear to you the preservation of the other.

These considerations speak a persuasive language to every reflecting and virtuous mind, and exhibit the continuance of the Union as a primary object of patriotic desire. Is there a doubt whether a common government can embrace so large a sphere? Let experience solve it. To listen to mere speculation in such a case were criminal. We are authorized to hope, that a proper organization of the whole, with the auxiliary agency of governments for the respective subdivisions, will afford a happy issue to the experiment. It is well worth a fair and full experiment. With such powerful and obvious motives to union, affecting all parts of our country, while experience shall not have demonstrated its impracticability, there will always be reason to distrust the patriotism of those, who in any quarter may endeavor to weaken its bands.

In contemplating the causes which may disturb our Union, it occurs as a matter of serious concern, that any ground should have been furnished for characterizing parties by geographical discriminations Northern and Southern, Atlantic and Western; whence designing men may endeavor to excite a belief that there is a real difference of local interests and views. One of the expedients of party to acquire influence, within particular districts, is to misrepresent the opinions and aims of other districts. You cannot shield yourself too much against the jealousies and heart-burnings, which spring from these misrepresentations; they tend to render alien to each other those who ought to be bound together by fraternal affection. The inhabitants of our western country have lately had a useful lesson on this head; they have seen, in the negotiations by the Executive, and in the unanimous ratification by the Senate, of the treaty with Spain, and in the universal satisfaction at that event, throughout the United States, a decisive proof how unfounded were the suspicions propagated among them of a policy in the General Government and in the Atlantic States unfriendly to their interests in regard to the Mississippi; they have been witnesses to the formation of two treaties, that with Great Britian and that with Spain, which secure to them every thing they could desire, in respect to our foreign relations, towards confirming their prosperity. Will it not be their wisdom to rely for the preservation of these advantages on the Union by which they were procured? Will they not henceforth be deaf to those advisers, if such there are, who would sever them from their brethren and connect them with their aliens?

To the efficacy and permanency of your Union, a Government for the whole is indispensable. No alliances, however strict, between the parts can be an adequate substitute; they must inevitably experience the infractions and interruptions, which all alliances in all times have experienced. Sensible of this momentous truth, you have improved upon your first essay, by the adoption of a Constitution of Government better calculated than your former for an intimate Union, and for the efficacious management of your common concerns. This Government, the off-spring of our own choice, uninfluenced and unawed, adopted upon full investigation and mature deliberation, completely free in its principles, in the distribution of its powers, uniting security with energy, and containing within itself a provision for its own amendment, has a just claim to your confidence and your support. Respect for its authority, compliance with its laws, acquiescence in its measures, are duties enjoined by the fudamental maxims of true Liberty. The basis of our political systems is the right of the people to make and to alter their constitutions of government. But the constitution which at any time exists, till changed by an explicit and authentic act of the whole people, is sacredly obligatory upon all. The very idea of the power and the right of the people to establish Government presupposes the duty of every individual to obey the established Government.

All obstructions to the execution of the laws, all combinations and associations, under whatever plausible character, with the real design to direct, control, counteract, or awe the regular deliberation and action of the constituted authorities, are destructive to this fundamental principle, and of fatal tendency. They serve to organize faction, to give it an artificial and extraordinary force; to put, in the place of the delegated will of the nation, the will of a party, often a small but artful and enterprising minority of the community; and, according to the alternate triumphs of different parties, to make the public administration the mirror of the ill-concerted and incongruous projects of faction, rather than the organ of consisted and wholesome plans digested by common counsels, and modified by mutual interests.

However combinations or associations of the above description may now and then answer popular ends, they are likely in the course of time and things, to become potent engines, by which cunning, ambitious, and unprincipled men will be enabled to subvert the power of the people, and to usurp for themselves the reins of government; destroying afterwards the very engines which have lifted them to unjust dominion.

Towards the preservation of your government, and the premanency of your present happy state, it is requisite, not only that you steadily discountenance irregular oppositions to its acknowledged authority, but also that you resist with care the spirit of innovation upon its principles, however specious the pretexts. One method of assault may be to effect, in the forms of the constitution, alterations, which will impair the energy of the system, and thus to undermine what cannot be directly overthrown. In all the changes to which you may be invited, remember that time and habit are at least as necessary to fix the true character of governments, as of other human institutions; that experience is the surest standard by which to test the real tendency of the existing constitution of the country; that facility in changes, upon the credit of mere hypothesis and opinion, exposes to perpetual change, from the endless variety of hypothesis and opinion; and remember, especially, that, for the efficient management of your common interests, in a country so extensive as ours, a government of as much vigor as is consistent with the perfect security of liberty is indispensable. Liberty itself will find in such a government, with powers properly distributed and adjusted, its surest guardian. It is, indeed, little else than a name, where the government is too feeble to withstand the enterprises of faction, to confine each member of the society within the limits prescribed by the laws, and to maintain all in the secure and tranquil enjoyment of the rights of person and property.

BY GEORGE WASHINGTON.

I have already intimated to you the danger of parties in the state, with particular reference to the founding of them on geographical discrimination. Let me now take a more comprehensive view, and warn you in the most solemn manner against the baleful effects of the spirit of party, generally.

This spirit, unfortunately, is inseparable from our nature, having its root in the strongest passions of the human mind. It exists under different shapes in all governments, more or less stifled, controlled, or repressed; but, in those of the popular form it is seen in its greatest rankness, and is truly their worst enemy.

The alternate domination of one faction over an other, sharpened by the spirit of revenge, natural to party dissension, which in different ages and countries has perpetrated the most horrid enormities, is itself a frightful despotism. But this leads at length to a more formal and permanent despotism. The disorders and miseries, which result, gradually incline the minds of men to seek security and repose in the absolute power of an individual; and sooner or later the chief of some prevailing faction, more able or more fortunate than his competitors, turns this disposition to the purposes of his own elevation, on the ruins of public liberty.

Without looking forward to an extremity of this kind (which nevertheless ought to be entirely out of sight), the common and continual mischiefs of the spirit of party are sufficient to make it the interest and duty of a wise people to discourage and restrain it.

It serves always to distract the public councils, and enfeeble the public administration. It agitates the community with ill-founded jealousies and false alarms; kindles the animosity of one part against another, foments occasionally riot and insurrection. It opens the doors to foreign influence and corruption, which find a facilitated access to the government itself through the channels of party passions. Thus the policy and the will of one country are subjected to the policy and will of another.

There is an opinion, that parties in free countries are useful checks upon the administration of the government, and serve to keep alive the spirit of liberty. This within certain limits is probably true, and in governments of a monarchial cast, patriotism may look with indulgence, if not with favor, upon the spirit of party. But in those of the popular character, in governments purely elective, it is a spirit not to be encouraged. From their natural tendency, it is certain there will always be enough of that spirit for every salutary purpose. And, there being constant danger of excess, the effort ought to be, by force of public opinion to mitigate and assuage it. A fire not to quenched, it demands a uniform vigilance to prevent its bursting into a flame, lest, instead of warming, it should consume.

It is important, likewise, that the habits of thinking in a free country should inspire caution, in those intrusted with its administration, to confine themselves within their respective constitutional spheres, avoiding in the exercise of the powers of one department to encroach upon another. The spirit of encroachment tends to consolidate the powers of all the departments in one, and thus to create, whatever the form of government, a real despotism. A just estimate of that love of power, and proneness to abuse it, which predominates in the human heart, is sufficient to satisfy us of the truth of this position. The necessity of reciprocal checks in the exercise of political power, by dividing and distributing it into different depositories, and constituting each the guardian of the public weal against invasions by the others, has been evinced by experiments ancient and modern; some of them in our country and under our own eyes. To preserve them must be as necessary as to institute them. If, in the opinion of the people, the distribution or modification of the constitutional powers be in any particular wrong, let it be corrected by an amendment in the way which the constitution designates. But let there be no change by usurpation; for, though this, in one instance, may be the instrument of good, it is the customary weapon by which free governments are destroyed. The precedent must always greatly overbalance in permanent evil any partial or transient benefit, which the use can at any time yield.

Of all the dispositions and habits, which lead to political prosperity, religion and morality are indispensable supports. In vain would that man claim the tribute of patriotism, who should labor to subvert these great pillars of human happiness, these firmest props of the duties of men and citizens. The mere politician equally with the pious man, ought to respect and to cherish them. A volume could not trace all their connections with private and public felicity. Let it simply be asked, Where is the security for property, for reputation, for life, if the sense of religious obligation desert the oaths, which are the instruments of investigation in courts of justice? And let us with caution indulge the supposition, that morality can be maintained without religion. Whatever may be conceded to the influence of refined education on minds of peculiar structure, reason and experience both forbid us to expect, that national morality can prevail in exclusion of religious principle.

It is substantially true that virtue or morality is a necessary spring of popular government. The rule, indeed, extends with more or less force to every species of free government. Who, that is a sincere friend to it, can look with indifference upon attempts to shake the foundation of the fabric?

Promote, then, as an object of primary importance institutions for general diffusion of knowledge. In proportion as the structure of a government gives force to public opinion, it is essential that public opinion should be enlightened.

As a very important source of strength and security, cherish public credit. One method of preserving it is, to use it as sparingly as possible ; avoiding occasions of expense by cultivating peace, but remembering also that timely disbursements to prepare for danger frequently prevent much greater disbursements to repel it ; avoiding likewise the accumulation of debt, not only by shunning occasions of expense, but by vigorous exertion in time of peace to discharge the debts, which unavoidable wars may have occasioned not ungenerously throwing upon posterity the burden which we ourselves ought to bear. The execution of these maxims belongs to your representatives, but it is necessary that public opinion should co-operate. To facilitate to them the performance of their duty it is essential that you should practically bear in mind, that towards the payment of debts there must be revenue; that to have revenue there must be taxes; that no taxes can be devised which are not more or less inconvenient and unpleasant; that the intrinsic embarrassment, inseparable from the selection of the proper objects (which is always a choice of difficulties), ought to be a decisive motive for a candid construction of the conduct of the government in making it, and for a spirit of acquiescence in the measures for obtaining revenue, which the public exigencies may at any time dictate.

Observe good faith and justice towards all nations; cultivate peace and harmony with all. Religion and morality enjoin this conduct; and can it be, that good policy does not equally enjoin it? It will be worthy of a free, enlightened, and at no distant period, a great nation, to give to mankind the magnanimous and too novel example of a people always guided by an exalted justice and benevolence. Who can doubt, that in the course of time and things, the fruits of such a plan would richly repay any temporary advantages, which might be lost by a steady adherence to it? Can it be that Providence has not connected the permanent felicity of a nation with its virtue? The experiment, at least, is recommended by every sentiment which ennobles human nature. Alas! is it rendered impossible by its vices?

In the execution of such a plan, nothing is more essential, than that permanent, inveterate antipathies against particular nations, and passionate attachments for others, should be excluded; and that, in place of them, just and amicable feelings towards all should be cultivated. The nation, which indulges towards another an habitual hatred, or an habitual fondness, is in some degree a slave. It is a slave to its animosity or to its affection, either of which is sufficient to lead it astray from its duty and its interests. Antipathy in one nation against another disposes each more readily to offer insult and injury, to lay hold of slight causes of umbrage, and to be haughty and intractable, when accidental or trifling occasions of dispute occur. Hence, frequent collisious, obstinate, envenomed, and bloody contests. The nation, prompted by ill-will and resentment, sometimes impels to war the Government, contrary to the best calculations of policy. The Government sometimes participates in the national propensity, and adopts through passion what reason would reject; at other times, it makes the animosity of the nation subservient to projects of hostility instigated by pride, ambition, and other sinister and pernicious motives. The peace often, sometimes perhaps the liberty, of nations has been the victim.

So likewise, a passionate attachment of one nation for another produces a variety of evils. Sympathy for the favorite nation, facilitating the illusion of an imaginary common interest in cases where no real common interest exists, and infusing into one the enmities of the other, betrays the former into a participation in the quarrels and wars of the latter, without adequate inducement or justification. It leads also to concessions to the favorite nation of privileges denied to others, which is apt doubly to injure the nation making the concessions; by unnecessarily parting with what ought to have been retained; and by exciting jealousy, ill-will, and a disposition to retaliate in the parties from whom equal privileges are withheld. And it gives to ambitious, corrupted, or deluded citizens (who devote themselves to the favorite nation), facility to betray or sacrifice the interests of their own country, without odium, sometimes even with popularity; gilding with the appearance of a virtuous sense of obligation, a commendable deference for public opinion, or a laudable zeal for public good, the base or foolish compliances of ambition, corruption or infatuation.

As avenues to foreign influence in innumerable ways, such attachments are particularly alarming to the truly enlightened and independent patriot. How many opportunities do they afford to tamper with domestic factions, to practice the arts of seduction, to mislead public opinion, to influence or awe the public councils! Such an attachment of a small or weak, towards a great and powerful nation, dooms the former to be the satellite of the latter.

Against the insidious wiles of foreign influence (I conjure you to believe me, fellow-citizens), the jealousy of a free people ought to be constantly awake, since history and experience prove that foreign influence is one of the most baneful foes of republican government. But that jealousy, to be useful, must be impartial; else it becomes the instrument of the very influence be avoided, instead of a defence against it. Excessive partiality for one foreign nation, and excessive dislike of another, cause those whom they actuate to see danger only on one side, and serve to veil and even second the arts of influence on the other. Real patriots who may resist the intrigues of the favorite, are liable to become suspected and odious; while its tools and dupes usurp the applause and confidence of the purpose, to surrender their interests.

The great rule of conduct for us, in regard to foreign nations, is, in extending our commercial relations, to have with them as little political connection as possible. So far as we have already formed engagements, let them be fulfilled with perfect good faith. Here let us stop.

Europe has a set of primary interests, which to us have none, or a very remote relation. Hence she must be engaged in frequent controversies, the causes of which are essentially foreign to our concerns. Hence, therefore, it must be unwise in us to implicate ourselves, by artificial ties, in the ordinary vicissitudes of her politics, or the ordinary combinations and collisions of her friendships or enmities.

Our detached and distant situation invites and enables us to pursue a different course. If we remain one people, under an efficient government, the period is not far off when we may defy material injury from external annoyance; when we may take such an attitude as will cause the neutrality, we may at any time resolve upon, to be scrupulously respected; when belligerent nations, under the impossibility of making acquisitions upon us, will not lightly hazard the giving us provocation; when we may choose peace or war, as our interest, guided by justice shall counsel.

Why forego the advantages of so peculiar a situation? Why quit our own to stand upon foreign ground? Why, by interweaving our destiny with that of any part of Europe, entangle our peace and prosperity in the toils of European ambition, rivalship, interest, humor or caprice?

It is our true policy to steer clear of permanent alliances with any portion of the foreign world; so far, I mean, as we are now at liberty to do it; for let me not be understood as capable of patronizing infidelity to existing engagements. I hold the maxim no less applicable to public than to private affairs, that honesty is always the best policy. I repeat it, therefore, let those engagements be observed in their genuine sense. But, in my opinion, it is unnecessary and would be unwise to extend them.

Taking care always to keep ourselves, by suitable establishments, on a respectable defensive posture, we may safely trust to temporary alliances for extraordinary emergencies.

Harmony, liberal intercourse with all nations, are recommended by policy, humanity and interest. But even our commercial policy should hold an equal and impartial hand; neither seeking nor granting exclusive favors or preferences; consulting the natural course of things; diffusing and diversifying by gentle means the streams of commerce, but forcing nothing; establishing with powers so disposed, in order to give trade a stable course, to define the rights of our merchants, and to enable the government to support them, conventional rules of intercourse, the best that present circumstances and mutual opinion will permit, but temporary, and liable to be from time to time abandoned or varied, as experience and circumstances shall dictate; constantly keeping in view, that it is folly in one nation to look for disinterested favors from another; that it must pay with a portion of its independence for whatever it may accept under that character; that, by such acceptance, it may place itself in the condition of having given equivalents for nominal favors, and yet of being reproached with ingratitude for not giving more. There can be no greater error than to expect or calculate upon real favors from nation to nation. It is an illusion, which experience must cure, which a just pride ought to discard.

In offering to you, my countrymen, these counsels of an old and affectionate friend, I dare not hope they will make the strong and lasting impression I could wish; that they will control the usual current of the passions, or prevent our nation from running the course, which has hitherto marked the destiny of nations. But, if I may even flatter myself, that they may be productive of some partial benefit, some occasional good; that they **may now** and then recur to moderate the fury of party spirit, to warn against the mischiefs of foreign intrigue, to guard against the impostures of pretended patriotism; this hope will be a full recompense for the solicitude for your welfare by which they have been dictated.

How far in the discharge of my official duties I have been guided by the principles which have been delineated, the public records and other evidences of my conduct must witness to you and to the world. To myself, the assurance of my own conscience is, that I have at least believed myself to be guided by them.

In relation to the still subsisting war in Europe, my proclamation of the 22d of April, 1793, is the index of my plan. Sanctioned by your approving voice, and by that of your Representatives in both Houses of Congress, the spirit of that measure has continually governed me, uninfluenced by any attempts to deter or divert me from it.

After deliberate examination, with the aid of the best lights I could obtain, I was well satisfied that our country, under all the circumstances of the case, had a right to take, and was bound in duty and interest to take, a neutral position. Having taken it, I determined, as far as should depend upon me, to maintain it, with moderation, perseverance and firmness.

The considerations which respect the right to hold this conduct, it is not necessary on this occasion to detail. I I will only observe, that, according to my understanding of the matter, that right, so far from being denied by any of the belligerent powers, has been virtually admitted by all.

The duty of holding a neutral conduct may be inferred, without anything more, from the obligation which justice and humanity impose on every nation, in cases in which it is free to act, to maintain inviolate the relations of peace and amity towards other nations.

The inducements of interest for observing that conduct will best be referred to your own reflections and experience. With me a predominant motive has been to endeavor to gain time to our country to settle and mature its yet recent institutions, and to progress without interruption to that degree of strength and consistency, which is necessary to give it, humanly speaking, the command of its own fortunes.

Though, in reviewing the incidents of my administration, I am unconscious of intentional error, I am nevertheless too sensible of my defects not to think it probable that I may have committed many errors. Whatever they may be I fervently beseech the Almighty to avert or mitigate the evils to which they may tend. I shall also carry with me the hope that my country will never cease to view them with indulgence; and that, after forty-five years of my life dedicated to its service with an upright zeal, the faults of incompetent abilities will be consigned to oblivion, as myself must soon be to the mansions of rest.

Relying on its kindness in this as in other things, and actuated by that fervent love towards it, which is so natural to a man, who views in it the native soil of himself and his progenitors for several generations; I anticipate with pleasing expectation that retreat, in which I promise myself to realize, without alloy, the sweet enjoyment of partaking, in the midst of my fellow-citizens, the benign influence of good laws under a free government, the ever favorite object of my heart, and the happy reward, as I trust, of our mutual cares, labors, and dangers.

INAUGURAL ADDRESS.

New York, April 30, 1789.

FELLOW CITIZENS OF THE SENATE AND OF THE HOUSE OF REPRESENTATIVES.—Among the vicissitudes incident to life, no event could have filled me with greater anxieties than that, of which the notification was transmitted by your order, and received on the fourth day of the present month. On the one hand, I was summoned by my country, whose voice I can never hear but with veneration and love, from a retreat which I had chosen with the fondest predilection, and, in my flattering hopes, with an immutable decision as the asylum of my declining years; a retreat which was rendered every day more necessary as well as more dear to me, by the addition of habit to inclination, and of frequent interruptions in my health to the gradual waste committed on it by time, on the other hand, the magnitude and difficulty of the trust to which the voice of my country called me, being sufficient to awaken, in the wisest and most experienced of her citizens, a distrustful scrutiny into his qualifications, could not but overwhelm with despondence one who, inheriting inferior endowments from nature, and unpracticed in the duties of civil administration, ought to be peculiarly conscious of his own deficiencies. In this conflict of emotions, all I dare aver is, that it has been my faithful study to collect my duty from a just appreciation of every circumstance by which it might be affected. All I dare hope is, that if, in executing this task, I have been too much swayed by a grateful remembrance of former instances, or by an affectionate sensibility to this transcedent proof of the confidence of my fellow-citizens, and have thence too little consulted my incapacity as well as disinclination for the weighty and untried cares before me, my error will be palliated by the motives which misled me, and its consequences be judged by my country, with some share of the partiality in which they originated.

Such being the impressions under which I have, in obedience to the public summons, repaired to the present station, it would be peculiarly improper to omit, in this first official act, my fervent supplications to that Almighty Being, who rules over the universe, who presides in the councils of nations, and whose providential aids can supply every human defect, that His benediction may consecrate to the liberties and happiness of the people of the United Siates, a government instituted by themselves for these essential purposes, and may enable every instrument employed in its administration, to execute, with success, the functions allotted to his charge. In tendering this homage to the Great Author of every public and private good, I assure myself that it expresses your sentiments not less than my own; nor those of my fellow-citizens at large less than either. No people can be bound to acknowledge and adore the invisible hand which conducts the affairs of men, more than the people of the United States. Every step by which they have advanced to the character of an independent nation, seems to have been distinguished by some token of providential agency. And, in the important revolution just accomplished, in the system of their united government, the tranquil deliberations and voluntary consent of so many distinct communities, from which the event has resulted, cannot be compared with the means by which most governments have been established, without some return of pious gratitude, along with an humble anticipation of the future blessings, which the past seems to presage. These reflections, arising out of the present crisis, have forced themselves too strongly on my mind to be suppressed. You will join with me, I trust, in thinking that there are none under the influence of which the proceedings of a new and free government can more auspiciously commence.

By the article establishing the executive department, it is made the duty of the president " to recommend to your consideration such measures as he shall judge necessary and expedient." The circumstances under which I now meet you will acquit me from entering into that subject farther than to refer you to the great constitutional charter under which we are assembled ; and which, in defining your powers, designates the objects to which your attention is to be given. It will be more consistent with those circumstances, and far more congenial with the feelings which actuate me, to substitute, in place of a recommendation of particular measures, the tribute that is due to the talents, the rectitude, and the patriotism which adorn the characters selected to devise and adopt them. In these honorable qualifications, I behold the surest pledges, that as, on one side, no local prejudices or attachments, no separate views nor party animosities will misdirect the comprehensive and equal eye which ought to watch over this great assemblage of communities and interests—so, on another, that the foundations of our national policy will be laid in the pure and immutable principles of private morality ; and the pre-eminence of a free government be exemplified by all the attributes which can win the affections of its citizens, and command the respect of the

I dwell on this prospect with every satisfaction which an ardent love for my country can inspire; since there is no truth, more thoroughly established than that there exists, in the economy and course of nature, an indissoluble union between virtue and happiness—between duty and advantage—between the genuine maxims of an honest and magnanimous policy and the solid rewards of public prosperity and felicity—since we ought to be no less persuaded that the propitious smiles of Heaven can never be expected on a nation that disregards the eternal rules of order and right which Heaven itself has ordained—and since the preservation of the sacred life of liberty, and the destiny of the republican model of government, are justly considered as deeply, perhaps, as finally staked, on the experiment entrusted to the hands of the American people.

Besides the ordinary objects submitted to your care, it will remain with your judgment to decide how far an exercise of the occasional power delegated by the fifth article of the constitution is rendered expedient, at the present juncture, by the nature of objections which have been urged against the system or by the degree of inquietude which has given birth to them. Instead of undertaking particular recommendations on this subject, in which I could be guided by no lights derived from official opportunities, I shall again give way to my entire confidence in your discernment and pursuit of the public good. For I assure myself, that, whilst you carefully avoid every alteration which might endanger the benefits of an united and effective government, or which ought to await the future lessons of experience, a reverence for the characeristic rights of freemen, and a regard for the public harmony, will sufficiently influence your deliberations on the question, how far the former can be more impregnably fortified, or the latter be safely and more advantageously promoted.

To the preceding observations I have one to add, which will be most properly addressed to the House of Representatives. It concerns myself, and will therefore be as brief as possible.

When I was first honored with a call into the service of my country, then on the eve of an arduous struggle for liberties, the light in which I contemplated my duty, required that I should renounce every pecuniary compensation. From this resolution I have in no instance departed. And being still under the impression which produced it, I must decline, as inapplicable to myself, any share in the personal emoluments, which may be indispensably included in a permanent provision for the executive department: and must accordingly pray that the pecuniary estimates for the station in which I am placed, may, during my continuation in it, be limited to such actual expenditures as the public good may be thought to require.

Having thus imparted to you my sentiments, as they have been awakened by the occasion which brings us together, I shall take my present leave, but not without resorting once more to the benign Parent of the human race, in humble supplication, that, since he has been pleased to favor the American people with opportunities for deliberating in perfect tranquillity, and dispositions for deciding with unparalleled unanimity, on a form of government for the security of their union, and the advancement of their happiness, so his divine blessing may be equally conspicuous in the enlarged views, the temperate consultation, and the wise measures on which the success of this government must depend.

FAREWELL TO THE ARMY.

Princeton, November 2, 1783.

THE United States in Congress assembled, after giving the most honorable testimony to the merits of the federal armies, and presenting them with the thanks of their country for their long, eminent, and faithful services, having thought proper, by their proclamation bearing date the 18th day of October last, to discharge such part of the troops as were engaged for the war, and to permit the officers on furloughs to retire from service, from and after to-morrow; which proclamation having been communicated in the Public papers for the information and government of all concerned, it only remains for the Commander-in-chief to address himself once more, and that for the last time, to the armies of the United States (however widely dispersed the individuals who composed them may be), and to bid them an affectionate, a long farewell.

But before the Commander-in-chief takes his final leave of those he holds most dear, he wishes to indulge himself a few moments in calling to mind a slight review of the past. He will then take the liberty of exploring with his military friends their future prospects, of advising the general line or conduct, which, in his opinion, ought to be pursued; and he will conclude the address by expressing the obligations he feels himself under for the spirited and able assistance he has experienced from them, in the performance of an arduous office.

A contemplation of the complete attainment (at a period earlier than could have been expected) of the object, for which we contended against so formidable a power, cannot but inspire us with astonishment and gratitude. The disadvantageous circumstances on our part, under which the war was undertaken, can never be forgotten. The singular interpositions of Providence in our feeble condition were such, as could scarcely escape the attention of the most unobserving; while the unparalleled perseverance of the armies of the United States, through almost every possible suffering and discouragement for the space of eight long years, was little short of a standing miracle.

It is not the meaning nor within the compass of this address, to detail the hardships peculiarly incident to our service, or to describe the distresses which in several instances have resulted from the extremes of hunger and nakedness, combined with the rigors of an inclement season; nor is it necessary to dwell on the dark side of our past affairs. Every American officer and soldier must now console himself for any unpleasant circumstances which may have occurred, by a recollection of the uncommon scenes of which he has been called to act no inglorious part, and the astonishing events of which he has been a witness; events which have seldom, if ever before, taken place on the stage of human action nor can they probably ever happen again. For who has before seen a disciplined army formed at once from such raw materials? Who, that was not a witness, could imagine, that the most violent local prejudices would cease so soon; and that men, who came from the different parts of the continent, strongly disposed by the habits of education to despise and quarrel with each other, would instantly become but one patriotic band of brothers? Or who, that was not on the spot, can trace the steps by which such a wonderful revolution has been effected, and such a glorious period put to all our warlike toils?

It is universally acknowledged that the enlarged prospects of happiness, opened by the confirmation of our independence and sovereignty, almost exceed the power of description. And shall not the brave men, who have contributed so essentially to these inestimable acquisitions, retiring victorious from the field of war to the field of agriculture, participate in all the blessings which have been obtained? In such a republic, who will exclude them from the rights of citizens, and the fruits of their labor? In such a country, so happily circumstanced, the pursuits of commerce and the cultivation of the soil will unfold to industry the certain road to competence. To those hardy soldiers, who are actuated by the spirit of adventure, the fisheries will afford ample and profitable employment; and the extensive and fertile regions of the West will yield a most happy asylum to those who, fond of domestic enjoyment, are seeking for personal independence. Nor is it possible to conceive that any one of the United States will prefer a national bankruptcy, and a dissolution of the Union, to a compliance with the requisitions of Congress, and the payment of its just debts; so that the officers and soldiers may expect considerable assistance, in recommencing their civil occupations, from the sums due to them from the public, which must and will most inevitably be paid.

In order to effect this desirable purpose, and to remove the prejudices which may have taken possession of the minds of any of the good people of the states, it is earnestly recommended to all the troops that, with strong attachments to the Union, they should carry with them into civil society the most conciliating dispositions, and that they should prove themselves not less virtuous and useful as citizens than they have been persevering and victorious as soldiers. What though there should be some envious individuals, who are unwilling to pay the debt the public has contracted, or to yield the tribute due to merit; yet let such unworthy treatment produce no invectives, nor any instance of intemperate conduct. Let it be remembered that the unbiased voice of the free citizens of the United States has promised the just reward and given the merited applause. Let it be known and remembered that the reputation of the federal armies is established beyond the reach of malevolence; and let a consciousness of their achievements and fame still incite the men who composed them to honorable actions; under the persuasion that the private virtues of economy, prudence and industry will not be less amiable in civil life than the more splendid qualities of valor, perseverance and enterprise were in the field. Every one may rest assured that much, very much of the future happiness of the officers and men will depend upon the wise and manly conduct which shall be adopted by them when they are mingled with the great body of the community. And although the General has so frequently given it as his opinion in the most public and explicit manner that, unless the principles of the Federal Government were properly supported, and the powers of the Union increased, the honor, dignity and justice of the nation would be lost forever; yet he cannot help repeating on this occasion so interesting a sentiment, and leaving it as his last injunction to every officer and every soldier, who may view the subject in the same serious point of light, to add his best endeavors to those of his worthy fellow-citizens toward effecting these great and valuable purposes, on which our very existence as a nation so materially depends.

The Commander-in-chief conceives little is now wanting to enable the soldiers to change the military character into that of the citizen, but that steady and decent tenor of behavior which has generally distinguished, not only the army under his immediate command, but the different detachments and separate armies through the course of the war. From their good sense and prudence he anticipates the happiest consequences, and he congratulates them on the glorious occasion which renders their services in the field no longer necessary, he wishes to ex-

g obligations he feels himself under for the
has received from every class and in
e. He presents his thanks in the
and affectionate manner to the general
l for their counsel on many interesting
r their ardor in promoting the success of
d adopted; to the commandants of regi-
)s, and to the other officers, for their great
ion in carrying his orders promptly into
he staff, for their alacrity and exactness in
duties of their several departments; and
missioned officers and private soldiers, for
ary patience and suffering, as well as their
tude in action. To the various branches
General takes this last and solemn oppor-
ssing his inviolable attachment and friend-
es more than bare professions were in his
e were really able to be useful to them all
He flatters himself, however, they will do
to believe, that whatever could with pro-
pted by him had been done.
ow to conclude these his last public orders,
mate leave in a short time of the military
to bid a final adieu to the armies he has so
nor to command, he can only again offer in
recommendations to their grateful country,
to the God of armies. May ample justice
here, and may the choicest of Heaven's
e and hereafter, attend those who, under the
, have secured innumerable blessings for
these wishes and his benediction, the
chief is about to retire from service. The
ration will soon be drawn, and the military
ill be closed forever.

IN THE APPLE TREE.

O, that first kiss,	That first seesaw,
It was bliss, bliss,	That first courtship,
Abba and me,	That first marriage,
That apple tree,	Up in a tree,
Abba and me.	Abba and me. Ab.

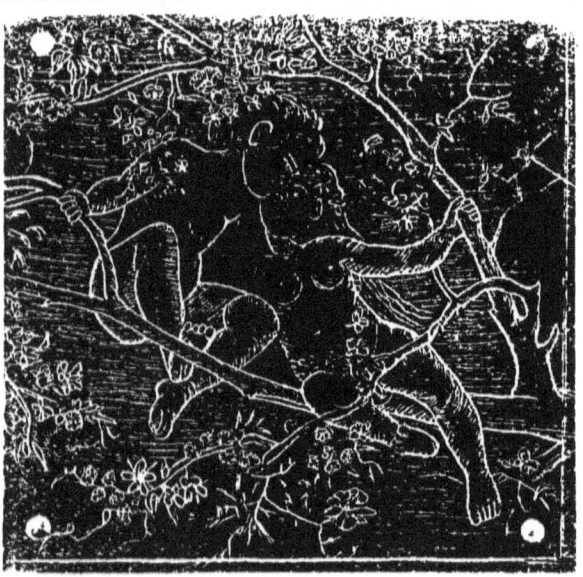

Home's not mearely four square walls,
 Though with pictures hung and gilded;
Home is where AFFECTION calls—
 Filled with shrines the Heart hath builded!
  Home! go watch the faithful dove,
   Sailing 'neath the heaven above us,—
  Home is where there's one to love!
   Home is where there's one to love us!
Home's not merely roof and room,
 It needs something to endear it:
Home is where the heart can bloom:
 Where there's some kind lip to cheer it!
  What is home with none to meet?
   None to welcome, none to greet us?
  Home is sweet— and only sweet—
   When there's one we love to kiss us!
                                  Abba.

OUR BEGINNING, ILLUSTRATED.

GEOLOGY, BOTANY, GEOGRAPHY and actual facts all go to prove that the Amerikas was the first, and not only the original home of man, but they now present the most magnificent and extensive variety of every thing that is kuown to exist. All of this go to prove beyond a doubt that the Christian's Mosaic account of our beginning is eronius. This bosting murder was born over two thousand years after their said creation, and wrote only from hearsay rumors, not knowing one thing of the Amerikas, that was the beginniug point of every thing! When the factst are he was born thousands ofyears after our beginnins.

The yearly overflow of the river Amazon, the most extensive river on earth, it causes a specific deposit of earth fare out over the pampus. Count the strattas of this formation and you know at once that this earth is thousands of yéars older than Christians tell us! So they have missed its formation and beginning as bad as they hav its end and destrution. For we know they have been prophesying its distruction for hundreads of years!

Count the strattas of the big trees that is now found on the Andes along the pacific, peaceful coast where earth was first oncovered, and you find that they are thousands of years older, yea, much older than anything in the eastern world; and give the lie to Mr. Christian and his presumed book from God.

IN the accompanying slate cut you can see a comparative representation of the giant descendents of the spontaneous age of generation, compared with that of the present age of special procrative generation. They, as did all vegetable and animal life lived longer and grew larger than their procreative descendence.

Ab and Abba are represented standing by one of those mammoth trees and looking down on a cotillion party of today as it dances on a stump of one of these mammoh trees that waved over Ab and Abba thousauds of years ago! and the hollow of which served them as Home Sweet Home!

The Andes mountains, the highest! the grandest! and the most extensively inhabited mountains on the globe! are represented in the background, towering far up above the stormy clouds, snow, frost, thunder, ligrhtning and rain!

CUT 1, figure 1, big stump, 13 feet high and 25 feet in diameter. 2, Ab, 3, Abba. 4, big tree, 4 hundred feet high. 5 falls of Tequendama, 6 hundred feet high. 6, the Andes mountains, 30 thousand feet high. 7, the elevated inhabitable vallies; up above the stormy sky.

See the Falls of Tequandama that is the grandest, highest and the most extraordinary cataract in the world! The river dashes over a perpendicular rock of over six hundred feet into an unfathomless abyss! See cut 2.

CUT 2, figure 1 is the large trees and high water falls; 2 the hight of the storm clouds. 3 Lake Titicaca, vales and vallies of the Andes; where rain seldom falls, thunder and lightning is now unknown; and where perpetual spring and light are shone by figure 4 and the sun.

On we go assending higher and higher into these extensive vales and plains of the Andes till we reach an extensive rich and fertile plaine at a hight of thousands and thousands of feet above the sea. A paradise, far, far above the stormy cleuds as is pictured in our cuts.

This is the original home of man, and the most elevated inhabited country under the sun. Here is the Lake Titicaca, and the ruins of the first city! See page 54-5.

And my god! only think, it is, and always have been far, far beyond anything in existence on this earth! Notwithstanding the absurd blowing of the Jews and Christians as to the superiority of their hateing, hateful man-god and their accursed holy land!

And as I have stated the first men, those of the age of the spontaneous growth, lived longer and grew larger than the men of to-day. Precisley so with all created animals; they lived, only they lived much longer than man, and as primitive man did not expose himself to the frozen regions this is why we do not find primitive man's remains imbeded in bogs and ice as we do that of the extinct mammoth!

And as primitive vegetation lived longer than primitive man or animals is why we now have the mammoth trees of the Sierra Nevada Mountains; yet living thrifty, and at an age as old as the earth! Growing at an altitude of 7 thousand feet above the level of the pacific ocean. They now occupy a space of only 250 miles. The great secret of the remarkable growth of these trees is their wonderful vitality. They never have been known to die of old age like man, animals and other trees. In every instance where they have been found dead they have been killed! This accounts for the fable of Methuselah, or the presumed great age of the Jew patriarchs, Gen. v.

Tradition tell us that our ancestors of the spontaneous age of generation and their children grew so numerous, large, lived so long, and grew so rich, wise and powerful as to have not only cover the most favorable parts of the Amerikas with immense cities and plantations, but they had filled the world with explorers, emigrants and adventurers both by land and sea. Till all mankind burry their dead facing east, south-east or south, as acquired from our fire or sun worshiping fathers of the Amerikas!

Again, our Amerikan traditions tell us that the two brothers, the Amerikas, went to war, fought each other— and the one with the cane-brakes, which was North Amerika, anihilated South Amerika! But, not till every city and pueblas was levled to the ground and those fine and luxurient plantations, factories and temples was destroyed!

THEN it was that the curse of Nature and Nature's God pounced upon these ignomineous murders with an awful scourge! Black-death, that terable unmanagable and uncurable epidemic of death swept the whole of them from the earth! Then it was that the Braves of the mountains the forest the rivers the valleys and the plains taken quiet possession of the Amerikas from pole to pole! Soon these sun-burnt, beardless Incas or Indian Fathers paternally ruled from sea to sea with a fathers love and care never no where else ever known mtchless equaled! They wittingly claimed to be too youug to have beard and that they never grew old! old enough too. So blow about your murder of a Jew Moses, your nigger Solomon and their boasting mongrels, and yet, their own history is black with their infamy and ignorance! Making them demons when compared to our brawney-brown Amerikan fathers.

One of the oldest epitaphs, perhaps in the world, is that inscribed to Ptolomato, the founder of San Augustine, Florida. As far back as tradition goes San Augustine was then an old walled coummunal city, and an extensive trading port for Africa and all Europe. The hateing hateful hand of the Christian has defaced its original hieroglyphic inscription and substituted an "Ingin burlesbue." This Ptolomato or Ptolemy was only one among a number that had long ruled as the "good fathers" not only in Amerika but also, in Egypt. This hieroglyphic writing found all over the Amerikas and Egypt, the peculiar shadeless, single line sculpture the ancient cities, pyramids that are found only in Egypt and the Amerikas, go to prove them one and the same people, that traded and lived together.

Again, our Amerikan tradition are the only ones that aver and point out to you the very exact spot where they or. riginated. And it is literally in the sky, or heavens, far above the storm clouds, and can be seen to-day in all of its Eden beauty and lovliness, flood or no flood! And here is how all of those unnatural songs and stories of gods, angels men, devils going up into heaven or the sky orriginated! They are premature births, abortions or downright Christ. ian lies! See page 133.

ONLY think! this religious madness! this god-chozen! god-favored! royal boss to rule the whole world, God! man, and the devil, is as rampant to-day as at the beginning, notwithstanding the awful lessons in utter anihilation that has been given them from the beginning.

The American Sentinel, of New York, of the 20th, of Feb., 1896, is so crankey as to speak thus on page 58: "The Eastern question points to the soon coming of the "King of kings and Lord of lords, Rev. 19, 16 " " Ask of me, and I shall give thee the heathen for thine inheritance, and the uttermost parts of the earth for thy possessions!" And says only this will settle it! And adds, that England, Austria and Russia, three great Christian Kingdoms hove been asking their lords and their gods for this heathen Turkey for hundreds of years! They have prayed, lied, murdered set all manner of traps for this Turkey! Why? Why thus Ignomineously meddle with and seek the destruction of your fellow man? Because this is Christianity! They are hateing meddlers and fishers of men! And pretend to believe that our heavenly father is going to thus murder and devour Mr. Turkey! in a supper for the aboue SCRIPTURIAL reasons; and give them their life, home and country!

They, these Christian nations, to-day, are a mear compromiseing, cowardly, blating, blasphemous set of heathens, that Turkey frailed the stuffing out of, and drove them trom their boasted god-given country in 1453! That's what ail 'em brother Jones! Then, Christian Spain, after clanning together witn these Christians, murdered, robbed, and plundered all South Amerika and Mexiko, of untold billions of gold, silver, wealth, and precious life! At that time she was the leading power in all Europe! Owning Spain, Sardinia, Sicily and Naples Then this addition of Amerika's fabulous wealth and unlimited resources, soon led Christian Spain victoriously to Rome the boasted eternal city! Rome's immense wealth, learning and life like that of the Amerikas was given to this Christian Spain as a Supper of the Great God! And never before, nor since did any city suffer as did this city of learning and refinement, from these Christian demons! ☞ The sack! the ravishing of Female Infants and children lasted for months! just as they did in the conquest of Mexico! This was genuine Christianity fresh from Christ and his apostles! It was ended only by a plague, a scurge, a wipe-out from hell! that swept the cowardly Christian ravishers and murders from the face of the earth—god or no god! supper or no supper! While the Infidels Tomahawk and the heratics diger, powder and shot' soon shook them loose from the Amerikas!

Yes, after this great Christian Spain murdered, ravaged pillaged and devastated Christian Rome and mother Amerika, then it was that Ifidel Turkey again in 1529, settled this heathed Christians supper by using the very same cannon on them that they used to annihilate the Christian murder Constantine in 1453, see page 129! They now drive the villions: these Christian barbarians, these Shrouded Knights of St. John, out of the isle of Rhodes! Subdued Egypt, devastated Hungary, and even appeared under the walls of Christian Vienna and sold Millions of Christtans into Slavery even in the streets of Christian Marseille, France! And if

the Christian bible is true—then this, or anything is right!
Was this not fair preferable to ravishing of them to death as
the Jews and Christians did! and are uow proposing to do
to this refined and humane Turkey?

CUT 3, the above cut, represents one of those SUPPERS
of the Christian's GREAT GOD! Where is eaten the
flesh of Kings, Captains, Horses and Mighty men, Rev. xix,
17, 18 ! See figure 1, it is a correct likeness of Jesus and the
Christian's god! He is the host that is entertaining a set of
genuine Christians! He says I come not to send peace on
the earth, no, but hate, fire and the sword! He says follow

me and I will make you a set of hating, hateful, pie hunting fishers of men!! And to do this you must hate your father, mother, brother, sister, every body and every thing!! And be able to devour without mercy your fellow man!!!

See figure 2, that Jackass Angel in the sun! See figure 3, its dear, dear, darling grandma, who like Elijah is swiftly wafted forever away! while figure 4 is a Christian cock that crows even for the devil! 5, Mr. Owl, who has found a fair damsels lower leg! 6, millions of dam fools on their knees begging mercy of a lunatic! 7, an infernal Christian police dragging his addled betters in! 8, Mr, Condor, the god of all, while 9 and 10 are Christian hyenas devouring both bad, good, great and small! While the Vultures, the Buzzards, the Crow, the Blackbird and the English Sparrow, that soar on high waiting for their part of the pie! This is the Great God that devoured the Christian's Little God Jesus———— to him Jesus did cry—— My god! my god! why hast thou FORSAKEN! me? ·Yes! forsaken! What an awful condition! Yet, this has been the fate of all Christian adventures! They live in hell! they die in hell! and they are fizzing, frying and blubbering in hell to-day! See, what went with these Christopher Columbus liars. What went with Cortes? Pizarro? Desoto? and all of those unholy murders? Thirty-seven thousand Christian children were devoured by this god in these unholy crusades See p, 143.

So on this religious craziness, this Christian avarice, murder and slaughter of the innocent has went, and think you, all in the name of, done by, or sanctioned by God! Yes, on the villions go, plotting against the life, liberties and persuits of their fellow man! And swiftly receiveing an awful and just retrebntion, both in this life and the life to come!

This is why our Amerikan Fathers declared this conutry forever free from such religious madness! Yet, while I am penning this book the civilized world is amazed and horrowfied at the abject poverty and degradation of this once lordly hell favored Christian Spain! Her barbarian war that she is now waging against Cubian Freedom, and the threats of our subjugation is damnable! The facts are, she to-day is a mear hateful, hating, preast-ridden, distressed heathen pauper! Owing billions! and owning nothing but disgrace! Swift retribution has justly overtaken her. Verily, she as is all Christians crazy or infamous! For by their infernal infamous fruits we know them!

But, let us return to your infalible scripture, that means what it says, and it must be carried out, concience or no concience, life or no life!

CUT 4 is a companion picture to CUT 3. It is the Christians Lord's Supper— Where they claim to EAT the body of their little "damphool" Jew, man-god Jesus! and even drink his hearts blood! See Matt., xxvi, 26-7-8!!!

FIGURE 1, 2, and 4, represents how they, the first Christians went for their Lord and Master before PAUL put his big brogan veto down on it! See 1, Cor., xi, 21. Then why did Jesus choose one of the Devil's CAROUSING customs? Because birds of a feather flock together! Train up a child in the way you want 'im to go and, like Solomon, he wont depart there from! See page 190-1! Jesus orriginated nothing! His Supper is only a —wildcating—of the horrible custom of human sacrifices, that they would carry out to-day as did their infamous Abraham if it was not for the American Ram that is not hung in a bush! So, they lick their carousing cannibal chops and content themselves by vividly presenting before you their blessed Jesus' crucified body and they vividly, with unhuman yells and tears! display before you the Sacred Bleeding Heart of thair defunct God!

See cut 5. above it is a mountain of hateing hateful Christian SKULLS at Gerba, Africa! For centuries the Christians have been sending immense armies to subjugate, ravish murder and feast upon Turkey in Africa, and this Mountain of Christian skulls tell to the world of the many, many bully good Suppers that the Great God, good Devil, or some body else has honored the Infidel world with! See figure 3, in cut 4, but dont look at figure 4, for it is one of the most correct likenesses of the spirit and actual doings as is seen at one of these LOVE-FEASTS! Agape! agape!

Yes, yes, brother Jones, what else did this god-forsaken, hell-inspired, hydrophobia saint see? He saw an Angel in the sun, proclaiming— The Supper of the Great God; which was the FLESH of Kings, horses, and mighty men! Rev. xxi, 17-8. And the fowls was specially invited. And in May 1453 these very identical Turkeys, that you are now expecting to devour, was honord with a Supper of the Great God, right in this god-chosen, god-favored and god-protected Christian City of Constantinople! Ah, my god! they feasted upon king Constantine's Christian carcass and that of over a million of his mighty god-inspired men! They spared the women and children however! Did your good Christian god-father Spain spare them in Amerika? Mexico? and Peru? Did she even spare them, her own blood, her own god-children in the destruction of Christian Rome in 1527? No, no, but they sexually ravished and murdered them!!!!

READER? this religious madness has had its day. Man has learned enough of it to see that Nature and Nature's God has not created one man, nor no set of men, to rule over the other. No! but each individual is a law, a rule unto himself. So, it is time for some mode of government to be inforced upon religionists that cannot, donot or willnot attend to their own salvation, and quit meddeling with that of their fellow man. Why? because, you and you alone can know any thing about your own concientious beliefs.

These beliefs are your own consciences' private matters that aught never to be made public! For, according to tradition, history and your own experience man's public religions has done ALL harm! and NO good!!!

A CONCORDANT INDEX.

A, b. c, 1, 2, 3; .... see page 4. 63, 136.
A, b, c. d, e, f, g, God, Job and the Devil, . 163 199, 215¾.
Aaron. 16, 77, 204, 278. Ab, Abba, 72. Above the clouds,
60, 68. Absent minded, 242. Absurd, 47, 272. Abolitionist, 140. Abcess, 228, 235. Abortion, 249, 250. Ablutions
and affusions, 221.· Abnormal or inaction 220. Abel, ...33,
68, 134, 140, 193. Abraham. 15, 21, 33, 75, 122, 247. Abrahamites, 60, 122. .... 167.
Accountable, 40, 145, 186, 194. Ackteekites, 65, 76. Acts,
86, 132. Accursed, 127. Acid Arsnic, 259. Acknowledged
additions, 134. Acknowledged imperfections, 134, 135, 179.
Acquisitiveness, 199· Accidents and not brains, 204. Ac-
cute or chronic, 234, 235. .... 261.

Additions and subtractions, 185, 194. Adhesive straps, 245,
256. Adam and Eve, 2, 4, 66, 74, 134, 137. Adamites, 1. 2,
5, 56, 66, 75, 125. Adam Porwigle, 114. Adventures, 61.
Address.or remonstrance,110. Adultry, 124. Adriatic, 143.

Africa, 35, 55, 6 1, 72, 126, 172, 130, 138, 143. Africans, 128.
Affusions, 221. After--birth, 251. Affraid to investigate, 194.

Age, 73, 74, 22), 231, 248. Age of peace, 129. Age of reason,
43, 87. Agencies of life and health, ... 217.

Ails us, 40. Air, atmosphere, ... 181, 241, 260, 271.

All, 91, 95, 101, 109, 114, 115, 118, 120, 121, 122, 123, 125, 126,
228, 131, 133, 138, 143, 146, 182, 189, 241, 247, 272, 273, 278,
279, 284, 285, 293. All power! 19, 23, 27, 32, 33, 36, 61, 63, -4,
65, 66, 71, 72, 74, 75, 77, 86, 87, 89, ... 186.

Alliance, 100, 104. Allopaths, 106 to 113, 217. All in the
name of God, 129. All wise, all good and all powerful, 138,
139. All animal or all human, 189, 190, 194. All alike, 180,
278, 280. All are vicious, all are virtuous, 280. All things
for my use, ..284. All made for one, or one for all, ...284.
Alaska, .11. Alecks, Smart ...34, 269. Alex Ammon, ...269.
Alexandrian library,129. Albino, 57, 197. Albino-Irish, 74.
Altitude, 95. Alphabets, 4, 63, 136. Aliments, 218. Alteratives, 239, 240. Always, 95. Alcoholized, 259. Almighty
cause, 269.. 293.

Amerika, 2, 6, 30, 35, 37, 68, 73, 74, 75, 84, 95, 97, 126, 129,
132, 136, 142. American Sentinal, 25, 143. Americus Vespucius, 30. America dear native land, 95. America in the
front, 97. Amerikas discovered, 62. Amerikan Indian, 74.
American Continant, 95. America, 97, 98. A. Central, 127,
140. American Constellations, 98. Amerikan Empire, 126.
Americans, 128. American Yankees, 129. Amazon River,
8, 58, 84, 88, 89. Amazonian female warrer, 87. Amendments, 130 to 138, 261½. Ample provisions, 144. Amour,
the god of animal love, or puppy religion, ... 255.

Analyze, 78. Analysis of man, 180, 182. Andes, 63, 69, 72,
84, 88. An American, 12, 28, 40, 123. An Ape, 189, 192
An Essay on man, 262. Angel, 64, 133. Antiquity, 74.
Ancients, 76, 283. Ancient books, 136, 183. Ancients Ac-
tecs, 127, 183. Antesolucents, 84, 85. Anihilated, 128, 130.
Anatomy, 180 to 200. Animal man, 196,--7. Antiseptic purification, 219.

Anodyne, 222, ·3. Anasarca, amaurosis, ... 244.
Apoplexy, amaurosis, 240. Apetite lost, 240. Apostles. 18
127. Application, 92, 136. Appeal, 107. Appropriated it, 136.
Aqua Amonia, ... 238.
Arab, 4, 2), 106, 126, 128. Arabia, 37. Arabians, 128. Arizona, 10. Arest, 18, 108. Aristocracy, 35. Art, 40, 41, 62, 72, 126, 127. Arcturus, 46. Arnon, an American author, 4. Arrested fined and imprisoned, 108, 110. Armies of fools, 108. Army of Christians, 128, 143. Arch Devil Washington, 129. Argo, 114. Arrogance, 129, ...130.
Asia, 35, 55, 150. Asylum, 14. Ascended, 32. Astronomy, 54. Association, raising, 190, -4. Astringent or relaxant, 218. Asthma, Phthisic, Croup, 239. Astronomy, ... 265.
Atoms, 283. Attracte l, 284. Atlantic, 58½, 72, 88, 94. Atlantic Ocean, 58½. Atlantica, 55, 83, 126. Attacted by the Faulkners, 114 Attorney-General, U. S. Court caught, 111.
Authority, 120. Authority at Washington, 110. Australia, 126. Aurilinus, 299. .... 274.
Avarice, 37. Avalanche, 92. Avanue to health, 109.
Avoiding, 239, 242, ... 250.
Awful follies, 130. 142, 163 174, ... 261½
Aztecs or Ackteeks, 56, 57, 50, 72, 76, 127, 132, ... 136.

Baal, Baala, 72. Babel, 140, 180. Babylon, 10, 61, 77, 137, 138, 142. Bacon, Lord, 302, 301. Bad Spirit, 83. Bad Man, 83. Bad to worse, 133--4. Bank, 8. Bipsoused, 12, ..19. Bapsouser John, 3, 18, 19, 123--4. Bapsoused a billion, 124! Bastard, 17, 28, 33, 75, 86-7, 138. Bastards "cant, or shant go to the Chriritian heaven, 138." Bathe l, 109. Baths and bathing, 216 to 261. Bandages and Compresses, 227, 250--1, 226. Balanced, 125, [145,] 146--9, 184--7,--8,--9, 190, 206--7, 242--4, 250--7, 277. Baptist bible society, 133. Baptist make a bible, 133, 204. Back-ache, 219. Barnness, ... 250.
Beast, 40, 74, 134, 187, 194. Beasts of burden,1, 21, 32-3, 40. Beacher, 15. Before Cain and Able, [Gen. iii, 17.] 68, 286. Begging, 28, 31. Beggars and tramps, 125. Beginningless, 53. Beginning, 53, 60--3, 73, 86, 95, 131, 193, 275, 286. Begat, 34. Begetting, 64, 73, 95, 258. Begot by a god, 33. Bells, bells, awful bells, 29. Belong to-- 12, ... 100. Believe or damed, 19, 126, 138, 142, 203, 242. Bellevue Hospital, 251. Belly-band, 254. Bell-weather leaders, 40. Benevolence, 191, 199, 290, 303· Better than Christianity, 13. Best adminesterd is best, 13, ... 291,
Bible making, 4, 63, 136. 138, 261½, Bible Catholic, 140. Bibles and laws, 2 to 43, 75, 127, 131, 184, 216. Bibles of errors, 130, 135, 261½. Bibles altered, 135-6, 261½. Bible collected altered and compiled, 129, 261½. Bible, King Jim's, 140, 185, 261½. Bibles destroyed, 135 to 140. Bible declared infalable, 133. Bible and woman 247. Bible gods, 123. Bible rule, 163 to 170, 178 to 180, 284. Bible Septugenc, 138. Bible, Uncle Sams, 135, 165, 170. Big country, 10. Biga·

mist, 29. Bishop, 11, 127. Birds, 74. Birthplace of man, 58.
Billow, Amazon, 88. Bitter, bitter enemies, 130. Big me
little you, 141. Big-belly, boils, 242. Birds of a feather, 2-
58. Bites and stings, 259. Birth of mankind, 69, 72, 74.
Black-mail, 25. Blasphemy, 32--3, 130. Blating, braying
missionarys, 181. Bleeding, 237, 245. Bleed, blister, puke
and purge, 109. Blenders, 66, 125. Bless or curse God, 131
Blood 18, 125. Blood-money, 29, 112. Bloody shirt, 119.
Blood and thunder, 99, 112, 125. Blood, cold blood, 112, 125-
Blood thickened, 237. Blood suckers, 240--2. Blown up, 1-
02. Blunders and errors, 19, 24, 101, 135, 143, 185. Blue pill
and salts, 239, 240,--1,--3,--4, 256, 260. Blue laws, 35, 135.

Books, 4, 44. Book City, 4. Book of religions, 122. Book
of books, 127, 131. Books and maps, 126. Books that make
the Christian bible, 120 to 139. Book Coron, 140. Book mormon, 138. Boycott, 23. Bond lords, 9, 30--2--9. Bonds and
taxes, 39, 46, 111. Boss, 40. Booger, 61. Bohemoth, 73.
Born, 34, 73, 89, 193, 274. Born developed, 188, 193, 274.
Born undeveloped, 188, 193. Born but to die, 274. Born
germs, 190, 193. Boils, bruses, burns, 235. Borgia or a Cat-
aline, 269. Boys or girls at your will, ... 258.

Brain, 44. Brain and nerve, 181, 190--2-3. Brain and body
190--3--4. Brains and honors, 204, 301. Bread, 18, Bread
and meat, 241. Bread and meat plant, 66. Bread winner,
249. Breasts sore, inflamed, 254. Briceville, 35, 102. Brit-
tans, 128, 134. Brittish armies, 134. Brittanica Encyclo-
peda, 73. Bridget's letter, 138. Brother, 13, 68. Brown,
John, 35. Bronchitis, 239. Broken bones, 245. Bruses and
burns, 243. Brutality and Humanity, 178, ... 179.

Buckeyed, 259. Buchanan, 100, 112. Burnt up throat and
stomach, 240. Burial of my father, 12. Burning, biting, 2-
59. Burnt out bum, 169, 240. Bull, John. Business, 100-8.
Butterfly, 66, 74. Butler, 119, 187, ... 204.

Cactus, 5. Cachexy, 243-4. Cadets, 143. Cain and Abel,
2, 33, 68, 74, 134, 140-3. Campbellites, 203. Came to his
own, 126. Canebrakes, 73. Cancer, carbuncle, 243-5. Candy and cradles, 255. Cannon, 118. Calvin and hell, 297.
Calandar, 132. Capitols, 63, 108. Cardinal points, 220, 240.
Caricatureing, 102. Carthage, 139. Castration, 39. Cases,
251-4. Cataract, 92. Catalepsy, 240. Catarrh, 235. Cata-
pillar, 66. Catheter, 239. Cathartics, 257. Catholics, 15, 19
25, 33, 38, 55, 62, 139, 204. Catholic lies, 62, 126, 138. Catholics make a bible, 139, 140. Catholic church, 127, 204.
Cathedrel at Rome, 61. Catiline, 279. Caught, 111, 113.
Cause and effect, 241, 251. Cause of the causes, 242. Cause
of all torpid diseases, 241. Cautiousness, 199, 200, ... 215½.

Celestrial, 65, 66-8-9. Ceres, 74. Cezar. 127, 139, 269, 297.

Chain of life, 286. Change, 66, 71, 181 2, 272. Change of life,
255. Change of color, 243. Charity, 13-4, 29, 30-7, 55, 170,
181, 193-7, 204, 291, 303. Character, 4, 9, 20, 29, 202. Chart
and character, 214, 179½. Chaos and destruction, 25, 143.
272-5-9. Charms, 16. Chemestry, 64. Cherokee, 35. Chattanooga Sunday Times, 141. Christians, 2 to 75, 118, 120,
188. Christianity, 26, 29, 37, 54-5 7, 204, 241. Christian

Women, 15, 16. 30, 86. Christian home, 29, 37, 55. Christian mind, 30, 55-7, 241. Christian, heart, 30-7, 57. Christian, knowledge, 30-3-7, 54 5-6, 86. Christian astronomy, geography, and mathematics, 30, 54-5, 261½. Christian gods or devils, 28 30-3-4, 46, 57, 77, 86, 120, 163. Christian god-head, 34, 89. Christians's god, christ, or savior, 16-7, 20-1, 34, 86, 163-4, 186-7-8. Christian's Jew bible, 40, 55, 86, 130 to 140, 161-3 to 179, 261½· Christian persecutions, 112, 116, 178. Christian frauds and life, 114, 140, 192-3. Christian army, 128. Christian armies slaughterd, 128. Christian slaves, 129, 143. Christian slavery war, 140. Christian's christmas, 21, 65. Christian's sunday, 20-1 Christian christites, 203. Christian's thirst for gold, 268. Church, 26, 31-8-9, 100-2-8, 133-8-9, 142, 193, 204. Church of England, 11, 261½. Church, E. W. Evangelical, 142. Church and state, 142. Church bells, 202 -3. Church rule, 11 to 37, 138-9, 195. Church ridden slaves, 10 to 37. Church teaches, 11 to 30, 1-38-9. Church driven, 35, 55 to 57 Child, 72, 146, 193-4, 2-51, 256, 281. Children, 40, 146, 194. Children of men, 33, 40,146. Children of this world, 5, 28, 38. Child's god, 77, 146. Children's Crusade, 143. Child-birth, 247, 252. Children to beget, 258. Chinese, 8, 123-6-8. Chinese wall, 138. Chiefs, 131, 197. Chief Justice, 200. Chill and fever, 233, 234· Chills, congestive, 233-4. Ceill and fever remedy, 234. Chilblains, 228, 235. Chinches, chigers, 19, 36, 240-1. Chicago, 32. Chicken eating, 29. Chlorosis, 248. Cholery, 90, 238. Choped off his head, 124. Chokeing, 238-9. Choke-damp, 289. Chronic, obstinate swellings, 223. 1st. Chronicles, 1st., chapter. 23 verse, ... 122.

Cider, 38. Circular, 103-9-10. Circulation, 128. Circulation, to reduce, to strengthen, to equalize, 222. Circumcision, 122. Cities, 72, 84. Cities in the skies, 259. Civilized,63.

Claims, 125. Class laws, 100 to 120, 193. Class of man, 190. Clap, gleet, whites, 235, 250. Cleansing, 218, 238, 240, bowels, stomach, skin, 260 Cleavland, 7. Cliques, parties, or_ders and churches, 5, 11, 14, 31, 33, 41, 100, 126, 129, 141, 144, 202. Clothing. 68, 90. Closed hymen, 239. Clouds, ...89.

Cocoa, 71. Cooksy momux, 25. Colors, 61, 66, 74. Columbus, 56, 63. Commissioner, U. S., 101. Commandments, laws and ordinances, 3, 5, 20. Commissioned from God, 12, 13, 15, 20, 21, 125, 179, Commerce, 62. Comprehend, 78, 197, 198. Complanant, prosecutor, witness, persecutor, and a United States commissioner, judge and jury all in one villian 110. Combined intrigue and treachery, 127. Commentary, 129, Comstock, 191. Combativeness, 199, 215½. Coma, convulsions, 239, 240, 241. Constitution, 43, 107. Constitution, U. S., 3, 11, 23, 33, 308 to 327. Confidence, 29, 231. Conscience, 13, 23, 31, 110. Condemn,14, 68. Convict, 102. Constellation, 98, 103, 105. Contending power, 125. Constantine, 126, 7, 8, 139. Conquest, 127, 134, 289.˜ Contradicting, 130. Confusion and madness, 143, 193, 272, 275.. Oonciousness, 145, 197, 280. Concubines and slaves, 189. Continueing natures of man, 189 Continuity, 197, 215½. Contrast them, 87, 198. Conscience is dependent, 198, 20)· Consumption, 238, 243. Constipation, congestion, 238, 239. Convulsions, 249. Conjugal love, 286. Conception, immaculate, 65. Copper, 67. Corn, 66, 73, 131.

Coblar, 298. Cock of the walk, 194, 204. Coffee, tea, 239, 259. Cornfields, 140. Corn shucks, 68. Colors, types, species of man, 74, 190. Cold and heat, 218, 223. Colds, 223, 235, 256. Colic, croup, congestion, 228, 235, 256. Compilation, 127, 130 to 139, 261½. Comparative man and beast, 190, 198. Congress, 103, Contageon, 238. 2. Corrinthins, 123, Corrosive, caustic, 259. Courts of the minb, 196, 200. Court house, 15. Court, 15-6, 108, 116. Court, U. S., 102, 112. Council trap, 112. Courtship, 247. Course of time, 71. Cow--tree, 71. Cow--boys, 123, ... 131.

Cradle of man, 69. Crane, Dr. 108. Cramp, convulsions, Croup, 235--8--9, 240, 256. Cravings, crankiness, 242. Crawfish bate, 125. Craziness, 13, 17, 20-2-3-5, 30 1·2-7, 119, 130, 146, 186, 241. Crazy drunk fools, 122. Creator, 55, 77, 80-2, 127, 159, 183. Create, 63-5, 131, 140, 183, 188. Creature, 19. Creeds, 19, 129, 123-4. Creosote, 238. Crime, 25-6, 32-4, 55-7, 74, 120, 134, 193, 204. Crime and the church, 192-3. Criminals, 61, 142. Crime against criminals, 25-6. Crime of the Christ'ans, 118, 178! Cross mark, 16. Cross and the lash, 140. Cromwell, 301. Cry, grief, fret, 1, 148, 157. Cruelty and crime, 120, 178. Crow, 113. Crown, center, fulcrum, 200. Cross bone, ... 254.

Cultivated, 72. Curse, 32, 68, 74, 120-3, 131-5, 140, 199, 207, 215½. Cursed the world, man and the devil, 135, 199, 247. Cussin mad, 120, 123, 199. Cursing, killing, 163, 178, 238. Currents, tides and winds, 59. Cure yourself, 251. Curtains, 279. Cut fice dog, 7, 33, 39. Cut and dried case, 111. Cut stone paved way, 128. Cut or burn it out, 245. Cutting the gums, 257. .... Cyclone, 85, 145. Cyncus or camp fever, 233. Cystis, ... 244.

Dads, 75. Daddy air, 181, 266. Dairy woman, 247. Damnation, 17. Damascus, 6. Damp, chilly air, 223. Daniel's god, 77. Dark ages, 37. Dark ignorent age, 128. Darling of the Lord, 191. Dating, 11. Daughters of men, 86, 120. Davis, 101. David, 75, 103, 169, 188. David and Goliah, 1, 88. David damnation, 103. Davidson county jail, 103. Day and night, 30, 84, 94, 132-6, 142. Day never ends, 132. Days work, 39, 46. Days of the week, ...• 132.

Dead, 19, 27, 36, 84, 267. Death bed, 27-8, Death not a punishment, 146, 281. Death by poison, 258. Dead beat, 1-24. Dead meat to eat, 123, 167. Deacon, 100 Debars, 107. Debility, 243. Decius, 279. Declaration of Independence, 3, 5, 11, 23, 43, 87, 241. Declared war, 86. Decoration day, 42. Decency, 87. Deeds, 47-8. Deeds not words, 118, 157, 268. Debased minds, 194. Defenders 26, 118 140. Deity 72, 75, 84, 268, 290. Deification, 73. Delirium tremens, 2, 236. Demoivre, 286. Democrats, 100-2. Democrat gods, 9. Den, 38. Deny, 108, 140. Depend, 74-5, 188, 205. Depraved, 26-8, 188, 268. Depuration. 241. Dependent depravity, 241. Derbia, the book city, 136. Derivatives, 239, 240, 241. Desolate, 93–4. Destitute, desolate home, 117. Destroy, 32-7, 86, 118, 128, 130-5, 140-4, 193, 168. Destructiveness, 199, 295-6. Destruction, expulsion, purification, 244, 2-96. Destiny, 53, 188, 199. Desert, 89. Descent, 32. Design,

262. Detection, 83, 110. Deuteronomy, 87, 121, 123, [xiv, 21.]
Deuling, 42. Developed natures, 188. Developed organs, 1-
90. Develop, 40, 67, 71, 188, 162. Devil, 2, 4, 19, 20,1, 33-6,
64, 76, 83-4-5-8, 100-2, 130, 141, 199, 290. Devils or gods, 86.
Devils writing a bible, 130-1. Devils made through fear, 290.

Diabetis, diuresis, 237. Diaphoretic, detergent, 222. Diarrhea, dysentery, 237, 249. Diet, 239, 240. Die, dying, 71, 1-07, [144,] 281. Difficult urination, 249. Difference, 86, 138, 180.,5-8, 200 62-94. Different religions, 124, 294. Digestion and nutrition, 242. Digby 295. Diluent, detergent, depurative, 218. Dinah, 122, 168. Discriminate, 108. Discoveries, 30, 62, 126. Discovery of the Amerikas, 126-7, Discharges, 237. Disease, 22, 127, [146.] 278, 286. Disease is remedial effort, 217. Diseases and remedies, 216. Diseases given by groups, 231. Diseases are of high or low energy, 231. Diseases of puberty, 128. Diseases of married life, 249 Diseases of child birth, 259. Diseases of infants and children, 255. Disgrace, 127, 193. Disgorged, 238. Dislocations, 244-5. Disposition of man, 4, 160 to 170. Disputes, 161, 178, 194, 261½, 262. Dispondency, 242. Dissatisfaction 11, 13, 296. Disturbed minds and sleep, 252, 261½. Distress, pain, sickness, 258. Disputed points, 132! Disturbance, 13 Divine, 11, 76, 125. Divine decree, 128. Divine slavery, 1-23, 140-1, 162. Divine heir to rule, 34, 86, 122, 125. Dividing the world, ... 130.

Doctors, 43, 159, 242, 278. Dogs, 17, 19, 23-4-7, 33, (145,) 268! Dollars, 24, 39, 46, 134. Down they went, 114-5, 128. Downfall, 32, 37, ... 128.

Dress, 258. Dress and fashion, 247. Dressing the infant, 2, Drink and food, 230-9, 242, 259. Drink agreeable, 259. Drinking, 153. Drunk, 100, 121, 153. Drunkenness, dirt-eating, 242. Drunken prohi-- 109. Driven, 35, 60. Dropsy, 243. Drugplaces, 109. Drugged gizzards, 112. Drummers, 109. .... 151.

Dues, salaries to masters, 203. Duty, 110, [144,] 188, 268, 290. Dutch war, 35 Dying, [144,|| 154, 284. Dynamite, 103, 104. Dyspepsia, 239, 540, ... 256.

Earth, 30, 68, 83-5.9, 93, 132-6, [142,] 181, 217, 271,2, Earth flat and square, 30, 132. Earth round, 30, 93, 132. Earthquakes, 61, 83, [55,] 269. Earthly paradise, 65-9, 85, 136. Eating, drinking, 132, 193. Eat, drink and hug strange women, 192. .... Ebb and flow of the eea, 84. .... 88.

Ecclesiastes, 26, 184-5. Eclectics, 106 to 120. Economy made practical, 211. Ecuador, 58, 63, 66, 68, 69, ...83.

Eden, 57-8, 60, 83-4. Education, reason, association, 190. Education and cultivation, 199 .... 200.

Eggs or germs of man, 63, 73. Egg-plants—human, 65-6-8-9, 73. Egypt, 10, 33-4, 127-8, 137, 142. Egypt's god, ... 266.

Eldorado, 61, Elders, 139. Elect, 23, 126. Electricity, 2-40-3-4. Electrical minds, 197. Elements, 71, 193, 268, 277. Elements of life, 269, 262. Elementary colors, 66, 277. Elephant skin, 243. Elevated, 69, 72, 88, ... 89.

Emancipation, 26. Emetic, 228, 240, 243, 256, 259. Empty pates, 32. Empire of Russia, 107. Emphysiema, ... 244.

End, 275, 286. End of time, 18, 39. Endure, pity, embrace, 280. Enemy, 11, 242. Energy, 92, 140, 272. Energy or Inteligence, 145, 169. Energy, high or low, 222. Energy low and bad, 242-3, England, 42, 94, 129. English people, 42. English language, 142. Enlarged glands, 238-9, Envy, 120 279. Enslave, 41-6, 202. .... 215$_4$.

Ephesians, 3, 85, 131. Epidemic, 186. Epluribus Unium, 197. .... Equal and exact justice, 17, 39, 293. Equator, 68, 83, 93-4. Equal in law and privilages, 125. Equal, 126, 169, 272. Equalizers, 239, 241, 293. Equalize the heat and the blood, 220, ... 260.

Er, Onan and that murdering Lord, 34, 122. Error, 11, 268. Eruptions and rashes, 60, 83, 235-7. Eruptive diseases, 236. Erysipelatous diseases, 235, ... 236.

Esther, 137. Esteem and love, 146-7, ... 298. Eternity, 146. Eternal cause, 268. Ethiopian mothers, 57. Ethiopian, African, 74. Ethics, 263, ... 278.

Europe, 35, 89, 94, 127, 130. Europe's infamous laurels, 301. European continent, 58½, 95. Eugene, ... 300.

Ever existing proof, 95. Every vile poison, 109. Every creature, 19, 126. Evils organized, 142. Evil designing rascals, i08, 118, 142. Evidence, 53, 74, 89. Evil one, 83, 120, 130, 163 to 170, ... 215¼.

Exalted, 72, 84. Excited minds, 202. Exercise and rest, 229, 249. Execute, 146, 182-3. Executive minds, 183, 268. Exempt property, 14. Existence, 74-5, 95. Exodns, 14. 121 123. Experience, 72. Expenses, 35. Extreamests, 189, 2-68, 280, 293. Extra good or extra bad, 189, ... 268.

Fables, 127, 187. Facts, 67, 75, 120-1, 134, 140, 143. Faith, 13, 23, 197, 267, 291, 302. Faith, hope and charity, 13, 24, 158, 199, 204, 210. Fainting, 249. Failure, 23, 32, 113. Fall of man, 290. False, 87, 101, 112, 184-7, 198, 275, 290, False pretenses, 14, 29, 87, 108, 112, 121-7. False and absurd bible, 128 to 130, 261½. Falce scales, 301. Famine, 41. Family records, 179. Family duties, 247. Fashion, 258. Father, 11, 25, 30-7, 57-9, 127, 180 Father, mother and son, 33, 183, 286. Father, son and ghost. 75-6, 286 Father, mother and child, 76, 183. Fate, 267, 275-6. Faulkners, 109, 113. 1-15, 120. Falkland, ... 295.

Feasts, 22, 41,67, 74, 290. Feast days, 132, 299. Fear, 288. Fear forced religion, 242. Febrifuge, 222. Federalist, 35. Fed to dogs tigers and lions, 129. Feet, keep them always hot, 255-9. Feed, 90, 109, 114, 129. Feeling, 78, [183]. Festival of Ceres, 74. Fever heat, 250 6. Fevers, 90, 232-3, 2-37, 254-6 Fevers, treatment for all, 233, ... 234.

First, 2, 45, 63, 73-4,5, 90, 131, 141. First love, 68 to 71 First courtship, 71-2. First marriage, 71-2-3. First senses, 78, 183 to 250. First age of the earth, 68, 289. First temples, 63. First cities, 63. Fire, 59, 83-5, 125-8-9, 131-3, 140.

Fire worship, 59, 75. Fishers of men, 36, 40, 67, 85, 119, 124 245, 290. Fitest, 40, Five colors, 64. Fight for them, 121. Fighting and murdering, 134, 290. Filthey, lothsom diseases, 191. Finished man, 195. First man, 73, First festival, 73, 134. First trouble, 193. First born Jew a murder, 134. First bible, 131 to 136. First Jew bible, 136. First, just, free, liberal—134. First trouble, 193. Fire and heat, 125, 128-9. Firmness, 197, 215½. Fire–damp, 259. Fish, snake. and ghost stories, 99. Fistulas, 245. Fits, 239, 256. Five miles high, 72, 84. Five senses, 78, [183,] 182. Five cent novels, 99. Five ways to feel. Fizz and fry, ...112.

Fleas, flies, and such bloodsuckers, 19, 240, 243, 261. Fled ignomineously, 128, 261½. Florid Scotchman, 74. Flood, 55, 83. Flux-like diseases, ... 237.

Fool, 21, 36, 103--4, 128. Fools, 108, 140-1, 275-6-8, 280-1-4, 2-95. Food and water, 67, 71, 90, 109, 216, [217] 230 8, 241, 284. Foot bath, hot! hot! 240-3, 257. Foment, 256. Fomentations, 228, 239, 244-5, 250. Follow me, 27, 40, 67, 85, 119, 290. Force, 15 67, 71, 92, [143,] 217. Fortunes, fabulous, 8, 36-7. Forsaken, 18, 44. Foreigners, 35. Fortified, 40. Forgiveness never! 114. Forty years starving, 122. Forging slavery fetters, 129. Forced upon us, 129. Forced into virtue, 190. Force of arms, 143, 289. Forehead, 201. Fortifying, 238. Fossail remains, 73. Fourth of July, 11. Foundation. 75. Fourth commandment, 21. Four corners, 30. Four times attacted, 114. Four runner, 123. Foundation, 125, 1-38, 243. Fountain of life, 183, Foxglove, 109. Foxtail, 1-02, 109, 110, 130. Fox and grapes, ... 150.

Fraud, 17, 101 France, 94. Franklin, 32. 46. Fractures, dislocations, 245. Fraid to think, 204. Free and equal, 1-40-1-2. Free will, 142. Freedom's sons now and then, 154, Free, 7, 32-3, 46, 87, 127, 197, 276. Freedom, 5, 11, 25, 32,3-7, 40, 87, 100 -29-30, 140-1-3, 154. Free government, 24.5, 87, 108, 141-3, 291. Freemasonry, 32. Free moral agent, 32, 87, 140, 197, 267, 276. Free religion, 33, 87, 127, 140, 287. Free salvation, [Matt. xv, 26 --dogs!] 108, 140-1-3. Freethinker, 42, 87, 140-1-3, 197, 276. Free men, 104, 127, 140. Free souveriguty, 108, 140-1-3, 181, ... 186.

Fret, never, 1, 148, 157. Freezing cancers, 245. Friend, 19, Frog and man, 206. Frosts and dews, 90, 261. F ost-bitten 235. Fruits, 30 2, 67, 71, 90, 100-1-4, 121-7-9, 131-8, 140, 187. Fruits and vegetables, ... 242

Full-blood, 138. Further gone than he, 28). Future rewards, 146, 186, ... 298.

Gad, ged, gid, god gud, are the words the guessed at vowels make. 133-4. Galatians, 122. Galling gizzards, 103, 112. Gambeling, 14, 29. Gaping, 239. Garbled extracts, 130-7. Garfield, 32. Garment, 124. Gaseous poisocs, ... 258-9.

Gease, 104. Genesis, 1, 2, 3, 4, 15, 34, 86, 120.2-3, 130, 134.6. Generation, 64, 75, 200. Generative love, 286. Geography, 94, Georgia, 35. Germs, 63, 190, 237, 241, 243, 261. Germin Empire, 94. Gestation, 65. Getters up of the first bibles, 1-33 to 138, and .... 261¼. .... Ghost, 34, 75, 87, 99.

Gilbert, 114. Girdle, wet and hot, 227. Gittin ligin, 13, 26, 28, 184. Give, 23, 39, 124. Give to the borrower and the beggar, [Matt. v, 42.] 124. Gizzard, ... 32, 103, 108, 112. Glaciers 89, 92. Glandular enlargement, 243. Glass flour, 259. Gleet and catarrh, 236, ... 250. God and Nature, 5, 6, 18, 21 to 27, 30 to 37, 43, 75-7-8-9, 82-4, 103, 140, [142] 181, 272.-4-7, [286) 291, 302. God, what he is, [53, 72, 77, 80,] 103, 180, 216, 272, 277. God--space, 72, 103, 2-72. God of principle, 78, 277. God wrote no book, 186. God's son wrote no book, 186. God's only son and book is nature, 186, 274. God within the mind, 280. God and man's 186. God or man's 266. God, man as— 268, 278. God as a beast, 274, 290. Gods made through fear and weak hope, 2-74, 290. God sends not ill, 296. God's love, man's 149, 303. God's attributes, 79, 83, 290. God's earthly, 77, 180-1, 268, 272. Gods of this world, 85-6, 103, 120, 123, 130-1, 277, 290. God of Israel, 191, 290. Gods or devils, 86-7, 120, 123, 134, 2 90. Gods of the Christians, 120-1, 290. God's special elect, 126, 138, 180. God made them ignorent, 135, 180, 271-2-3-4. Gods of Babylon, 77. God, Aaron's 16, 77, 204, 278. God and the Lord —make man, 1, 21. God's promises, 16, 30, 1 15, 125, 138. God's sons, 16. 30, 75, 126. God's only son, 18. God-sent, called, or god-favored, 23, 30-1-3, 180, 126, 138, 216. God perfect, 26, 30_3, 82, 125, 138, 274 5. God's lamb, 29. God rests, 29, 30- God's laws, 21, 33, 44, 31, 82, 103, 138, 272 373. God--head, 33-4, 75-6, 82, 183. God or Goddess of corn Cerese, 74. Goddess Amerikus or Liberty, 87. God done it ? 115, 120, 121, 138-9, 180. God fights for them ? 121. God of Gods ? 168. God of them all ? 123, 290, God's slave ? 87, 138, God so decreed ? 128, 272-4-7. God's set up throne ? 1-28. God's special agent ? 138, 180, 277. God's infallible a-gent ? 134-8. God's good guide ? 131 -8 180. God's only means and way ? 274. God and religion ? 140, 290. God a robber, thief, ravisher and a lying cruel murder? 141-2, 163 178, 290. God and Solomon ? 190-1. God of puppy love, 255. Godless books in King Jim's bible ! .... 137, 138.

Go not to others, 126. Go into all the world, 19, 126. Good 17, 23, 26, [144,] 292 tr 299. Good-father, 80 Good laws, 31 [144.] Good for evil, 124, 297. Good Ingin, 9, 125·6, 144· Good organs a fallacy, 198, 292 to 299. Good men ? 114, 190, 194, 279, [280,] 295. Goose-headed set, 100, 104 to 108 to 120 Golden rule, 144. Gold, 8, 30, 67. Gomorrha, 3, 34. Gospel, 119, 33, 126. Gout, rheumatism, 129, 278. Government 11, 13, 31-3-5, 43-4, 120, 126, 128, 143, 290, 291. Government paternal, 7, 31,3, 143, 289, 291. Government, religious, 15, 21, 33, 44, 143, 290. Government by the people, 129, [291.] Govenors, ... 100-1_3 9-12-20-91.

.... Grant, Gen 7, 123, 191. Grain, 71. Grandfather, 13. Granny, 31. Grass family, 73. Graduated, 107. Gravel, 239. Gravity, 93. Greece. 61, 133-7-8, 1 42, Greek and Romons, 6. Greek Slave, 87, 129, 258. Great age, 73. Great grandfather, 73, Greates Intelligence—God, 80-2. Greatest Good, 103,t299. Green sickness, 248. Guardian, 26, 31, 33, 131. Guarding, 108. Gulph stream, ... 58, 94.

Habit, 182, 220, 278. Hagar, 122. Hail republic, 99. Hare lip, 256_7.9. Harmony, 125. Ha rison, 31. Hare_brained, 242.

Hallucination, 242 261½. Half-breeds, 138. Half-made, 66
Hamilton, 35. Ham, 74. Haman, Brewn and Guiteau, 142.
Hanibal, 191. Harrison, 31. Harlot, 29, 122. Happiness,
15, 17, 87, 98, 258, 281, 286, 292, [293,] 302. Hanging gardens
of Babylon, 138. Hate commanded, 13, 25, 119, 125, 138. 140
277. Hate father, mothr, wife and children, 119, 277. Hate,
fear, grief, 277. Hatched, 63. Haunt, 34. Hayseed, 102, 110.

Heaven and hell, 5, 14, 15, 26-7 8, 37, 60-9, 80, 125, 130, [145,]
[188, 290.] Heavenly father, 55, 80, 60-3, 74. Heaven built
on pride; Hell built on spite, 290. Heaven, cast out of, 83.
Heat, 92, 218. 239, 244. Heath, 13, 31.7, 90, 104 to 117, (146,]
206. Heathen, 14. Hearing, 78. Hearsay evidence, 139.
Heart of man, 200.9. Heart said to the head, 209. Heart-
burn, head-ache, 249, 259. Heat and fever to reduce, 222
Healing wounds, and soars, 245. Heir, 33, 85°6, 125. Heir
Heir to heaven, 85-6. Hebrew, 14, 26, 133. Heli, 76. Hell,
if true, 99, 130.3, 191. Hell-fire and brimstone, 125, 130, 133.
Heratics, 99. Henderson, 114. Henbane, 109. Hernia, 2-
44. Hepetic, 222. Health, peace, comfort, 294. Head and
face cool, 259. Hemorrage, hysterics, 237.8, 249. Hennis-
ee, 31. Hermit, ... 290.

Hiccough, hysterics, 239. Hieroglyphics, 127, 133. 138. Hiena howl, 23 High, broad forehead. 200. High kickers, 1-
24 Higher powers, 86. Higher state of exiatence, 71. Hill
Ben, 141. High, 72, 86. Hireling, 39. His own, 17, 18, 191.
History, 32-4, 53.7, 106-20-5, 130-7-9, 140, ... 193.

Hobgoblins, 87, 254-5. Hog, 19. Home, 8, 36-7, 44, 60, 115,
181. Home, sweet home, 52. Homeopaths, 106 to 120. Honesty the best policy? 98. Honest Injin, 9, 108. Honest John,
113. Hoo-doo, 16. Hope, 13, 197, 267. Horrors of horrors,
30. Hosea, 123. Hot head foot and body, 220, 239, 240, 244,
252, 256. Hot water and soap, 238-9, 240-4, 251-6. Hot bath,
239, 240-4, 254-7-9. House of God, 30, 190-1. House of Israel. 17. Houchins, 113. Hovel, 8, 36-7. Hovel and stable, 2-
03. Hot irons, bricks or rocks to the feet, 240, 244, 251,-4-6-
9. Hot water injections, 250-1-4-6-7-9. Hot toddy, 259, 260.
Honey moon, 247. Honor, esteem, love, 298. Hope, happiness, 281, 291-3. How, when and wheare man fell, 290. How
religion debases, 194. How god answers prayer, 193. How
god helps, 193. Howling, 32, 100 to 120, 124. Howls and
bow—yows, 7, 23, 33, ...— 84.

Human liberty, 98. Human depravity, 138, 188, 190. Human gore, 140. Human body, 181, 200, 218. Human nature
188, 190, 200, 206, 209, 276. Hnman man, 198, 199, 200, 207,
276. Human head, 199, 200. Human food, 290. Humiliated, 27. Hunters, 150. Hungry, 27. Hundreds of religions
129. Hug, 28. Hurricans, 84, ... - 145,

I belong to them, 100. Icebergs, 89. Idiot, 40, 86, 134, [1.
45,] 204. Idlenss, 78. Ignorent, 18, 30, 44, 76. 288. Igno-
ramuses, 76, 275. Illustrate, to, 12, 15, 25-6, 30-2,3, 40-5, 77,
78, 83, 141, 199, 206, 251, 303. Illustrations, 20, 42. 45, 53, 58,
58-9, 69, 76, 88, 95-6 9, 100, 101, 102, 104, 105, 107, 108, 117,
118, 119, 130, 179, 180, 183, 187, 189, 190, 196, 199, 201, 205, 206
214 to 216, 219, 220, 221, 225, ...,........ .... 261.

Illegal, 31-2, 107, 111. Ills and woes, 247, ... 279,
Immatured, 6. Imperfect, 26, 64, 133, 272. Immortal, 40, 71
184. Immortal Soul or Spirit, 184, 186. Immoral, 59, 187.
Imputed discovery, 126. Impossible, 127, 191, 272. Immutable, 140. Impios, 128. Improve and control, 206, 272.
Imbecility, 242. Imposture, 74. Improve by balancing, 244,
272. Imaginary, 254. Impregnable, 258. Impiety, 128, 272.
Imprison, 109, 146, ... 114,

Incus or Chief, 56-7, 72-4, 131. Indian, 6 to 9, 35-6, 106, 192,
267-8. India, 33, 61, 141. Ingin, 133. Indian Corn, 68, 73.
Influence of the Sun, 91. Infidel, 12, 13, 24, 30-2-5.7, 56, 99,
128, 178, 247. Infidel poor-house, 14. Inspector, 15. ....
.... Insult, 23, 28. Intimidating, 22. Inquisition, 25,
107. Indulgence, 25. Innocent, 32-4. Insanity, 32. Independence, 32, 129, 181, 192. Innocent mothers and infants,
34. Insurection, 35 6. Inferior, 44, 190. Ingersoll, 42. Intelligence, 53, 71, 80, 140, [145,] 272, 288. Ingersoll and
Paine, 42. Increase, 71. Insect, 71, Industry, 72. Incarnation of the Sun. 73. Infaleable witness, 76, 133. Infinite
78. Injure, 109. In hell if true, 99. Indignation meeting,
101. Infamy, 107-8, 129, 143. Inquisitorial General, 107.
Inquisition, 108, 134, 239. Infidel Literature, 101. Infidel
Literature Mailable, 110, 113. Indict, 111. Inspector, 113,
114, 128. Investigation, 114. In and out of power, 118. In
the name of God, 118, 121, 129, 134-6, 178. Infamy commanded, 123. Intrigue, 127. Institutions of Learning, 128. Interpretation, 133, 272. Infalible Bible, 133. Infant, child,
man or woman, 145, 246-7, 252, 281. Infernal Infermities, 1-
86. Instinct, 193, [285.] Introductory Remarks, 216. Injection, 228, 238, [240,] 249, 250-4. Inflamation and Congestion, 220, 235, 244-5. Inaction or Torpor, 220. Inflamation
of the brain, 235. Inflamatory Diseases, 234, 244, 250-9. Indigo and hot water, 240, Intercourse, Sexual, 250. Intemperance, 153, 161, 257. Investigator, 114. Insuperable line,
271. Instinct and Reason, 186, ... 271.

Iron, 67. Iron Clad Age, 114. Ireland, 94. Irish type, 208.
Iritation, 240, 259. Isaac, 15, 29, 33. Island, 34. Is life worth
living? 142. Isolated parts for a creed, 131. Itallions, 8. I
think I thunk a lie, 148. It's money after all, 150. Italic
words in their bibles, 134. Italy, 126. Itch, tetter, ... 237.

Jacob, 15, 29, 74, 122. Jackass, 19, 22, 126, 128. Jail, 109,
James, 27, 123. Jason, the Amerikan Historian, 4. Jaundice, 249. .... Jealous, 86, 120, 138. Jealousy limited their life, 120. Jefferson, 10, 32, 44-6. Jeruselam, 16, 18-9, 24, 123, 138. Jesus, 3, 10, 13, 17, 19, 21-4-7, 32,
33, 74-5, 85, 118-9, 124-5-6, 131-2-8, 192. Jesus' god, 24, 77, 86.
Jesus' bible, 137. Jesus' Letter to Bridget, 128. Jesus and
John, [118,] 124-5. Jesuses, how many, 126. Jesusites, 60,
203. Jesus the Tramp Doctor, [Mark, vi, 5.] 248. Jezy. 85,
86. Jews, 4, 9, 10-4-7-8, 50, 123_7, 136-7-8, 143, 208. Jews' god
33. 119. Jews' bible, 138, 184. Jew Slave, 129. Jew Joseph,
122. Jew Beginning Day, 143, 192. Jewite route te Heaven,
203, ... 178.

Jimson, 109, 259. Jine de church, 28. Jine, backslide and re-jine de church, 191. Joshua, 16, 21, 121, 123, 132, 136. Jorden, 19. Jones, 27, 141. John, 14, 17, 19, 30, 76, 85-6, 130. Job, 85, 136, 184, 199. Job's wife, 131. Joel, 87, 113. Joseph, 76, 86. Joseph's wife, 86. Jove, Mike and Nick, ..163. Judges, 122, 200, 294. Judgement, 185, 200, 231. Judge, Justice, [197,] 198, 200, 298. Judea, 19, 34, 123. Juda and the Lord couldent— 122. Judas, 19, 27, 298. Justice, 16, 20-3, 26-9, 39, 43, 87, 141, 190, 193, 200. Justice Conscience, [190. Just men, 26, Justice or Injustice, [198,] 200, 290-2 to 300. Juno, 84. Jupiter, ... 84.

Keturah, Abes' Concubine, 122. Keeping up, 238. King, 2, 11, 16, 18, 20-1, 17, 31-2-9, 75, 86, 122, 124, 229. Kings, gods and devils, 87, 129, 130, 134. 1.°Kings, 87, 191. King gods, 38, 86. King Dollar, 39. Kingdom, 18, 78, 85. Kings of this Earth, 86-7, 130. Kiugs of this World, 85-6-7, King Jim, 87, 122, 261½. King Jim's Bible, 40, 55, 75, 87, 99, 122, 133-5-9, 140-6, 160 to 170. King Jim's god, 146, 163. King, Ruler or a Great man, 125. King's Concubine Slaves, 87! King George, 25, 32-7. King Philip, 35 King of the Jews, 143. King William, 35. King Louis, 43. King Jim, the Simpleton, 129. King Jim's Bible declared Infalable, 133. King Jim and Lord Bacon, 301. Kill, 38, 43, 86, —121, — 122. Kill all except the [women] children, 121. Killing, murdering, 242, 244. Kill with caustic, [245,]. Killing, curing, 2-38, [245,]. Killing Insect Life, 244. Killing of Abel, 33, 193. Killing of Er, 33-4, 86, 122. Killing of Onan, 33 4, 86, 122. Killing of all violators, 20, 32-4, [Ex. xxxii, 27.]. Killing of Jesus, 20-4-7. Knaves, 21. Knowledge, 56, 67, 71, 126, 128, 143, 193. Knowing, 71, 126, 143. Knock down proof, 73, 87 126, 143, 193. Knew nothing of the World, 126. Know thyself, 193, 274, 304. Knowledge doth destroy, 282. Knowledge is thyself to know, 204.... .... 304.

Labor, 8, 21, 29, 32, 39, 123. Labor and Slavery Ordained, 123. Labor or Travail, 254. Labrador, 94. Lakes, 63, 68. Lard, butter or greese, 259. Large, open, perceptable parts, 262 Land of liberty, 87. Land of perpetual light, 65-8. Lamb, 29, 68. Lamb or Lion, 119. Lash and the Cross, 140 Last day, 18. Last witness, 86, 131. Latin, 133. Laudanum, 259. Law and Gospel, 143-4-5-6. Laws then and now, 5, 6, 16, 20-1-6, 30, 64-8, 87, 143, [142,) 290. Laws of God? 87, 131, 144. Law, 283, 274, 290, 293,302. Lawyer, 30, 76, 100 to 114, 197, 242. Laws of Nature. 16, 17, 21, 64-6-7-8, 87, 144, 180, 258. Laws of Man, 87, 131, 141-4, 180, 290. Law-breakers, 25, 31-2, 87, 100 to 114, 136, 268. Lawless, 9, 31, 102. Lawsuit, 197. Laws of the world, 140-4, 288, 290. Laws of life, health, disease, and death, 216, 288. Laws partial and general, 269, 270. Law census, 106. Law Oral, 137-9. Lay it all on God! 136, 178, ... 184.

Learning, 4, 5, 6, 32, 123, 128, 92, 197, 288. Learning good and evil, 120, 130. Leader, 40. Leather or prunella, 260.

Lectured and taught, 192. Legally eat, drink or do—12.
Legends, 58, 63, 68. Legislature, 102-5-8-9, 110, 112, 141.
Lemonade, 259 Length of day and night, 94. Length,
bredth, hight, 200. Leopards, 74. Leprosy, 243. Let U.S.
make Man, 180. Lewedness, 250-7. Leviticus, ... 14, 121-3.
Liberty, 11, 15, 24, 37, 39, 98, 114, 129, 141. Liberator, 45, 1-
41. Liberel Infidel Literature, 114, 126, 129. Liberal, 126,
128, 131. Library, 128. Lice and like bloodsuckers, 240.
Lie, 18, 22, 31-2-6, 42, 56, 62, 87, 126-7-8, 180. Life, 15, 37, 40
63-8, 89 to 95, 114, 182-4, [220,] 226, 271, 284. Life to come,
87. Life blood, 34, 240. Life-long persecution, 114. Life's
center, 196. Life force 217, 288. Life is only inherant within us, 217. Lifes play is o'er, 281. Life before religion, 286.
Lightning, 40, 92, 128. Light, 91-2, 129. Likeness, 123.
Liniment, [259,] 251. Lime fresh and quick, 238. Lint or
old rags, 250. Lincoln, 32, 140. Lincoln and Washington,
45. Lion of Judea, 119. Livly and Harmon, 114. Living
and dead matter, 217, 228. Liver diseases, 239. Like or
balanced, 258. Live, how to, 71, 154 to .... 159.
Lock-jaw, 239. Longings, 249. Lord, 21. 30-4. 86, 122, 137.
Lord's Supper, 74. Lord-god, 21, 137. Lord's day, 29, 30,
132. Lord's school, 21. Lord-man-god, 67. Look to me,
87. Lost Sheep, 17, 126. Loss of the Senses, 241. Loss of
right, justice and honor, 241, 290. Loss of semen, 237, 241.
Lot and his gals, 34, 120, 122, 134, 248. Louse, 19, 240, 241.
Love your enemies, 124. Love, 16, 17, 64, 72, 277, 283, 298.
Love, hope, joy, 277, [286,] 288, 300. Love, puppy, 192.
Love, procreative, 286. Low down, 99, 100 to 119, 121, 122·
Luke, 3, 4, 13, 14, 18, 19, 68, 75-6, 85-6, 119, 123. Lust, inordinate, 248, 290. Lye soap, 250. Lying with, 121-2. Lying
in, 247, 253. Lying Commanded, 123, 146, ... 180.

Made every thing in six days out of nothing? 131. Madness
272. Maddens and destroys, 134, 143, 272. Mad opinions,
17, 76, 134, 142. 192, 202, 272. Ma! ma!! 72, 193. Magistrates, 11, 14. Making of bibles closed, 140. Making an offence, 110. Malaria, 90. Malefactor, 76, 86. Mammoths,
73. Mc Minnville, 116. Making a man, 1, 2, 137, 192, [193,]
194, 199. Making Adam and Eve, 1, 2, 66, [137,]. Making
us mad or glad, 195, 199. Main god, 86, 182. Maker, 20, 1-
31-7, 193. Man, 1, 2, 21, 22, 40, 67, 71-2-4, 137, [144, 180,] 2,
[188, 192,) 190,3-4 7-8, 200, 277-8, 280, 291. Man when finished
194. 199. Man is double--double, 197-9, 200, 276, 291. Man's
nature, 182,3-4-9, 198, 200, 270 6, 291. Man, mortal, 144, 145.
Man, immortal, 144, 145. Man's proper study, 181-2, 199, 200.
Man's destany, (188,]199, 283, 285 Man's nature and estate,
262-4, 270-6. Man in the abstract, 262, 276. Man's extent,
limit and conuection, 263, 291. Man as GOD, 268 Man or
fellow, 298. Man is for me says man, 284. Man is made for
me says a goose, 284. Man before religion, 286. Man's fall
was in art, 56, 282-6. Man is as perfect as he aught to be,
267. Man is not without a plan, 265, 291. Man and Beast,
185 6-7 9, 199, 200 70-4. Man's maker, 68-9, 70, 173, (193,) 199,
267. Man's needs, 76, 144, 193, 199. Man, matter, and mind,

67, 193, 198, 199, 200. Man's birth, 58, 74, 144. Man's beginning, [193]. Man's standard, 67, 144, 156, 183 to 189, 190, 192, to 199, 266-91. Man's daughters, 16. Man's gods, 3, 17, 27, 33 64, 65, 67, 75, 119, 138, 139. Man deserves no pity, 186! Many sign boards, 130, 191-2. Mars, 84. Mastodon, 73-4. Manifest, 71. Manhood, 40. Marriage and divorse, 29, 42. Mansions, 36. Master, 31, 100. Mark, 19, 25-7, 76, 123. Mason, 12, 100. Map of man, 263, 276-8. Marcellus, 30). Mariner--like, [not Columbus--like,] 286. Marriaze, 246-8. Master, servant, friend, 281. Marsselles, good bishop, 295, Matured, 6, 180-1-2. Matter and life, 284 Masters or rulers, 2-03. Mastication, 242 Marseilles, 143. Massive Cities of rock, 72. Mathematical certainty, 159. Matthew, 17, 18, 19 26, 33, 75-6, 85 6-7, 119, 123-4-6, 193. Maupins, 113. May--pole festivals, 65, 76, 125, ... 359.

Mean as hell, 26-9. Meat to eat, 71, [Deut. xiv, 21.] Measels, 237. Measuring the size of the Organs, 199. Measuring will power, 200. Meconium, 255. Medical students, 19. Medical law, 108. Medicine, 104 to 113. Meddling, 22, 100, 137. Meddlesom insolence, 127. Mediator, 39, 65, 126. Mediation, 242. Medula Oblongatta, 199. Melancholly, 242. Melted Mount Sinai, 122. Mental, 34, 180 to 200. Mentology, 258. Mental action, [196,] 198-9, 200. Mental diseases, 242, 272, 261½. Menstration, 248-9, 255-8. Merry--go--round 61. Merchants, 123. Mercury, 84. Methodists, 12. Methodist Rout to heaven, 203. Meeting Indignation, 101 Mexico, 10, 56, 58, 127, ... 127.

Microbe or Germ diseases, 233, 241, 261. Midwife, 252. Middle man--Perfective, 188, 199, 200. Mighty works, 76. Mideonites, 122. Milk, 71. Milk, honey and fritters, 122. Millions of years to write a bible, 131. Millitary craze, 143. Milk, 71. Milk-leg, 254. Milk-sick, 259. Midnight, 44. 44. Millions, 24, 63-5, 123. Millionairs, 8, 9. Millerites, 39. Milkey corn, 69, 73. Minds, 71, 145, 181-3-4, 194-8-9, 280. Minerva, 84. Miners, 102. Mineral medicine, 259. Mineral and vegetable, 216, 259. Minds of man, 183, 198-9, 200. Mind and matter, 144, 181, 198, 199, 270. Miracleously, 125. Misrule, 6, 280. Missionary, 31,7, 76. Mistaken, 27, 133. Missouri, 35. Missapplication, 92. Missnomer, 114. Missprints, 135.6. Mistakes and frauds, 135, 136, 180. Miserable deaths 191. Mismenstration, 239. Misplacements, 244. Mitchigan 114. Mixed, 152. Mixing and momixing up man, ... 86.

Mob law, 6, 23.4, 89, 100.2.3, 140. Moccasins, 68. Mohammed, 140. Momix, 76, 103. Money, 8, 9, 11, 17, 29, 30, 35,9. 46, 102, 114, 125, 134. Money changers, 9, 10, 102, 125. Money-begging, 12, 29, 125. Monk, 294. Mouroe, 10. Monarch 43, 107, 190. Monopoly, 41. Monkeying, 86, 108. Moral law, 5, 29. Morocco, 59. Mormons, 36, 39, 97, 137, 143, 203. Mortal, 71, 188. Mortality, 120, 191, 198. Morton, 109, Morality and religion, [198,] 199, 200. Morality and health, 187, 190, 200, 262. More human than good, 193. More favorable eternity, 144. More mistakes than any thing, 135·6. Moral or good organs a fallacy, 198-9, 200, 262, 270, 276, 291. Morose, 242. Morbid appetite, 242. Morphine, 259. Mosaic order of worship, 138. Most subtle or wise, 137. Mos Jesus, 32. Moses' god. Morgan, 32. Mother India, 6, 33, 57. Moses, 3, 5, 16, 21, 29, 127, 136 7-8-9, 141. Mother Earth, 281, 266,

278. Mother of all life, 90, 193, 278. Mother and child, 246
247. Mothers, 13, 57, 87, 90, 193, 278, 286. Mother-marks,
243. Mortality, 29, 34, [190,] 302. Moors, 59, 62. Mount
Geriziom, 138. Mountains of humain remains, 216. Moon-
eyed, 237. Moist heat, ... 240, 244.
Multitude of minds. 194, 199, 200. Murder, 16, 20-3-4-5 8. 30
to 34, 42, 56, 63, 109, 118, 120, 141-2, 202, 242, [286. Murder
commanded, 123. Murdering gods and devils, 134. Musketo, 66, 240. Mustard and warm water, 259. Music, 44, 95,
96. Mumps, 235, ... Myself, 37-8-9. 109, to 114, i-
34, 143, 216. My reasons, 143. Mysteries, 72, 73, 93, 199, 2.
80. Mystery of things, 197. [183,] 198-9, 200, 241, 272, ... 276.

Naked, 68. Names of diseases, 231. Nankeen Chinaman,
74. Narcotic poisons, 260. Nasty religion, 121. Nathen a
prophet, 191. Nation, 27. Nature, 53, 64-5-7, 73-6, 84, 182,
188 [231,] 272-8 284. Nature's Path, 17, 25-7, 64-8, 76, [144,]
216, 248, 272, 279, 302. Nature and destiny of man, 53, 67,
72, 84, [144,] 182-8. Nature SPOKE man obeyed, 58, 68, 2-
88. Nature and end of man, 192. 282-5. Nature and reason,
278. Nature errors not, 268 9. Natural passages, 238. Nausia, reaching, sick headache, vomiting, etc., 218, 249, 256.
Naval cord, 253. .... 253.
Nearer, nearer, death to thee, 285. Nearly starved, 124.
Nearly naked, 124. Nebulous matter, 72. Nebuceadnezzar
137. Negro, 7, 8, 10, 13, 16, 35, 42, 106, 208, 247. Negro--Af-
rican, 74, 140, 192. Negro--Slavery, 42, 140. Negro--Slave,
87. Neptune, 84. Nero, 269. Nervousness, 249. Nervine,
222-3. Nerves, 195, 249. Nettles, 237. Never dying, 144.
Never dying mind, 71, [186,] Never known a man, 121.
Never yet revealed, 138. Never yet equaled, 138. Never
recover, 109. New Orleans, 32, 204. New York, 38, 42.
New World, 119. Newton, 275. New Testament religion
virtue, and morals, 76, 76½, 139, ..., ... 142.
Nick, 83-5, 131, 163, 215¼. Nick-nacks and candy, 255.
Night and day, 21-7, 30, 84, 94, 132-6, 142. Night demon or
mare, 239. .... 239.
No tax, 61. No bishop, 127. No bible, 127. No pope, 1-
27. No miricale, 124. No coat, 124. No forgivness, 186.
No power but of GOD, 86, (186,). No voice in choosing
nor paying, 240. Noah, 2, 21.—drunk and naked, 122. North
America, 89. Nostrum, 109. Not new, 125. Note preface,
and title page, 0. Nothing better to offer, 106, (188,). Not
change man but control him, 139. Non resistance, ... 124.
Nubends, 66. Numbers, 123. Nurse, 247, 255. Nuts, 71.

·Oake, 73-4. Oath-bound, 33, ... 40.
Obey your parents, 144. Obey the laws, 144. Objeet of
this book, 0, 189. 199. Obstetrician, 252. Obstructions, 2-
38 9. Odscene, 59, 99, 124. Obstructed stomace and bow-
ells, 239. .... Occupied, ... 250.
Odd-fellows, 100. Odor pure, 250, ... 250,

Of the devil, 130. Offensive breath and looks, 256. Office, 32-3, 100. Officers, 25, 31-2, 40, 101, 107, 113, 118, 123, 193, 204. Officers of God, 18, 25. Official letter did it, ... 112. Oil of worm seed, 257. Oil of castor, croten, 257 Oil of anise, 257. Oily substances, 259. .... 259. Old illiterate pauper, 124. O! Lord a! 28. Old books, 4, 5. Old Testament, 139, 142. Old countries, 33, 66. Old age, 1 - 94. .... Onan, 34, 86, 121. Onanism, 122, 250. On oath, 113, 132. On it goes, 122, 193, 194. Only route, 27, 29, Only son, 33, 122, 142. One, two, three, 4. One and the same, 72, 192. One god, 43, 87. On the field of battle, 128. Once a man, 194. One stupendeous whole, 272. One calls it virtue, 280 Only son of god, 142. Oely way past away, 129, ... Oppression, 32, 106. Opinions, 118, 259. .... Order, 31, 33, 123, 269, 272, (294,), 231, 212, 278. Ordained slavery, 123. Organization, 182-6, 194, 197, 206, Organs of brain and body, 195-7, 205, 207, 270, 278. Organs of the mind, 215½. Organs of the mind indefinite, 199 270, 278. Organs of mind or mustication, 195, 270, 278. Organs for goodness a fallacy, 198, 292 to 299. Organic quality, 231, 170, 278. Origin, 4, 5, 6, 20, 33, 53, 64, 66 75,77, 92-5, 114, 127, 133, 138. Origin, nature, and destiny of man, 53, 91-2, 135 to 139, [193-4,]. Original Scriptures, 133. Origin of masonry, ... 133.

Osirus, 34. Others, 72. Othea citizens, 124. Others call it vice, 280. Our beginuingless, 53. Our beginning, 53. Our maker, 131, 191, 193. Our's point to heaven, your's to hell, hell, 230. Our officers to be examined, 110. Outlawed, 104, 107. Our Buck, our Bob, 104. Our god, 65, 92, 131. Our Religion, 65. Our work, 241, 244 Our theory of disease, 2-16. Our theory of religion, 216. Our cardinal principals, 2-40. Our safty must our liberty restrain, ... 290.
Overthrow, 35. .... Own testamony, 135. Owned but not controled, ... 139.

Pa, pa, 72. Pacific, 58¼, 72. Pagans, 5, 65, 125. Pain, dstress, sickness, 258, 259. Pains, strains and aches, 223. Pain in the side, back, etc., 219, 249, 250, 253. Paine, 32, 28, 42, 44, 87, 133. Pain and Ingersall, 42 to 45. Paine, Prof., 251. Palsy, paralysis, palpitation, 239. Palms, 65, 69. Palaces, 36. Pantheism, 5. Pards with a whore, 121. Partiality, 1-20, 121, 132. Parties, 31, 41. Parent, 72. Pardon, 39. Paradice, 58, 63, 69. Paralize the mind, 240. Partners, 284. Part and not the whole, 266. Paregoric, 250-3-6. Paralytic, 259. Passions, 78, sexual, 248, 259, 269. Paternal class, 9, 108, 144. Patriot, 38, 43. Patriotism, 97-8-9. Patterson, 1-09. Pauper, 31, 182. Pauper graves, ... 115

Peace, 125. Peasant, 39, 106. Peddlers, 19 Pedigree, 125. Pension money, 11, 35. penitentiary, 101. Pentateuch, 136, 138. People, 40. Peopled the world, 60. People yonng and old, 22. Personal god, 27. Perfect, 26. Persia, 10. Peter, 19. Perpetual Spring. 69. Peru, 58, 63-9. Persecuted, 106, 101. Peruvians, 63. Persia, 10, 137. Perfection. 64, 79 Perpetuation of man, 76. Perjury, 101. Perfect as God, 125.

Peace, 31, 85, 125. Perfectly plain to all, 133. PERSONAL MATTER, 78, 145. Personal identity, 145. Perceptive minds, 183, 198, 200, 275. Perfective minds, 183, 198, 277. Pessary, 251. Peviousness, 256, 258, ... 259.
Phenicia, 62-3, 136. Pheajcians, 4, 72, 126. PHILOSOPHER'S GOD, 78, 145. Philistians, 131, Phrenology, [1-99,]. Phthisic, 256. Physical, 34. Physicians sphere, 217. Physiognomy, physiology, phrenology, 180 to 216, ... 258.
Pictures, 44, 69, 118. Picture--graph, 62. Pie hunters, 36, 126. Piles, 219, 239. Pimples, 243. Pirat, 42, 133, ... 298.
Plato, 275, Plat-hair, 237. Pleasure, 277. Plowing, 32. Plunder, 37. .... Pneumonia, pleurisy, ... 235.
Pock, 237 243. Pocket-book, 61. Poisons, 19, 216, 240, 256, 259, 298. Poets, portraits. 290. Peison-oak, 109. Polititions, 102, 152, 242. Popular opinions, [117,] Polyog, 74. Pope, 11, 108, 204, 285. Pope Sextus, v, 135. Pope's, p, 304. Polyp, 74. Polypus, 244. Poles, 93-4. Portraits, 108-9. Porwiggle, 32, 74. Postmaster, 112. Postmaster--Gen., 110. Post Inspecter Settle, 114. Potency to reason, 188, 275. Poultices and fomentations, 239, 240-3-4, 254, 260. Pouring down the throat, 240, 259. Power accumulatory, 188, 197-8. power manipulatory, 188. Power of government, 1-10, 186. Powers, 85-6, 91, 107, 125, 186, ... 297.
Prayer, 15, 23-4-7-8, 31-2-8-9, 140, 242. Prayer, faith, and works, 24, 31-8-9, 129, 140. Prayed and preached, 192, 290. Prayed out of hell, 204. Practice depravity, 193. Practice 231. Pregnancy, 247-9. Preachers, 242, 275. Predispose to misfortune, 207. Predominate is boss, 207, Preventive, 2-38. Preach against, 140, 275. Presumpteous thieving set, 136, 266. 275, 281. Presumpteous Blasphemous Imposters, 1-27, 136, 275. Predudice, 115. Pre-eminence, 403. Pretend, 29, 31. Preacher, 11, 27, 30-1-5, 44, 76, 87, 108, 113-4, 204, 242, 285. Prefatory remaaks, 1 to 46. President, 23, 39. Priest, 39, 43, 76, 114, 275. Priest ridden, 11, 25, 31-7-8, 108, 275, 285. Privilage tax, 8, Prince, 85. Priority, 73. Primative, 92. Prisoners, 60, 129. Prison, 19, 42, 108, 114, 124. Printing press, 110, 125. Prisoner and council, 112, 124. Printers, 139. Principles of treatment, 240. Pride, 272-5, 297. Procreative Love, 286. Prolapsus, 244. Prolapse, 2-51. Profess perfection, 193, 275, [277,]. Proverbs of Solomon, 190. Propagating minds, 189. Provisions for all, 144. Prophet, 139. Proselytes, 22, 29, 31, 124, Proof-sheets, 111. Proof, 20, 31, 73-4-8, 126, 129, 130-1, 140-4, 193. Protection, 15. Protective minds, 183, 198, 275. Prophicy, 37, 216. Presecuter, 110, 112. Prusic acid, ...,......,......,.......... 259.

Psalms, 15. Psalmist, 185, ... 185.
Puberty, 247-8. Puck, 114. Pulce and the tongue, 731-2, 250-5. Punished to protect, 146. Puppy love, 74. Puppy religion, 192, Purge, purify, 218, 237. Purge or vomit, 218 237, 257. Purification, 238, 249, 250, 275-7. Put to death, 1-18, Pyramids of Egypt, ... 138.

Quakers, 9, 104 to 106, 203. Quality, 71. Queens, 122. Queen Anne's war, 35. Quinto, 93. Quinsy, 235. Quieting, 218, 250.

Races and colors, 61, 207. Rags and brocade, 298. Rasing, education, and association, 190. Rally with our fever syrup, 259. Rampant, maniackal screaming, 203. Rantings, 140. Rape, rapine, ravish, 25, 28, 61, 120 to 123. Rapper, wet and hot, 227. Rashes, 237. Rascals, 21. Rascality, 39, 111, 112. Rate of earth's motion, 93. Rational, 40, 71, 75, 184. Rat poison, 259. Raw eggs, ..., 259. Reasoning, 40, 71-5, 141, 184-5, 276 8. Reader, 100. Reaping, 32, 122-3.- Reasoning minds, 183, 265, 278. Reasoning pride, 268, 278. Reason and passion, 275-6 8. Reason and self-love, 276-8. Reason or Intellect, 285. Reason dethroned, 194. Reading. references, 120. Read nor write, 141. Rebuilding Signal fires, 129. Rebls, 99, 114, 125. Rebellion 35, 141. Re-converted a billion, 124. Recieved him not, 1-26. Recollections, 133. Re·constucted, 141. Receiveing, investigaing, acting, 183, 195. Redress, 107, 110. Red, yellow, white baby, 253. Redress for injuries, 15. Reflection, 286. Refrigerant, 222-3, 245. Refuges, 61. Registration or count-out law, 107-8. Regular old bum, 124. Religion, as or what it is, 1, 5, 9 13, 16, 23-7, 124-9, [142,] 186, [190,] 193 215, 241. Rejected, 17, 124. Religious theory of scales, 1, 9, 10, 199. Religious alters, 1, 9. Religious standard, 9, 15 to 14, 23-4-6, 39, 124, 190-3-9. Religious morals, 9, 13 to 17, 26, 129, 190. Religious government, 7, 10, 14-5,6, 24, 33, 124, 129, 190-1-3. Religion done it, 9, 10, 14-5-6-7, 20-3-5-9, 32-9, 55, 87, 108, 117, 120-4 9, 134, 186. 191-3-9, 202, 241. Religious laws and lawsuits, 9, 10, 14, 23-5, 124-8-9 191, 193. Religion, 27-9, 32-6, 40, 65, 87, 102, 108, 120-6, 141-2, 190-3,9. Religious rule, 11, 14, 16, 23-5 7-9, 33-9, 120-4-8-9, 163 to 179, 191-3. Religionists, 13, 14, 15, 16, 20-3°5 7-9, 32 3 9, 40, 120-4-8-9, 140 1 186, 291, 192, 199, 202, 215, 247, 277, Religious men, 40, 1-00 to 121, 108, 115, 134, 141-3, 191-3-9, 277. Religious ringsters, 100 to 114, 108, 193, 199, Religious govenors, 100 to 114, 191, 193, 199. Religious cranks, 108, 185, 215, 261¢. Religion caused the first enmity! the first murder! the first curse! the first slavery! and the first destruction! 120. Religion and blasphemy, 130, 199. Religion and God, 140, 199. Religion is no mark of goodness, 193, 202, 203. Religionist are brutal beasts, 194, 215. Relax, relieve rigidity, 240. Reliability, trust, 277. Released, 115. Relaxant of astringent, 2-16, 230, 240, Remedy, a universal, 218. Remedial effort, 2-17. Remedies and diseases, 216. Remains, 73, 123. Renounce, 107. Republican gods, 9. Republican, 107. Representation, 39. Replaceing and retaining, 245. Repose, 56. Reproductive organs, 73. Reproach, 127. Repealed their god's laws, 140. Rest and exercise, 13, 21, 29, 67, 132, 229, 250. Researches, 89. Resurection, 184. Retrograde, 144. Revolutionary fathers, 25, 26, 32, 39, 40, 57, 98, 118, 133, 141, 143. Revolutionary war, 25, 33, 57, 141. Revelation, 36, 85, 86, 139. Rewards and punishments, 146, ... 186.

Rhode Island, 35. Rheumatism, 228, ... 235.

Riches, repute, trust, 298, Rigidity of the muscles, 239, 258 Right is the matured man always, 186, 286. Right and Festrval, 73, 107, 200, Ring, streaked and striped, 92. Ringworm, 237. Rivers, 87, 92. River Amazon, 58, 69, 72, 73, 88. River Nile, 60, ... 60.

Road to hell, 29, 260, 203. Road to destruction, 216. Roasting-ears, 73. Rob, 28, 37, 55. 56, 61, 114, 118, 120 to 123, 127, 1, 41-2, 193. Robbery commanded, 123. Rock, 67. Rome, 10, 56, 61. Roman, 75, 86, 126,7, 134. Roman Soldier, 123-4. Roman Empire, 126-7, 134-7-9, 142. Roman Army, 128· Rome's Cross, 3. Rman captivity, 135. [Romans, 3, 14, 26.] Rose of Sharon, 191. Rosin flour, 245, 256, 260. Routs to heaven, 12, 23, 203. Routs to hell, 203. Round about there 124. Royal religion, 33, 86, 120 to 123_5 134, 191 3-9. Royal heir, 34, 86, 122. Royal son, 86, 125. Royal gods and devils, 125. .... Ruin, 37, 63, 72 3, 84, 120.8, 191-3. Rulers, 86, 98, 114, 203. Rule or ruin, 41, 98, 134,.......... 142.

Sabbath, 3, 9, 20-1, 24-5. Sabbath school, 107. Sabbath for rest, 121. Sacrificed, 61. Sacred weekness, 106- Sackcloth, 124. Saddusee, 137. Safty, 39, 46. Sagegrass, 102-9.10. Sagar, 103. Salivation, 237. Salts and fever syrup, 254. Salts and blue pill, 239 244, 260. Salts and paregoric, 238, 254, 260. Sallaries, 9, 203. Saloon, 14. Samaritian Jews, 138. Samson, 131. Samuel, 123, 190. Sane, moral, or healthy, 37, 43, 190. Sardiens, 27. Sassafras tea, 260. Saviour, 21, 65, 76, 126, 142. Savage, 103. Saturne, 84, Satan, 83-4-5, 130, 163, 165, 215¼. Saint Asa, 110. Saved seed, ... 135.

Scavengers of the world, 90. Scaldhead, scurf, etc., 237. Scholars, 134. School, 31_6-8, 107. Scrofula, 38. Science of human nature, 262, 275. Sciences, 72, 126, 194, 275. Scientest's god, 78. Scotland, 98. Scrubbing bath, 238, 239. Scrofulous swellings, 243. Scrubbing generally, 247. Screaming fits, 257. Scrubbed, 109.· Scribes, 139. Scum on tongue, 256.

Seasons, 66, 84. Seasons come and go, 142. Seamstress, 247. Sea and its use, 89. See or believe alike, 180, 266. Sees feels and knows, 186, 266 Sees thinks and reasons. 193-4, 266. Seeing, 78, 180. Seed time and harvest, 132. Secret, 63, 92. Secret oath bound clans, 7, 31, 100, 204. See! cant you see? 40. Secret characters, 133. Sectarian, 23, 141. Sedition, 17. Seduction, 15, 86. Self-rule, 11, 141. Self-control, 231, 266. Self-contradictions, 20_1-6, 76, 76½, 99, 119, 122 4-5_6, 131'3"4, 139, 143, 163 to 179, 185-6, 190, 202, 215¼, 261½. Self-knowledge, 200, 231, 266, 274. Self-love, 276, 290, 302-3 Self-preservation, 285-6, 202. Self-polution, 242, 250. Self-murder, 2-76. Selected eleet, 125, 130. Senses, 38, 185. Sensibility lost, stupor, 239, 240. Sense, common, 17. Septugent bible, 138. Sermons, 23. Serpent, 84-5. Serving, 98. Set of men, 108, 180 Set the Negro free, 140 Sexual organs of generation, 64. Sexual indulgence, 250, 286. Sexual derangement, 242. Sex-strength, 192, 220, 231, 247, 257, ... 286.

Shame, shame, 23-3, 95, 100, 129, 134, 143. Sham, 41. Shape and hue, 92. Shed not a tear, 148. Ship, shipings, 61, 143. Shaking Quakers, 203. Shankers, sinuses, 245. Sheckemites, 122. Sheep, 17, 21, 29, 40, 126, 250. Shows, 8. Shook down the heavens and meltedMount Sinai, ... 122.

Sick, 71. Sick howling winds, 90. Sickness and death, 258. Sidney, 295. Signs, 19, 25, 30, 141, 142. Siek folks, 76. Silver, 67. Simites, 9, 36, 143. Sins of others, 28, 143. Sin shame and crime, 34-5_6-7, 60. Sin, shame and crime rewarded, 120. Sin and sinners, 268. Sire, 286. Sirene, 86. Sister 13, 68. Sitting and foot bath hot, 251. Sixteen wars, ... .35. Skedaddled, 108. Skill, mechanical, 244, ... 244 Slavery, 10, 14, 16, 26, 32-3-4-5, 46, 87, 100, 120.9, 137, [140-3], 189, 202, 247, 302. Slavery bible, 26, 38, 46. Slave pens, 202, 203. Slave pens make the man! 204, 302. Slavery of parties, cliques, churches and secret oath-bound orders, 129, [189.] Slave of fashion, 258, 302. Sander, 23, 141. Slaughtered, 16, 128, 143. Slay your brother, companion, and neighbor, 120, 140, 143, [Ex 32, 27.] Sleep much for infants, 255, Sleep, snooze or rest, 230, 241. Sleepiness, stys, salivation, ... 249. Smart Alex's, 36, 103, 141. Smash out your brains, 20. Smelling, 78. Smith the lawyer, ... 117. Snake stories, 99. Sneezing, suffocating, 239. Snow-bound, and desolate, 95. Snow-capped mountains, 89, ... 90.

Soap, strong lye, 243. Soap and hot water, 238-9. Soaping, scrubbing hot bath, 244. Society and states before priests or kings, 72, 288. So-called, self_styled– 140_1. So-called word of god, 143. Sodom and Gomorrah, 3, 34, 121. Soldiers, 32, 118, 123, 143. Solar system, 54, 56, 83-4 Solomon, 15, 16, 74, 137, 190-2. Solomon's songs and temple, 16, 61, 74, 138, 191. Sold without a buyer, 121. Solvent, the only, 218. Songs, 61. Songs of Solomon, 137. Sons of the gods and the devils, 86, 120, 189. Soother's, 241-4, 250, 260. Soothing inducing sleep 222. Soothe, strengthen, sweat, 218, 241, 250. Soreness of the breast, 249. Sores, abcesses, boils, etc., 235. Sore stomach, side, back, etc., 235. Sore eyes, 235. Sour, bitter, foul stomach, 118. Soul or spirit, 144,5, 184. Soulless, 140. Soul's salvation, 76. 140. Source of life and mind, 183. 186, 195. Source of light and heat, 91-2, [142]. South, 35, 88,141. South Carolina, 35. Sovereigens, 23. 25, 28, 30, 181, 186, 193. South America, 34. 55-6, 66-8, 83-4-8, 127, 133, 138. Sounding brass--40. Sour throat, 225_6, ... 226.

Spasmodic diseases, 239, 260. Spells, 16, 87, 239. Spells of Proteus, 92. Species, 63, 92. Special gods, 145. Spirtualists, 39, 87, [144-5,] Spirit, 87, 145. Spider and the fly, 153. Spots, sores, scurvey, syphilis, 243. Spooning an infant, 256. Spring perpetually, 40, 79. Spraker, 192. Sprains, soures, 219. Spirit for murder, ... 142.

Stars and Stripes, 3, 38. Star--Spangled Banner, 175. Stables, 8. Starved, 10. St. Peter of Rome, 62. Statue shaped rocks, 84. Statues, huge, 84. Standing army, 108. Starved to death, 109. Standard, 123, 141. States Att'y 117. St. John 124-6. Standard of Justice, 125, 140 l. State and the church, 142. Stations, 193. Stars and stripes, 140. Steam and water doctors, 109. Steam and electricity, 244, 260. Steam and sweating bath, 260. Stearing betwixed extremes, 262. Stiff_ joints, St. Vitus's dance, 239. Still born, 255. Stimulant, 220 Steal, 28. Sticks and stones, 32. Stone forts, 34. Storms, 60. Stomach and bowels, 238. Stomachache or heart_burn, 239. Stopages, 238-9. Stone, stricture, 239. Stomach pump, 259. Strong drink, 153, 161-2. Strife, 26, 56, 68, 84, 125, 141. Stratagem foiled, 111. Strychnine, 109. Strong seculao arm, 120. Stratta, 74. Stranger still to me, 134. Strangling facts, 138. Strengthening, 238, 250, 277. Students of medicine, 109.

Study thyself to save thyself, 181, 266, 274. Stupor, mental and physical, 240. Stupify the mind, 240-1, 259. Strychnine, 259. .... Subjugation, 127. Success, 99. Such are saved, [188]. ...... Sudorific soporific, 222. Sufferage, 46. Suffocative, 259. Suffering, 125. Sulphur, 243-4, 256, Summer and winter, 84. Sun and its influences, 91. Sun, 54,5-6-7, 72-3, 84, 91˜3, 132 4, [142], 272. Sun worship, 56, 73, 83. Sunday whiske hells, 100. Sum-totle, 276, 304. Sun of life 183. Sunday, 20˜3. 39 8, 73, 132. Sunday laws, 9, 23. Sunday at the poles, 94, 132. Sunday feasting, 29, 73. Sunday school, 21, 31, 36, 143. Supremacy, 11, 84, 125, 126. Supreme law of the world, 140, 145. Supposed superior, 203, 266. Suppressed diseases, 238. Supports, 245, 250. Suppers 239. Superstition, 40. Supplemented sense, 188. Superior and inferior, 1˜88, 266. Superseeded the prayer meeting, 143. Superseeded, 131. Supposed, 75. Support, 75, 90, 203, ... 203.

Sweet land of liberty, 96. Sweating, 221-2-3. Swelling and Soreness, 246. Swelling of the limbs, 249. Swelling, pain and spasms, 259. Sweet milk and flour, 259. Sweet or castor oil, 260. Sweeten one, sour the other, 279. Swelled to gods, sunk to beasts, 293. Sworn, 119, 129, ... 133.

Symptoms, 231, 251_7_9. Symptoms, pathognomonic, 257. Sympathise, study and preach, 192. Syrup, Dr. Thompsons' for fevers, [234], 241, 244, 250, ... 253.

Take natures path, 293. Tallow, hot, 254. Talking in the sleep, 242 Talmud, 139. Taylor, Gov., 107. Tamor, the harlot, 122. Tasting, 78. Taxes, 8, 9, 14, 39, 61, 203, 247. Tax-tackey-school, 31. Taxation and no representation, 247. Taxation and no protection, 247. .... 248.

Teachers, 27, 132, [190], 303. Teaching, 40, 60, 191, 271. Tea kettle tea, 241. Teeth, 195. Tearing down, 140. Teething, 257. Telling the truth, 120, 290. Temperament, 206-7 8, 231. Temptation, 153. Temple, 17, 36 8, 62-3, 84, 134. Temperate, 250. Tents, 71. Tenn., 73, 100 to 117. Terror, 134, 241. Tetanous, tremons, trembeling, 239. Tetter, itch, ringworm, 237. Text, 133. Texas, 10, ... 10.

Thankfullness, 74, Thank God, 128. Thoughtful, reasoning judgeing, 189. The proper study of man, 181, 274 to 276. Theology, 5, 61, 87, 120, [190], 193_4, 203, 247, 276, 290. The triune three, 130. The gods made man, [180]. Theaters, 8. The sweet by and by, 51. The bad man, 83. The mighty river Amazon, 88. The church meeting, 101. The two pictures, 118, 294. Thief, 111, 120'7. Third god, 182. This that, tit tat, 134 Third witness, 33. Thief of a god, 33, 109. Thief, 42, 61, 120, 109. Thinker, 43, 194. Theory of disease, 216. Think THRICE before you fight once, 211. Throat, stomach and bowels, 240. Thrush, redgum, 237, 256. Thunder, 60, 72, 91, ... 92.

Tickling the throat, 259. Ticks, 240, 255. Times or the seasons, 132. Time, 29, 30, 63, 132, 182, 241, 276. Timothy, 14. Time for rest, 21, 132, 241. Titus and Cczar, 279, 297. Titicaca, 58, 62, 72, ... 69.

To think and reason, 194, 276. Tools, 67. Tooth and earache, 235, 248. To keep healthy and strong, 250. Tobacco tea, 118, 239, 259. Toddy, 250-3-6. Tolerated, 191. Thomas Paine, 133. Tomboy, 247. Tongue-tied, 256. Tonics, 239, 241 Torrid zone, 55. Tornadoes, 84, Torture, 118, 129, 133, 199. Torment, tortue, 140-1. Torpor, inaction, 220. Torpid diseases, 240. T'other side of Jorden, 255. Totaly depraved, 26, 28, 189, 190. Tougher sex, 252, ... 251. Tramps, 8, 72, 120. Tramps religious, 247-8 Travler, trade, 30, 72. Travlers, 84. Traitors, 35, 99, 106, 127, 142, 187. Traditions, 53-8, 60-6, 72-3, 84, 127, 133-8, 289. Tranquility, 37, 56, 68-9, 242. Transmutabillity, 64. Translation, 127, 133. Training, 190, 290. Tragedy, after tragedy, 122. Travail, 252, 224. Treatment for all diseases from page 216 to 262. Trees of life, 65-9. Treatchery, 127. Trinity Church, 8, 14, 61. Triton, 84. Trixters, 101-2. Troubles, 22, 84, [193,] 242, 266, 260. Tropics, 65. Truss, 256. Truth, 43, 200, 262, 276, 290. Truth Seeker, 114, 290, Trust, 187. True religion, justice, morality 65, 190, 289, 290. True story of Jesus, 76½, 125. Try, try keep trying, 146-7, 159, ... 159.

Tubercles, 243, Tumor like diseases, 243-4. Turn of life, 245. Turenne, the godlike, 295. .... Twins, 68, 72. Twin Brothers, 35, 72. Tyndall, 93. Types, 74, 208. Typographic printing, 62. Tyrants, 99, 284, 289, 290, ,.................... 293.

Ulcers, 245, 256. .... Unanoyed and uninjured, 255. Unbalanced, unwell, 13, 22, [146,] 184, 186, 188, 190, 2-06. Unbalanced, do rong, 188, 106 Unbalanced not sane, 1-88, 191, 206. Unbalanced, unbarable, 191. 206. Unconstitutional, 110. Unbelief, 19. Uncle Sam, 5, 7, 9, 24, 35, 57, 102, 125*, 6, 128. Uucle Sam's Farm, 115. Uncle Sam's religion, 125, 144 to 147. Unchangable, 74, 140, 181. Uncurable craziness, 186. Understanding, 133. Undue stimulous, 241. Uufading, 74. Ungodliness, 137-8. Unhealthy, 13, [146,] 184, 2-06. United States of, America, 10, 13, 20, 29, 35, 43, 66, 125-6 128,140. Union the bond for all, 286. Universal cause, 17, 46, 144, 181, 283, 293. Unimpeachable witnesses, 95, 180. Universal hate commanded, 123. Universal, 144. Unjust, 74, [1-46]. Unmailable matter, 109. Unpardonable blasphemy, 161 Unpurforated hymen, 239. Unrest, 13, 184. Unreasonable, 74, 124, 186. Unreparably injured, 114. Unseen hidden, 197. Untimly death, 216. Unwise laws, 7, 9, ... 9. Upas, 61, 216. Urania, 84. Urine retained, 239. Usurpers, 1-26, 191, 192. .... 192.

Vagabonds, 120, 124. Vagrant, crazy wild man, 124. Vagina 250-1. Vally people whiped the Lord, 122. Valey of the Amazon. 73, 89. Value, 46, 89. Varicos veins, 239, 244. Vegetable, 71, 89, 129. Vegetated, 1, 66, 71, 89. Vegetable and mineral, 216. Vegetables and fruits, 242. Vegetable medicins, 259. Veneration, 197. Venus, 84. Vermifuge, [257. Vespucius, 126. Vcto, 39, ... 39.

Vicious, 59, 99, 134, 187, 247. Vicious virus, 134. Vice or Virtue, 279, 280. Vica Versa, 95. Violent hands, 17, 18, 1-42. Vilest Violaters, 100 to 114, 120, 142. View them, 87, 99.

Victuals and drink, 211 2, 230. Violating their gods laws, 1-42. Vinegar, 18. Virtue, 15, 22, 26, 34, 98, 99, 193, 247, 277-9. Visiting iniquity of fathers upon their children, 14. Vision Seeing, 242. Virtue's prize, 298, 302. .... 302. Volcanic, 55, 61. Vomit or purge, 218, 240.1, 257. Vomiting cholery, 237. Vote of the people, 39. Vulgar, 99, 114. Vulcan, 88. .... 84.

Wages, 39, 46. Wall street, 8. Wars, 118-9, 128, 130, 140.1, War, American Revolution of 1776, [11], 35, 43, 45, 57, 172-3 War of 1812, 35, 119, 140.1. War declared, 86. Wars— Barbary, 35, Blackhawk, 35, French and Indian, 35, Indian, 33, Mexican, 35, 127, Seminole, 35, Southern rebellion, 35, 1-41, Tecumseh, 35, 57. Warms us, 90 to 68. Warming up pa tients, 222. Warm water and indigo, 240, 257. Warm water emetic, 257. Warrant, U.S, 191. Washington. 32, 44-5, 98-9, 120. Washington and Lincolin, 45 to 47. Washing and dress ing the infant, 253. Wast of waters, 89, 94. Washed, 109. Wating for a Christ, 108. Water, its use, 89, 94, [217,] [218] Watering places, 109. Water, cold or hot, 217. ☞WATER WILL PURIFY BY VOMITING SWEATING AND PURGING, 218. Water, tepid warm or hot, 218. ...... 218. Wealthy beggars, 14, 22. Wealth, fabulous, 16, 22, 86. Wealth and learning, 136. Weak organs, dislocations, 244-5. Weak, little and blind, 266. Webster's dictionary, 185. Webster, daniel, 97. Webster's brain, 187. Webster, Calhoun, Martin Hillings, 201. Webster, Calhoune and Butler, 187, 203-4. Weigh thy opinion against Providence, 268, 282. Well balancede, 187-8, 220. Wesley, 15, 288, 300. Wet girdle, 239. Wet, dirty nor cold, 255, ... 255

Whatever is, is right, 36, 89 to 95, 273, 297. Whatever is, is best, 94, 146, 273. What is God? 75, 77, [144], 272. What ails us? 30, 31, 40, 108-9, 134-5, 268, 272, 290. When and where man was made, 1, 63, 90. Whoreing religion, 15-6, 1-20. Who are the law breakers? 23, 30-1, 140.1, 268, 275, 290. What is bibles? 127, 261½. What it means, 134. What must balance, (190], 220, 272. What to eat, drink and avoid, 230-9 241. What shocks one person will please another, 297. When to suckle the baby, 255. When to give it water and food, 255. Wher's the north, 94.5 When man fell, 260.

Whores, whoremongers, 120-2-3. Who are the sinners? 268, 272, 290. Whiskey, 118, 239 Whiskey hells, 100-61. Whites, gleet, clap, etc., 235, 250. Which day is Sunday? 29, 30 132. Whither I go ye cannot come, 131. White and black, 280. When to work or rest, 132. Whoredom and wickedness, 1-22-3. 142. Whoremongering Judah, 122. Whoredom commanded, enjoined and rewarded, 123. Whole world, 126, 128. Whole creation, 61, 90, 272. Who gave you freedom? 141. Whole duty of man, 144-6, 272. Who and how saved, [188]. Whe knows but he? 269, 272. Who but God can judge us? 297. Whoping lie, 12½. Why has not man a microscopic eye? 270, 272, ... 272.

Wife winers, 124, 247. Wiggle tail, 66. Wigwams, 71. Wild-cat brandy, 111, 112. Willing witness, 110. Wilderness, 124. Will, what it is, 198. Wine, 16, 18, 22, 239. Wine, woman and song, 138"9, 163 to 173. Wine bibbing, 29. Winter. 69, 84, 90-4. Winds, 60, 69, 84, 90-4. Wisest and meanest, 301. Wise skilled woman, 252. Wiser, 125. Witness, 33 57-8, 58¼, 67, 75-6, 86, 94_5, 112-3, 120,131-5, 185. 195, 231, 232, 261½. Witness, Infalable, 75-6, 86, 94-5, 261½. Witness, human, 197. Witness, double-barreled, 113. Witness, prose-persecuting, 113. Witness, Paul, 86, 131. Witness, lawyer and judge, 195, 177. Witness, animal, 197. Witness, unimpeachable, 58¼. 76, 94-5, 120-1-2_3, 163, 179, 180, 215₄, 261½ Witches, 87, ... 87.

Wolf like, 29. Womb-man, 68. Woman, 1, 2, 15. 16, 68, 87. Womb, 257. Woman in heaven, 86. Woman and the devil cast out, 86. Women and children, 128, 220. Woman's first need, 246. Woman and her charge, 247. Woman and the bible, 247. Women, Lords, Gods and Devils, 247. Woman's most damnable enemy, 248. Wonderful, 94, 272. Wonder what it is? 197. Wonder and mystery, 241, 272. World, 62, 74, 84 5, 90, 131, 133, 272. World in 1492 and now in 1895, 2, 38, 62, 131-4-5, 141. World's Fair, 9. 23, 25. World's good enough, 160 World beyond, 72-4, 85, 90_4, 272. World's fountain of life, 89, 94. 🖙 World makers, bible makers and Sunday makers, 64. World's congress of all religions, 118. Works of art, 40_1. Worship, 73, 85, 126, 141. Worm water, 94, 217, 218. Word nor work of God, 129. Words and explanations, 134. Word of mouth, 139. Worm sickness, 257. Worry, 242. Worms, 256, 261. Worm seed, 251. Wounds, ... 245. Writing King Jim's Bible, 130. Wrote it with his tail, 130, Wrong to you, right to me, 280. Wrong and right, 146, 2⁻ 66, 280. Wryneck, whooping cough, 239, ... 239.

Yankee, 35, 57, 66, 114_5, 194, 208. Yankee American, 129, 141, 194. Yankeeite, 65, 194, 217. Yankee doodle, ... 172. Year of time, 132, 142. Yellow fever, 233, ... 234. Yoke, 251. Yonger, 74. You cannot be, 141 You are sure for hell, 203. Your sphere, their skies, 268. Youth, manhood, age, 281, ... 281.

Zea maze, 73. Zea celestrial, 73. Zea caragua, 73. Zeal not charity, 299. Zinc chlorid, 245. Zones, 94. Zephyr, ... 145.

You know that people misrepresent what you say or write. You know that they change what you say or write. You know we are told that the Devil and Eve made God change what he had said and done!! — Gen. i, 31; iii, 17-8; vi, 6, 13. Then, from this experience is it reasonable to suppose that your bible or anything else is as it first was?

You know it is impossible to prevent the changes of time man and the devil. Every subject presented in this Index is a Text to talk, lecture, preach or write about.

FREE MUTUAL PROTECTION; both in this life and the life hoped for! Any man, woman or child can join this association by writing or calling on us.

HOW, when and where to get all kind of books free. See below our list of books. We will swapp with you. Send me your book or books and we will send you the worth in my books as you may choose them.

Send us one-cent and we will send you a liberal or infidel sermon. Send us 25, 50 or 100 dollars and get our magic lantern shows. Photo-galleries, tents and exhibitions for out door work made to order.

Send us your likeness and we will engrave it from one dollar up. Send us your likeness and one dollar and we will copy it into one 8 by 10 inch size, or into 4 cabinets, or into 6, 8, 10, or 12 nice card photographs. Send us your printing and we will soon do it up cheap and in good style.

BOOK first. Fletch Woodward's fights with those bad, bad town-boys. It is a two years fight on the gallows and in four filthy Christian jails. It involved cliques, churches, parties and oath bound secret orders! Price, ill., . 20 cents.

BOOK second. That Kooksy momix. It is Woodward's prison-life, escape, rescue. compromise, removal, final trial and acquital. With his views on government, religion and medicine. Handsomly illustrated. Price, ... 20 cents

BOOK third. Gives another new religion, proving all and showing how all bibles or presumed words of God was gotten up and how they came to contradict themselves.. Giving hundreds of self-contradictions both in theology, history, morality, doctrin and beliefs. Price, . . . 30 cents.

BOOk fourth. A universal system of Photography; making all kind of Daguerreotypes, Ambrotypes, Ferrotypes. Pearltypes, Transparencytypes and Negativetypes by a wet, dry-wet process. Price ..,.. .... 25 cents.

BOOK fifth. Your own phrenology. If you want to know all about that head, heart, body, and mind of yours call on us, or send us youur likenes, and a description, and two dollar and we will analyse you. If you are diseased or unbalanced it will tell you what is the difficulty, and how to cure and to control it at but little time and cost

We give in writing and illustrations your physical and mental natures and condition. Price .... $2.00.

BOOK sixth. The American Scriptures, Uncle Sam's Bible, or a universal diagnosis. The greatest and grandest book on earth! Containing the greatest truthes ever given to irring man! It proves the American Continents and their peoples were first! That Europe, Asia and Africa cannot, exist without our CURRENTS! our circulation! All other countries owe their very existence to the Amerikas. And hundreds of facts, like this one, are given, explained, wrth illustrations, making a medical book of near four-hundred pages. Price............. .... 1$. 25 cents.

BOOK seventh. The oceans of human blood that religion has shed! Enough to float the largest ships! Illustrating the two roads from Cain on down. Price...25 cents.

BOOK eight. Chaos, or great god what ails us! Is an awful book of many large illustrated pages, just showing one years destruction and confusion. Price .... 10 cents.

BOOK nine. The All-o-pathic System of medicine, religion and government. Giving all known diseases and their treatment, illustrated. Price. .... 50 cents.

Address or call on Woodward & sons, Mc Minnville, Tennessee. Liberal Publishers. Y. A. I: 121, 7, 10.

www.ingramcontent.com/pod-product-compliance
Lightning Source LLC
Chambersburg PA
CBHW022105300426
44117CB00007B/591